THE ICONIC NORTH

THE ICONIC NORTH

CULTURAL CONSTRUCTIONS
OF ABORIGINAL LIFE
IN POSTWAR CANADA

Joan Sangster

UBC Press • Vancouver • Toronto

25 24 23 22 21 20 19 18 17 16   5 4 3 2 1

Printed in Canada on FSC-certified ancient-forest-free paper
(100% post-consumer recycled) that is processed chlorine- and acid-free.

LIBRARY AND ARCHIVES CANADA CATALOGUING IN PUBLICATION

Sangster, Joan, author
    The iconic north: cultural constructions of Aboriginal life in postwar Canada / Joan Sangster.

Includes bibliographical references and index.
Issued in print and electronic formats.
ISBN 978-0-7748-3183-3 (hardback). — ISBN 978-0-7748-3185-7 (pdf).
ISBN 978-0-7748-3186-4 (epub). — ISBN 978-0-7748-3187-1 (mobi)

    1. Native peoples – Colonization – Canada. 2. Native peoples – Canada – Social life and customs. 3. Native peoples – Canada – Government relations. 4. Indians in popular culture – Canada. 5. Popular culture – Canada. I. Title.

E78.C2S27 2016   305.897′071   C2016-900818-5
                                                         C2016-900819-3

Canadä

UBC Press gratefully acknowledges the financial support for our publishing program of the Government of Canada (through the Canada Book Fund), the Canada Council for the Arts, and the British Columbia Arts Council.

This book has been published with the help of a grant from the Canadian Federation for the Humanities and Social Sciences, through the Awards to Scholarly Publications Program, using funds provided by the Social Sciences and Humanities Research Council of Canada.

UBC Press
The University of British Columbia
2029 West Mall
Vancouver, BC V6T 1Z2
www.ubcpress.ca

Contents

Illustrations

Acknowledgments

Research, as Zora Neale Hurston once wrote, is simply "formalized curiosity. It is poking and prying with a purpose." My pathway into this book was sparked by an interest in Indigenous labour, combined with a historian's innate curiosity about the genesis and connections between primary sources. An informal curiosity led me from Arctic memoires to formalized curiosity about other archives, films, photos, people, and texts, and to questions not just about what I found, but what may have been lost, as in the case of Paulette Anerodluk's lost photographs. My intent to write about the North initially sparked some teasing from colleagues – understandably so. I have an unremitting fear of flying (so, like other Canadians I cling close to the 49th parallel); I've never been part of the hardy Great North canoe trips of my Canadian Studies colleagues, and I am a firm advocate of snow-birding – just about anywhere – to escape the winter.

Even though my interest in this new research initially appeared out of academic character, colleagues have been unfailingly generous and helpful throughout the research process, reading sections of the monograph or making suggestions about possible sources. My thanks in this regard to Sarah Carter, Julie Cruikshank, Shelagh Grant, Peter Kulchyski, Caroline Langill and Veronica Strong-Boag. I have also appreciated conversations about the North with Sherrill Grace, Peter Raymont, Carol Payne, and Annis Mae Timson while they were at Trent for our Northern Lecture series.

Throughout the writing process, my involvement in the Frost Centre for Canadian Studies and Indigenous Studies has been important to my conceptual framing of the monograph, given our emphasis on teaching and research relating to Indigenous history and Canadian colonialism.

Frost graduate students and faculty Molly Blyth, Sean Carleton, John Milloy, Julia Smith, and Kim Wilson were good sounding boards, as were students in my MA and PhD seminars. Graduate students at Trent and beyond also provided research assistance: my thanks to David Tough, Kelly Pineault, Meaghan Beaton, and James Onusko. While I was involved in Administration, staff members Loretta Durst, Jen Richardson, and Cathy Schoel made my life a little easier, and while I was organizing an international Canadian Studies conference at the end of the manuscript process, Lisa Pasolli and Bill Waiser helped immensely with their good-humoured energy. Tom Symons has offered a ready ear and sage advice over the last years: I appreciate his support for my scholarship. My thanks, finally, go to my colleagues in Gender and Women's Studies, and to the engaging group of Canadian historians at Trent, especially the indefatigable Dimitry Anastakis.

Irene Baird's granddaughter, Nora Spence, has been exceptionally generous, sharing conversations with me about her grandmother and providing me with a copy of Irene's CBC radio interview so I could actually hear her voice. Monroe Scott kindly lent me a copy of his play about Budge Crawley, and Tom Matthews and Elizabeth Knox at St. Georges Anglican School found pictures of Irene Baird for me as well. My research was also facilitated by a Social Sciences and Humanities Research standard research grant; and talks delivered for the Canadian Historical Association, Canadian Studies at Queens, and the York University History Graduate Student Association allowed me to share and refine my ideas. In the publication stage, Darcy Cullen, Holly Keller, and others at UBC Press have been models of efficient and enthusiastic professionalism, a delight to work with.

My family, now expanded to include the young Jack Long, continues to offer me love and joyful diversion, as does my partner Bryan Palmer, without whom my life and writing would be much impoverished. He has promised to go down North with me to see the polar bears as soon as this book is published. This book is dedicated to him.

THE ICONIC NORTH

Introduction

They glamorize and romanticize the Inuit ... and give us status the others
don't have. Canadians like to talk about us eating frozen meat and living in
the cold. It gives Canada something that other countries don't have.
Everybody likes the Inuit.

> — *Nellie Cournoyea, "The Independent Inuit,"*
> Maclean's, *14 July 1986*[1]

Nellie Cournoyea's sardonic take on how southern Canadians imagine
the Inuit North is a pithy summation of decades, if not centuries, of our
northward gazing. Since the earliest days of Euro-Canadian incursion
into Indigenous lands, the North has been rendered exotic, romantic,
terrifying, sublime, enigmatic, otherworldly, and intrinsically Canadian,
and some of these adjectives are equated not just with the landscape but
with the original inhabitants of the North: its First Nations. Is there
really any more that can be written about this fascination with the North
and Canadian nordicity, given its firmly entrenched place and multitud-
inous expressions in artistic production, social science, and historical
writing? Should we not turn the North, including its cultural construction, over to its own First Nations and peoples for re-visioning as they
work through the project of decolonization and self-determination?

While I wholeheartedly support that re-visioning project, the recent
politically orchestrated announcements, and attendant media hoopla,
concerning the discovery of Sir John Franklin's shipwreck in the Arctic
are a salient reminder that we need an ongoing critical analysis of a romanticized North "discovered" by white explorers.[2] My examination of
northern contact zones — defined as places of cultural interaction characterized by asymmetrical power relations[3] — does not attempt to define the

North from the perspectives of Indigenous peoples and northerners but, rather, contributes to a critical interrogation of the colonial relationships that have underpinned Native-newcomer relations in Canada, interlaced as they are with North-South relations. By uncovering and analyzing cultural discourses about northern Indigeneity that circulated in the post–Second World War period, this book extends the discussion of our troubled history of colonialism as it was mapped out on the landscape of popular, educational, and more "highbrow" cultural production.

My questions about how the North was perceived emerged from my previous work on Indigenous women and paid labour. When the federal government introduced labour placement programs for Aboriginal women in the 1950s, it was assumed that women of many First Nations needed a cultural makeover in order to transition to a modern capitalist economy, despite the fact that many had been participating in the market economy since the last century. Cultural suppositions about an "Indian personality," about the cultural baggage Aboriginal women brought with them from reserves, and about how Native cultures inevitably clashed with modernity figured prominently in these policy discussions. "Industry is moving north," notes one government pamphlet, and Indians, now "living in simple style ... in places far from cities ... provide a nearby source of labour." The Indian character, attuned to the "sun, moon and tides" rather than "clocks and calendars," and Native aversion to material acquisition and individualism, are "disadvantages" to their integration into the life of working-class affluence. While this public-outreach pamphlet also speaks of the need to preserve aspects of Indigenous cultures, it constructs an essentialized Native person it equates with northern "wilderness," while associating whites with modernity and "industry."[4]

Understanding the nexus of culture and labour, and how the former became a totalizing explanation that left colonialism unnamed, hidden, and forgotten, thus became an important question for me. How, I asked, was cultural representation an integral part of persisting colonial relations? How were images, understandings, and communications implicated in public perceptions and state policy, in media and education, all part of the daily fabric of life, so "taken for granted" that they allowed

Indigenous people to be seen as both romanticized and reviled, at the same time backward, childlike, heroic, vanishing – but always needing reinvention? How did relations of gender, class, and colonialism interconnect, and was there appreciable change in the northern imaginary over time?

The northern part of my question emerged in a more happenstance way, typical of historians' innate curiosity and wandering eye for textual artefacts from the past, as evidentiary clues lead us from one source to another. Since I spend a lot of time in second-hand bookstores with my book-collector partner, I began to sit in the Arctic section and read women's travel narratives. They became an entrée to my previous question, the first of a series of detours, leads, and queries pointing in other cultural directions. The question of northern colonialism also preoccupied me because I am situated in a research centre with a long-standing interest in the North and a commitment to understanding and critiquing Canada as a colonial project.

It is a fundamental argument of this book that cultural constructions of the North must be framed within the changing political economy and history of postwar Canada. A focus on culture need not generate a *culturalist* discursive determinism or assume a rejection of historical materialism, feminism, or traditional empirical methods of historical research, all of which assume there is a reality out there to be grasped – perhaps not definitively known, but grasped. This study is materialist in its assumption that the economic and political underpinnings of settler colonial relations are born of struggles for control over land and resources and, thus, domination over other humans: "territoriality," as Patrick Wolfe concludes, "is settler colonialism's specific, irreducible element."[5] Questions of power cannot be separated from the defining elements of material life, including the forms of production and social reproduction that create and sustain societies, and the social and political relations shaping how people survive and produce cultures over time. Colonialism is, however, far more than a set of changing political and economic structures with its own contradictions; it is also a lived experience of domination, negotiation, and resistance – and a profoundly gendered one at that.

Historical, materialist, and feminist questions should prompt us to ask: Why these images at this point in time? How might the depictions of Aboriginal peoples have emerged from past cultural resources, yet been reshaped in the postwar period, leaving a profound legacy for the future? Which groups benefited from these images and how? Such an approach recognizes that the commodities, ideologies, and human interactions of northern colonialism were part of (and sometimes replicated) larger global and spatial processes, but they took on historically and regionally specific contours: in the North, Cole Harris argues, dispossession and development were often "telescoped tightly" together within a short time frame, with the former justified in the liberal modernization language of the latter.[6] Similarly, Lisa Piper shows that development in the northwest was distinct from Prairie agricultural settlement: in the North, the state and private enterprise primarily "sought resources suited to industrialized marketplaces" and to "fuel[ling] industrial capitalism." While Aboriginals perceived a northern landscape integrated into their culture, Euro-Canadians could only see a "physical landscape" that could and should be plumbed for its riches.[7] It is hardly surprising, then, that a dominant anthropological perspective of the time assumed one should study the inevitable: modernization and acculturation.[8]

As a concept of space and place, the North had exercised an important role in the imaginary construction of the Canadian nation-state since the nineteenth century, influencing political visions and economic power, and it was also shaped *by* those forces. From the 1940s onward, however, the North assumed a new economic and political significance in Canadian life. Although the fur trade was facing economic difficulties, the North was promoted by other business concerns as Canada's last economic frontier of development, holding the promise of generating wealth for all and *requiring* development, just as the western frontier had been portrayed as empty, unused, literally wasted by communally centred Indians until it was developed by white settler-farmers and corporate property holders.[9] Even when Prairie Aboriginals attempted commercial farming, as Sarah Carter shows, the state favoured white agricultural development, rationalizing its policies with a cultural explanation for Aboriginal disinterest in farming.[10] Although situated in a different landscape, her research should raise our critical antennae when we read later cultural constructions of the Indigenous North.

The state saw Canada's best interests tied up with northern development, whether this new northern "National Policy" was articulated through Conservative John Diefenbaker's electioneering vision of a new North or Liberal Jean Lesage's ministerial call to include Indigenous peoples in resource development.[11] The close connection between the fate of the North, resource development, and Indigenous peoples was symbolized by the changing nomenclature of the federal departments responsible for these areas. Until 1949, many aspects of northern administration came under the Department of Mines and Resources, which was later transmogrified into the Department of Resources and Development, and merged again in 1954 into the Department of Northern Affairs and National Resources. In 1965, responsibility for "Indian Affairs," previously centred in the Department of Citizenship and Immigration, was transferred to the newly created Department of Indian Affairs and Northern Development.[12] In Ottawa's eyes, the North was about minerals, resources, and development.

By examining cultural production in this context of political economy, space, and power, we are able to better understand how it was defined by different "positionalities, possibilities, and contradictions."[13] This "realist" and historical materialist outlook does not assume that cultural representations are the mere epiphenomena of economic structures or the conscious creations of state and capital,[14] any more than it assumes that they flow freely in an ether of ideas, unmoored from social relations. They are linked in a complex process of ideological engagement, in which cultural discourses do the work of communicating, explaining, legitimating, and justifying. Rather than defining culture as a "bounded domain," Gramscian theorists suggest, it is better conceived of as an organic part of society, encompassing ways of thinking and social practices that explain the world. These are always positioned and precipitated within specific social and historical contexts. Cultural discourses may be shot through with contradiction, and they are neither fixed nor unchangeable, as human agency has a role to play not only in constructing but also in questioning the relationship of culture to "real" lives, identities, and goals. What is important, then, is not just to define what culture is but to explore how it circulates and how it is implicated in "constellations" of power relations.[15]

Finally, an approach that explores colonial images predominantly from the perspective of the more powerful – the colonizers – does not assume that the contact zone was a one-way street, with colonizers exercising power unidimensionally. As the documentary *Qallunaat! Why White People Are Funny* shows, Inuit people had their own critical, cynical, humorous, incredulous constructions of the Qallunaat.[16] While some excellent studies explore Aboriginal-settler dialogic "exchanges,"[17] or, like Mary-Ellen Kelm's investigation of western Canadian rodeo, human experience, and "hybridity,"[18] this study focuses more on the culturally dominant settler images employed to define the northern contact zone. As a consequence, it does not attempt to speak *for*, or even definitely *about*, Indigenous actors, a presumption that colonized groups have repeatedly criticized.[19] However, by suggesting some tensions between and within historical sources, and some disjuncture between colonial images and the reflections of northern Indigenous peoples, it implicitly validates the importance of bringing to light alternative Indigenous understandings of history and colonialism.

KEYWORDS: DEFINING NORTH, COLONIALISM, RACE

This exploration of various representational contact zones is situated at the intersection of a number of historiographical and theoretical literatures, all of which have been deeply concerned with definitional "keywords" that shape our writing in crucial ways. While I use a shorthand vocabulary of generalized terms, like "North" and "colonialism," I acknowledge the importance of recurrent debate over the suppositions behind such terminology. The North, as other scholars ranging from geographers to literary theorists have suggested, is not only defined by geography and climate or the officially designated line of the Arctic Circle: it is also an imaginary construct, a "state of mind,"[20] and, for Canadians, an ideal linked to our national identity. As ads told us during the last Olympic Games, Canadians "*are* winter": we *are* the North. Like

Sherrill Grace, whose writing has influenced my thinking, I understand the North in Canadian cultural production as an "idea" and a "creative process" as much as a "physical space." For Grace, the North is a "creation in words, sounds, signs and symbols of northern mentality," and, while normalized as essential to Canada, it is a product of "habitas, a human construct we have learned to accept as a 'given.'"[21]

While indebted to the expansive literary perspectives of Grace and others, I am primarily concerned here with the work of culture as it was expressed in the thirty years after the Second World War through practices and images depicting the eastern Arctic and the Northwest Territories (the current Nunavut, Inuvialuit, Nunatsiavut, Yukon, and NWT), and, in one chapter, the western provincial North. Indeed, I selected case studies from a range of northern geographical locations precisely for the diversity they provide. Historians who suggest that our knowledge of the North is best built upon an understanding of the historical and structural characteristics of the region – with an eye to the physical, human, economic, and social "struggles" and conflicts of the area – make eminent sense to me. One of those arenas of struggle identified by Kenneth Coates is that explored here: "the struggle between popular culture and reality."[22]

Since the North in this time period was constantly invoked in the mainstream media as Canada's last frontier – one where settlers and Indigenous peoples were engaged in constructing *new* relationships, in contrast to the old, tattered antagonism of (southern) Indian and white – it provides a scene ripe for the analysis of cultural messages about Natives and newcomers, which many observers equated with the meeting of tradition and modernity. Postwar visitors, sojourners, and state officials often claimed that the Inuit were *different* from the southern Natives in personality (evidenced by their hospitable relations with whites) and even in their willingness to adapt to Western ways. Was this, however, little more than a rationalization of colonial incursion as this white frontier/Native homeland was increasingly occupied, valued especially for its strategic position in the global Cold War and the resources it might yield?[23] The European "obsession" with the romanticized image of stoic but happy Inuit, facing environmental adversity with unending cheerfulness, was not entirely new. Writers had long been fascinated with Inuit hunting culture, so diametrically different from "peasant, soil-based" agricultural cultures, as Hugh Brody argues. The political economy of the postwar period could only accentuate this perceived contrast between northern and southern First Nations: while the southern Indians had been "warlike," standing in the way of "progress" as whites spread aggressively across the western frontier, the Inuit now "smiled happily from the sidelines" as whites carved out their new frontier in the North.[24]

Indigenous peoples are not categorized in this book as they were by the government of the time – as status Indian, non-status Indian, and Eskimo – though when describing and paraphrasing sources, I sometimes use those designations as if they were in "scare quotes" to replicate the true flavour of the discourse and sensibility of the time. More often I use the terms "Native," "Indigenous," "First Nations," or "Aboriginal" as the Royal Commission on Aboriginal Peoples (RCAP) has, basing this designation primarily on people's self-identification. In some circumstances, nevertheless, it is necessary to disaggregate general terms in order to analyze a more precise cultural construction of Métis, Inuit, Innu, or Indian – because this is what colonial discourse did, creating distinctions between groups that, in turn, revealed much about those creating colonial ideologies.

This is a complicated issue for historical sources sometimes distinguish between, but more often homogenize, Indigenous peoples in the northern imaginary: the Innu and Inuit, no matter where they lived across the vast expanse of the North, from Coppermine to Baffin Island to Labrador (today Inuvialuit, Nunavut, Nunavik, and Nunatsiavut), were often collapsed in popular parlance into one category – the Eskimo – even though these groups were not just geographically but also socially and culturally distinct.[25] Even well-travelled knowledgeable white sojourners succumbed to this unifying tendency, as filmmaker Doug Wilkinson did when he noted of different Inuit regions: "The Eskimo problem is universal; it is present wherever there are Eskimo."[26] Because this book touches down across the North, I inevitably relay images of different First Nations: blurring them together is not my intent, even if discourses at the time did so. The chapter on women's travel narratives focuses predominantly on women posted in the eastern Arctic, particularly current Nunavik and Nunavut, while the one on the Royal Commission on the Status of Women (RCSW) is briefer in its treatment of Inuit settlements since the commission only heard testimony in Yukon and the Northwest Territories, primarily about Athapaskan First Peoples, for example, the Gwich'in (Dene), who were simply described as Indians. The Dene at the time were multiple, comprising about eight language groups, with different resource bases, social groupings, and cultural practices – distinctions not absorbed by the RCSW.[27] My discussion of the National Film Board (NFB) films offers specificity where it can, for example, when the Netsilik or Tununermiut Inuit are featured, but filmmakers also veered towards generalization when they outlined development across the entire Mackenzie district in *Canada's Awakening North*, taking in different Dene groups, northern Cree, and Inuit. The *RCMP* television series was the most unconcerned with ethnographic naming: First Nations were fluid in their hands, hybridized and re-imagined into fictional entities.

Even more contested are the descriptive categories "colonialism," "Eurocentric," and "race." They are all distinct, yet they overlap and may inform or reinforce each other: racism, as Ella Shoat comments, is "not unique to the West" but has often been colonialism's "ally and by-product."[28] "Colonialism" is a term now commonly used in Canadian history books dealing with the First Nations, yet a generation ago it often described Anglo-French Canadian or Canada-US relations and, generations before that, Canadian-British ones. If we take "colonial" to denote the power exerted by a metropolitan area over a peripheral one, and the concurrent economic, political, or cultural domination of peoples through formal and/or informal means – ranging from disciplining jurisprudence to acculturating education – then the maxim that the Indigenous North existed in a colonial relationship to the South seems self-evident.

In the postwar period, many northerners used the word "colonial" to evoke their unhappiness with the North's "colonial status" since the NWT was administered from within a federal department and lacked the

autonomous powers exercised by the provinces.[29] Not until 1967 did this
territorial government move north. As Kenneth Coates and Kerry Abel
argue, the term "colonial" is particularly meaningful in northern history
given the direct control that Ottawa exerted over northern lands, governance, and peoples: "In geographic terms," they note, "Canada is
the largest colonizing power in the contemporary world."[30] Indigenous
peoples increasingly employed the term "colonialism" after the late 1960s
quite differently, as a political keyword to describe their relationship to
white-dominated governments. Colonialism as a form of rule was critiqued by a growing anticolonial movement that wanted to name the previously unnamed relations of subordination and exploitation Indigenous
peoples had experienced. Until that time, non-Indigenous northerners
seldom described Native-newcomer relations as essentially colonial in the
sense we think of the term: with connotations of race, Eurocentrism, and
imperialism. That was to change after the 1960s as some non-Indigenous
allies threw their support behind the First Nations political project of
decolonization.

Current definitions of colonialism in the Canadian context have been
shaped by decades of historical literature detailing Euro-Canadians' aggressive efforts to lay claim to Indigenous lands and to alter Indigenous
cultures and social practices in ways deemed to be better for them: all this
rationalized as necessary progress. This is not to designate good and bad
people, colonial actors and colonized victims, as popular and conservative historians claim feminist academics do whenever we write critically
about past injustices. Rather, it speaks to the importance of understanding historical processes, whereby forms of political, economic, and social
power were exercised over less powerful or subordinated groups, and
also to identifying the rationale for these power relations. Understanding
Canada as an "evolving colonial entity,"[31] with layers of colonial relations that change over time and involve different groups, is an apt way of
describing colonialism in its Canadian incarnation. While there can be
no doubt that economic, political, and cultural control and regulation
of Indigenous lands and peoples is an integral part of our history, the
Indigenous North may not always fit comfortably into theories and models of colonialism.[32]

Colonialism remains an overly general term. As Marx and Engels noted in the nineteenth century, the need for markets "chased the bourgeoisie" across the whole world so that colonialism became global: "It must nestle everywhere, settle everywhere and establish connections everywhere."[33] Colonialism might have nestled everywhere, but settler colonialism, which more accurately describes the dominant Canadian experience, is a distinct variant within the general rubric of colonialism, though this term, too, is highly contested. The older, British definition of "settler colonialism," which stresses demography – necessarily meaning a numerically dominant white majority – does not apply universally to the Canadian North.[34] Patrick Wolfe's definition, which equates settler colonialism with differing relationships to land and labour and the dispensability (or not) of Indigenous bodies and work to the colonial project, has far more relevance. Still, his assertion that the settler-colonial project usually replaced Indigenous peoples is also out of kilter with the Nunavut experience, as are Australian definitions of settler colonialism, which emphasize the complete segregation of Indigenous peoples.[35]

Even if colonial and settler-colonial forms "interpenetrate" one another, as Lorenzo Veracini argues in his theoretical text on the subject, they are still "antithetical" in nature, with settler colonialism characterized particularly by its desire and capacity to "control the population economy" as a "marker of its sovereignty."[36] Settler colonialism is not only shaped by a different political economy from "trading post" or "franchise" colonialism,[37] but it also develops distinct means of self-legitimation, particularly that of storytelling, with respect to its meaning and existence. Veracini's characterization of these "narratives forms" as modes of "transfer" is useful to my discussion of the Indigenous North because he emphasizes multiple forms of transfer, or of control, that range from forceful relocation to far more subtle marginalization. The transfer of Indigenous peoples from their homeland might involve not only their physical and geographical removal but also forms of conceptual, narrative, accounting, or assimilative transfers – to name a few.[38] Still, this characterization of settler colonialism might also be understood within the conceptual framework of ideology, which, as Patrick Wolfe argues, is also peppered with contradictions. Ideas that promote "elimination" of the Native from the land (because settlers "use it better") may be accompanied by the symbolic celebration and recuperation of Native cultural forms, claimed by settlers as part of their nationalist self-construction.[39]

Since the 1960s, some have also used the designation "internal colonialism" to describe Indian reservations and minorities of colour in the United States as well as Canadian Indigenous-settler relations; indeed, the concept burst into northern studies with particular force in the Berger Commission era, when it was employed by Mel Watkins to describe Canada and the Dene nation.[40] The concept of internal colonialism, when first advanced by Robert Blauer (and more recently reiterated by Russell Benjamin), embodied a strong political and moral critique of US imperialism. They argue that colonialism may involve both transnational *and* internal political and economic domination, with both Native and Mexican Americans key examples of the latter.[41] E. San Juan makes a strong case for its continuing effectiveness in the theoretical toolkit of anticolonial analysis. He explicates the areas of overlap between transnational and internal colonialism, arguing that the latter term remains a compelling descriptor of the cultural domination of people of colour within the United States who are "alienated from their land base" and "structurally disadvantaged" by the way they are "integrated into the national polity."[42] There are obvious similarities to the Canadian Indigenous North.

It is no accident that the term "internal colonialism" was first taken up during the 1970s, when Marxist concepts such as exploitation, underdevelopment, and imperialism were au courant and radicals outlined clear winners and losers in the processes of the capitalist search for marketable resources on Native lands. For Aboriginal activists at the time, internal colonialism became a Fanon-like description of the daily racist assaults on Native peoples' inner being as well as an economic model that involved economic dispossession, political paternalism, and ideologies of racial superiority.[43] Such political concerns have not evaporated. Shari Huhndorf's more recent study of American whites "going Native" uses the term "internal colonialism" as a means of disputing popular misconceptions of American "exceptionalism" to global imperialism: she wants to remind Americans that they, too, were involved with the "dis-possession" of their own Native peoples.[44]

Attempting a Canadian definition of internal colonialism, J.S. Frideres developed a model denoting requisite indicators, including incursion into Native territory, destruction of social and cultural norms, political control, economic dependency, reserves as hinterlands to a metropolitan centre, the provision of low-quality services, and an ideology of racism.[45] While ideal-type models like this one have been refined, they have also been critiqued. The historical process of colonialism may need a less stiffly reified mode of analysis, one that takes into account historical complexity, changing modes of production, Aboriginal agency, and differences within and between Aboriginal communities.[46] Colonialism proceeded unevenly and in a different manner across the country; moreover, the internal-colonialism model often focuses primarily on reserves, which are home to only some Indigenous peoples. The term also simplifies a complex history of racialization in Canada that encompasses many groups and homogenizes the assumed opposing interests of white versus Indigenous. Such a polarized model fundamentally sidelines class and gender divisions within these overly homogenized categories, as if all whites have the same economic interests. The state, too, can become a singular, unified, and purposeful enterprise of domination when research suggests a more complicated picture.[47] For all its failings, however, the term has a particular political and moral resonance, especially for the North, even if it lacks rigour as a confirmable model for all Indigenous nations. As Linda Gordon suggests in her rethinking of the term for American usage, it may be an apt political *metaphor* for a historical relationship that,[48] on the one hand, involved dispossession, segregation, and cultural denigration, yet, on the other hand, also created forms of resistance, self-definitions, and longings for self-determination.

Colonialism may or may not be buttressed by Eurocentrism, the ethnocentric view emanating from Europe of an advanced Western culture, political institutions, and economic organization. Eurocentric ideas often assume a linear history with Europe at the centre of progress, spreading superior ideas, science, and culture outward to the less developed (or perhaps "slower to develop") peripheries. Various rationales – race, culture, environment – are used to explain why the West is a unique and autonomous world leader, always the "Inside diffusing its culture to the Outside."[49] European norms (better termed "Euro-Canadian" in this book) are equated with the necessary path of progress, including development and democracy – ironically, as some European nations "appropriated [the] culture and material production" of other groups, and suppressed their own forms of democracy.[50] Rather than seeing Eurocentric ideas as mere "prejudice," argues J.M. Blaut, it is important to analyze their ideological role and subtle incorporation into expert, academic, scientific forms of knowledge, so taken for granted that they appear to be reality or truth.[51]

Moreover, explaining colonialism only through the power of Eurocentrism ignores the history of non-European colonial relations, problematically occludes class, and denies diversity and distinctions between European groups – some of which were also racialized. Nor does it fully explain the timing and intensity of colonial activity, such as the nineteenth- and twentieth-century imperialist era of European conquest – in Marxist terminology, the "last stage of capitalism." Eurocentrism is better seen as a set of "historically situated discourses," not a "genetic inheritance" of all white Europeans or the sole cause of colonialism.[52] Moreover, critiques of colonial power and oppression are also part of the European, Western political tradition. These theories provide useful tools in scrutinizing colonialism in all its varieties. As Andrea Smith and Joyce Green show, for instance, feminism is not a theory fatally encumbered by its Western origins: it offers insight into the connections between colonialism, patriarchal ideologies, and capitalist social relations.[53]

"Eurocentrism," Blaut argues in his classic on the subject, is the "colonizers' model of the world." But Eurocentrism has a complex association with "race," which must always be historically situated in relation to specific colonizing projects. Race, most academic writing agrees, is a socially constructed category, even though it was often equated with identifiable physical differences, such as the "Oriental look" and "slanted eyes" on which whites commented so often in their writing on the Inuit. Like class, race is better thought of as a process or evolving formation rather than as a thing or objective category. It is "relational, contingent and contextual," always created within a historical dialectic of structure and agency.[54] The connection of race to colonial projects also shifts over time: in the nineteenth century, race increasingly became the "organizing grammar" for colonialism, supplanting a more varied list of organizing principles and justifications.[55] As this transpired, race became a means of ideologically ordering humans into unchanging categories, linking "natural essences and physical characteristics" to unchangeable "social hierarchies."[56] Most often, these categories constructed an axis of white supremacy and black inferiority, with other peoples situated in complex manifestations along a continuum in between, though this varied with the colonial project. Ideologies of racial difference may be theoretically dismissed as ideological constructions, but they are remarkably resilient, often anchored in material relations of power, privilege, expropriation, and exploitation. Renisa Mawani's work on Canadian legal discourses exposes the shifting truths asserted by colonial powers about race, showing how these categories never had any "ontological essence." Still, it is revealing that, no matter how they shifted, they consistently buttressed white European authority and state policies.[57]

Writing on race in a postcolonial vein points to its fluidity, hybridity, even capricious redefinitions, but the effects of racism have been undeniably real: violence, dispossession, hatred, both external and internalized. Its manifestation in Canadian history is evidenced in writing on culture, law, immigration, education, the economy, politics, and in many specific examples of racialized groups constructed as "other" to the preferred white nation. That "white" nation was itself a construct rather than a reality. While I may abstractly juxtapose the "white" South to an "Indigenous" North in this book, this schematic shorthand does not mean that I assume that the southern population was undifferentiated by class, race, and ethnicity: quite the contrary, for it, too, was rent with differentiation and division. Such racial categorization may have been invoked at the time, but contemporary critiques of race would now militate against pronouncement about a white South. Indeed, scholars interrogating the national narrative of race, space, and nature are now directing their attention to the "imaginary" of the "Great White North."[58]

Although some classical racist ideas about innate physical differences grounded in biology still existed in the post–Second World War period, it was expositions of cultural difference that more profoundly shaped writing on Indigenous peoples in Canada – a reflection of international intellectual trends in the "transposition of racial arguments into cultural ones."[59] Most academic and cultural writing equated ideas about the natural superiority of the white race, negatively, with the Ku Klux Klan or Nazism, ideas that had supposedly been overthrown along with Hitler. The post-1945 era saw new human rights claims articulated in intellectual circles and international organizations like the United Nations as well as some emerging rights-based legislation in Canada. When the word "race" was still used, as it was for French Canadians, it might actually be a synonym for culture or ethnicity. Even if classical racism was subdued in postwar Canada, the term "culture" could act as a stand-in for "race" – still denoting evolutionary ideas about superiority/ inferiority through concepts of progress, development, and cultural sophistication. As in Britain's imperial colonies, ideas of race still "underwrote the distinctions of colonial rule" long after the colonizers adopted the rhetoric of racial equality.[60] Cultural relativism and a rhetorical nod to racial equality could coexist alongside practices of racialization. As Blaut argues, racial thinking became more difficult to identify and critique for precisely this reason. In depictions of the Inuit especially, race was sometimes reinscribed as a "false compliment" through an emphasis on Inuit people's "primitivism and exoticism," which idealized their "natural" state but also kept them encased in a static history of the past.[61]

HISTORY AND THEORY IN DIALOGUE

My understanding of the cultural construction of northern contact zones has been shaped by intersecting areas of scholarship on cultural production, debates about colonialism and postcolonialism, and analyses of northern history. Each chapter delves into more specific debates about using novels, women's travel writing, documentary film, television studies, and so on. Because my case studies are so diverse in nature, I have kept much of this expository discussion chapter-specific. Nonetheless, broader debates about history, culture, and colonialism have provided an overall framework for *The Iconic North*. Since context is critical to how I interpret texts, I am indebted to the extensive northern historical scholarship in Canada. It would be impossible to reflect on images of the North without an understanding of the state, the politics of northern development, and histories of settlers and Indigenous peoples, among other topics explored by historians of the North. Moreover, both historians' and political economists' modernist assumptions about the importance of excavating human experience, grasping evidentiary reality, and uncovering the interplay of social and material structures with human agency resonate in important ways for my research.

The North as a symbol of national identity has its own extensive historiography. It has preoccupied historians, from the late-nineteenth-century Canada First nationalists to W.L. Morton's twentieth-century claim that the nation is an ever-moving northern frontier to more recent Foucauldian claims that the Canadian North is produced through a "discourse of power."[62] Though historians may differ on the exact origins, meaning, and effects of this equation of Canadian history with nordicity, they find common agreement that the "country as North" has been a changing theme in interpretations of history.[63] As Sherrill Grace points out, this extends to art, music, fiction, and theatre.[64] That many of the earliest Euro-Canadian historians integrated assumptions of white racial superiority into their interpretation of nordicity and obscured Indigenous peoples as the North's first inhabitants is now widely understood. Contemporary historians, whose work is more attuned to a critique of racial hierarchies and colonial relations, are attempting to create different debates, themes, and understandings of Canada as North.[65] While they point to unanswered questions and debate the best conceptual frameworks for researchers, historians' academic production of northern histories has proliferated and diversified remarkably in the last few decades and is often characterized by a vibrant interdisciplinarity.

Overviews of northern history, studies of the evolving political institutions and government policies in the territorial and Arctic North, and examinations of the interface between foreign and domestic policy interests, especially over the sovereignty question, have been critical in setting the stage for my work, as have more in-depth studies of Indigenous-settler relations, including relocations of Indigenous communities.[66] Without understanding the government's priorities on economic development, one cannot understand the NFB films funded and produced in this time period. Without historians' discussions of the immense political, economic, and social changes over the postwar period in the North, including the contradictions these changes created, one cannot read Irene Baird's fiction productively. Moreover, one cannot interpret any of this cultural change without attention to history, the environment, and political economy. As Frank Tough argues of subarctic Manitoba, an approach lacking political economy can, ironically, "generate a history which exculpates colonialism" by overemphasizing culture and ignoring differing modes of labour,[67] the accumulation and distribution of wealth, and the resulting processes of dependency and exploitation.

Historians have also been sensitive to the sensual and spatial difference of the North, pointing to the importance of cold, space, and distance "not only as a physical reality but as a state of mind" in writing on the North.[68] Comparative thinking about the structural characteristics of the North, in comparison to other remote regions also faced with "struggles of human populations against external and internal forces, both conceptual and physical," has opened up into studies of land, resources, and conflict between groups, both Indigenous and non-Indigenous.[69] One of the more transformative shifts in northern historical work since the 1980s has been the focus on First Nations histories as well as the importance of gender as a category of historical analysis.[70] While some historians have redeveloped concerns articulated years ago in staples writing on the fur trade, now giving agency and presence to Aboriginal peoples, others have explored Indigenous cultures, legal traditions, health, and political mobilizations.[71] Writing on Indigenous-settler relations has emerged not only from documentary and archival research but also from methodologies of anthropological fieldwork, participant observation, and oral histories collected both by outside researchers and Indigenous and non-Indigenous northerners on a path of historical self-recovery.

The documenting of life histories, as Chapter 7 notes, was a nascent method used in one of the northern studies conducted by feminist and socially conscious anthropologists for the Royal Commission on the Status of Women.

Historical writing on Native-newcomer interactions through trade, missions, law, labour, and white exploration – the latter not only a predominantly masculine enterprise but also one *in masculinity* – have been invaluable, and they sometimes serve as a revealing foil to the cultural constructions of the North during the 1940s and 1950s.[72] While contributions to *The Beaver* and/or sojourner narratives suggest a battle between Christianity and "primitive" shamanism or paganism, for instance, historians have unearthed a more complex story of the interchange and overlap of religious beliefs.[73] Historical and anthropological research on economic shifts in men and women's work in northern communities have altered our understanding of gender, challenging the simplistic postwar image relayed through film of universally patriarchal hunting cultures.[74] (Admittedly, more stereotypical images of the northern male prospector, red-coated policeman, and venturesome white woman entrepreneur may still find their appeal in popular histories.)[75]

Understanding the changing cultural construction of Indigeneity has been a major preoccupation in cultural history and cultural studies, although, with a few notable exceptions,[76] authors have focused more on Indigenous peoples in the United States and southern areas of Canada than on Indigenous peoples in the North. Indigenous scholars have spoken powerfully about the dominant mass media images that historically bombarded their own communities, distorting Native experiences and cultures and, tragically, internalized by their own people. Harold Adams, a Native rights advocate in the 1970s, urged his fellow Native peoples to simply abandon efforts to "improve our image ... because native people did not create these images," and, if Indigenous peoples tried to improve them, white society "would simply create new racist images."[77] Contrary to Adams's pessimism, many Indigenous writers and artists subsequently took up the project, creating their own cultural imaginary and sometimes turning the colonial images back on themselves.[78]

Critical investigations of the disjuncture between a colonial image of Indigeneity and "real" Indigenous peoples were thus increasingly stimulated not only by Indigenous organizing, self-articulation, and objections to the stereotypes that had long plagued them, but also by sympathetic historians' recognition that racism and colonialism were integral parts of the Canadian nation-building project. Most historical writing assumes that one can disentangle racist construction from historical reality: the very use of the word "stereotype" discloses this assumption. Uncertain about imposing their own decisive images on Indigenous peoples, non-Indigenous historians may protest that they don't want to "argue" with the stereotypes but simply have us "think about them" – yet their writing indicates that this line is not so easily drawn, with all judgment avoided.[79] Stereotypes, as Homi Bhabha writes, are the mainstay of imperialism, but, unlike his postmodern-inflected writing, historians tend to operate under the assumption that stereotypes can be dissected, challenged, and differentiated from interpretations that come far closer to the truth.

The imaginary Indian, in particular, has been the subject of many studies, drawing on a wide array of textual and visual sources from photography and film to literature, folklore, cartoons, art, mass media, history, and other expert academic discourses.[80] Historical analyses have the advantage of encouraging *historicization*, with their attendant emphasis on contextualization and change over time. American studies opened up discussion of the ways in which changing constructions of the Indian were also efforts to articulate a truly American white identity, often through whites encountering an "authentic" antimodern, primitive, traditional Aboriginal identity: the modern and premodern were thus "mutually constituted."[81] "Playing Indian" and "going Native" were not just exercises in cultural exchange: they were tied up with processes of domination and subordination, and with efforts to assuage white anxiety, creating comforting justifications for white political domination and the dispossession of Native land.[82]

The "Imaginary Indian" in Canada, as Douglas Francis similarly shows, reflects the "changing values" of whites, revealing a process whereby Euro-Canadians defined and redefined themselves in distinction to the Indigenous other.[83] Euro-Canadians wanted to make themselves into what Indians were not: that is, committed to progress, development, rationality, and cultural sophistication (often seen as masculine attributes as well). The precise nature of this "othering" altered over time: the early idealization of the noble Native gave way to demonization when Aboriginal peoples were perceived to be standing in the way of political and economic objectives – namely, settler control of land and resources. The created fantasy of the Indian therefore had an important legitimating task – though it was also fraught with contradictions, with Indians both othered and integrated as folkloric mementoes into the Canadian identity. The latter observation was true of the Inuit, too, as Nellie Cournoyea's opening comment indicates. Some postcolonial theorists of settler-colonial societies place this contradictory process of "desire and disavowal" at the heart of their analysis: the settler occupies a place between two worlds of authority and authenticity, the "imperial culture from which he is separated" and the world of the First Nations whose authority he "replaced and effaced, but also *desired*."[84]

The legitimization of white settler societies also buttressed a particular gender as well as racial order. Fantasies of the female Indian acted as a foil to idealized, middle-class, white female identity by suggesting an opposite – the Native "wild woman."[85] If Indigenous women were integrated into or appeared to justify the colonizing project, they were assessed more positively, as the extensive literature on the Pocahontas myth and its opposite, the debased "squaw," suggest.[86] Many nineteenth-century studies of colonial image making indicate how gender ideology literally underwrote the formation of the settler-colonial nation-state. Sarah Carter's work on nineteenth-century captivity narratives and the political ferment surrounding the 1885 Rebellion, for instance, highlights how normative discourses about white women constructed in opposition to images of Indigenous women became forms of regulation that, in themselves, were "useful to those in power," fitting into a settlement-and-pacification agenda.[87] The imperative of protecting white women from the danger of Indigenous men and the need to transform Indigenous women's moral values were both part of the rationalizing ideology of colonial domination. Moreover, these colonial ideas were transnational, shared across white settler societies through colonial discourses and shared policy objectives, including efforts to "domesticate" Indigenous women into appropriate familial roles.[88] The part that white women play in the colonial project does differ across time, place, and according to women's social location. I argue that this nineteenth-century emphasis on the vulnerability of white women and the imperative of instructing Aboriginal peoples on the virtues of a patriarchal family could no longer be employed in 1950s Canada. Instead, white women were now portrayed as beneficiaries of the modern family, enjoying equal and companionate relations with men: this was the contemporary version of femininity to which Indigenous women were to aspire in their cultural makeover.

Contextualizing Indigenous imagery in terms of the prevailing social formation and historical period is also critical for visual historians who explore the changing representation of Canadian Native peoples in state-sponsored images produced by the NFB. For Carol Payne and Zoe Druick, for instance, we can only understand the intent of images and film, and the objectives they accomplish, within a political context of power relations: they ask what kind of citizen identity was being created at this time, why, and by whom.[89] Their writing defines power relations in a more Foucauldian manner than mine, with more emphasis on governmentality and the "impersonal networks of power that buttress authority;"[90] however, they also trace processes of cultural hegemony and are acutely attuned to the power of the state without reducing NFB personnel to historical actors lacking agency or complexity. As Payne shows, many NFB photographers embraced an idealized image of the multicultural Canadian nation, inclusive of Indigenous peoples. Their intended project was to convey this message of tolerance to the wider population. Moreover, what we interpret as colonial and racialized images can also play a different role for Indigenous peoples when these images are repatriated to Indigenous communities for their reinterpretation and use.[91]

Understanding the manufacturing of consent through an ideology of multiculturalism is critically important for this era. As Eva McKay argues, after the Second World War, but especially after the 1960s, the state promoted a discourse of multicultural tolerance that many civil society organizations took up with considerable enthusiasm. On the one hand, Indigenous peoples were still represented as racialized others – the case of the stoic, happy, childlike but adaptable Eskimo being a case in point. On the other hand, cultural diversity and tolerance were increasingly popularized and became "intrinsic to the Canadian identity," literally a "national resource" to be treasured.[92] This, too, reflected international shifts in the meaning of race as "cultural pluralism, value relativism, and mutual tolerance" became the liberal means of "discussing social difference." The end goal, however, was not equality but, rather, "an alternative society of tolerance of difference,"[93] an ideal that left colonial relationships, including an imaginary "ladder of progress" from primitive to modernity, unquestioned.

THE ELUSIVENESS OF REPRESENTATION

Many cultural historians raise the thorny question of whether representation can be understood outside its discursive creation, pointing out that "we only have access to the real through representation."[94] The elusiveness of representation is often discussed with relation to how the reader or viewer negotiates the image or text. As Peter Geller points out in his analysis of northern photography before 1945, most visual historians try to analyze the "production, circulation and reception" of the image, but the latter always remains something of a question mark in comparison to the other two categories.[95] The ambiguous "unreliability" of texts,[96] visual or otherwise, produced about the Indigenous North is particularly obvious and concerning because many forms of representation were purposely – but also unwittingly – produced in the service of the colonial gaze, often by non-Indigenous people. An interpretive middle ground is explored in one collection on photography and the Arctic "imaginary": while the legacy of postmodernism no longer permits a completely "realist" interpretation of images as literal reflections of the past, representations are created and interpreted within identifiable historical and social contexts, which suggests that there are not unlimited interpretations to be extracted from them. If representation can no longer be cast as a vehicle of truth, it does construct "certain truths about certain categories of people."[97]

When studying colonialism and representation, it is impossible to escape the immense influence of postcolonial theory – especially in visual and literary studies, where postcolonialism has arguably had its most profound impact. Writing labelled "postcolonial" is so diffuse in theoretical approach that it is risky to make generalizations. Critics have also equated this vagueness, and the universalizing assumptions of its most enthusiastic advocates, with its lack of explanatory rigour. All forms of colonialism, they point out, cannot be homogenized across time periods, peoples, and empires; attempting to do so effectively collapses temporal, spatial, and historical specificities into a linear story of moving "beyond colonialism," highly problematic nomenclature in a world of continuing colonial relations.

The most general intention of much postcolonial theory – to better understand and challenge the discursive means and methods of colonialism's cultural reproduction – is congruent with the project of this book.[98] Insights from postcolonial writing are apparent in the way I read the texts and images in *The Beaver*, for instance. Works like Edward Said's *Orientalism* immediately come to mind. Drawing on Foucault and Gramsci, Said explores the Western imaginary of the Orient, created through an array of expert knowledges and producing powerful discourses of white and colonial superiority. The North, similarly, was orientalized, particularly in writing on the Inuit, which often stressed the exotic, primitive, and spiritual nature of Inuit life, with the latter simultaneously impugned and idealized as distinct from Western modernity. According to Said, orientalism obscured not only certain histories but also the "interests" of those involved in "this perpetuation."[99] The connections he makes between Western forms of knowledge and political power, and his argument, via Gramscian theory, that the exercise of colonial power was "purposeful" in serving political and economic ends, also resonates with *The Iconic North*.[100]

So, too, do feminist arguments that postcolonial writing has productively championed more critical analyses of sexuality, subjectivity, and gender as part of the overall "social fabric" of colonial relations.[101] Orientalism was never gender neutral: it relayed interconnected ideologies of race and gender, and women colonizers were also active participants in *creating* orientalizing texts and images.[102] The emphasis in postcolonial writing on analyzing the metropole and its periphery as part of the same discourse of power; on tracing the transmission of, and resistance to, colonial power through narrative, text, and discourse; on questioning narratives that link the higher "good" of modernizing progress with Eurocentric ideas; and on interrogating varying categories of race as they interconnect with gender and class are all themes important to this book.[103]

However, many of these very general theoretical aspirations are also integral to other approaches to history, and the "post" part of postcolonialism raises troubling questions about its apolitical positioning, lack of historical rigour, and idealist suppositions.[104] The "failed historicity" and homogenized "singularity" of postcolonialism, Sara Ahmed argues, limits its effectiveness as an explanatory historical tool. Ironically, postcolonial theory also ends up not "decentring, but recentring time around Europe and capitalist modernity."[105] It is no accident that the critiques of postcolonialism that I find most powerful are advanced by authors concerned about its denial of history. They insist on more attention to social and material context, on a more realist analysis of power relations, and on a truly political critique of colonialism rather than on a playful dance around its fluidity, ambiguities, hybridization, indeterminacy, and so on.[106] While the latter preoccupations may be particularly characteristic of the postcolonial writers who are most indebted to postmodern French "high theory," such as Homi Bhabha, their influence has been so pervasive that these problems trickle down into other writing. Ironically, as critics such as Benita Parry point out, postcolonialists often deviate from the very originating anticolonial namesakes they would like to claim, like Frantz Fanon, who saw discourse born *out of* the politics of active, even violent, anticolonial struggle, not the reverse. Alfred Memmi, too, often claimed as postcolonial, was clear about the origins of colonial ideologies: "colonizers' basic economic needs became the logic of colonialism."[107] Glen Coulthard's critique of the liberal politics of recognition currently hindering Indigenous resistance in Canada perhaps best draws these strands of critique together. His prognosis for "anticolonial empowerment" unites the original insights of Fanon concerning the external and internal subjectifying nature of Indigenous oppression with a thorough critique of capitalist social relations and the colonial state.[108]

As global historian Arif Dirlik argues, postcolonialism, with its aversion to grand narratives and structural explanations, its emphasis on narrativization rather than evidence, its obscuring of class relations and global capitalism, and its sidelining of human agency, is limiting as a theory aimed at understanding the history of colonialism or addressing the actual experiences of exploitation and marginalization suffered by Fourth World Indigenous peoples. Ignoring the international division of labour and global capitalism are only two of the many problems identified by literary theorist E. San Juan, who critiques the way many postcolonial writers over-emphasize cultural differences, ignore the nation "as a historical product," and narrativize social relations so thoroughly that they disappear into "the realm of floating signifiers and exorbitant metaphors." The result: the "asymmetry of power relations and resources between hegemonic blocs and subaltern groups ... disappears."[109] The most trenchant critics see postcolonial theory — the word itself distorted from its original meaning — as symptomatic of the crisis of late imperial culture, promulgated by a Western-situated class faction of Third World intellectuals cut off from the material realities of Third World life, creating a politics quite compatible with that of the global bourgeoisie.[110] Postcolonialism is thus just one more "product of flexible post-Fordist capitalism, not its antithesis."[111]

Indigenous writers also suggest that the more relativist "post" disavowals of essentialism and authentic identity can become another form of paternalism, effectively denying Native peoples the ability to define their identities in ways distinct from existing negative and dehumanizing ones. Fourth World First Nations may "wish to lay claim to their history, their land, and their rights based on a very real or authentic Aboriginal identity or ideologies."[112] The celebration of hybridity, ambivalence, border crossing, immensurability, and multiculturalism suggests we set aside the search for, and preservation of, "original" communities — such as the First Nations. This not only "glosses over processes of global hegemony" but can also undermine the very premises on which calls for redress, land, and survival are based.[113] As Coulthard argues, the "place-based" self-determination sought by the Dene as an alternative to dispossession relied on the mobilization of national, political, and cultural discourses of distinctiveness.[114] Native American Philip Deloria puts it more bluntly: it is fine for academics to talk about the infinite constructedness of culture, space, and border crossing if you *have* control of your borders, if you have not been *denied* a cultural and material space.[115] Even if I avoid defining an essential identity for Indigenous peoples, in other words, I recognize their political reasons for wanting to do so.

Of course, not all literary approaches embrace postcolonial theory uncritically. Some writing on the Canadian northern imaginary draws on theories of discourse, but with an eye to incorporating Bakhtin's dialogic of social, reciprocal relations. Discourse and narrative are analyzed as textual expressions of power but also as part of a larger historical context.[116] Renée Hulan confronts the contradictions of postcolonial theory, with its postmodern aversion to truth claims, in her excellent study of the North, noting the "unresolveable tension between the claim to expose colonialism" and the "acceptance of postmodern play of invention and indeterminacy."[117] Her approach also puts the construction of masculinity and femininity, as socially and historically generated processes, at the heart of the national mythology of Canada as North, also a feminist goal of *The Iconic North*. By highlighting the incongruence of postcolonial theory with Aboriginal women's stated goal of reclaiming their authentic experiences, one can also highlight the current political intentions of Indigenous women in the North. As one recent collection makes clear, Inuit women want to speak back to some constructed images of themselves in colonial literature, correcting texts in which they appear as pathetic victims of patriarchal cultures, with "men mak[ing] the decisions and women obey[ing] orders."[118]

A critique of the gendered nature of colonialism, Sara Mills argues, is better served by incorporating insights from feminist and materialist perspectives stressing context and causation. If we explore stereotypes, for example, we must account for their different meanings, the functions they fulfill, and their relationships to political and economic structures. The goal of writing about the white-Indigenous colonial encounter, she contends, should be a critique of the politics of "colonial destruction" rather than a postcolonial "obsession with text and discourse" or with psychoanalytic analyses of "fantasy and desire."[119] Colonialism raises feminist questions not just about the oppression of the colonized but also about the privileges of some women in relation to others and the ways class intersects with colonial power, a key theme in the chapters on women sojourners and on the Royal Commission on the Status of Women.

Similarly, *The Iconic North* assumes that we can never fully discern colonial representations as text without attention to context: in the case of the North, this meant the economic and political promotion of a northern frontier of resource development, the marketization of goods and peoples, the increasing alienation of Indigenous people from their land, more intensive interventions by state and civil society institutions in managing Indigenous lives, an augmented presence of white sojourners, and emerging articulations of Indigenous resistance. As many international theorists of imperialism argue, we should never underestimate the "cultural work" associated with colonialism, but the conditions of cultural production are constituted in specific, local, material and social relations.[120] Thinking of the "work" that culture does – entertaining, explaining, exemplifying, legitimizing, rationalizing – directs us to the concept of ideology, in contradistinction to a more Foucauldian emphasis on the "truth effects of discourse." The latter obscures centralized power and "opposing social forces" in society, while the former opens up questions of lived ideas and practices that are bound up with social relations of power and processes that create and sustain hegemony.[121]

The cultural practices and products discussed in this monograph were shaped by inherited traditions from the past as well as the possibilities and conditions of the present. Perceived audiences and "tastes," narrative conventions, local and national knowledges, aesthetic practices, and expert and scientific discourses (among other contingencies) are deeply embedded in the "social," which connects to the "cultural," arena. Cultural producers, in Gramsci's terms, do not just produce for their "own recollection ... Every artist-individual is 'historical' and 'social' to a greater or lesser degree."[122] Cultural production also embodies a dynamic of reproduction – and possible contestation. As Frank Tester argues regarding his reading of government records about the North, texts can be seen on one level as "representations" and interpretations, yet they become "events in themselves," sustaining and reshaping the "textual means by which relations of ruling" operate.[123] A contextualized and historicized reading of cultural texts also implies that we can identify some disjunctures between representation and real lives by looking for tensions and contradictions in and between our sources. It is these very gaps and tensions that the Indigenous women discussed in my conclusion identify in their objections to white constructions of their lives.

In the chapters that follow, I approach the overarching questions of how colonialism is mediated by and constituted through culture by using quite different case studies. Chapter 1 examines white women visitors and sojourners who popularized their northern experiences in published memoirs. Women's recollections indicate common anxieties, observations, and self-positioning in this literary format, but I also argue that, over time, there were some differences in their views as well as changes in their perspectives. Chapter 2 explores *The Beaver*, a popular magazine produced by the Hudson's Bay Company that drew on expert knowledge, visual display, and first-hand settler accounts of northern living to create a distinctly nationalist story of the Canadian North. Two examples of the visual North follow in Chapter 3 and Chapter 4: the former explores documentary NFB films, particularly those to which the federal state gave "two thumbs up" or down; the latter looks at constructions of white and Indigenous masculinity in *RCMP*, a popular television show. Chapter 5 explores the writing of a northern traveller, commentator, and federal civil servant, Irene Baird, whose northern oeuvre has been too long ignored by literary scholarship. In Chapter 6, an exploration of the Royal Commission on the Status of Women's trip to the North, the construction of Indigenous women by those testifying, the commissioners, and the media, takes the reader into the 1960s and early 1970s. Finally, in the conclusion, I reflect briefly on the lives of three northern Indigenous women who, in this same time period, gazed back at white colonizers.

This chapter is a call for further explorations of northern Indigenous views of white sojourners, colonialism, and the South, reversing the dominant trends in writing – including my own. Suffusing *The Iconic North* is this very contradiction: my understanding that, however useful it is to critically analyze cultural contact zones of colonial encounter, we always run the risk of refocusing our attention on the metropole. Contemporary cultural production in writing, film, art, and performance emanating from the North, especially from First Nations, suggests that the traditional colonial gaze is being subverted in no small part through their retelling of history.

CHAPTER ONE

Narrating the North

Sojourning Women and Travel Writing

In her travel narrative describing her 1946 trip to Povungnetuk, at the north of Hudson Bay (Nunavik), to become the wife of a Hudson's Bay Company (HBC) trader, Wanda Tolboom recounts her anticipation of her perfect wedding, with bouquet, cake, and ceremony, in the land of ice and snow. There were few couples (like she and her partner), she noted, who could boast that their wedding was "attended by every white couple within 600 miles."[1] The promotion of these white weddings as romantic firsts in an uncharted, empty land was symbolic of changes in the Arctic in the post-Second World War period, denoting an increased influx of white women sojourners, the promotion of new domestic and marital roles linked to the Euro-Canadian presence, and also a cultural erasure of the existing Arctic bride – the Inuk woman.

The images of Indigenous life in white women's travel narratives published from the 1940s to the 1970s are the subject of this chapter. Since the eastern Arctic was often cast as the newest of untamed lands, I concentrate on narratives set in this geographical space, but I also draw comparisons with women's accounts of sojourning in the subarctic provincial and territorial North.[2] What was the "reciprocal relationship" between politics and the "textual practices" of colonialism in this travel literature,[3] the likely readings, and the political and social consequences of the knowledge circulated? Even if the images of Indigenous peoples presented by these authors bore little resemblance to the identity of the First Nations, the potential power of these texts as arbiters of public opinion was important, particularly given the timing of their publication. These sojourners' portraits of Indigenous life, consumed as authentic accounts of exotic or primitive peoples, helped to create the cultural landscape on which political and economic decisions could be rationalized.

White wedding in the North as portrayed in *The Beaver* in 1943. | Hudson's Bay
Company Archives, Archive of Manitoba, 1987/205/1156

Indeed, some of these sojourner authors, like Donalda Copeland, were
participants in state modernization projects in the North: she was not just
observing but justifying her role of bringing scientific medicine to a
superstitious, backward people.[4]

Coinciding with other forms of information, such as film, popular anthropology, and government propaganda, these narratives contributed
to the southern fascination with the North as a frontier of development
in need of white aid, intervention, and expert guidance. Some authors
commented on the contemporaneous extension of the welfare state in the
Far North, often explained to their readers as integrating Inuit peoples
into equal Canadian citizenship. Yet the simultaneous portrayal of the
original inhabitants as fatalistic or stubborn adherents to a premodern
culture could only reinforce the view that they required expert direction
in this turn of events – not just on how, but on where, they should live.
These images thus helped to sustain Canada's distinctive brand of internal colonialism, which involved not only the "geographical incursion" of

whites but also the ideological construction of a hierarchy of white progress, culture, and history.[5]

This view of history and progress had much to do with orientalist ways of seeing. The white person's Inuit, for example, was manufactured using discursive strategies such as disregarding, essentializing, generalizing, and sometimes idealizing aspects of their culture.[6] As a consequence, their subject position was erased, and they remained objects of curious scrutiny, often counterpoints to whites' self-portrayal as modern, rational, progressive, and scientifically superior. Hugh Brody puts it well: the "Eskimo are seen by whites only as Eskimo," never as individuals. Drawing on stock, repeated stories, whites constructed tales depicting the true, original essence in all Eskimo people, often doing so by pointing to the bizarre in their culture: "they are illustrations."[7] Brody echoes Alfred Memmi's classic text on the colonizer and the colonized in which he argues the latter are always characterized by "the mark of the plural ... They are 'this,' they are 'that.'"[8] Photographer Richard Harrington's private diary of northern travel likewise captures the incessant discussions he heard about a generalized, singular Native: "Conversation topics here among the white population ... swing back to the natives, how bad or good they are; above all what should be done about them; how they differ from us; how they could be made like us; how their lives should be arranged differently and better; what ails them; how they deteriorate; how hard they are to handle; how dependent they have become on white men."[9]

Orientalism was also gendered: white women played an active role in constructing orientalist discourses through cultural forms such as travel writing, which translated Indigenous women into objects of a colonial gaze. They were culturally foreign, sometimes sexualized, and often rendered passive subjects of both masculine Aboriginal and white governing practices. At the same time, women sojourners' renditions of their encounters with Indigenous peoples, particularly the Inuit, invariably argued for friendship, understanding, and tolerance between races and cultures. Yet this cultural relativism could also operate as a form of "anti-conquest,"[10] articulating liberal tolerance while nonetheless reaffirming Euro-Canadian cultural and social superiority. Contemplating the strange behaviour of the other – the Eskimo – sojourners' accounts suggested dichotomized images of civilized and primitive, modern and premodern. Some women's accounts of living with subarctic Indian and Dene peoples similarly stressed the cultural chasm between Native and newcomer, though there were changes over this period, symbolized well by the contrasting narratives of Jean Godsell, who, in her 1959 book, celebrates the last glory days of the white-led colonial Hudson's Bay Company, and Sheila Burnford's more self-reflexive attempt in 1969 to understand her Indians neighbours in the context of cultural tolerance.

WOMEN IN AN ALIEN ENVIRONMENT

Looking primarily at women's narratives foregrounds the question posed in writing on women, travel, and imperialism: What was the role, rationale, and meaning of white women's participation in colonial ventures, their investment in the racial hierarchies of colonialism?[11] The risk in over-valorizing a singular binary based on race or colonialism, however, may be the erasure of other axes of power, such as class, age, and gender, thus eclipsing the complexities of social relations as they were lived out in colonial contexts. Women's travel accounts were to some extent shaped by their gender, and they are useful texts precisely because women were especially curious about Indigenous women, their work, and family life, topics that potentially brought attention to the labour of household production – a theme often ignored in expert accounts.[12] At the same time, white women's responses were also shaped by age, race, social position, and occupation. For instance, although white women sojourning in the North were less likely to adopt the masculine persona of the "bold hero adventurer,"[13] their narratives sometimes overlapped with those of male northern travellers, revealing a colonial, superior surveillance of Aboriginal ways.

White women's accounts of life in the North did vary in style. While I use the term "travel narrative," these were primarily stories of temporary sojourners living in the North for a time. Like classic travel stories, they were written for a "middlebrow" home audience as forms of first-hand "witnessing" of non-European cultures. Travel narratives have historically assumed a myriad of forms, variously stressing exile, personal quests, geographical exploration, anthropological observations, even "rest cures."[14] Many of these authors combined conventions of the autobiography and the exploration narrative; some used anecdote, irony, and humour more than others; one author recounted scientific and environmental data; and some women were more openly pedagogical in their presentation.[15]

Women's views of the North were also shaped according to whether they came north as wives accompanying husbands or as single career women, whether they were merely observing their surroundings or trying to alter them through educational and nursing work. Despite these important differences, many of the northern sojourners discussed in this chapter came from similar class and cultural surroundings: most were high school- or university-educated Anglo-Celtic Protestants from farming or middle-class families. Godsell, who accompanied her HBC husband North, was a middle-class Scottish immigrant who often idealized her Scots heritage and had met her husband while working as a secretary in the HBC office in Winnipeg. Ella Wallace Manning had a degree from Dalhousie and subsequent nursing training at the Royal Victoria Hospital in Montreal, while Donalda Copeland went North as the "first public health nurse" on Southampton Island.[16] Marjorie Hinds, a British-born welfare teacher, was lauded in reviews of her book as a "cultured English-woman" and "pioneer in Eskimo education."[17] Katharine Scherman, although she was part of a group expedition, was educated as a scientist in her own right. Miriam MacMillan, who accompanied her older explorer husband, came from a cultured, middle-class New England family. Mena Orford, also a wife following her husband's lead, came from a comfortable Prairie family whose members saw her marriage to a poor rural doctor as something of a decline in status. Elsie Gillis, who had attended university, actually joked that she was a "spoiled city girl" whose farthest travels had been to New York City.[18] Wanda Tolboom, the wife of an HBC trader, came from rural Manitoba but was also educated and middle class in outlook. Sheila Burnford and Edith Iglauer, whose books were published in the 1960s, were educated, established writers: both were immigrants to Canada who brought with them a fascination with the North.[19]

Book cover of Wanda Tolboom's *Arctic Bride*, published in 1956.
Many white women's memoires were reviewed positively as insightful
pictures of Indigenous life in the North.

The public reception of their books was also quite similar. While one review of Godsell's book was slightly frosty – an issue discussed below – most reviews of these sojourner accounts were positive, uncritical, and laudatory. In some cases, sojourners reviewed each other's books, approving their "vivid narrative" and engaging historical sketches.[20] Reviews in *The Beaver* were common, and commonly positive, revealing a shared project of white cultural observation of the mysterious Inuit. Tolboom's *Arctic Bride*, for example, was "delightful and readable," with

memorable Eskimo characters whose "simplicity created many a hilari-
ous incident."[21] Members of the Arctic Institute, writers, academics, and
government officials all wrote reviews that extolled women's command
of history, their evocative descriptions of the "pristine beauty" of the
landscape, [22] and their "expert knowledge,"[23] which was based on first-
hand experience in the North. Not surprisingly, an influential bureaucrat in the Department of Northern Affairs and National Resources
was extremely pleased with Edith Iglauer's positive interpretation of the
government's cooperative projects in the North: while Iglauer was not
a seasoned northern "expert," she was "an observer of rare talent and a
reporter of outstanding competence."[24] Women sojourners like Manning
were praised not only for enlightening the public about the North but
also for providing an engaging story of, in Manning's case, her own
transformation from "city girl to the woman of a primitive country."[25]
Authors were also commended for their descriptions of Indigenous cultures, and, in this regard, they were presented as tolerant as well as highly
knowledgeable: Mena Orford, said the *Canadian Geographical Journal*, is
"full of praise for the happy, placid nature of the Eskimo people and their
unfailing helpfulness."[26] The reception for many of these books, in other
words, was trusting and complimentary. Notably, white women's expertise on Indigenous life went largely unquestioned.

While women had different reasons for going to the North, there were
commonalities in their descriptions of the environment. Most women
stressed that they were anomalies in a land inhabited by few whites. "I
was a museum curiosity," remembers Wanda Tolboom of her arrival at
Povungnetuk, "fingered by old women."[27] Sheila Burnford's first encounter with northern Ontario Ojibway, along with an artist friend,
Susan Ross, is one of discomfort as she senses their suspicion of strange
white women: "I would have liked to [stay] but the old women were un-
easy and shy and could not speak English: they were obviously unhappy
at the sight of Susan's sketchbook."[28] Donalda Copeland, still using
the terminology of race in 1960, puts it more bluntly: "[There was that]
prickly awareness that dozens of strange slanted eyes are watching you ...
and thinking hidden thoughts ... There was a sense of being queer, of
being alien and different, of being one member very much alone of a race

among members of another race whose tongue and thoughts and values are completely foreign to you."[29] However, even this recognition of Indigenous women's unease, or the rhetorical technique of self-effacing reversal, as Mary Louise Pratt argues, can also mask, as much as undo, relations of power and hegemony.[30]

Women's sense of difference was also relayed in the language of exploration and conquest as they stressed their presence in an empty, silent, unknown land, a technique that negated the Indigenous human presence. Women writers identified their travels with the histories of famous white explorers, and their accounts proclaimed their place as "firsts": the first white woman on a particular island, the first white woman to negotiate a particular journey, or the most northerly white wedding.[31] Especially because of language differences, when white women spoke of loneliness, they usually longed for the company of other white women. In Jean Godsell's autobiography, she praises the few older white women within travelling distance, like "Mrs Gerald Card," who "adopted me like a daughter," and whose daughter, in turn, Godsell treasures as a special visitor: "During the summer months, Katie would return from Bishop Strachan School in Toronto ... the only white girl of her age in the country she was, truly, The Sweetheart of the North."[32] Yet, as Mena Orford recounts in her *Journey North*, the same longing was not true for her children, who quickly made Inuit friends, with whom they chatted, played, and visited in their homes.

White women saw themselves bonded by their common isolation, and many claimed that divisions of class or female rivalry were not a part of their northern experience. Women's autobiographical reluctance to reveal uncomplimentary views of themselves and others is understandable, though teacher Margery Hinds did address some of the different views whites had of the Inuit in her small Port Harrison settlement. The autobiography of HBC trader's wife Jean Godsell, set in the western provincial and Far North, is an anomaly in this regard as it is replete with tales of hostile, nasty, competitive white women.[33] Godsell discusses the intense competition between white women for social status in isolated northern enclaves. In some respects, this was the corollary of their husbands' business competition between rival fur trading companies. She is implicitly critical of less cultured, lower-middle-class white women who tried to use their racial status to enhance their social capital.

Her memoir also stands out among others for its disparagement of Indigenous women, and, as such, it is contrasted in more detail later in this chapter to Sheila Burnford's memoir. Historical context is important: Godsell's book was published in 1959 but recounts the interwar fur trade of northern Alberta and the Northwest Territories as well as her trip to the Arctic Ocean with her fur trader (and well-published author) husband, Philip. Godsell claims that, at this point in time, her presence in the North threatened the "dusky daughters" and "swarthy" women in the area, the "half-breed" women who had come to play a prestigious role in fur trade society: "I represented, without realizing it, the very thing these native-born members of the old regime viewed with such suspicion."[34] These women are routinely cast as uncultured and inhospitable – with a few exceptions, such as Godsell's "loyal and devoted" maid Rosa.[35] Métis women's pretension to whiteness was ridiculed, as in the following description of a wife's attempts to elevate her status through material household decoration, a ploy that Godsell simply scorns:

> As his swarthy spouse, attired in a beaded, black satin dress and silk-worked moccasins, passed around steaming mugs of tea, I glimpsed a veiled hostility in her dark, brooding eyes. On a massive sideboard that went ill with the garishly-painted walls, Coalport, Wedgwood, Crown Derby and other expensive china stood cheek by jowl with chipped-enamel plates and Indian beadwork, while trail worn socks and moccasins dangled by the stove to dry.[36]

Far more predominantly, women offered respectful assessments of their fellow northern sojourners. This polite solidarity among white women was likely shaped by women's experience of life in very small enclosed communities where whites "stuck together." It was perhaps also a product of these writers' common class and educational backgrounds. For women who accompanied their husbands North, the cultural distance between themselves and Indigenous women was accentuated by the fact that the latter were often employed by them as domestic servants, thus making the racial relation simultaneously a class relation. White women embraced the use of paid help in a domestic environment in which they found it overwhelmingly difficult, if not impossible, to survive. Manning's ability to get by entirely on her acquired skills was seen as extremely unusual and "courageous" by local HBC traders, who dubbed her a veritable "white Eskimo."[37] Far more common was the experience of Mena Orford, who, when she arrived, was told, in the language of household effects, that her maid Nukinga "went with the house."[38] Faced with unending dishes, Gillis looked around the settlement for an Inuit woman who might "have some vague idea of white man's ways." "I would be glad to have Inooyuk as my maid," she told her husband, who then had the HBC trader strike the "bargain" for Inooyuk by paying her in HBC credit.[39] Most sojourners, publishing in the 1940s and 1950s, would not have portrayed themselves as imperious employers; rather, they tried to employ humour and anecdote to describe their cultural estrangement from their hired help, though this often exposed a clear sense of racial hierarchy. Again, only Godsell was different, openly discussing her attempts to teach her male servant who was "master."[40]

White women were generally understood to be a potential liability due to their inability to weather the physical surroundings. As a result, some narratives were characterized by ambivalence, awkwardness, and a need to justify their presence, dissimilar to the tales of many men. Of course, unlike nineteenth-century middle-class women travellers, these modern sojourners had citizenship rights and were more likely to have participated in the world of paid work. Canadian women had only recently been exalted during the war for their equal embrace of male labour. Even some of the professional women, however, commented on the difficulties they encountered in going North. "It's a man's country," was the recurring theme Hinds found when she applied for jobs in the North: "Had I been a man it would have been fairly easy to find a job in Arctic Canada at that time ... Nursing and teaching had been undertaken by [female] missionaries – but neither missions nor matrimony attracted me!"[41] Manning, who accompanied her husband on his geodetic surveys, had trouble persuading the government to make her an assistant on the second expedition, nor could she initially even find an RCAF person who would fly both of them into the North. The idea was initially greeted with bursts of laughter from the pilot, and only a strategy of immense persistence succeeded.

Hinds, Copeland, and Manning could better situate themselves as adventurous, path-breaking explorers, as could Edith Iglauer, an American journalist whose travels in the Canadian North were published in 1962 as *The New People: The Eskimo's Journey into Our Time*. Yet writer Sheila Burnford, even in the late 1960s, took great pains to justify her travel, unencumbered by husband or family, both to the people she visited and to her readers. Like Hinds, she explains her presence as a single female northern sojourner by positioning herself outside of the normal expectations of womanhood, as someone likely seen by others as "eccentric or Amazonian." Burnford stresses how out of place and unhappy she was in the expected housewifely role of postwar Canada, attending "teas, PTA, Brownie Flypups." Going to the North was, for her, "breaking out of purdah."[42] Those women who went as wives, in contrast, were more likely to cast themselves as reluctant or intrepid partners in their husbands' northern ventures.

Women were still considered potential problems in an environment associated with hostile natural forces, danger, masculine bravery, and contact with primitives. Writing of her earlier travels before the Second World War, Miriam MacMillan describes how she had to prove herself relentlessly, taking on task after task to prepare for her husband's expeditions and, when she was finally allowed on board, also taking her night watch like the men. Despite her husband's claim that the "crew would not want a woman on board,"[43] they eventually produced a petition calling for "Lady Mac's" participation in the trip. Women also found their distinct space by stressing their feminine roles and attributes. In *North Pole Boarding House*, Gillis, like some other narrators, becomes a social, domestic focus of the all-male community, a surrogate mother or sister to other local white, single men, helping to celebrate birthdays and to provide domestic rituals and Christmas celebrations. Godsell clearly played the same role at Fort Fitzgerald, though her parties and popularity with the local RCMP men (so she tells us) resulted in other white women resenting her.

However, in the post-Second World War period, a small group of white women was increasingly moving North in feminized professions (as nurses and teachers) and also as wives of fur traders or government officials. The earlier HBC practice of traders marrying Indigenous women was now discouraged, and every effort was made to ensure the comfort of white HBC wives by provisioning their households with chesterfields, canned food, even washing machines. Not surprisingly, these white women often portrayed liaisons between white men and Native women as undesirable or unworkable. This suspicion of "half-breed" relations was not simply articulated in Godsell's memoir. Some writers, for example, depicted Inuit/white liaisons as a remnant of the white whalers' (irresponsible) past, though others, drawing on nineteenth-century racial theory, implied that their mixed-blood progeny might produce a "superior" type of Eskimo.[44] A man from white "civilization" who married an Eskimo woman, an RCMP constable told scientist Scherman, "would be dragged down."[45] Gillis relates an incident in which a young white man at their weather station was teased about the attention he was receiving from an older Inuit woman. He then received a jocular warning: "An Eskimo woman's skin, so I was told, looks very brown to a white man during his first year in the Arctic. In the second year, it may not look so brown. If, in the third, it looks white, then it's high time for a man to get out. He's in danger of becoming bushed."[46] Hinds was not at all critical of interracial marriage, but she was scathing about white men's sexual use of Inuit women, and she suspected that the fascination with the wife-trading tales of the Eskimo had much to do with the predatory voyeurism of white males. She was likely astute in this regard. Occasionally, a white man's northern memoir might discuss his relationships with already-married Inuit women in a manner that stressed the woman's choice in the affair.[47] More often, as Richard Harrington notes privately in his northern diary, white men exhibited simultaneous desire and fear of Inuit women. He mocked men's prurient preoccupation with women's supposedly loose sexuality, though he was clearly fascinated too.[48]

Women, then, were conscious of their status as precarious outsiders even though they were favoured as partners for white men. Like white men, they were preoccupied with physical survival in an environment that was equated with danger: the North was described as physically inhospitable, frightening, literally at the end of the universe. Both men and women invested considerable detail in discussions of the making and wearing of Arctic dress, travel by komatik, the building of snow houses, hunting for food, and the preparation of skins and meat afterwards. Their detailed descriptions of daily survival became a form of anthropological and scientific classification,[49] a technique that carried with it an air of authorial certainty. Women, however, were more self-deprecating about their own uselessness and vulnerability. When she first arrived, Manning imagined the Inuit women thinking – with justification – "Who is this useless woman who knows nothing about preparing skins and clothing?"[50] Still, there was a decided contrast between women's descriptions of their husbands' integration into the environment and their own alienation from it. Some of the sojourning wives informed their readers that their white husbands became such skilled outdoorsmen that they were almost Eskimo, highly respected for their survival skills. They also waxed eloquent regarding their husbands' paternal kindness to the Eskimo. "He loved these simple people,"[51] says MacMillan of her husband, and, according to her, they revered him.

Ice and snow were not the only dangers described. More than one woman recounted the tale of an RCMP wife mauled by huskies.[52] Since this one incident took place in the 1920s, and was still being recounted in the late 1940s across the North, it had clearly become a stock story symbolizing the vulnerability of white women in the North. The Inuit were also a potentially menacing presence. Despite the dominant picture of the passive, jolly Eskimo, many narratives included at least one tale of a vicious murder or supposed cannibalism, when humans consumed the flesh of the dead, suggesting the Inuit might lack an evolved sense of humane compassion. Since many women had read standard Arctic travellers' accounts, they called up incidents from these works that reinforced this point of view – sometimes citing the very same "cannibalistic" event depicted in Peter Freuchen's book.[53] Common to these descriptions of death in the Arctic is a lack of contextual explanation or knowledge of Inuit culture and a fascination with gruesome details. Some did explain cannibalism by its connection to imminent starvation and the need to sacrifice some lives in order to prevent a family's complete annihilation. However, it might also be portrayed more negatively, suggesting that Indigenous people perpetrated it, knowing it was morally wrong. Godsell, quoting from a nineteenth-century HBC journal, notes the case of a Cree man who "frequently prevaricated" when questioned about his family, so the other Indians suspected "he murdered and devoured them."[54]

Patriarchal violence within Indigenous cultures is occasionally suggested and is often detailed in Copeland's memoir, which begins on the very first page by designating the Inuit North as a land "where woman was still a chattel [and where] a man might possess more than one alone."[55] Copeland repeatedly asserts that females were not as valued as were males. She discusses infanticide as though it had been routine rather than occasional, as most anthropological accounts suggest: "though girl babies were no longer being put out in the snow to die, they were frequently handed out for adoption."[56] Copeland also recounts treating an emaciated, limping Inuit woman, a second wife who had not lived up to her husband's expectations and thus had been "badly beaten," with bruises over her entire body. Her husband's translated, matter-of-fact explanation contained no remorse: "I had to make her obey."[57] To suggest all Indigenous peoples are pristinely free of all violence against women is itself an idealized, essentialized view – as current Indigenous feminists remind us. However, to imply, as this memoir does, that violence was essentially an Indigenous problem, inherent to their patriarchal cultures, is similarly simplistic and, in this case, colonialist in tone.

Nor were authors' accounts restricted to only male violence. Hinds relays a much-repeated story of a woman in her community who, years before, had participated in a religious-crazed, cold-blooded murder of some of her family, sending them out to the ice floes. On one of their ship's stopovers going North, Gillis's husband was commandeered onto a makeshift jury trial for an Inuit woman accused of murdering her husband. Gillis characterizes her as a woman without remorse, creating an image of an amoral primitive: "Her beady brown eyes looked unconcernedly at us and her face broke into a happy grin. This is really serious business, I thought[,] shocked at her deportment ... Then I remembered that here was a daughter out of another era, a child out of the stone age, suddenly thrust among people thousands of years distant from her ... Obviously she was completely unable to understand all this colour and ceremony to teach white man's ways to her and her people."[58] Even a quick glance at Gillis's account suggests a more complex situation: the woman, pressed into a marriage she did not want, claimed she was abused and threatened with a knife; a signed confession in syllabic was produced, even though she did not read or write; and the trial was undertaken in English, which she did not speak. Gillis, a newcomer to the North, ventured that the Inuk woman *desired* her sentence of banishment as a mark of prestige, providing further proof of the need to impose new values on those who could so cold bloodedly take a human life. Since the interwar period the state had slowly tried to impose its superior legal norms on the Indigenous North. Travellers' accounts could only reinforce support for this project since they evoked a sense of fear about the occasional, but unpredictable, violence of the Inuit.[59]

The more preponderant image of the Inuit was that of a primitive and simple, happy and good natured people, echoing the photographic displays in *The Beaver* of "The Cheerful Eskimo."[60] Descriptions of the Inuit as Stone Age peoples were so numerous that one cannot begin to recount them. Katharine Scherman's first impressions will suffice. Entitling her opening chapter "Back to the Ice Age," she describes the northern Baffin Inuit as "exotic gnomes" with oriental eyes, men of the "Stone Age" who had the "simplicity and directness of children" and who taught her scientific party what it was like to be "uncivilized" again. Describing Joseph Idlout, the guide who led and sustained their expedition to Bylot Island, Scherman's use of temporal metaphors stresses a cave man image: "he was cut off from us by a barrier of many thousands of years" of progressive civilization, the counterpart of our Asian ancestors who drifted east and west out of an unknown, faintly remembered Garden of Eden."[61] While Scherman was there to study birds, her stature as scientist also endowed her observations of the Inuit with the force of veracity.

In their descriptions of Inuit society, writers used orientalist techniques, such as generalizing and essentializing, to create an image of premodern peoples on a collision course with modernity. Scherman's book recounts many Inuit stories collected by the local HBC trader from elders. These myths, she explains, with their animalistic spirits, were not "abstract or symbolic," as in more developed cultures; rather, they were merely full of "magic."[62] Other writers claimed that the Inuit had no real forms of governance, only hunting leaders; that they embraced superstitious fantasies, especially about the spirits of the dead; and even "drilled holes" in the heads of those who appeared insane.[63] Although some women also wrote of Inuit emotion and intelligence, even this was dependent on white assessment. MacMillan, for example, cites her expert husband: "they could be as intelligent as whites ... and my husband had evidence to prove it."[64] This repeated language of primitiveness inevitably had a cumulative ideological impact. "Primitive" denotes a people marked by their prehistoric state, designated as less technologically and intellectually advanced, without a complex social organization, cultural world, or history. Denying non-Western Indigenous peoples a history, as David Spurr argues, is one of the key rhetorical means of denying them humanity.[65]

The designation "primitive" was sometimes invoked romantically to celebrate Indigenous peoples' less complex, less competitive, less materialistic culture. Manning notes that she found the "interior" Eskimo "poor but gentle," their character proof that those Eskimo with "the least contact with whites were the finest."[66] Hinds asked the government for a transfer from Port Harrison to more remote Baffin Island, where the Eskimo had less contact with whites. It is "well known," she writes, that the "best type of Eskimos prefer to live in their own camps near to their hunting grounds and that the poorer type tend to congregate around the posts."[67] The Inuit were often presented as a communal people lacking in individualistic selfishness, an image that idealized, but also essentialized, in its simplicity.[68] Some northern travellers saw themselves escaping the pressures and spiritual vacuum of modernity, claiming that the simple Inuit had not yet absorbed the bad traits of a materialist society: Eskimos, Gillis relates, never stole even when they were hungry.[69] A more pragmatic Hinds disputes such romanticization, noting that there were good and bad in all peoples and that Inuit could certainly steal, including from her: when Eskimos know the English language well enough to read what has been written about them, she concludes sardonically on this score, "they'll get enough laughs to last a life-time!"[70]

THE STATE AND INDIGENOUS PEOPLE

Despite immense respect for Indigenous peoples' environmental skills and practices, whether these involved gathering wild rice in the provincial North or making fur pants in the Far North, whites were still portrayed as those in leadership roles, with the best interests of the Native in mind, a view also reflected in some progressive social democratic attempts to improve the lives of northern Indigenous peoples at this time.[71] Using the language of British imperialism, some authors described the Inuit as children and whites as their paternal protectors. Others saw themselves as guides and role models, offering rescue and amends. Federal government employees Donalda and Harold Copeland, a nurse and welfare teacher, respectively, were on Southampton Island (Nunavut) to "devote" their lives to "our people ... the Eskimo, the people to whom we were to try and make some amends for all the woes besetting them following their contact with our race."[72] While fur trade history does suggest relations of some reciprocity between whites and Indigenous clients,[73] HBC sojourning wives portrayed the company as paternalism incarnate, emphasizing instances of credit, food, and medicine humanely extended. When families faced "hunger and hardship," and men came to post destitute, Tolboom explained, we gave away our old clothes, and "spread the biscuits thick with lard" (the HBC ration) to help them out.[74]

Like the traders, the police and other state representatives were generally cast as benevolent and fair. Discussion of the various arms of the federal state in these sojourning narratives is particularly significant given the consolidation of white law and order and the expansion of the welfare state at the time, not to mention very direct intervention in moving some northern Inuit to new settlements. Retired chief of the Eastern Arctic Government Patrol, Major D.J. McKeand, notes Gillis, had been "a great white father" to the Eskimo, while Scherman accepts the self-description of the RCMP constable she encounters who tells her: "you get a different type of man up here nowadays – you get men who really want to do something for the Eskimo, not exploit them."[75] Because the Inuit did not understand what was best for their children, many writers explained, payment of family allowances was overseen by the RCMP. Yet, as Frank Tester and Peter Kulchyski later document, Inuit family allowances were treated less as a universal right and more as a form of regulated "welfare," which was monitored by white overseers and used to force children into schools.[76]

Wanda Tolboom remembers that she and her husband were "thankful" when the RCMP corporal arrived from Port Harrison: "[The] police are the guardians and friends of the native people, whom they protect from possible exploitation by the White Man and the only occasional harm they do to each other." The RCMP offered comprehensive state services, recording vital statistics, attending to fur export permits and game laws, as well as disbursing "Old Age Pensions and Family Allowances and other forms of relief to needy natives." The corporal was the local registrar of family allowances, keeping track of the amount allowed each family by Ottawa, while the HBC trader was the sub-registrar. Together, they monitored Inuit spending since "primitive native parents" could not simply be sent a cheque to "spend at their discretion." The baby bonus given by the government, Tolboom stresses, was a great boon to local parents, but they needed lectures from the RCMP so that they might purchase wisely, buying "powdered milk, baby cereal" and blankets, not "tea, tobacco or a new dress for mother."

Tolboom then adds an anecdote that ties together the need for supervision of family allowances and the supposedly primitive attitudes towards sexuality and family. The RCMP constable was part "doctor, dentist and part Dorothy Dix," the latter referring to his paternal role as informal adjudicator of familial and local conflicts. Two young men came to the constable to settle an argument about who was the father of a young woman's new child about to receive the allowance. The constable negotiated a truce, but, much later, a "very decrepit old Eskimo" appeared at the door and insisted that he was actually the father. This suggestion of casual profligacy left the RCMP "perplexed," though Tolboom's husband was reduced to "gales of laughter."[77]

The many examples in which whites cited their paternal, guiding roles for Indigenous inhabitants are numerous, yet, of course, ironic, given the way that the Inuit saw whites. Describing the early RCMP on Baffin Island, elders remember they were "just like kids ... like children, as they had to have everything done for them – clothes made for them, posts cared for, igloos built, and even their tea mugs held in the cold!"[78] Also telling is the laughter that spontaneously erupts in the modern film *Qallunaat! Why White People Are Funny* as older Inuit are informed that the police are always there to help them.[79] Clearly, the Inuit have their own historic interpretation of the RCMP, which does not mimic that of the police force.

For those writers who had been in the North working for the state, such as Marjorie Hinds or Donalda Copeland, their very presence justified increased federal intervention in northern Inuit lives – though privately Hinds was critical of the planning and timing of state interventions in the relocations.[80] Copeland's memoir is full of stories of her frustration with Indigenous amateur healers who thought they could cure illness or injuries but often made the situation far worse, endangering Inuit lives with their ignorance. She is clearly dedicated to improving the health of her constituents, working day and night with few resources, but her vivid descriptions of living conditions (as "filthy hovels") and of emaciated, infected bodies (often with TB) sends a very clear message about the absolute necessity of the state bringing modern scientific hygiene and health care into the North. That the inadequate housing conditions she witnessed might have been shaped in part by inadequate responses to migration and centralization, not laziness or slovenliness, is not entertained. And, while Copeland had some sympathy for the Inuit who feared going south for TB treatment in alien circumstances, she was still insistent that they must go.

Writers like Farley Mowat were known for their sharp critiques of the state's role in the North, but these women authors were more complimentary. Journalist Edith Iglauer's *The New People* details her trips through the eastern and central Arctic observing the government's attempts to establish an Indigenous cooperative program in the late 1950s and early 1960s. Iglauer's book opens by asserting that Canadians had little knowledge of, or interest in, the Inuit (a rather curious statement for an American), though Donald Snowden, an employee of the Department of Northern Affairs, was cast as a dedicated antidote to this ignorance. Iglauer was less preoccupied with detailing survival in an alien environment than in exploring how social change – in this case cooperatives – happened in the North. Like "embedded" journalists today, she became a part of Snowden's entourage as it tried to establish cooperatives to market fish, lumber, seal, and handicrafts, primarily around Ungava Bay. As they travelled, she also commented on the environment, Indigenous social relations, and other government programs. Her rendition of the federal state's role in the North was positive: she lauded efforts to help the Eskimo move from "an ancient and primitive world in which each family battled alone against cold, hunger and death" into the modern world –"our world" – characterized by an "economically interdependent society" of "self-sufficiency and dignity" rather than the old "pathetic relief handouts."[81]

A statement of racial progress could hardly be more baldly put, though Iglauer does not mention the internal disagreement within the Department of Northern Affairs and National Resources about the usefulness of co-ops. More progressive bureaucrats supported them, but more conservative naysayers dismissed them as "communistic."[82] Snowden becomes the hero in her story: he was respected by the Eskimo," she writes, and, over time, the federal co-op promoters were able to resurrect some settlements that were in such a bad state that the Eskimo were simply ready to give up and accept starvation. A central event in her account is a cooperative conference that drew both federal civil servants and Inuit delegates from across the North. This meeting was evidence, Snowden explained to her, that their leadership training was paying off as some Inuit were beginning to take the initiative and become architects of their own fate: "[The] Eskimo are showing signs of learning how to tell us when we are wrong. I don't believe the government is infallible and the co-ops make it possible for the Eskimo to give us hell."[83] Iglauer's emphasis on Snowden's positive belief in Indigenous self-governance and the potential for Inuit self-sufficiency is significant, especially in contrast to earlier sojourner narratives, even if many of the co-op instigators described in her account are still white experts.[84]

The RCMP's and federal government's roles in the North were often portrayed more positively than were those of the religious missions, which were treated with some ambivalence. Some women praised devoted individual missionaries whom they admired and knew personally. Elsie Gillis had kind words about the dedication of Anglican missionaries Canon Jack Turner and his wife, while Miriam MacMillan assured her readers that the Moravian missions had a "definite influence for good" on their Inuit charges.[85] But other writers were far less adamant about the need for Christian conversion than were nineteenth-century writers. Reflecting a more secular age after the Second World War, authors like Katharine Scherman worried that judgmental, moralistic missionaries had destructively disparaged Inuit traditions. While some authors assumed mission-run schools were a necessary, even a positive development in the North, there was a discernible uneasiness with the cultural disparagement that accompanied religion. Despite her ever-crusty sense of white, British superiority, Hinds laments the denigration of Native performance and dance as "heathenish," as something to be simply expunged from their culture.[86]

Burnford tries to put herself in the shoes of the Indigenous person being missionized by comparing an old Roman Catholic religious tract disparaging her own kind (Protestant Scot) to the Christian disparagement of Indigenous religion. Notwithstanding her use of the word "heathen," her analogy is meant to open up a critique of Christian proselytizing as narrow- minded in both contexts: "I read with much interest a prayer [in the Roman Catholic tract] for 'the appalling evil of mixed marriages,' religiously mixed of course ... How far, or how narrowly could bigotry extend? And what presumption ... For the first time I had a glimpse of how it must feel to be a happy innocent heathen and suddenly wake up one day to find an influx of strangers in your midst, impertinently praying over you, and doing their dedicated best to convert you to another way of life, a life having no bearing whatsoever, either spiritually of physically, on the life you were leading."[87]

Many sojourners' accounts debated the pros and cons of whites' incursions into the North. Though framed within relativist terms that stressed the need to protect Indigenous cultures, these invocations did not always reflect a true "reciprocity" of equals as much as a subtle paternalism premised on some of the same sentiments as missionization.[88] Furthermore, in the case of the Inuit, the repeated image of a less materialistic people living a timeless "gypsy" life was used not only to idealize but also to suggest the Native person's lack of initiative, shiftlessness, and premodern fatalism.[89] Recounting the three most noteworthy things about the Inuit (who, ironically, had been indispensable to keeping them alive and fed) Scherman lists: "no sense of time, laziness and unending sociability."[90] Her understanding of a boundary line between decisive work, on the one hand, and leisure, on the other, is both highly Eurocentric and judgmental. Indigenous cultures often had very different notions of work, leisure, and communal time as well as of the boundaries between them.[91]

In Orford's account, her doctor husband becomes exasperated, if not enraged, because he claims that the Inuit won't save food and plan for the future. As a result, families are starving: "they are just too bloody fatalistic and improvident to provide for tomorrow."[92] Yet most whites learned from the Inuit how to cache food under rocks, and material goods always had a different meaning for hunters who had to carry things with them. Like the poor blamed for their own unemployment, the Inuit were viewed as architects of their own fate. Inuit fatalism – not trade conditions, the depletion of resources, inadequate federal planning, and/or social dislocation – explained why the Inuit were starving. According to Ella Manning, Eskimo conservation practices were completely inadequate due to their lack of modern understanding of firearms. Citing her husband as expert, she claims that the Inuit fired wantonly on seals and that they needed whites to oversee the walrus hunt in order to protect the species.[93] While some white scientists at the time echoed fears about "wanton" hunting, more recent analyses of Inuit history are sceptical of such culturally determined claims.[94] Hinds's harsh judgment about one instance of Inuit relocation is especially salient in its stress on Inuit fatalism: "they had their ups and downs." But most of the "downs" were "their own fault, for now that there is a good market for Eskimo handicraft there is no need for any Eskimo to be penniless."[95]

Indigenous culture was thus celebrated as a remnant of a nobler, simpler past but impugned for its primitive, fatalistic ways. The image of the Indigenous woman as a "post Native," living close to government or HBC buildings, made this clear: she *should* become civilized, but she can never really do so. Inuit women might act white, but they can never embrace whiteness.[96] While the "dispersal" of the Inuit away from settlement posts was encouraged by the RCMP in the 1950s, over the next decade other state actors and events eventually reversed that pressure.[97] Indigenous labour was essential for northern whites working for the government, the HBC, and missions, yet sojourners warned of the danger of post Natives – their neighbours – becoming spoiled as they wanted the same luxuries as whites but without working for them. Describing a woman working as a servant for the HBC in the Arctic, Scherman notes that "Makpa was one of the few examples I had seen of Eskimos ruined by coddling. They were easy to spoil, being adaptable and lazy ... It was obvious that this elegant, neat, lazy girl could never again live the life of her people ... She was no longer a true Eskimo but neither was she anywhere near being a woman of our civilization."[98] Since it was children who were normally spoiled, this language suggests the infantalization of the Inuit in the eyes of their white parents.

FAMILY, SEXUALITY, CONSUMPTION

According to many writers, one of the signs of the "spoiled Eskimo" was her taste for the dress and make-up of white women. Women sojourners' narratives offer detailed descriptions of Inuit women's dress, work, family life, domesticity and consumption – categories of particular fascination because Inuit women were portrayed as highly valued for their work but nonetheless as subordinate members of patriarchal households. Authors often equated primitive with patriarchal, referring to a recent past of Inuit men fighting violently for women, of female infanticide, or arranged marriages. The problem of too much in-marriage in small settlements was also noted by writer Edith Iglauer.[99] Iglauer relays to her readers the interpretation of patriarchal Indigenous family and social relations offered up by her government handlers. One explained to her why local women could not be involved in the cooperative board: because Inuit men would not sanction it. Indigenous girls were married off by their parents as teens, it was explained to her, due to the deeply held belief that "when they are old enough to work they are old enough to marry."Moreover, once married, "the woman belongs to the man she marrys, just as his dogs do."[100] Some authors express an interest in accounts of polygamy and wife trading, though this is discussed far more in men's accounts of their lives in the North than in women's accounts.[101] Downplaying evidence of cooperative familial relations between Inuit men and women, white narratives adhere to the image of their own familial and social order as more progressive, egalitarian, and fair to women. Although white women are sometimes equated with vulnerability, they also become symbols of modernity, particularly in discussions of sexuality, family, and consumption. As in other colonial situations, the imposition of superior white norms, especially relating to domesticity, was to be accomplished not by direct coercion but, rather, by repeated example, image, and subtle ideological persuasion.[102]

Inuit childbirth is often endowed with notions of the primitive, portrayed as easily accomplished, with less pain and disruption than is experienced by white women.[103] Writers commented on how soon Inuit women were back at their work, though this may have been a necessity (as, historically, it had been for white working-class women). While there is some evidence that white nurses in the North were trying to relate Inuit practices to new ideas of natural childbirth,[104] many sojourners' accounts still invoke images of primitive reproduction. Manning's one example is telling: "The [woman] was too lazy to do more than she had to do any time, but I did think she would make something ready. As an Eskimo baby's layette consists of a single garment, a hood, there is little sewing to be done ... there wasn't even a hood ready, and as soon as the baby was wiped – with her hands – she snatched the filthy rag of a hood that Lizzie had made for her doll. Neither did a sepsis have any place in the whole procedure."[105] Donalda Coleman's expertise as a graduate nurse makes her similar descriptions of unsanitary, haphazard home births all the more powerful. Mena Orford was horrified to find out that her young daughters had witnessed a home birth and did not want them to give her curious husband a description (especially at the dinner table), fearing the children might be damaged by witnessing this primal scene. Pressed on by the doctor who had not yet seen a Native birth, their description convinced him that midwives were ignorant, not tying the cord properly, and causing women's deaths. Mena's most modern northern birth, in contrast, took place in the hospital, while she was under anaesthetic, "out like a light."[106] Yet, in a revealing discussion about childbirth in the North, Maud Watt, an HBC trader's wife who spent her entire life in the North, told her biographer that she secretly sent for a knowledgeable "Indian midwife" when she went into labour because she did not trust the local doctor, a "hard-faced woman" with the reputation of being a "butcher" and a drinker. While the doctor slept in the house, the midwife quietly slipped in and delivered Maud's baby.[107]

Family rituals such as marriage also became markers of domestic difference between Indigenous and white. Bouquet, dress, bridesmaid were all in place for Tolboom's wedding, and though she is gently self-mocking in her description of her vigilance to custom, it is clear that this symbolized the proper standards of marriage. The fact that a white wedding denoted a virginal wedding was made clear with contrasts to Inuit weddings. When the Anglican minister made a visit to Povungnetuk, he was perturbed to find an Indigenous couple who had had their child baptized and then announced that they wanted to be married. Facing an impatient and annoyed minister, "the couple grinned foolishly" and, in response to his lecture about the proper place of marriage, they explained, "we forgot."[108] Some women's accounts laud the existence of long-lasting Inuit unions, a deliberate attempt to counter sensational accounts of wife trading, but the underlying sense that marriage might be taken less seriously by the Inuit remains.

Nowhere was the difference between the primitive and the modern more evocatively symbolized than in descriptions of food and dress. Consumption defined white domesticity, indicated by the pantries of white women, often provisioned for a full year by the visit of the *Nascopie* (or other ships after its sinking in 1947). Describing the arduous work of unpacking, Tolboom notes that her shelves included everything from staples to "shredded coconut, olives and strawberries ... and cases of fresh potatoes, eggs and oranges."[109] Gillis's shelves were so full after ship time that they looked like "a full grocery store." Using ready-made ingredients, she describes their desserts alone of "canned fruit, pies, cakes, puddings, jello ... Apple pie, raisin, dried apricot, pumpkin, caramel, chocolate, butterscotch, lemon."[110] The contrast with the "biscuits covered in lard" served to the Inuit is striking. On a visit to a local tent, Tolboom realized that her garbage was being recycled and used as their household items, while Gillis recounts her charitable donations to the thankful locals: rotten eggs and potatoes.[111] For white women, now accustomed to consuming rather than to producing food, the thought of losing ship provisions was disastrous. The nine hundred pounds of meat sent north for Gillis's house never made it, resulting in her images of "starvation" and her incessant public "complaints." The latter outbursts so embarrassed her husband that he became publicly enraged with her.[112] Some women, however, came to value Inuit food, especially the meat provided by local hunters, and Hinds was understandably critical of the problematic introduction of infant formula in the North as well as of the government's paternalistic attempts to tell Indigenous women how to preserve game.[113]

Household items and dress also marked out "the modern." Many white women wanted to create familiar domestic space, importing everything from wallpaper to crystal, silver, china, and a full closet of clothes. Sojourners had to have winter clothing made for them by Inuit women, otherwise they would have perished: yet white fashions – from nail polish to stockings – remained a symbol of social prestige. Edith Iglauer comments on the incongruous dress of a Port Burwell white female school teacher: at home she dressed warmly, but, when facing her pupils, she wore a "pearl necklace and earrings, tailored skirt, silk stockings, and high heeled shoes." This was a costume meant to convey respect for her "authoritative" position.[114] In contrast, some writers portrayed the advent of the catalogue, the harbinger of consumption, as a ray of hope for the untidy Inuit women, dressed in "shapeless, long, ugly cotton skirts [admittedly a Christian mission influence]."[115] Although Elsie Gillis accuses her maid of being spoiled by proximity to whites, she explains how she had acted as a role model in terms of fashion and manners: "On Sundays, of course, I always wore one of my best silk dresses [for dinner]. On Inooyuk's first Sunday [as an extra maid] with me she came dressed as usual. She did not again make that error."[116] Like many an imperial explorer before her, Gillis was using dinner attire to make a public statement about proper femininity and "imperial rank" as much as she was dressing for her own enjoyment.[117]

Yet when Indigenous women imitated white manners and dress they could be ridiculed. Jean Godsell mocks the Indigenous women who ordered countless parcels from the Eaton's catalogue only to realize COD meant they had to pay on arrival (unlike traditional HBC store credit). Soon, she claims, Eaton's realized "that Marie Chandelle, Rosalie Squirrel, Elise Lame-Duck et al were not ... the type of customers they desired." The catalogue showcased all the "baubles and luxuries" that might aid these women's search for some "tricks in beauty treatment. Half-breed and Indian girls now bobbed their hair in imitation of the whites, only to be referred to as Buffalo heads by the less advanced of their kind who refused to be high-hatted." According to Godsell, a physical brawl between fashion groups ensued: Aboriginal women are again portrayed as uncouth in comparison to herself.[118]

In Gillis's account of Christmas celebration in their home, she describes her maid, Kowtah, appearing incongruously in a mix of white and Native costumes: "She wore a lady's maroon felt ribbon trimmed hat, over her black braids ... a wine-coloured coat, draped with a huge fur collar. On her feet were ladies fur trimmed velvet overshoes. In her ears were ear-rings, and her lips and finger-tips were daubed with bright red ... It was all I could do to keep the smile from becoming a shout of laughter. Kowtah imagined herself a fashion plate straight out of one of the magazines she had seen at Jimmy's. Her fifth avenue costume had no doubt come out of some missionary bale."[119] Reviewers of these books clearly found such accounts amusing.[120] Could these Indigenous women dressed up as whites be characterized as instances of colonial mimicry? Perhaps this was the case for Indigenous women, but those with the discursive power were white women whose texts reinforced mocking colonialist images rather than subverting them with post-colonial "hybridity."[121]

Christmas also became a means of establishing new modes of consumption and cultural practice. Women sojourners offered detailed descriptions of Christmas celebrations as they tried to recreate home in an alien environment. They transported Christmas trees, candles, decorations, serviettes, and other paraphernalia to celebrate properly amidst the Natives. At their celebration for the Inuit, the Tolbooms offered up party favours: "[unsold HBC items from the trading post], games and refreshments: what a party we had ... into the office and waiting room porch crowded eighty-seven men, women and children. Never since have I seen so many joyful, perspiring Eskimo faces." The HBC couple distributing the party favours were impeccably dressed parents, imperial in image: "I felt gala in my red woollen dress, high heels and nylon stockings. Perfume, nail polish and a little corsage of evergreen and holly berries provided special touches. [Wulf] wore his good suit. Oh, but we did feel like the Lord and Lady of the Manor."[122]

The fact that Indigenous women's bodies were objects of merriment in some of these descriptions is similar to, but also different from, earlier accounts of southern First Nations women, the latter represented most clearly in Godsell's account.[123] The fact that whiteness was equated with cleanliness, while Indigenous women were portrayed as dirty, greasy-haired, and unkempt, was found in both sets of racist discourses. However, Inuit women were not sexualized as degenerate or promiscuous temptresses in quite the same manner as were some southern Aboriginal women. Inuit women were rendered more childlike than voluptuous, with Inuit men cast in the cave man role of sexual possessors – a stereotype, argues Hugh Brody, reflecting white sexual desires/anxieties more than anything else.[124] Nonetheless, Inuit women's sexual availability was implied, with references to their easy liaisons with whalers, their past acceptance of polygamy, their lack of inhibitions concerning privacy in one-room homes, and their supposedly seasonal sexual coupling. "In early summer in every Eskimo encampment," writes Tolboom, "Sex rears its head. But here it is not an ugly one. It is looked on as ... the changing of the seasons. It is accepted as simply as the matings of all wild things in this Land."[125]

In Arctic memoirs, however, Inuit women's domestic labour, especially their provision of food and dress, is vigorously extolled as readers are offered many examples of concrete material aid without which whites would have perished. Even journalist Edith Iglauer, only in the Arctic temporarily, admitted that Native-made dress was essential to her survival as she travelled to research her story on cooperatives. Despite these descriptions of Indigenous women's crucial labour, writers nonetheless absorbed the reigning anthropological and popular images of a patriarchal Inuit culture, with male hunting at the pinnacle of prestige and power. Since many sojourners saw men trapping, trading furs, and acting as guides, and women doing "inside" labour, such as sewing and child care (deemed feminine and valued less in their own culture), it was assumed that the gendered division of labour reflected the power of men. This assumption was not necessarily shared by those few writers who spent more time immersed in Inuit culture and who spoke the language. One HBC fur trader stressed the cooperative partnerships of Inuit husbands and wives as well as women's crucial role in directing decisions about extra-marital liaisons.[126] Though women sojourners were sometimes critical of the sexual status of Inuit women, they easily accepted the gendered division of labour, some even recommending more and better domestic training for Inuit girls. Many saw handicraft sales as the one area in which women could contribute to the domestic economy.

Some women's narratives also became tales of increased respect for the Inuit over time as they gained a better understanding of their cultural mores. In one incident, Tolboom's favourite dog had to be shot, and her husband warned her that the skin absolutely had to be used by locals, who were in desperate straits, for warm mitts. Initially upset, she came to understand that the careful use of all resources for daily life was a positive part of Inuit life. When Gillis first saw her maid polishing the glasses by spitting on them, she recounts, "I was just sick with disgust."[127] But after a discussion with her husband, she admitted that, in a culture where so much of women's work involved chewing, this was simply a logical use of a human tool.

Discussions of child rearing were used, most notably, to relay positive comments on Indigenous lives. Copeland, who tends to misunderstand Inuit adoptions as the casual "handing off" of children to other families, comes to recognize the intense love for children behind her own maid's repeated efforts to secure an adopted child. Many accounts note the lack of discipline for children but then laud their good behaviour and the intense love of parents for their offspring. Burnford makes such comments about both the northern Ojibway and the Inuit. "Children are indulged, but never spoiled," she notes of the former. No one ever "said 'no' to children," she later recounts of her Nunavut trip, "children learned what was out of step within a family group by observation and experience. The children at Pond were the most happy, self-contained and naturally courteous little people I have ever met."[128] Mena Orford's transformation from critic to acolyte of Inuit culture is symbolized by her comments on children. Her first impression of her Inuit helper, Nukinga, literally betrays physical disgust, yet this is followed by the quick revelation of her children's very different response: "A churning started in the pit of my stomach ... as I watched this gross woman with the dark-skinned perspiring face encircle my two in her wide arms and in turn, rub each of their noses with her own ... but as [the children] left, their faces shone with a contentment and happiness I hadn't seen for some time."[129] More dramatic is her realization that the Inuit aversion to physically disciplining children is perhaps more compassionate than her own belief in spanking. When she hit one of her children in front of her two Inuit helpers, she saw pure horror in their eyes. She began to question her superior knowledge, acknowledging that the Inuit make "a pretty good job of child rearing."[130]

SHIFTING SENSIBILITIES

While there are similarities between these sojourner accounts, there are also some differences – and not only that between wives and career-women already noted. If we look, for example, at two discussions of northern Native and Inuit women published ten years apart, we can see some change over time. The contrast between books by Jean Godsell and

Sheila Burnford makes this point clearly, though perhaps almost too extremely. While Godsell's autobiography details the interwar period in the North, it was published in 1959, and the very fact that it was published is significant. So, too, is its reception. One uncritical review notes that, even if Godsell's tell-all "over-the-tea-cups" memoir did not reveal the names of the other wives "she rubbed shoulders with," they might still recognize themselves in this revealing text.[131] Many reviews in western Canadian newspapers played up Godsell's role as an "expert" on Indians and her honorary induction as a "chief" into two Indian tribes. Most commentators noted the "colourful characters," humorous vignettes, and stunning physical landscapes presented in her book. It is true that Godsell and her husband had complicated relationships with Indian culture and heritage, which they ostensibly promoted, but the lack of any comment on her belittling descriptions of Indigenous peoples is noteworthy.[132]

One slightly critical review notes that her "racy" account, with its "many adjectives and exclamation marks," could make "tiresome reading," and the reviewer picks up on the contradiction between Godsell's claim that she was a most virtuous, non-gossipy woman and the fact that the book is saturated with nasty gossip. The reviewer also refers, though more obliquely, to Godsell's racist description of Indigenous peoples.[133] The passage in which Godsell describes how she asserted her authority over her servant, John James, is only one example of many. When James appeared with a hangover and was not doing his work, her husband gave her advice she claimed was "very sage":

> "He's just trying you out," he remarked, "he wants to see how far he can go with you. It's a typical Indian trick. Give him hell," he reiterated, "if you don't master him now, you never will." Never will I forget the look of stupefaction on John's face when I finally sailed into him ... From then on, on my husband's advice, I gave him what-for on an average of once a month. Often I had to make an excuse for doing so. At first this seemed rather mean but I soon learned, as everyone does who handles Indians, that it was the only way to keep him in line. As a result, John James would, ever after, have gone to Hades and back for me if I had told him to do so.[134]

Godsell's description sounds much like advice given to owners of slaves and indentured servants. As we have seen, Godsell also highlights the competition between Indigenous and white women for social standing in a manner that ridicules Métis women, although she is somewhat equal opportunity in her denigrations of other women, claiming some white women, too, are vicious and competitive. While there are many instances of racism in her book, what is most important is her lack of self-consciousness about these: her use of pidgin English for Native dialogue, her bragging about keeping Indians in their place, her celebration of a fur trade society built on white initiative and hierarchy.

It is hard to imagine a publisher embracing a book like Godsell's ten years later or reviewers glossing over her descriptions of Indigenous peoples. In contrast, Burnford's books, one detailing her visits to the northern Ontario Objiway-Cree and one focusing on her travels to Nunavut, were promoted differently a decade later. *Without Reserve* was marketed as a decidedly non-colonial view of the Indigenous North. Burnford, the publisher claimed, did not go north to "exhort, to teach, to heal, to snoop" but, rather, to be "absorbed into the daily life of the reserve" and to appreciate the culture and legends of these "vulnerable people whose ancient values have meaning for us all."[135] What actually marked out the book in comparison to other sojourner accounts was Burnford's constant attempts to put herself in the shoes of Indigenous peoples, to understand the world from their perspective: her books offer some credence to Ronald Haycock's claim that "humanitarian awareness and guilt" began to characterize some representations of the Canadian Indian in this time period.[136] Her effort at empathetic relativism is characteristic of postwar cultural discourse about oppressed others, including those who reported on African American life-as-lived in the United States,[137] and it was likely also shaped by a changing political context – namely, the vocal, public mobilizations of Indigenous peoples for radical change in the 1960s.

Without Reserve shares some of the romanticization of exotic Native peoples reminiscent of earlier sojourner accounts of the North, and it repeats the common trope of an ancient, traditional society awkwardly making its way towards modernity. Her Indigenous neighbours are

sometimes essentialized and rendered silent and passive, though somewhat mystical in outlook, immersed as they are in a "timeless" ancient
past.[138] Yet she is also critical of badly planned state interventions, and
she attempts to make interesting connections between racism and the
class prejudice she knew first hand from her Glasgow background. She
repeatedly surmises that her actions and appearance must appear excessively strange in the eyes of her Indigenous neighbours, and she struggles to remain "open minded," rejecting the stereotypes of Native peoples
she hears from other whites.

Burnford both succumbs to, but is critical of, white expert knowledge
about Indigenous lives. While referring to the reserve as "occupied territory," she nonetheless portrays the occupiers – "priests, school teachers,
nurses, welfare officers" – as well intentioned.[139] On the one hand, she
repeats without critical commentary the paternalistic view of a visiting
Catholic missionary that the Indians were "like children spending all
their allowance at once on candy; and like children they must be patiently taught."[140] Yet she is also suspicious of overbearing whites who
have less than noble motivations for being in the North, including a
white man who has adopted a Native boy, she suspects for all the wrong
reasons.[141]

Burnford's 1972 Arctic memoir, *One Woman's Arctic*, based on the two
summers she spent on Baffin Island, Nunavut, shares some of these same
contradictions. She criticizes racial stereotypes but then returns to essentialist generalizations about the Eskimo personality, all the time declaring
her ability to move beyond them: "To me, the Eskimo became individuals, some more appealing, some wittier, wise or warmer, no longer a
group of ethnic strangers behind a language barrier."[142] Burnford mocks
and questions her own cultural assumptions and self-preoccupations, but
she sometimes falls back on them or assumes that superior white knowledge will explain and aid the Inuit. Still, her memoir is markedly different from those written by Tolboom or Gillis. Unlike wives following
their husbands North, Burnford relishes the opportunity to go hunting
with the Inuit, throwing off the persona of the fragile white woman,
though she does acknowledge her complete reliance on Eskimo environmental know-how. She writes positively about Inuit adoption (in contrast

to Copeland), the closeness of family life, and the inevitability of Inuit taking over their own governance. And she also gives credence to Inuit customary notions of justice rather than assuming they were violent, primitive, and uncivilized.[143]

A tendency to idealize the noble northern Inuit in comparison to the defeated and bitter southern Indian, however, is still apparent: "Long after the dignity of their cousins in the South had disintegrated under the influence of the white man, [northern Native peoples] remained complete and whole in the life that their people had led since time unknown ... [T]he Eskimo was the indigenous help without whom the white explorer could not have survived and on close acquaintance became a figure to be greatly admired: endearing and jolly, showing superlative ingenuity and endurance."[144] (Even within the North, she contrasts Frobisher Bay, which she dislikes for its southern-type ugly city sprawl, urban poverty, alcohol, prostitution, and alienation, to the more idealized, pristine, traditional, untouched, northerly Pond Inlet.) Burnford's liberal humanism is cross-cut with the exotic. Her optimistic hope in the commonality of humankind, the collapsing of barriers between the "sophisticated and primitive, exploiter and exploited," is perhaps overly romantic.[145] Yet, however fraught with contradiction, however much her view of the North is shaped by her own class and ethnic background, her travel narratives express a different sensibility than do those of Godsell or Tolboom.

THE POLITICAL IMPLICATIONS OF TRAVEL WRITING

The tone of women sojourners' superior surveillance of Indigenous life sometimes imitates that of male writers, although their less confident relation to the wild North – particularly if they came as helpmates – and their more detailed descriptions of women's lives, domesticity, and consumption also make their narratives distinct from men's. In some instances, women's narratives can also be read against the grain, revealing not the jolly, docile Eskimo woman but a far more complex human being, one coping with rapid social change and sometimes less enamoured with Euro-Canadian incursion than whites understood. Despite the claim of many sojourners that they understand the lives of Indigenous women, their own accounts suggest otherwise.

Inuit women, for instance, are often portrayed as passive and docile, but the skirmishes women describe over domestic labour indicate that they were not. If Indigenous women disagreed with the white women for whom they worked, they might either simply stop coming or quietly indicate their disapproval. White women often took silence for approval, yet Inuit women were likely displaying *ilira*, "a show of deference to intimidating individuals" that reflected the subtle but pervasive result of inequality.[146] Scherman, among others, recounts instances in which Inuit women and men seem to simply disregard advice or orders. Clearly, even those working for whites maintained a strong sense of their own needs, values, and judgments. Hinds was more likely than some authors to endow her Inuit neighbours with complex reactions and agency, and she, too, notes instances in which Inuit would simply not do things that they were ordered to if they judged them to be unsafe or unwise, no matter how insistent whites were. One might also interpret the negative reactions of northern Indigenous women to Godsell differently than she did: as hostility to her racism and as a rejection of her derogatory views of their culture.

However, assessing the dominant messages behind these sojourning narratives is still important. How would northern Indigenous peoples, especially those in the eastern Arctic, have been imagined by readers in postwar Canada? Sojourners' views of the Inuit did not simply replicate earlier writing on the southern First Nations. Within colonialist discourses, there was some distinction between a language of northern Inuit "primitivism" and the language of Indian "savagism," with the latter being even more pessimistic and negative in character than the former. Also, some women conveyed messages of tolerance, respect for Indigenous women's skills, and compassion for other human beings. Burnford's books suggest that an embrace of cultural relativism and liberal humanism increased over time as the historical context in which women wrote altered. Moreover, some white women, especially those who had been in the North for some time, did come to identify Inuit women as their friends, not just their neighbours. When she was teaching the Loucheaux Dene at Fort McPherson, Marjorie Hinds detailed her pleasure in spending days accompanying "her friend Sarah" out on her traplines.[147] Mena Orford could not forget the night she went to have tea and chat with an Inuit neighbour and saw her boy badly mauled by a dog. Orford's recounting of this tragic story made it clear that she felt deep compassion for this devastated mother, a woman she called a friend.

But tolerance and compassion can coexist with paternalism, also a theme in many of these narratives. The image of primitive and/or fatalistic Indigenous cultures, facing the painful fact of inevitable adaptation, appears repeatedly, along with the notion that whites were well placed to oversee the difficult, uphill path to modernization. Rhetorical and discursive strategies of colonial representation – superior surveillance, scientific classification, modernist idealization, and eroticization – are woven into sojourners' accounts. As a result, the non-Indigenous South is portrayed, in the light of modernization theories of the time, as more progressive, modern, urban, and industrial, as the repository of knowledge that might allow Indigenous peoples to develop more fully.[148]

These representations of Indigenous life were deeply political in an era when the North was an increasingly important economic frontier and military concern, and as government intervention in Inuit lives was increasing. Within the ongoing public debate about the fate of the northern Indigenous peoples, the images created by white sojourners assumed to have direct experience of Inuit life were endowed with the weight of a certain veracity, authenticity, and memorability. As cultural producers of travel narratives, women thus played an active, constitutive role in the creation of colonial texts and ideologies. Nonetheless, sojourners' own admissions that Indigenous women and men retained different views and values, and sometimes disagreed with them, indicates that paternalist traditions did not go unchallenged and that the culture of colonialism was never monolithic or unassailable.

CHAPTER TWO

The Beaver

Northern Indigenous Life in Popular Education

A visual equivalent of Wanda Tolboom's description of her wedding in *Arctic Bride* was displayed in the 1943 issue of *The Beaver*, Canada's "magazine of the North," sponsored by the Hudson's Bay Company. Two photos of white Arctic weddings are featured, one with fashionable bride and bridesmaid in long dresses, groom, best man, and no fewer than two ministers in robes, and the other featuring a formal wedding party that also included Bishop Fleming, an RCMP officer, and Superintendant Major McKeand. Both shots are taken against a dramatic backdrop of ice and snow. The caption for one explains that the small "dark object" protruding into the picture was "the head of an Eskimo child," who of course remained unnamed.[1] These pictures are but one example of the celebration of the white Arctic bride in the pages of *The Beaver*, offering a marked contrast to the magazine's images of northern Indigenous women, who were more often shown in traditional Native dress, engaged in productive and domestic labour or, by the late 1950s, adjusting to modern familial and work roles. These contrasting displays of femininity, juxtaposed by culture and race, are illustrative of *The Beaver*'s use of imagery and text to create an ideology of Canadian northernness that ostensibly promoted ideals of anthropological discovery, historical pride, and cultural tolerance while also reinforcing colonial images of northern Aboriginal peoples.

This chapter explores the visual and textual rendering of Aboriginal peoples, crafted for a predominately white, middlebrow audience in the South, by focusing on four themes: the expert account, the nostalgic picturesque, the development narrative, and the visual representation of Inuit women. Rather than measuring the ethnographic accuracy of *The Beaver*, I want to examine the "imaginative spaces" that Indigenous peoples occupied for magazine readers searching for entertainment and education, the "tropes and stories that ordered [Indigenous] existence" in their minds.[2] In this textual contact zone, interpretations of Aboriginal life often assumed an ambiguous tone for the magazine was infused with the cultural relativism characteristic of much post-Boasian anthropology,[3] and many authors advocated cultural tolerance and interracial cooperation in the development of the North. Much like American inter-war intellectuals and avant-garde artists who appropriated aspects of Indigenous cultures, *The Beaver* attempted to create a Canadian national identity by celebrating its links to First Nations history and culture.[4] Yet the magazine also reflected a cultural hierarchy that, by recording the primitive, strange, and alien behaviour of the Eskimo, cast white Euro-Canadian modernity as superior and inevitable. It drew on symbols and stories already a part of a racialized ideology that explained the culture and history of northern First Nations, and on orientalist ways of seeing the non-Western other, often implicitly contrasted to white Canadians who were modern, rational, progressive, and technologically advanced.[5] Adapting orientalism to visual anthropology, Fatimah Tobing Rony advances the notion of an "ethnographic gaze": in the case of *The Beaver*, Indigenous peoples are placed within an exotic "mise-en-scène" in which the individual Native is made "real" by the objectifying ethnographic gaze of white observers.[6]

While *The Beaver* was initially developed as a public relations endeavour by the HBC, the magazine gained readership over the post-Second World War period as a *National Geographic*-style publication offering authentic images of the North, Canadian history, white exploration, and Aboriginal peoples, especially those from the Canadian west and the North. By examining the recurring images of Indigeneity in *The Beaver*, we can better understand the dominant ideologies concerning race and Indigenous cultures circulating in Canadian society, how they were conveyed, and where they found a close fit with the ideas conveyed in other media (such as memoires and documentaries). *The Beaver* is an excellent example of the way in which the cultural and political realms were closely connected because its image and text worked *as ideology* to legitimize the persistence of internal colonialism in Canada's North and to proscribe economic and social solutions to the problem of how to go about ensuring the inevitable and necessary modernization of traditional Aboriginal cultures. The magazine's ideological work overlapped on two levels: first, it was a conscious, *interested* project of meaning making on the part of the HBC, an attempt to create a narrative of nation building that idealized and rationalized the company's economic history and involvement in the North; second, its messages about Indigenous peoples were part of a broader hegemonic ideology of race and culture diffused through civil society, deeply interwoven into this educational, popular magazine itself.[7]

The Beaver's reciprocal construction of a primitive North in need of guidance from a modern South masks relations of ideological power that had potentially profound consequences for Indigenous peoples, and it also hints at the magazine's popular appeal for its predominantly English-speaking, white audiences. Although reader response remains outside my purview (and granted consumer readings may always be unexpected or ambiguous), *The Beaver*'s dominant images of the Aboriginal North generally reaffirm an uncritical acceptance of post-Second World War Canadian society. The stress on progressive development that would liberate Indigenous peoples from ill health and environmental insecurity, on white-Indigenous collaboration, and on the image of a happy Eskimo being integrated into a history of Canadian progress, all fit comfortably within the cultural and political milieu of the period. As Catherine Lutz and Jane Collins argue of *National Geographic* images, readers could both see themselves as culturally tolerant and still fall back on racial explanations for cultural differences, thus avoiding troubling questions about the international division of colonial labour and structural questions of race, power, and history.[8]

EXPERT ACCOUNTS

The Beaver had long been a deliberate public relations effort on the part of the HBC to align its commercial image with positive interpretations of Canadian nation building. Originally an HBC staff publication established in 1920, *The Beaver* altered its agenda in 1933–34; it shifted from romancing its personnel to romancing its customers and the public, presenting material designed to "create a feeling of pride" in the HBC empire.[9] The latter was conceptualized as an integral part of Canada's nationalist story. As one enthusiastic reader wrote to the editor: "I *envy* you [the great job] of circulating Canada's history. You *sell* Canada to Canadians and the world!"[10] Subscription fees were introduced, circulation substantially increased (including new American readers), and free giveaways – for example, to the troops during the Second World War – were used to boost readership. By 1960, a typical run was twenty-four thousand.

In the post-Second World War period, the magazine circulated in public libraries, schools, and to a wider public. It was marketed as educational and informational as well as entertaining, appealing to a middle-brow audience, which, though smaller than that targeted by the mass media, remained a socially significant readership. Like the American-based *National Geographic*, which purported to document the lives of the global other for white middle-class Americans, *The Beaver* mixed pedagogy and pleasure, projecting a liberal humanism and stressing the importance of scientific research, objective knowledge, and tolerant understanding of racial and cultural difference. Promotion of a positive HBC image lingered on as a key goal, signified by the inside-cover tag line, which accompanied the picture of an Inuit man holding a mass of beautiful white fox furs: "This is the Arctic, Canada's newest frontier, served now, as in the past, by the men of the HBC."[11] That the HBC offered benevolent *service* rather than extracting wealth was clearly the message. As photographic historian Alan Sekula argues, who owns or controls the archive profoundly shapes the relationship between culture and economic life, creating "a hidden connection between power and knowledge." Archival holdings become a convincing voice of documentary authority, legitimating existing power relations even while purporting to offer a cultural "exchange between equal partners."[12]

The magazines' editors in this period were well-educated professionals, with backgrounds in popular writing, journalism, and museums. After editor Douglas MacKay was killed on HBC business in an air crash in 1938, Clifford Wilson, a well-connected journalist and, like MacKay, an established author on the HBC, was hired to oversee all the company's public relations projects. Undoubtedly the key architect of the post-Second World War *Beaver*, Wilson saw his tenure at the magazine coincide with his connection to an increasingly professionalized museum world, and, in 1958, he left to run the Glenbow Museum in Calgary.[13] After 1959, the new editor, Malvina Bolus, added material on arts, crafts, archaeology, and nature, though the staples of Wilson's magazine – namely, articles on travel, exploration, vignettes of daily life in the North, and writing extolling the HBC's record of "enterprise in opening up the vast territories of North America and in serving their peoples"[14] – remained important. The magazine prided itself on its "good taste" and its objective adherence to "the facts."[15] And in tandem with this positivist claim is Wilson's stated mission to promote a Canadian history that might inspire national pride – a goal apparent in his earlier writing of historical children's literature.[16]

At a time when academics, along with other experts and journalists, "had a virtual monopoly on how Aboriginal peoples were represented to the rest of society," the ability of the editors to showcase prominent expert voices was important.[17] The magazine's contributors encompassed scholars from anthropology, history, science, and economics, both those professionally employed and amateur raconteurs and historians, including a significant group of women writers, marginalized within academe at the time, yet still employed in archives, museums, American colleges, or working freelance. Some of their contributions are noteworthy for their early interest in women's history. Marjorie Campbell's title "Her Ladyship, My Squaw," might sound discordant to our ears, but the actual article could be considered an early feminist reinterpretation of the fur trade that stressed the value of Aboriginal women's labour and social contributions to the HBC.[18]

Respected scientific groups such as the Arctic Institute of North America were featured, along with internationally known writers whose very reputations were the product of their northern travel, writing, and research. Invoking the knowledge of anthropologists offered an especially impressive seal of authenticity to *The Beaver*. In 1951, for instance, the magazine invited prominent spokespeople from the anthropological profession to write on the theme "Enter the European," looking at the impact of whites on the Arctic Eskimo. Anthropologist Diamond Jenness surveyed a number of Western countries involved in Arctic areas and was critical of some of the negative influences instigated by white incursion, whether it be the exploitation of the Inuit by whalers or the government's inattention to its Indigenous "wards." However, he tended to cast the Inuit as "pawns" of white ingenuity and deviousness, noting that they were "inarticulate and helpless, for in their own primitive communities they had never known any organized government."[19] He judged that the RCMP and traders in the Canadian North were usually "just and humane" towards the Natives, but the HBC was a victim of the prevailing capitalist business climate and the profit imperative: the destruction of Eskimo self-sufficiency was thus just an unfortunate outcome of the HBC fox trade. Critical of the Canadian state for its failure to live up to its "moral responsibility" for the Eskimo, he lauded the more protective and assimilative policies of other governments and placed a high value on cultural and "racial" intermingling rather than on Inuit cultural preservation. His message that the Canadian state was morally responsible for the Inuit could be read as a call for attention to their voices, but his work also assumed a highly paternalistic view, assuming Inuit needs could be best defined by anthropological experts like himself and their needs taken care of by a benevolent state.[20] Indeed, unlike many Boasian anthropologists, Jenness still relied on evolutionary paradigms, often seeing Eskimo culture as static, even doomed to obsolescence.[21]

The Beaver also showed considerable deference to missionaries working in the North. Regular contributor and Anglican minister Donald Marsh weighed in on the "Enter the European" debate, arguing that the Inuit had gone from being wards of the government to citizens with equal rights who should not be forced into the mould of southern peoples but, rather, allowed to pursue their traditional lives as hunters. Yet he portrayed the mission encounter as progress incarnate, bringing the syllabic alphabet, writing skills, education, and religious enlightenment to primitives, and he warns that Eskimos were being spoiled by overly indulgent southern policies: "the issuance of relief to the Eskimo people has become one of the greatest problems of the arctic."[22] A Catholic missionary asserted even more forcefully that his religion had provided humanistic enlightenment to Indigenous peoples. "Child murder, desertion of the old and the cripples, wife-trading etc. are now things of the past amongst the Christians," he concludes concerning the legacy of the Roman Catholic Church.[23] Some residential school survivors would now disagree with this interpretation of the Church's overwhelmingly positive impact.

Long-time HBC traders invited to comment on this debate reminded readers of their positive roles as medics, advisors, even domestic counsellors to the Inuit. In the vein of much imperialist rhetoric, trader Pete Nichols saw his role as a white "father" to his Eskimo "children." The father, he writes, wants his children to "grow up gradually, to be introduced as painlessly as possible to the hectic tempo of modern civilization ... he needs to steer them between rocks of hard stone age existence and the sucking whirlpool of civilization." In this schema, the male Inuit are *prospective* paternal role models as they are already manly heroic hunters, symbols of the unspoiled, natural, human past. What makes these men quintessentially Eskimo, adds Nichols, is their struggle with a harsh environment, "their courage, dependability and manliness – all those things which make the race so admirable in the white man's eyes."[24]

As Ann Fienup-Riordan notes, for southern audiences, *all* northern Eskimo were popularly constructed as the mirror image of the ideal white explorer, exhibiting bravery, independence, and perseverance. They were idealized as the "ultimate survivors," uncorrupted by civilization – though, ironically, not as people who should control their own fates.[25] Nichols and other *Beaver* authors relied heavily on the views of earlier white explorers like Peter Freuchen, whose own writings were reprinted in a series entitled Out of the Stone Age, accompanied by sketches of Eskimo hunters as unkempt wild primitives with long hair, tearing on raw meat, and using bows and arrows. Not surprisingly, Freuchen's claim that "the HBC has done more than any other company in the world to make life simpler and easier for people living in the north" also made its way into the magazine.[26] This cave man persona also subtly reinforced images of primitive sexuality found in other travel writing on the Inuit. The image of the Eskimo caveman, club in hand, claiming his woman by force, as Hugh Brody suggests, is in some respects a projection of white sexual desires/anxieties: "the caveman is our primitive ancestor ... the original version of ourselves. What they feel is deep down at our core. The stereotype is whites' version of the essence of ourselves."[27] Joanna De Groot, too, comments on the Western fascination with archetypes of the primitive exotic woman or male hunter, both products of the forces of nature. These images, she contends, represent the other to the white self; they are both attractive and repellent, representing the need of whites to control and "discipline *themselves* in order to maintain their claim to superiority."[28]

Anthropologists, as respected scientific commentators on non-Western cultures, were often incorporated as authorities on topics ranging from Inuit and Native art to history, culture, and subsistence practices, with some of this writing reflecting the lasting influence of salvage ethnography.[29] This expert surveillance often celebrated aspects of Inuit and other Indigenous cultures, particularly their environmental and survival skills, but it simultaneously echoed the need to document cultures liable to be swept aside by the tides of modernity. Scholars connected to American and Canadian museums were frequent contributors, reflecting Clifford Wilson's connection to the museum world. Their mode of writing, like that of many experts, often drew on the rhetorical device of "classification ... an ideologically-charged procedure of demarcating non-Western cultures from the benchmarks of more sophisticated European ones."[30]

Marius Barbeau, to note only one example, wrote on topics ranging from the fur trade and voyageur songs to settler buildings, Indian tobacco, art, the silver trade, and so on. Using a theme like tobacco, he unravelled a historical and anthropological discussion of its use, significance, and meaning over time. His keen eye for the meaning of the material produced short, accessible articles that were undoubtedly meant to stress the value of Indigenous history and culture. At the same time, his rendition of the fur trade, to use another example, reinforced a narrative of white civilization coming to the primitive wilderness. Writing of Port Simpson, he admits that the fort offered a "new regime of [economic] benefit to the [HB] company," but it also bestowed "peace and order" on the "warlike" Natives, long "demoralized by contact with predatory seamen and now addicted to a slave trade of their own." The accompanying sketch shows the "Haida and Tsimsyn" doing battle outside the fort, reinforcing an image of war-like Indians.[31] Barbeau's complex relations with Native peoples not only reflect the imprint of Boasian salvage ethnography, a desire to record and value Native cultures, but also the influence of "prevailing social prejudices," sometimes harnessed by the state to its policy goals.[32]

Harry Hawthorn, a professor of anthropology at the University of British Columbia and co-author of two reports for the state on Indians in Canada, also contributed to the Enter the Europeans debate.[33] Hawthorn, whose wide-ranging assessment of Indians in Canada (known as the Hawthorn-Tremblay Report) was an important policy statement of the time, introduced the idea of Indians as "citizens plus" within the Canadian nation-state. Though ultimately the Hawthorn-Tremblay Report was sidelined by the government, it offered an optimistic prognosis for the progressive integration of "Indians into Canadian citizenship" through the provision of social services and education. Indians, he argues in *The Beaver*, must now conform to "a highly literate, industrialized modern nation." As they become full "citizens" they might also find "practical expression" for their cultural past in cultural conservatories such as the museum. The sketches chosen by the editor to accompany the article are C.W. Jeffreys's well-known drawings of early exploration and colonization (offered by permission of Imperial Oil), many of which underscore the theme of the white settler as leader, instructor, and treaty maker.[34] One could argue that this visual message does not accurately reflect Hawthorn's policy ideas and views on Aboriginal cultures. If this is the case, then their proximity to the article becomes an interesting comment on how the magazine's editorial control might subtly skew the expert's intent or message.[35]

The editors occasionally secured pieces from international scholars outside Canada, like Margaret Mead, known for her commitment to the popular dissemination of research. In one article, Mead's children's book on the Eskimo way of life, drawn from Boas's work, was reproduced.[36] In another Enter the European contribution, Mead offers a historical analysis of Western incursion into the South Pacific, extolling the positive,

progressive role of anthropologists in an internationalizing world as promoters of respect for all cultures and as expert advisors on how to ease
fragile, primitive Indigenous cultures into the complex technology associated with modernity.[37]

These contributors' pieces were not only shaped by the dominant anthropological paradigms of the time but also moulded to fit the aims of
this HBC publication. Their writing was selected, edited, and presented
according to the magazine's public relations program, including its aim
to entertain as well as to inform. Indeed, it is important to stress that anthropological opinion was not of one mind, and some anthropologists
defended Aboriginal practices such as the potlatch in the face of state
repression.[38] But the magazine was not a forum for complex argument
and critique. In more than one contribution, anthropologist and curator
Douglas Leechman describes the historic Cree and Chipewyan in negative, essentialized terms, and he stresses practices like polygamy, with
powerful men fighting each other for "seven or eight wives." Years apart,
two Leechman articles describe Indians "wrestling for wives" in almost
identical words. Was he re-using old writing or were these "sensational"
details of the Native past replayed in this manner precisely because they
spoke to popular images of the Hollywood Indian?[39]

Since the early twentieth century, anthropologists have debated the
popularization and commercialization of ethnographic research, concerns
perhaps intensified with the consolidation of the discipline within univer-
sities in the post-Second World War period.[40] These *Beaver* contributors
undoubtedly saw their writing as a positive effort to educate a lay audience and were not very mindful of its unanticipated effects. Their expert
commentary must be situated within the reigning theoretical preoccupations of the time,[41] including contemporary scholarly debates. Differences
were aired, for instance, about the best way to successfully integrate Inuit
and Euro-Canadian cultures, and, by the 1960s, a new generation of anthropologists used *The Beaver* to report on and, significantly, to valorize
aspects of Indigenous cultures.[42] A few *Beaver* expert commentators also
raised political concerns about the social and economic marginalization
of First Nations peoples. Why is it, asks Dr. Morris Shumiatcher, a lawyer

known for his civil liberties work in Saskatchewan, that Canada's oldest nationals – the Indians – rank lower in status than its newest immigrants? His answer includes a critique of the federal system of "wardship," and his solution embraces a "citizens plus" solution in which Indians share the "full benefits of their treaties and Canadian citizenship" until they can become "full-fledged Canadian citizens."[43]

While the occasional editorial piece (such as the one just mentioned) challenges the status quo, perspectives critical of the HBC, or, indeed, of colonialism as a system, do not appear, and the experts ultimately reflect fairly homogeneous ideological and professional networks and ideas. Many anthropological experts interpret federal policies benignly, or quite positively, as, for example, one anthropologist who, in the vein of the Cold War, praises the Canadian state for its employment of social scientists like himself to search for "working solutions" to Inuit problems in comparison to the Soviets, who would never engage in "objective" research about their northern peoples.[44]

Other expert voices in *The Beaver* include professional historians such as A.S. Morton, Donald Creighton, and W.L. Morton, who provide accessible, short excerpts from their longer works (such as Creighton's article on Sir John A. Macdonald) as well as studies of the fur trade. While differences in their interpretations are evident, much of the writing nonetheless betrays a dominant narrative of the West and North, in which white settlement represents the march of inevitable progress and development, with Native peoples, however noble, doomed to displacement. Even George Woodcock's sympathetic version of Louis Riel depicts him as a "defender of a dying race."[45] An early piece by W.L. Morton on the emergence of Red River similarly celebrates its dualistic culture, though he describes this distinct society as the unification of white "civilization" and Indian "primitiveness."[46] Twenty years later, however, Morton's discussion of the vibrant culture of difference that thrived at Red River reflects changing historical terminology: gone was the term "primitive Indian," though the Métis are described for this popular audience as "picturesque Indian-French peoples." Nonetheless, the change in language is important.[47]

Woman cleaning ice window of snow house. Indigenous women's labour was portrayed as arduous and primitive. | Hudson's Bay Company Archives, Archives of Manitoba, 1987/363-E-324/66 (N15959)

Scientific and medical experts are also featured, with the latter lauding the displacement of Indigenous superstitions by the scientific certainties of modern Western medicine. Nurse Donalda Copeland's memoir of battling Inuit superstition through her nursing practice thus overlaps with *The Beaver*'s message on medicine in the North. One study, funded by both the federal government and the "generous aid of the HBC" was undertaken by a list of distinguished medical, anthropological, and scientific experts whose findings were published in the *Canadian Medical Association Journal*. Their *Beaver* article, published under the tongue-in-cheek title "Voyage of the Medicine Men," documents malnutrition in James Bay Indigenous peoples (who, according to the study, experienced starvation before the arrival of family allowances) and advocates for better medical and dental care, refrigeration, and TB tests. Malnutrition, continue the medical experts, may well have been the cause of characteristics such as "shiftlessness, indolence, improvidence and inertia, so long regarded as inherent traits in the Indian race."[48] While professing a liberal questioning of racism, such studies reinforce the view that one *could* generalize about the Indian character through the use of such categories as "laziness."

Many whites sojourning in the North also adopted the roles of amateur anthropologists or "ethnic tourists," contributing vignettes that assumed intimate knowledge of Indigenous cultures. One suspects that pieces like the "Windigo Woman" were chosen as illustrations of the exotic, unusual, or unexplainable Native, with the exotic providing a reassuring mirror to the reader's own conception of his or her rational normality.[49] These amateur anthropologists crossed the spectrum from the culturally tolerant to the resolutely superior observer. A "Resident Nurse" who describes her local "Medicine Man" depicts him as a "pseudo-doctor" but still "no quack." Some of his natural remedies worked, others did not, but she concedes that he had long "dreamed of his role" and was dedicated to curing his fellow Ojibway. "Healing is in his soul," she writes sympathetically, reinforcing the Indigenous viewpoint that healing has a spiritual dimension.[50] Yet, in the same issue, HBC manager George Anderson's "Pagan Eskimo" portrays the angakooks, the spiritual Inuit leaders, as "crude," uninformed, and superstitious, peddling "taboos," even abusing their power. One "lazy" female angakook, he claims dismissively, conveniently had the spirits tell her that she should not gather fuel for her family.[51]

Photographers also became important documentarians of the natural landscape as well as of Inuit and Dene life.[52] Indeed, photography, text, and art acted "intertextually": photography drew on pictorial conventions stretching back to the nineteenth century, and textual explanations of visuals could dramatically alter the way they were interpreted for readers.[53] Many photographers were northern sojourners, like missionaries J.H. Webster and Donald Marsh, or HBC employees encouraged by their employer to create a photographic record of the North. Following in a long history of explorers and missionaries who returned home with lantern slides to display the Native to their audiences, some photographers clearly "stole" their images, capturing authentic, "dying" tribal rituals for white eyes.[54] Philip Godsell, a former HBC trader, offers his rendition of practices of the "warlike" Assiniboines. His article is paired with a photo of the (banned) Sun Dance, with "skewers piercing the chest muscles" of the young men.[55]

In contrast, Richard Harrington, a professional photographer who was renowned for his wide-ranging depictions of the Inuit North, offers both informal shots and posed portrait studies such as "The Cheerful Eskimo," a portrayal of healthy, smiling Eskimos from a range of age groups. These portraits, explains Harrington, represent "what was noble about the Eskimo" as they show the "finest types" of Eskimos – "cheerful, hardy, resourceful, and brave."[56] Harrington's immense and impressive oeuvre of northern photos is not easily categorized or pigeonholed; however, the photos selected by *The Beaver* tend towards depicting an essentialized Eskimo, and it is doubtful the editors would have considered publishing some of Harrington's more disturbing, tragic portraits of starving Inuit, captioned in his later book with comments like "Near death. Note Government identification tag."[57] The trope of the "cheerful" Eskimo – happy, childlike, naive, and welcoming to whites – was of long standing in popular culture, including Hollywood films,[58] and could be easily integrated into *The Beaver*'s positive message of Inuit-white cooperation in the North. The practice of photographing the "vanishing races" as "racial types" was also part of a much longer history, stretching back to the nineteenth century, in which the "scientific" photo helped to establish the "imaginative geographies" of British imperial power.[59]

Some photographs were also juxtaposed with startling headlines suggesting that the present Eskimo was becoming an artefact of history. An article on the "vanishing" Eskimo is accompanied by a photo taken by Doug Wilkinson, writer and NFB filmmaker, who offers this judgment on Inuit life: "The Canadian Eskimo is on his way out and you and I are slated to be the interested spectators at his demise ... there will be a new race of northern Canadians with some Eskimo blood but they will be remote from their ancestors."[60] Wilkinson, as a subsequent chapter on the NFB shows, professed deep respect for Inuit hunting culture, which he tried to capture in the much-praised documentary, *Land of the Long Day*. In *The Beaver* text, however, his words are used to suggest the inevitable replacement, rather than preservation, of an Inuit way of life.

HISTORICAL NOSTALGIA AND THE COLONIAL PICTURESQUE

The HBC consciously promoted itself as a historic institution, as a key constitutive element of Canada's nation building. In a special 275th anniversary edition in 1945, Douglas Leechman asserts the value of timeless HBC traditions, declaring that "not much had changed" since the company discovered "the savages at the bottom of the Bay" almost three hundred years ago.[61] Articles on the fur trade celebrate early contacts between Aboriginal and white, perpetuating nostalgic and romanticized images of the fearless courier de bois, the brave trader, and the intrepid female traveller. A tour by Clifford Wilson through HBC buildings in Winnipeg offers him the opportunity to ruminate on the company's museum holdings. Gazing over the library, he pictures the fine old Scots traders, erudite in the wilderness, reading the "leather-bound" classics like "Dante's *Inferno*" in the cold of the winter as they warmed their feet by the fire.[62] Historic rituals and symbols of the HBC, from the London Beaver Club to the company flag, are featured; readers are reminded that the HBC had once ruled its own empire, presided over by its own governor, whose tenure and replacement were surrounded with pomp and ceremony. Even advertisements juxtapose products like the HBC blanket with Native art, fetishizing commodities as historical artefacts.

The magazine also links the HBC to the Crown itself – and what other commercial enterprise could connect its origins to Charles II? During the Second World War, monarchist connections were made frequently: "little did Charles II dream," one author writes, "that someday his Company of Adventurers would play their part in fighting for England."[63] A photo spread shows the HBC governor, Sir Patrick Ashley Cooper, leaving Buckingham Palace after he was knighted, accompanied by his son and daughter, both in the military. His wife, of course, wore HBC fur.[64] Linking fur to members of the royal family is also a promotional strategy that plays on cultural associations of fur with wealth, status, and grandeur.[65] Princess Alice is shown inspecting blue fox furs at HBC House in London, while Princess Elizabeth is photographed as she left for her honeymoon in 1947, wearing her wedding present from the HBC – a beaver coat. Accompanying the picture is a copy of her thank you note to the company.[66]

One of the most enduring staples of historical nostalgia in *The Beaver* is the travelogue, usually detailing the voyages of HBC employees, missionaries, and elite travellers. The dominant historical narrative of exploration is one of masculine perseverance and prowess in the wilderness, even when disaster or death intervenes. Christine Sawchuk's claim that "Canada has never boasted [northern] explorers of the popular stature known to other nations" should not be taken to mean that exploration itself was not a highly popular theme.[67] Although tales of rugged masculine bravery in the northern wilderness are plentiful, the magazine also offers accounts of women's voyages, which are noticeably attentive to gender, family, and relationships with the Indigenous peoples upon whom both white women and men depended for survival. Yet even women like the extraordinarily resourceful HBC wife Elizabeth Watt, who praises the Aboriginal guides who helped her trek from Hudson Bay to the Gulf of St. Lawrence, uses a language of discovery, suggesting the land was unused, unclaimed until whites appeared. Such travel stories are, simultaneously, symbolic narratives of conquest and domination. As Pratt argues, European accounts often operate as narratives of "anti-conquest," emphasizing white innocence in the wilderness while nonetheless establishing their hegemony through the very "possession of seeing."[68]

Beaver contributors wrote of the northern journeys of elite women travellers like Elizabeth Taylor, the daughter of a late-nineteenth-century American consul to Canada. Although one of Taylor's male descendants portrays her as a "frail ... mite of a woman ... braving the rigours of the wilderness," historian Grace Lee Nute stresses her impressive, detailed writing about both the physical wilderness and Aboriginal peoples. While Nute tries to cast Taylor as a sympathetic character, she cannot disguise Taylor's sense of superior cultural voyeurism. Taylor consciously sought out the most "primitive" Eskimos, "unchanged by whites," those whom she assumed would be "larger, more warlike and more treacherous and suspicious" than the others.[69] A similar series on Frances Simpson recounts her famous voyage west to meet her HBC governor husband. Undoubtedly, women authors identified with these white women travellers, whom they celebrated as pioneering role models and proof of women's ability and courage to create a northern Canadian nation. But the resulting erasure of Indigenous women – one of whom, after all, was also married to Simpson – constructed a white northern frontier even if it added women to the story. There *are* some exceptions. At least one piece, presaging a later feminist history written by Sylvia Van Kirk, argues for the important role Aboriginal women "in between" had played in fur trade history. Author Marjorie Campbell points to Indigenous women's crucial labour, providing "food, clothing and shelter" for white traders, as well as to the existence of some "loving" marriages "in the custom of the country." She concludes that, without Native women's essential economic and social contributions, "the discovery of the northwestern third of the continent would have been considerably delayed."[70]

Visual display was a key strategy used to convey the nostalgic picturesque to readers. In its earliest incarnation, the picturesque denoted "contrast and sudden variation," the evoking of feelings associated with "memory, death, the passing of time and distance – [with the] subjects [often] the remote and marginal."[71] While the picturesque also became a synonym for scenic, idyllic, even romantic scenes, it was easily fashioned into a colonialist genre of visual display that elicited sentiments of nostalgia for the imperialist past, the exotic, and the culturally marginal. As Rony argues, the picturesque was thus also "a shielding gesture," with "relations of dominance" preserved by playing up images of the "dying races" or playing down disturbing reminders of colonial power.[72]

In *The Beaver*, artistic renderings of landscape, HBC forts, and portrayals of action and adventure convey nostalgia for a grand colonial empire of the past: spectacle and history are co-joined in pictures of discovery, bravery, risk, and enterprise. Men encounter larger-than-life menacing animals, dog sleds career through the snow, and voyageurs plunge through massive rapids, suggesting a past of daring and heroism. Sketches of old HBC forts and encampments, long abandoned, rise out of the northern wilderness like ruined castles on a British landscape, marking past glory as well as the coming of white civilization. Accompanying texts reinforce the nostalgic picturesque. In Elizabeth Watt's description of her visit to the abandoned ghost Fort Nascopie, she recalls the "heyday of its existence – canoes arriving at the now deserted shores, and picturesque old-fashioned Indians, dressed in their painted deerskin coats ... while other Indians, equally picturesque, would sit on the bank, smoking their stone pipes ... A pageant of old-time post life passed in front of me – Now all was gone."[73] In keeping with imperialist nostalgia, these renditions of times past "mourn[] what was lost" while maintaining an image of white innocence on the frontier.[74]

While the visual archive of the magazine is immense and varied, its reproduction of nineteenth-century pictures by artists like Paul Kane and Peter Rindisbacher reinforce colonialist themes. Kane was promoted by the HBC as a documentary artist, offering ethnographic veracity, yet, as recent critics contend, his paintings are constructed images of feathered Indians created for white Victorian eyes.[75] Whether the artistic trope is the noble savage, the barbarous savage, or the vanishing race, much of this nineteenth-century Canadian art naturalizes a colonial hierarchy of white/ British superiority and Aboriginal inferiority.[76] Dramatic sketches and paintings of Aboriginal battle-making, pagan rituals, Inuit drumming, the herding of (extinct) buffalo, or the Aboriginal primitive in traditional *undress* (pictures of naked whites were certainly not shown) are featured in the magazine,[77] and when Indigenous and white meet, the latter are often depicted as offering leadership as well as the hand of friendship.

A sense of white superiority vis-à-vis Indigenous cultures, however, is not absolute or without ambivalence. Anthropological accounts, for instance, might use terminology that seems to replicate the evolutionist trope of people moving from ancient to modern life, yet they might also report Indigenous peoples' own *self*-designations, intended to signify humour or mark cultural preservation. When John Hongiman witnessed Inuit drumming and dancing, for instance, he notes that the older women joked about performing for him as "the ancient ones." If the title of his article, "Dance of the Ancients," means one thing to a white reader, it might mean something quite different to Inuit women.[78] Staged cultural performance often has a different meaning for Indigenous peoples than it does for whites, and the fact that the Inuit playfully posed for whites or mocked them by playing on cultural images was understood by those whites who spent considerable time in the North.[79] Discussions of Indigenous art also became a key means of validating First Nations cultures. As early as 1942, an article by the BC Society for the Furtherance of BC Indian Arts and Crafts praises west coast Native art; and, by the late 1950s, Indigenous art is featured prominently as the handicraft movement attempted to sustain and restore Indigenous arts – though some authors suggest that this movement was promoted by whites as a charitable process of protection and recovery.[80]

By the 1960s, attention was increasingly focused on Inuit art. Irene Baird may have seen Eskimo art through ethnocentric tropes, labelling its themes "mystical" since the Eskimo lived so "close to nature," but she also describes Baffin print making as energetic, original, and visionary: it represents not the past but new "lively" forms of Canadian artistic talent.[81] Inuit sculpture is also of particular interest, with experts deliberating on whether this was truly "primitive" art any longer or whether it was now better termed "Eskimo sculpture."[82] In 1967, a full issue dedicated to Inuit art suggests an interpretive shift from ethnographic curiosity to analysis of varied forms and meanings for Indigenous art.[83] Such pieces do offer some alternative to the theme of the colonial picturesque in that they analyze Indigenous art not as bygone relics but, rather, as new developments within the Canadian art scene.

The picturesque is sometime joined by the picaresque in the form of accounts of droll, mysterious, or wild colonial figures – though not all are Indigenous. Inuit customs are portrayed as quaint, endearing, or amusing but also as potential anachronisms in the new North. White sojourner Marion Nichols relays various amusing and "exciting moments" at the HBC Cape Smith post, including the time when "the little native Muk Kenuik" went crazy, being "full of devils" as the "locals" called it. Her own "maid," Betsy, is portrayed as an amusing hybrid of Annie Oakley and Calico Jane, with "billowy layers of red and pink calico over skin boots, bright hair clips and hefty rifle in hand."[84] She is very competent at hacking up a seal, Nichols tells us, but not very competent at cleaning the kitchen properly – the latter denoting a modern housewife's job. White authors occasionally admit that the Inuit found whites amusing, inept, and useless, but these observations may represent the appearance of openness and reciprocity rather than its actual practice.[85]

A revealing example of the droll Native contrasted to the normalized white is found in contrasting wedding stories. In the pictures described at the beginning of this chapter, the white wedding party looks the respectable modern role: a minister presides, with bride in long gown and men in suits. In contrast, in an account pitched as humour, one *Beaver* writer describes a hybrid Indian wedding combining white and Native cultures but ultimately lacking in basic social graces.[86] The bride, writes the author, "stalked up the aisle with the implacable purpose of a heavy tank, dragging the little bridegroom by the hand." A shrivelled little man, the groom is wearing clothes "liberally decorated with goose feathers adhered to with grease." The most derisive image is that of the overbearing bride, who appears in moccasins, purple dress like a flour sack, pink ribbon, and white rosettes, creating "an intense optical shock." She produces a ring from her former husband (clearly not mannerly wedding practice), which is placed on her finger by the "grimy paw" of her new spouse. The accompanying cartoon plays on a well-worn trope: the domineering large bride dragging a scrawny cowed man to the altar, but the bride is also a racialized version of Aunt Jemima. On the following page, another photo of an Indigenous wedding is far less derisive, though the worn clothing and demeanour of the participants still stands in contrast to the proper weddings of white Arctic brides featured in *The Beaver*.

DEVELOPMENT NARRATIVES

The Beaver's visions of the future for northern Indigenous peoples are coloured by cautious optimism and a deep belief in the progress associated with Euro-Canadian modernity. Most of their writers are in agreement that cultural collision and painful adaptation are inevitable, especially in the eastern Arctic, though they differ on how the authorities should manage less technologically advanced cultures like those of the Inuit. Narratives of development in *The Beaver* stress the importance of education, new forms of labour, a stable family unit, the centralization of communities, the introduction of Canadian law, and the value of racial cooperation. These themes reflect the dominant ideals of post-Second World War liberal modernization theory, with its emphasis on the "shift from the tribe to the city and the production of an educated, rational, modern man." As feminist critics point out, these discourses also rest on "gendered foundations" and reproduce "dichotomies of 19th-century thinking" that juxtapose the traditional (nature, superstition, and physicality) with the modern (man, science, abstract knowledge, and civilization).[87] Even though traditional societies are described positively, as "holistic, seamless webs of family, spirituality and community," they are still characterized as static, subsistence poor, in need of change.[88]

After the Second World War, both state planning and new capitalist ventures are promoted in the pages of *The Beaver*. Gordon Robertson, commissioner of the NWT, tells *Beaver* readers that the real wealth of the North lies under the ground, and the sooner it is exploited, the better. Since the fur trade can only "go in one direction – down," he urges Indigenous men to use education as a tool to prepare them for the new North of mining ventures.[89] One article promotes exactly the same mining venture in Rankin Inlet that the NFB film features in *Men of the Rock*: pictures of white and Inuit men descending below the surface to mine nickel not only promote mining development but also imply that this is a good example of white-Inuit collaboration.[90] Even those promoting the North as wilderness see entrepreneurial possibilities in the tourist trade: articles extol holiday by canoe, the perfect wilderness quest for urban dwellers from the South.

This northern frontier needed to be tamed as it was modernized. William Morrow, defence counsel for Judge Sissons on the northern circuit, lauds the judge's efforts to take a compassionate and culturally sensitive version of Canadian justice into Inuit settlements, but the end goal is still to introduce "modern law to primitive people" so that they could "study civics first hand."[91] The RCMP are featured often and, invariably, positively. Their job is to offer paternal justice, law, and order to the Inuit, "educating the native mind" to the mundane basics of Canadian income tax, estate law, and relief – a task requiring "infinite patience," as one RCMP author laments.[92] The Inuit's lack of investment in individual wage labour and wealth accumulation also needed altering, and the RCMP could help by encouraging more "thriftiness" as, unfortunately, the Inuit habits of "laziness and improvidence" meant that they were all too content to have the state support them.[93] Policing social provision also meant regulating family allowances, making sure that Inuit parents did not squander their allowances on needless luxuries at the HBC store rather than on the modern pablum they were thought to need. While the RCMP is pictured as paternal, benevolent, and fair in these accounts, the Inuit are seen as naive, childlike, in need of instruction and state "tutelage." *The Beaver* articles thus echo the views of white women sojourners presented in the last chapter.[94]

The importance of the debate on economic modernization is indicated by articles penned by prominent politicians such as federal cabinet minister Jean Lesage. Offering what might be an incipient version of "citizens plus," he suggests that the Inuit should be not only absorbed into the Canadian polity with equal "rights, privileges, opportunities and responsibilities" but also allowed to maintain their "cultural identity." His prognosis echoes prevailing liberal modernization theory: Indigenous peoples should be helped to adapt to the inevitable triumph of the market, given opportunities for new employment (such as in northern airfields), and educated to take over their own administration in a rational, efficient manner. There are potential pitfalls: citing Margaret Mead as his source, he worries that Natives might potentially lose all sense of initiative and self-reliance in this economic transition "up the ladder to civilization."[95] This development narrative is also gendered, with Lesage designating Inuit men as the "breadwinners" and negotiators with the public political world. He is not alone. The McGill anthropologist who relayed his research on the transition to a wage economy in Frobisher Bay (research largely sympathetic to all government policy and programs) assumes that the worker is inherently male, and only one lone, extraneous photo attached to the article tells us that "women also earn wages."[96]

By the late 1950s and 1960s, more civil servants and researchers completing studies for the government were drawn into discussions on economic development. As the Northern Affairs and Natural Resources information officer, Irene Baird was understandably upbeat about the creation of Inuvik, the new state-"planned" community created by an

Pictures like this one of an Aboriginal "modelling" fur as a consumer product are very rare. The group at Coppermine includes Paulette Anerodluk and Ann Webster, daughter of Anglican Canon Webster. | Nunavut Archives, Joe Osborne fonds, N-1990-006: 0441

alliance of men with "parkas and those with brief cases."[97] Federal welfare teachers Marjorie Hinds and Joan Ryan emphasize the value of retaining some Inuit and Dene traditions in the development process, but other academics and state consultants see Indigenous peoples as government wards in the true sense of the word. Arctic geographers puzzle over how a "redundant" people would be recast into a more "modern" society, while Diamond Jenness suggests that the Inuit need Ottawa's moral guidance and "wise" federal policies.[98] This paternalism, argues Hugh Brody, lasted well into the 1970s as whites in the North circulated countless stories of the Inuit as "temperamental children of nature" suffering disorganization as their "intact, traditional cultures" faced the trauma of modernity.[99] University-based researchers often construct their articles within the confines of this dichotomy: What happens when a "Stone Age" culture is "jettisoned into the jet age?" asks anthropologist Toshio Yatsushio. While he was an advocate of more Eskimo "self-governing institutions," he believed that these needed to be steered into existence by whites with the requisite knowledge and experience of government.[100]

The magazine's attempt to provide a provocative image of primitive cultures embracing modern ways is symbolized in descriptions of changing dress, beauty, and consumption. "Beauty is only skin deep," announced *The Beaver*, when it ran an article on tattooing that argues that the Inuit woman was leaving this primitive practice behind, now preferring to imitate her "white sister, not only in the things she does, but also in the things she does not."[101] One photo of a bevy of British models touring Canada shows them posing in the latest fashions at an HBC store as they ogle and finger "a bit of Eskimo haute couture " – a manikin in the HBC museum with braided hair and beads, moccasins, and parka.[102] This example emphasizes the importance of captions, titles, and text in conveying context and meaning for visuals: Eskimo women are quite literally museum pieces in comparison to modern white women. Although scholars contend that Indigenous peoples used performance and dress as a means of cultural preservation, and that they might "talk back" to the ethnographic photographer looking for authentic Native images,[103] the still photos collected and used by *The Beaver* have little potential for such agency and negotiation.[104]

Writers on modernization and development in the 1950s and 1960s often understood Indigenous societies as patriarchal, as societies in which women faced a devalued self and familial oppression, themes that harkened back to nineteenth-century writing in which Native women were "exotic specimens, oppressed victims, sex objects, or the most ignorant members of 'backward' societies."[105] While Marxist anthropologist Eleanor Leacock argued at this time that earlier Aboriginal societies were historically egalitarian, these views did not necessarily dominate in more popular writing. Development narratives, for instance, claimed that the companionate, monogamous marriage embraced by Euro-Canadian society was yet another benefit that modernization would bring to the Inuit. The male Inuit hunter was assumed to embody prestige and power, with women's domestic roles hidden, private, and less valued – assessments that reflected Euro-Canadian assumptions concerning familial labour. Ironically, this view of Inuit patriarchy contradicts nineteenth-century efforts on the part of the state to remake southern Native families in the image of Anglo, middle-class, and patriarchal families.[106] By the late

1940s, however, a shift in Canadian culture had occurred, with the ideal marriage increasingly portrayed as egalitarian and companionate. Pure patriarchy was increasingly out of style – or at least masked and hidden from view.

Finally, calls for racial collaboration were often woven into development narratives, as evidenced by Baird's claim that men of the parka and men of the briefcase were the architects of the new North. One *Beaver* article hopes that Canada's North might prove to be "one of the first spots on earth where the colour line is really dropped ... [This is] the most exciting single feature of our rapidly accelerating northern development." White, mixed-blood, and Inuit live in the same houses, their children attend the same schools, the author continues, and, as a result, every facet of economic production and administration will be decided on the basis of individual merit rather than on the basis of race. In keeping with modernization theory of the time, this outlook stresses individual achievement and the fair distribution of rewards. These are the positive contributions of Western cultures to developing areas or, as this author puts it, the consequence of "white civilization" moving north.[107] In the popular imaginary presented in *The Beaver*, race is ultimately an ambiguous and contested category. Some images of "Red and White" families in *The Beaver* suggest cultural opposites, yet other photos of white and Inuit children happily playing together, reprinted more than once, appear to be deliberate attempts to symbolize the racial collaboration needed to effect northern development.[108]

VISUAL DISPLAY: INUIT MADONNA OR DRUDGE?

The HBC saw its photograph collection as a means of carefully managing its history and image making, monitoring what and how it collected as well as what it printed in *The Beaver*.[109] While some *Beaver* photographers like Richard Harrington and Lorene Squire produced striking, humanistic images of daily life in the North, *The Beaver*'s cover often featured colourful renditions of the traditionally attired, feathered Native or noble warrior in canoe – images constructed for an approving white colonial gaze. Other visual representations on the cover provide stark contrasts between the primitive North and the modern South, with white men more closely associated with technology and modernity, sitting beside airplanes, and Inuit women more associated with traditional skills, such as sewing skins. The undeniably compelling photographic display in *The Beaver* was likely one of its most powerful selling points and, thus, an important means of conveying meaning to its readers. While photos are intended to communicate an empirical, realistic documentation of the North, some are also breathtakingly striking in affect: they are a fascinating example of a photographic archive "suspended between a discourse of science and that of art," making a claim both on science and truth, on the one hand, and on "pleasure and romantic aesthetics," on the other.[110] The magazine's selection, positioning, and captioning of photos are intrinsic to the ideological process of making sense of the North. The photograph is a "mobile" and flexible artefact: [111] the original encounter between a (usually white) photographer and an Aboriginal subject may be overlaid with power relations, but which photos are published and how they are displayed endows them with another layer of meaning. Whether they were taken spontaneously or posed by missionaries, anthropologists, state contractors, or HBC employees also matters, as each of these agents invested purpose and meaning in his or her respective photos. While generalization is thus difficult, a reflection on one thematic cluster of photos relating to women's dress, work, and bodies hints at *The Beaver*'s ambivalent pairing of humanistic intention with paternalist renditions of the primitive and the modern.

Reassuring images of the Indigenous mother, like the one labelled "Madonna of the North,"[112] suggest that domesticity for women was essentially the same across lines of race, a romanticized view that also fit well with an intensified culture of domesticity in the postwar era. A particularly popular photo of one Inuit woman, reproduced twice in *The Beaver* (once on the cover) as well as in the *American Magazine*, shows her in traditional Inuit attire, wearing "a costume of duffle decorated with beads and coins," with a young child at her side. The mother is well groomed, smiling, set against a striking background, and the pose resembles that of Western women: she is nestled close to the child, but not carrying him in her hood.[113]

"Fur as consumption," from the inside cover of *The Beaver*, summer 1955.

"Fur as work," cover of *The Beaver*, March, 1945

Pictures of children, unblemished by physical debilitation, happy, and often looking directly into the camera with a curious innocence and hope for the future, were also popular in *The Beaver*, as they were in similar publications.[114] Indeed, photo essays depicting young "Eskimo, Indian, white" children all at play together became didactic tools symbolizing the "universal" values that supposedly characterized all races. Children's disarming "lack of prejudice," editorialized the captions, should be the model for adults in the North.[115] Shots of mothers and children connected by affective ties, the latter held or coddled, were also common, in part because those photographers capturing Inuit daily life were intent on representing the gendered division of labour in which women were the primary caregivers of the youngest children. The image of the idealized Indigenous Madonna pulled at the heart strings of tolerance; it suggested that these "other" cultures were shaped by the same mother love as were Western cultures. "Under the skin," mothers were all alike, though it is revealing that Indigenous women were most idealized when they appeared to be similar to white Western women.[116]

However domestic and pleasing the portrayals of Inuit mothers, they did not always fit the dominant notions of white/southern beauty. Featuring a picture of the Calgary HBC store's beauty contestants (all white women in bathing suits), *The Beaver* explains that readers had complained that there were "too many natives and too much ice" in the publication, so it was offering up something more appealing.[117] Differences between the primitive and modern woman are symbolized in *The Beaver*'s dramatically different images of fur. Fur was esteemed for its use and exchange value by Indigenous women, but it is portrayed as a fetishized item of consumption for white women. Dichotomous presentations of fur as work and fur as consumption are numerous and reveal a stark racial contrast: in advertisements, bourgeois white women are swathed in glamorous jewels and furs, suggesting decadence, wealth, and sensuality, yet Inuit women are portrayed chewing skins, cutting and scraping furs across branch frames, or sewing fur by hand.[118] Indigenous women's work preparing fur is celebrated as an example of their traditional skills, but this addresses neither the declining, uncertain economy of fur at the time nor the importance of Indigenous women's unpaid labour to the production of value for the HBC.

As a visual record of Inuit and Dene women's unpaid work sustaining families and communities, *The Beaver* collection is quite remarkable. In its desire to provide popular anthropology for the masses, the magazine incorporated many photographic explanations of women's work, from how they prepared seal skins to their role in the creation of a kayak. The latter article offers a step-by-step picture-lesson in kayak making, with men and women alternating between various tasks, each important to the final product. Photographed by a white woman who had been raised in the North, the photo essay is especially attentive to the kayak as a communal project.[119] By encouraging their employees and other northern residents to become amateur photographers in documenting the North, the magazine did provide an opening for a more eclectic display of women's work.[120]

However, if *The Beaver*'s choice of photographs is any measure, the ambivalence about women's paid labour characteristic of postwar Canada insinuated itself into the magazine. Although Indigenous women's arduous labour is sometimes celebrated, it is also seen as potentially de-feminizing. Pictures of Indigenous women at work, shouldering immense physical tasks uncharacteristic of those performed by Western women, cast them as overly burdened, even masculinized toilers in a world of arduous labour. At ship time, notes one photo caption, women "do much of the carrying" of freight up from the shore. These "mothers," depicted with children in their hoods, are about to lift a "sack-laden stretcher" left by the ship.[121] Another photo of an aging Inuit woman bearing on her back a massive burden of sticks for fuel evokes not only wonder but also discomfort with her masculine physicality and a gendered division of labour more characteristic of peasant than of modern womanhood.[122]

Photographs of women's bodily labour often represent the contrast between Western/modern and Inuit/primitive cultures. Inuit women's work caring for a rudimentary one-room igloo, preparing skins, or swaddling a naked child belong to the traditional past; they speak to a salvage mentalité but also intimate the ongoing unity of past and present. Images of women squatting on an igloo floor with a sewing machine, suggesting the awkward mix of modern technology and traditional lifestyle, evoked a "reverse exoticism" for the viewer.[123] In one issue, contrasting visuals are quite striking. A colour spread of pictures of an Inuit family taken by a Catholic priest is used to denote things "as they used to be" – that is, before the acquisition human-made "alternatives" to the Eskimo's "dangerous, uncomfortable" existence, which was determined entirely by nature.[124] It is not only women's labour but also their bodies that suggest a less desirable existence: women are bedraggled, wrinkled, seemingly unwashed, somewhat emaciated, teeth missing. A second display of photographs, "Journey from the Igloo," stresses a different story – namely, the path to modernity. A new village at Rankin Inlet is displayed with canvas tents, a modern schoolroom, and a kitchen in which the teacher and children learn "to make the best use of food and equipment and become part of community life."[125] Their bodies are fully clothed, not naked; they are dressed in Western fashion; they look alert and eager to learn; and they are surrounded by the trappings of modernity.

Similarly, white women are often pictured in their well-furnished HBC post houses, which are indistinguishable from southern manses, while Inuit women are featured in snow houses using time-consuming utensils. The fact that the domestic comfort of white sojourners was premised on Indigenous labour is occasionally recognized but never emphasized, again masking a colonial division of labour within the North. *Beaver* readers are also led to believe that northern Aboriginal women ultimately yearn to imitate the domestic lives of their white counterparts in the South. Modernization is presumed to be a boon to the emerging modern Inuit woman – referred to in *The Beaver* as a woman "in between." Wage labour is an important part of this potential; Inuit women who had moved "from" the igloo could take advantage of new work opportunities within the existing gendered and racialized division of labour – as cashiers or, perhaps, teachers.

At the same time, Inuit women's domestic labour is depicted as being positively transformed by technology. A photo display and accompanying article written by Irene Baird offers an optimistic analysis of cultural adaption in the Inuit family. Due to the forces of modernization, she suggests, the Inuit woman had to be helped, especially by the state, to adapt to these positive changes. New schools, consumer items, and better food and housing are replacing the precarious living conditions of the past so that families are "no longer at the mercy of sickness, hunger and harsh weather." Old ways are "evil" and dismal; new ways promise more freedom and security. Modern living frees women from incessant toil, offering them "the electric oven," freedom from the hunting camp, and the prospect of something "*new* – leisure time." White women who now enjoy such things are situated on an evolutionary/historical trajectory of progress ahead of Inuit women who are only now "doing their pioneering." Despite the massive differences in culture, however, some gendered traits seem to be transcultural as the Inuit men are the "leaders ... and wage-earners" and Inuit women have the "quieter, more passive roles."[126]

Irene Baird's *Beaver* article does suggest that progress might bring with it potential problems, such as the possibility of delinquency, since teenagehood was so "relatively new" to culturally fragile Eskimo families.[127] But authors like Baird had immense faith in Eskimo cultural adaptability – this in contrast to other authors of her time, whose commentaries on southern Indians are tinged with far more pessimism. Photos of the potential new Inuit career woman are especially arresting: she is pictured in front of her new electric stove, with a small nuclear family, though also caring for other women's children as babysitting had become paid work. She is shown in Western attire as well as in a traditional parka. She has embraced modern religion and is having her child properly baptized by a minister, and she shops at an HBC store, where the uniformed clerk is also an Inuk woman. She is also employed in an emerging government sector. Paulette Anerodluk, whom I discuss in my conclusion, is shown in her capacity as a civil servant, providing carving material to men in the federal rehabilitation centre at Frobisher Bay. From Christianity to consumption, the pictures and text suggest that the ideal new Inuit woman is being remade in the image of Euro-Canadian women.

SUSTAINING *AND* DISMANTLING COLONIAL IMAGES

The Beaver's representations of Indigeneity were shaped by contemporaneous political and economic forces and by the dominant cultural ideology of Euro-Canadian society. The HBC was perhaps the most obvious ideological influence on *The Beaver* as the magazine consciously created a vision of the company's noble history, its concern for its Indigenous workers, and its prognosis for northern development. But the HBC was also part of a larger political economy, history, and culture of colonialism engendering orientalist ways of seeing that, as Said argues, with some pessimism, could become culturally hegemonic.[128] *The Beaver* portrays a northern frontier in which traders, the state, and missionaries are the enlightened leaders of northern development and First Nations peoples the exemplars of cultural tradition. The Inuit especially are seen as part of a fascinating but doomed Stone Age past now being "jettisoned" into a "jet age" present. Just as the nineteenth-century "photographic frontier" in the Pacific Northwest aided settler "expansionism," so, too, did these visual and textual representations of the North.[129]

The Beaver attempted to create a popular history of northern nation building by integrating Indigenous peoples into its celebratory narrative, yet it did so by simultaneously glossing over structural and systemic inequalities and, ultimately, by putting a modernized veneer on discursive strategies of colonial representation. Admittedly, this was a magazine created and marketed primarily for a white and southern audience. Although one posed photo shows two Inuit men smiling broadly as they look at *The Beaver*, there is little evidence that First Nations people themselves either contributed to or read the magazine. Perhaps Richard Harrington even took this picture as a tongue-in-cheek comment on the Inuit's amusement at how they were portrayed by others. A small piece on Eskimo hunting published in 1954 was heralded as "the first article by an Eskimo" in *The Beaver*,[130] and, by 1970, an occasional piece by an Indigenous person celebrated their movement into "non-traditional" work, such as piloting.[131] Yet these articles are exceptions to the rule. More often, Indigenous people remain the objects of an "ethnographic gaze" rather than active, creative, and contradictory human subjects.[132] Yet, in contrast to this ideological disposition, the magazine presents itself as an objective and scientific window on the North, a claim promoted espe-cially through the use of expert accounts and professional, first-hand surveillance by anthropologists, historians, state officials, doctors, and others. Their rendition of the Indigenous North promotes a liberal modernization narrative, and a gendered one at that: a Western, white, modern familial and gender order will eventually take the place of the primitive and patriarchal order in which Indigenous women's lives are circumscribed by ancient domestic technology and back-breaking labour.

The attraction of *The Beaver*, consumed as both education and enter-tainment, may have emanated from its presentation of a multitude of topics, ranging from ice to Inuit myth, and its fusion of various tech-niques and styles of presentation: eye witnesses accounts, academic experts, historical nostalgia, landscape and nature shots, ethnographic photography – to name only a few. The nostalgic presentation of the colonial picturesque and the pleasure of its compelling photo display are part of its middlebrow appeal. So, too, is its presentation of history as a spectacle of daring and discovery and as a reassuring linear evolution towards tolerance and modernity. Its colourful pastiche of themes and styles, however, does not produce an apolitical pluralism. Expert sur-veillance in *The Beaver* ultimately provides scholarly credence to the magazine's dominant theme of white settler progress in Canada's evolu-tion, and the picturesque, nostalgic rendering of the HBC's centuries-old empire offers Euro-Canadian readers a reassuring, uncritical view of a colonial past. Text and image work as ideology, presenting a dichotom-ized narrative of primitive and modern, with the former inevitably to be confronted and altered by the technical, rational, and scientific superior-ity of the latter. Celebrating the Eskimo's mystical connection to nature, the northern Indians' wilderness prowess, or providing photos of the "colourful Indian" confines First Nations peoples to the realm of nature, to a static, if romanticized, historical and cultural identity. As James Clifford notes of the long-lasting influence of the salvage paradigm in the twentieth century, there is a desire to "rescue 'authenticity' out of destructive historical change," with authenticity poised on the brink of the present, still salvageable before the inevitable onslaught of Western culture.[133]

The ideological assumptions of the magazine, however, are not without contradictions, and its character does alter over time. By the later 1960s, there is a shift in tone as ethnographic paternalism was under question in both political and scholarly circles. In anthropological writing, for instance, the value of Indigenous knowledge was now accented.[134] *Beaver* articles put more emphasis on emerging Inuit art as art in its own right, discuss Indigenous-led governance, and even feature some critical pieces on Indigenous living conditions. In his northern travel journal, for instance, George Woodcock is critical of an educational curriculum that was meaningless to the Inuit and of the local "ladder of [white] bureaucratic hierarchy" in which settlers could not even communicate in the local language. More damning are the pictures of Indian "shacks" that sufficed as housing at Churchill, and his description of Indigenous impoverishment and animosity to whites, topics rarely broached in the past: "most [Natives] are unemployed and on welfare. They accept this with a mixture of pleasure at not having to work – lacking our puritan ethic – and resentment at their second class status. They hate the white man the way the Eskimo do not – yet."[135]

Second, throughout *The Beaver*'s tenure, a humanistic *intent* is increasingly apparent: text and image stress tolerance for other cultures, the importance of racial harmony, and admiration for Indigenous environmental knowledge. This liberal humanism may have provided readers with some tools to dismantle the magazine's colonialist ideology. "Expressions of cultural relativism" in anthropology, warns Noel Dyck, "were more likely to produce generalized critiques of ethnocentrism than to expose colonial power,"[136] but the former might lead to the latter. While we may be critical of the essentialist tone of many *Beaver* articles, some of the sentiments expressed are remarkably similar to comments heard today in many a scholarly seminar on Indigenous peoples. Whites' cultural relativism is interlaced with their admiration for the more environmentally attuned, generous culture of the Indigenous other. A white northern government employee, for example, describes his hunting expedition for caribou with the Inuit in precisely these terms: "Soon this struggle for existence will be a thing of the past. I hope their philosophy will live on. If the Eskimo has food and good health he is happy. They share their all in times of plenty and famine. They never discipline their children, the environment does it for them. They are worthy of our respect. I feel privileged to have known them."[137]

The precise impact of *The Beaver* is ultimately open to some question. One cannot assume that its ideological messages about Indigenous peoples were imbibed by readers wholesale, without any negotiation; nor can one assume an instrumentalist reading of direct correspondence between state goals and HBC interests. The state and civil society are connected spheres, but they are also a messy "knot of tangled power," in which both coercion and ideological consent intermingle, altering their connection over time.[138] It is possible that those *Beaver* authors who were attempting to humanize and valorize Indigenous cultures ultimately raised some new questions, both for readers and for those represented, that would later engender more decidedly anti-colonialist views of Canadian history.

CHAPTER THREE

North of Schamattawa

"Indians," "Eskimos," and RCMP

When Crawley Films and the CBC announced that they were creating a television series based on RCMP cases, the newspapers reported that a BBC scriptwriter was being imported to help nudge the project along. An irate nationalist TV viewer wrote Budge Crawley, the head of Crawley Films, protesting this foreign intrusion into the making of home-grown heroes: after all, the Mounted Police "are our national emblem almost." She was sceptical that a British writer could really tell the "day-to-day story" of the Mounties and asked if he would be incorporating British-isms like "what-ho matey" into their lines. Reassurance came from production manager Peter Cock, who replied that the scripts were crafted by Canadians and that this interloper – Vincent Tilsley – was an experienced "script editor" who was there to help get the "action" scenes right. The sarcastic, hand-written internal memo circulated to the men involved in production, along with her letter, suggested a far more dismissive view: "perhaps we should take out this lovely woman and give her a good time."[1]

It goes without saying that the RCMP is a much mythologized Canadian institution, if not a veritable cultural industry.[2] Since the late nineteenth century, newspapers, magazines, novels, children's books, comic books, school texts, films, and TV shows have all featured versions of the heroic Mounties, both the earlier North-West Mounted Police and their post-1919 reincarnation, the RCMP. The Mounties' extended reach as a federal, provincial, and northern police force aided their ability to promote themselves, both culturally and politically, as a quintessentially Canadian symbol of hardy masculine heroism: the men who were tasked across many frontiers with "maintaining the right." This chapter examines the television series *RCMP*, which aired in English and dubbed French on the CBC and also abroad from 1959 to 1960, in order to probe both its cultural construction of Indian and Eskimo characters and its depiction of Indigenous/white settler relations in the postwar period. Using both textual and visual sources, I ask why production of the series took the shape it did, exploring the program's total "assemblage":[3] its plots, visual feel, characterization, and ideological lessons.

The representation of Indigenous-white relations in *RCMP* both mirrors and reproduces a particular moment of postwar expansion, state intervention, and colonial consolidation in the North, reinforcing the imperative that scholars pay close attention to history, social change, and social totality in our analyses of cultural media such as television. In the vein of "always historicize," we need to connect the *RCMP* TV stories to the contemporary political economy of northern development,[4] popular discussions of Indigeneity, and the dominant ideologies of gender, race, and nation, not least because the show drew implicitly on nationalist discourses that themselves were mobilized for northern development. How did the episodes dealing with Indigenous peoples reproduce a form of gendered colonialism, even though the program was also couched in a liberal discourse of tolerance for the Indigenous other? Were there also more subtle, contradictory messages in the show that challenged colonial renditions of power?

In this cultural contact zone, the Mounties are portrayed as a quintessentially northern police force. The film clips opening each episode feature dog sleds, bush airplanes, and snow-covered terrain, and the publicity photos launching the series present the lead character, Jacques Gagnier, in an arctic parka amidst the snow. In this imagined northern landscape, Indigenous peoples are endowed with some humanity, kindness, and wisdom, but they are clearly a marginalized group, in need of either care or leadership from the white law enforcers. The Mounties, far from being agents of colonialism, are paternal and benevolent, bringing insight, law, and justice to bear on Indigenous peoples and their problems. Cast in a particularly Canadian cultural mode of understatement and irony, with very little physical action, guns, or violence but, instead, a focus on everyday law, *RCMP* cannot be easily subsumed within the American police procedural genre, even if the Mounties always did get their man.[5] It might better be considered a hybrid form that features small-town Leacockian police stories, infused with the sensibility of the popular family melodrama of the 1950s, as the police provide paternal advice, stability, order, and happiness to their charges, just as the father did in *Father Knows Best*.[6] In the gendered landscape of Mountie-land, however, paternalism and benevolence could become condescension as colonized peoples were portrayed as the benefactors of the RCMP's stern but humane paternal care.

POLICING AND CULTURAL REPRESENTATION

In assessing the context that framed the production of *RCMP*, we need to take into account the reigning Mountie mythology, the production concerns of the Crawley organization, and their mutual reinforcement. Academic debates concerning the connections between law and cultural representation have ranged from literary examinations of crime fiction and film to sociological theories of policing in which culture and law play mutually reinforcing roles. Parallel debates in television studies have contemplated how best to analyze television within the overlapping academic areas of cultural studies, media/communication studies, and television studies.[7] Interpretive fashion has shifted over time, shaped by the rise and decline of neo-Marxist and structuralist analyses, and the later influence of postmodern thought, especially in North American cultural studies. Due to the latter, there is a lingering tendency to eschew straightforward readings of the meanings seemingly projected in television and to search instead for the contradictory "multifaceted terrain of power relations" expressed through cultural texts.[8] Some writing in communication studies since the late 1990s argues against an artificial division between political economy and textual approaches, claiming their mutual constitution.[9] This is a compelling line of reasoning. We cannot decode the stories in *RCMP* without taking into account the systems of cultural production that shaped them, asking what the structural and ideological limits on culture making were: "what can and cannot be said and shown."[10]

Television is a powerful form of representation, a site for the making, articulation, and interpretation of cultural values that must be evaluated as forms of power, ideology, and identity construction *in their own time*. As an influential form of imaginative meaning making, television shows subtly embed ideology or, at least, privilege some discourses over others. This is not to suggest we should read television as discourse; rather, we can explore how discourses work as a set of effects that justifies, legitimates, explains, as well as entertains and provokes, "shaping our imaginative sense of possibility" and also reifying certain relations as normal and inevitable.[11] My analysis thus recalls some of the keywords associated with early British cultural studies: "power," "social relations," "commodification," "ideology," "reification," "conflict." Drawing on these earlier insights of cultural studies allows us to analyze the way in which powerful group interests – of white men, for instance – were explained as caring rather than as oppressive, so much so that even liberal attempts at anti-racism were ultimately more conformist than oppositional. While I would not argue that images in this television show were deliberately created to justify colonialism, nor can we assume the wholesale internalization of ideology by the viewer, I am suggesting that there *was* a mutually reinforcing relationship between cultural production, ideology, and the reproduction of a gendered colonialism in this quintessentially Canadian police drama. "Modern colonial culture," vis-à-vis Aboriginal peoples, as Elizabeth Furniss argues, "works at the level of everyday life," particularly through cultural definitions of history, identity, and current issues.[12] *RCMP* aided the everyday circulation and consumption of an image of the North in which Euro-Canadian law brought inevitable progress to Indigenous peoples still enveloped in a premodern, traditional past.

The depiction of the RCMP offers a particularly vivid example of the interchange between law and cultural representation. As popular historian Pierre Berton points out, the Force assumed a key role in its own self-promotion, patrolling the boundaries of Mountie representation through embedded journalism and Hollywood consulting.[13] Mountie mythology was also kept alive by the Force's own many recollections and autobiographies, which echo the heroic white masculinity of the fictional Mountie. Police labour, as Christopher Wilson points out, encompasses considerable storytelling *about itself*, and this self-created "knowledge economy" about criminality has shaped both fiction and non-fiction versions of police work.[14] The narrative power wielded by the police, according to Ian Loader, is invisible yet immensely "affect- ive" for their voice is equated with wisdom and expertise on issues of both order and disorder. Their symbolic authority emanates from the fact that they "start from a winning position." Their "power of legitim- ate pronouncement" allows them to "diagnose, classify, authorize and represent both individuals and the world, and to have this power of legitimate naming not just taken seriously, but taken-for-granted."[15] In the postwar period, the RCMP's purchase on respect likely also eman- ated from the power of Cold War ideology, which justified a key ele- ment of their raison d'être: counter-espionage activities. The secrecy surrounding their spying on the Canadian population was rarely chal- lenged in the media – with a few exceptions.[16]

After it was created in 1919 out of the cauldron of state repression and fear of the working-class radical, the RCMP was both a key institu- tion of law enforcement and, at the same time, constructed itself in a particular cultural mode: as Anglo-Celtic, upholding British values and the Empire; as a model of brave white masculinity; and as defenders of the status quo against the threats of communism, radicalism, and foreign immigrants.[17] Operating as a police force across the North, the RCMP also took charge of many civil service duties – the post, prisons, and coroner inquests – making the Force essential to the "metropolitan" extension of multiple forms of regulation from the South.[18] Legal prac- tice and culture are interconnected in RCMP history since the cultural construction of the Mountie allowed the Force to operate with immense authority and discretion as it tried to introduce Euro-Canadian notions of law and order to Indigenous groups.[19] As historian William Morrison points out, the northern Mountie *especially* was "the perfect subject for mythologizing," incorporating themes of "heroism, inhospitable climate, difficult terrain, exotic natives and unruly foreigners."[20]

In the knowledge economy of policing, there was some distinction between the way the RCMP portrayed Indians as opposed to Eskimos in relation to the state project of frontier containment and modernization. The Inuit were seen as both more essential and more sympathetic to white settler survival. They were cast in a more benign light: as primitive perhaps, but not as hostile, antagonistic, and lazy, as were more southern Aboriginal groups.[21] Indeed, in the wider culture, the images of all Indigenous peoples changed over time; each generation of non-Aboriginals re-imagined the Aboriginal other, revealing as much about itself as about the image it was creating.[22] As the state was consolidating its northern reach in the post-Second World War era, RCMP interactions with Indigenous peoples, especially the Inuit, were repeatedly idealized in popular culture as mutually beneficial and as an example of the Canadian law-abiding mild frontier as opposed to the American law-breaking wild frontier. In popular histories, the RCMP were welcome arbiters of frontier law and order; in magazines, they were progressive conservationists teaching northern Aboriginal peoples needed environmental lessons; and in articles on social issues, they were valued emissaries of state welfare and citizenship.[23] This idealized alliance of "redskins and redcoats" became a subtle hat trick masking colonialism:[24] by absorbing the Native into constructions of (white) Canadian national identity, Margery Fee contends, we romanticized a relationship that "naturalized the appropriation of [Native] land."[25]

From the inception of the TV series, the Crawley production team saw the public's investment in this Mountie mythology as a key to *RCMP*'s success. The show was incubated within Crawley Films, an extremely successful independent film company based in Ottawa, the brainchild of Frank "Budge" Crawley.[26] In the post-Second World War period, Crawley Films grew exponentially, finding a ready market for informational films for industry, educational institutions, and government, though the company also made some animated and dramatic films. The idea of a series based on RCMP cases was discussed as early as 1955, though planning gained momentum in 1957–58, and, from the very beginning, Budge Crawley envisioned an entertaining show with a "documentary quality."[27] As David Hogarth contends, documentary was not merely a preeminent form of Canadian film making but also a desired aesthetic that filtered into other genres.[28] The original idea was prompted by a celebratory series on the RCMP, written by Alan Phillips in 1954 for *Maclean's*. Crawley encouraged him to create a pilot proposal for television stories based on RCMP cases, and, a year later, Phillips met with Crawley producer George Gorman and writer Monroe Scott to develop the series concept. Lister Sinclair was initially involved as a story editor, and Crawley himself had input.[29] The overlap in positive perspective between the *Maclean's* series, other newspaper columns, magazine features, and the TV series underscores the seamless interchange of popular culture ideals and dominant assumptions about the RCMP at the time.

PRODUCING *RCMP*

Aside from the major issue of writing the series, there were two other concerns at the outset: financing the series, particularly with sales abroad, and securing the RCMP stamp of approval. By 1957, Crawley was writing to and meeting with various corporations that looked after TV distribution in the United States. He was seeking financial partners, from major players like CBS to smaller distribution companies. The CBC was on board as a co-producer, though it wrangled with Crawley over foreign distribution revenues (since it already had all viewing rights in Canada), claiming it was interested not only in profit but also in fostering a Canadian television industry. To the CBC, the 80 percent Crawley versus 20 percent CBC split Crawley wanted seemed a little unbalanced.[30] By the time he started scouting American participation, Budge Crawley could commit to twenty-five episodes at thirty-five thousand dollars each, with a major share of his capital coming from two wealthy backers: media magnate John McConnell and Budge Crawley's father, Arthur Crawley.

Budge Crawley sought backing from an American company that would distribute the shows in the United States in return for help with production. In his appeals for funding, Crawley pointed to his company's stability, its past successes, and the advanced organization of the *RCMP* series. A quid pro quo was suggested: in return for distribution rights, there would be consultation from the US distributor "on the type of film story which will best succeed in the world TV market."[31] The process of searching for US backers was simultaneously a process of seeking advice on what would sell as popular TV. Crawley asked questions about production techniques, the appropriate format, whether there should be historical as well as contemporary stories, and if "there should be stories with violence, fights etc. [and if these] should predominate over off-beat stories like crime lab stories" (thus presaging the *CSI* franchise?).[32] Even lead actors were discussed: a relative newcomer, Sean Connery, was suggested to the Crawley team, but it did not pursue him.[33] The Canadians were secretly a little cynical about the Americans' assumption that only they knew "all the tricks of the trade," but Crawley was eager to secure their input on what might sell abroad.[34] Given sensitivities around the Mounties as a revered Canadian institution, and also likely the growing cultural nationalism in the wake of the Massey Commission,[35] Crawley did not publicize how much latitude he was offering an American distributor in terms of artistic input.

Eventually, Crawley found a partner in California National Productions, a subdivision of NBC Television Division, and he secured directorial aid from a Los Angeles-based writer and director, Bernard Girard, and, after him, another producer-director, Harry Horner. The US distributor claimed that "for years Hollywood motion pictures and television producers ha[d] been negotiating in vain for a working arrangement with the Royal Canadian Mounted Police" and, thus, that it was "fortunate" to secure the rights to the series.[36] In truth, Hollywood had long made films with and without the input of the RCMP, but the impression was intentionally given that the Crawley venture gave it access to the inner sanctum of the Force's treasured stories. The BBC came on board as a co-producer, though not before extracting a much better financial deal for itself, discounting the price of each BBC episode by two thousand dollars through negotiations deemed rather unprofessional by the Crawley group.[37]

If the woman who complained about a British scriptwriter had known Crawley was soliciting American advice, she might have been even more incensed. However, she likely would not have objected to Crawley's commitment to consult the RCMP. When promoting the series Crawley claimed that he and his crew had an "exclusive" arrangement with the Force and also that "every script and every sequence of each episode was supervised by members of the force."[38] From the inception of the series, the official imprimatur of the RCMP was seen as a cornerstone of the project's success. When they were still trying to decide the basic format of the series, one consideration was pleasing the RCMP, and Crawley promised that the Force would never be misrepresented in the scripts.[39] Indeed, one story that involved a less than edifying conflict between two officers over internal advancement went nowhere. D.R. Rivett-Carnac,[40] who succeeded Nicholson as head of the RCMP, was used as a technical adviser, and Vernon Kemp, a former RCMP official and now a private security consultant, also commented on scripts. These connections were a public selling point; however, privately, partners in the US had to be reassured by Crawley that Nicholson, as a "liberal, reasonable and sensible man," would not "unreasonably intervene."[41]

In order to secure authentic stories from the field, RCMP men were also encouraged through a circular from RCMP headquarters to send in script suggestions based on their real life experiences. Many did: there were stories of apprehending safe crackers, delivering babies in cars, murder, and one even paid homage to a trusty RCMP dog named Nikki who once saved the day. Some RCMP men in the field harboured ambitions to be hard-boiled mystery novel writers, offering up purple prose that extolled tough masculinity tested in the rugged field of the frontier. One such aspiring raconteur wrote of a young recruit "he noticed immediately" when he joined up. He not only admired his prowess in the boxing ring but also his skill with horses: "he knew a cow pony from a bronc and could handle either kind ... [In the ring] he was dead game. He was tough. He was accepted."[42] Tilsley placed all these scripts in the producer's proverbial bottom drawer, clearly disappointing some budding writers. He finally asked whether the RCMP could put an end to this stream of stories since he saw no benefit in paying Mounties for stories that he could just as easily find in the *RCMP Quarterly*.

Tilsley was also adamant that women scriptwriters were not welcome, a reflection not only of the prevailing gendered hierarchy in the film industry but also of his view that no woman could adequately capture the homosocial frontier masculinity exemplified by the RCMP. Two in-house female film workers submitted scripts. One was rejected outright and the other was turned away, then the author was told they might take her "story idea" but that George Salverson would rewrite it.[43] When an external experienced female writer submitted a script through her agent, Tilsley responded privately to the production "boys":

> I am of the stubborn opinion that no woman could write for this series. I don't suppose [she] is as good as Charlotte Bronte or Jane Austen, and I wouldn't have them writing *RCMP* either. The mere thought of the way in which even the best women writers would portray the relationship between Gagnier and Scott makes my flesh creep.[44]

Ironically, Tilsley had already adapted female novelists for British television – Charlotte Bronte (*Jane Eyre*), for one – and one suspects he would not have asked his male writers to be a Dickens or a Hardy.[45] At this time, however, police procedural writing was associated with male writers, who were supposedly able, by osmosis, to conjure up the feeling of masculine dialogue and action in police dramas.

Accuracy in presentation was to be facilitated by two RCMP officers who offered on-set advice (down to the proper haircut), and, when one of the major scriptwriters, George Salverson, required aid, the way was paved for him with an advance letter that introduced him to his local Toronto RCMP detachment.[46] Another key writer, Monroe Scott, first a Crawley employee and then a freelancer on the series, was given a formal introduction to RCMP headquarters, where he searched for cases that might become TV scripts. He also used a letter of introduction from Nicholson to connect with RCMP detachments throughout the Northwest Territories while on another writing assignment. The praise the RCMP received from Crawly for their "wonderful, generous" cooperation on scripts was almost sycophantic, though undoubtedly politically astute.[47]

Crawley had concerns about competing TV versions of the Mounties, but, as one friend reassured him, the famous *Sergeant Preston* series was no more than a "Hollywood" tale, a "standard western" designed to appeal to "children and adolescents and [was] not an authentic documented treatment of the RCMP."[48] In contrast, the Crawley version was to be *authentic*, a concept continually invoked, in part because some of the stories came directly from the *RCMP Quarterly*. The idea that *Quarterly* cases were themselves not just pure fact but, rather, dramatizations and interpretations created by their RCMP chroniclers was never entertained. When the RCMP advisors inspected scripts for authenticity they might advise not only on technical detail but also on the plot, tenor, and believability of the episode. Kemp insisted that he would remove his endorsement unless he saw "clean, interesting stories" (leaving aside what he meant by "clean").[49] One script, "The Gentle Executioner," which came out of the *Quarterly*, dealt with a husband slowly poisoning his constantly complaining hypochondriac wife. Consultant Kemp objected to minor aspects of the plot but never to the underlying message that the man had some justification for killing an irritating "shrew" of a wife. The men involved in production all agreed: the poor meek husband was "possibly justified" in his actions.[50]

It was taken for granted that the RCMP would appear as upright, law abiding, honourable, always "working within the law."[51] The Mounties always got their warrant before they got their man. It was not just the direct advice of the RCMP that aligned the TV series with images of heroic police behaviour but the reigning respect for the Force that the creators, writers, directors, and producers had all absorbed. The Mountie myth of muscular – but compassionate –white frontier masculinity was at the heart of early planning documents, which described the Mounties' heroism, dedication to justice, and legendary restraint when it came to policing Indigenous others. The Mounties, one internal document claims, faced moments of "bloodshed and violence," but they were "famous for being able to keep their guns in their holsters." They could literally stare down adversaries with their courage, though they might also engage in "feats of derring-do that are too James Bondish to be usable without watering down the facts."[52]

This does not mean that all *RCMP*'s script advice was followed, and Rivett-Carnac's own script was rejected. Tilsley felt that, once the real *Quarterly* cases were depleted, writers could create their own stories and that these would be no less "realistic" because both embraced the same image of brave frontier masculinity.[53] The ambiance of the series was also to be uniquely Canadian.[54] While some stories would have "suspense and tension," there would also be "off-beat" stories and ones with irony, "humour[,] and warmth," featuring atypical criminals, such as the old farm woman who was shooting at the RCMP to prevent the authorities from institutionalizing her husband, who had Alzheimer's.[55] *RCMP* was also supposed to feature a different variant of masculinity than that found in the "Hollywood hoodlum" police drama;[56] it sought a "distinctive flavor," with police characters neither approximating the British "Fabian of the yard" nor the American "Joe Friday."[57]

The originally proposed anthology format, with an RCMP officer, a very Irish-sounding Sergeant Mulholland, introducing RCMP cases from across the country and summing them up with a moral at the end,[58] was also intended to convey documentary authenticity. Under pressure from its American partners, the Crawley team reluctantly abandoned this format for one northern locale — imaginary Shamattawa in northern Saskatchewan — since it promised a sense of continuity and audience investment in regular characters. Describing this forced shift years later in a play, *Corpus Delectable*, whose lead character is a thinly disguised Budge Crawley, author Monroe Scott summed up this capitulation to Hollywood pressure: "First thing they said was there had to be a formula for police series ... with one principle locale ... My God, the whole key to Mountie drama was that they did more things and patrolled more territory than any other force on earth!"[59]

The small-town northern setting of Schamattawa, with nearby farms, mines, trapping, and an Indian reserve, allowed the creators to showcase the many-sided nature of the RCMP as the men solved big and little crimes, and dealt with the mundane dilemmas and character failings of local characters. Schamattawa had a recurring group of type-cast regulars: the local doctor, the judge, farmers, the token "Chinaman" who ran the local diner, the middle-aged town female busybody, and an Indian guide and interpreter, Ben Aptugan, played by Angus Baptiste from the Maniwaki reserve. Three regular characters anchored the RCMP detachment: the hero, Jacques Gagnier, and his two underlings, Constable Scott and Constable Mitchell. Historically, French Canadians were less

Quebec actor Gilles Pelletier, who played Jacques Gagnier in Crawley Films' *RCMP,* is shown in publicity for the CBC show. | LAC, Crawley Fonds, MG 28 III 99, box 191, publicity file

interested in joining the force than were anglophones, but there is no evidence his background was recommended by the RCMP as an antidote to the long association between the Force and British imperialism.

Jacques Gagnier, production notes tell us, embodied typically French "Gallic" cultural attributes, combined with heroism, good character, honesty, integrity, and bravery: he could literally face down death and "talk someone out of using violence of any kind."[60] He was an unusually cultured man: he loved gourmet cooking (since his parents owned a restaurant in Quebec); he had a wonderful voice (he sang at all the local churches, eschewing taking religious sides); he liked and impressed beautiful women (though never succumbed to their wiles); indeed, he had a "Gallic acceptance of sex," though he remained a much sought after bachelor. Gagnier was also extraordinarily perceptive about human nature. "Wisdom was the keynote" of his character; local citizens respected him, knowing he was both a "stern disciplinarian" and a compassionate man. He was to be akin to a "chaplain in the army, a father figure," dispensing wisdom and informal justice as well as maintaining law and order.[61]

Gagnier's compassion always extended to Indigenous peoples, and he also had a rare appreciation for their culture: collecting Eskimo art and music was featured prominently as his one "highbrow taste."[62] He also shared their wilderness skills as a canoeist, tracker, and hunter; indeed, this wilderness prowess made him more Native than the Native. That Gagnier's character clearly had some audience appeal is suggested by the few surviving fan letters. One devoted British fan was politely persistent, praising the handsome Gagnier as a "wonderful actor ... a great favourite of ours here." "I really fell for him," she admitted to the Crawley vice-president in one of her regular letters.[63]

Gagnier's second in command, Constable Scott, played by John Perkins, was supposed to be an ambitious young man who eschewed taking over his father's small business in British Columbia for "a life of vigour" in the RCMP. He was an excellent boxer, an avid horseman, "physically courageous ... a well brought up boy, naturally polite." In comparison to Gagnier, Scott is both "more complex and more straightforward," the latter indicating his "Teutonic" instincts, the former reflecting his methodical, careful examination of all sides of a story. And he is "utterly normal sexually." What that means is unclear, except that his heterosexual proclivities are emphasized: he has a "trace of envy" for Gagnier's charm with women. Don Franks was cast as Mitchell, the second symbolic son to father Gagnier. Mitchell, a budding scientist, is using his prized job in the RCMP as a stepping stone out of the working class: he wants to move up the RCMP ranks into the scientific study of crime. Coming from a modest background, he is the detachment's fixer and handyman, "a very nice little guy," although, when faced with a fight, he exhibits great physical toughness, a product of his class background.[64]

RCMP VERSIONS OF INDIGENOUS PEOPLES

As the Mountie myth came together with production priorities, another element of the police knowledge economy was also apparent: Crawley relied on the RCMP, and occasionally on other white experts, for an understanding of Indigenous peoples and the northern landscape. One script he wanted to produce, "Bear Walk," was not endorsed by the "Indian experts" (i.e., white administrators) at the Glenbow Museum, and this contributed to its being shelved. Crawley was keen to produce something that could use background filming of a Sun Dance ceremony, likely seen as exotic and compelling for both the domestic and international markets, and he tried to work with the local Indian agent in order to film on an Alberta reserve. This project floundered, in part because Crawley could not negotiate an acceptable deal with the local Blackfoot, despite the feeling of local white Indian administrators that the Indians should be "grateful for [some]one to come and take a record of their tribal customs."[65] Crawley staff members were also concerned about the presentation of Inuit characters. The Arctic stories, George Gorman mused, would not only involve a climate and "time problem" but also a casting problem: "Where do we get the Eskimos?" He did have a solution: "If we have a good make-up artist there is no problem. We can make our own Eskimos."[66]

Imparting a northern sense of landscape and location was also a central concern. Part of the RCMP job description was battling the northern elements – just as Indigenous peoples did – and this motif was commented on at some length by RCMP advisors. Former commissioner Rivett Carnac gave detailed advice on how the RCMP's tracking prowess would be manifested in one story in which Constable Scott is wounded and left to die by some very bad guys. That RCMP men had absorbed the skills of the Native went without saying, and, more than mere skill, this also denoted their masculine strength and courage: "respect is granted to [RCMP] men in these surroundings according to their endurance," advised Rivet Carnett, "but it must be efficient endurance. Eskimos especially admire this quality [in white men]."[67] In one story involving Aboriginal actors, Kemp was extremely detailed in his prescriptions for

Filming an "authentic" northern snow scene, with sled dogs, at the Wakefield production site. | LAC, Crawley Fonds, MG 28 III 99, box 191, publicity file

the appropriate racial hierarchy within policing personnel: A "half-breed constable" would never talk so "patronizingly to a [white] Constable" he cautioned. Looking over the "Moonshine" script, he claimed that no RCMP constable would ever call an Indian "Mister Smoke" as he "would hardly address an Indian as Mister anybody." Naming had to be exact in its representation of racial authority and authenticity. His counsel extended to generalizations about the economic and social situation of First Nations peoples. The issue of treaty money was initially mentioned in one script as a means whereby an Indian character would pay off his debts, and Kemp thought this should be excised since "treaty money does not amount to very much." "Indians in Saskatchewan have farms and are usually well-heeled," Kemp claimed in a rather sweeping generalization that was surely a surprise to some Indians living below poverty level. This decidedly paternalistic view of Indigenous peoples was accompanied by claims to know exactly how Indians would respond to other characters and events. A scared Indian kid, he warned the writer of "Moonshine," would not hide in a tree but, rather, would run home.

Nor did he want the RCMP hero to appear *too* domestic. Because Gagnier was a gourmet cook, he once offers to cook something for Wilson Lee, the local "Chinaman." To Kemp, this scripted reversal of racial work roles was simply ludicrous.[68] Kemp was also extremely critical of "Silent Companion," a story of a constable in the North crossing the wilds with the body of a murder victim covered up on his sleigh, accompanied by the unknowing murder suspect. While taken from a *Quarterly* story, the writer changed this incident of *Eskimo* murder into a *white* murder, a major faux pas for Kemp. No doubt, the RCMP advisors with northern experience were promoting *their* version of authenticity, and some of their objections indicated sensitivity to the specificities of Indigenous cultures. If there is Cree dialogue, Kemp said, then speak it in Cree, not another language. He also took issue with the script first entitled "The Unhanged Indian" because he felt the title was somewhat "sordid," racially "prejudicial,"[69] and in bad taste. It was altered to "Moonshine."

Nonetheless, there was nothing in the advice proffered that deviated from the image of the Mountie as northern white male hero and the Indian and Eskimo as more marginal populations with a noble history but in need of white guidance. There are remnants of the doomed warrior implied in *RCMP*'s version of the Indian and Eskimo, combined with a sense that they had fallen on hard times.[70] This was both part of a broader cultural ideology that *RCMP* had absorbed and the ideology that the RCMP itself reproduced. Moreover, even if RCMP veterans from the field were more attentive to the language, culture, and differences between First Nations, the members of the production team were

less so: Indian and Eskimo characters were imagined as simply inter-
changeable. When discussing a new script, "An Epidemic Story," they
noted that it could be potentially set in "an Indian Village" but could just
as well be done with "Eskimos."[71]

Indigenous characters often became "types," something symbolized
well by the casting of Indian roles, which was primarily an exercise in
finding the right racial look rather than in finding someone who had acting skills or who could develop them. Staff scouted out Indian-looking
actor possibilities at local reserves. George Gorman reported to producer Bernard Girard that he had visited the woman playing Mrs. Mathew
Smoke in "The Unhanged Indian" ("Moonshine") in order to meet related boys who might play her grandsons, but one "had a stammer and
the other was cross-eyed." A contact took him to the Maniwaki reserve
so he could "see all the Indians [he] could see" in a short space of time.
After a day he reported: "I had seen nine male Indians between the ages
of 35 and 50," plus some others for the other adult role. His lists of possible actors always stress the physical: "Xavier Cizar (picture number 1)
... is stocky full-chested, very Indian looking. Picture number 2 could
play Joe in Storm O'Brien," although, unfortunately, "he could not read"
and would have to be taught his lines by rote. Another prospect, Gabriel
Cooper, looked "more French than Indian" (whatever that meant) but
could be used as an extra, while Angus Dancy (picture number 4) was a
"very Indian looking Indian."[72] And so on.

Despite the fact that their racial looks were important to the script,
Indian actors who were extras received only fifteen dollars a day, which
was problematic in terms of their travel time to the Gatineau set (the few
designated "principals" received more). Girard's acting scout near the
reserve warned him that their travel time would take up to two days and
that they would not give up three days in total for a mere fifteen dollars.[73]
While the work may have been welcome for some Aboriginal people, the
two surviving letters from regular Angus Baptiste indicate the marginal
nature of their economic existence. Baptiste received a regular weekly
advance so that he would be on call when needed, but later the company
tried to reclaim over-paid salary from him, despite the fact he worked at

low-wage, intermittent jobs. It appears Crawley staff helped to find him work as a fishing guide, then in lumbering, but it is clear that Baptiste lived hand to mouth.[74]

INDIGENOUS PEOPLES ON CAMERA

In analyzing the available thirty-some episodes of *RCMP*, one conclusion is inescapable: women do not fare well in these scripts. Suffice to say, they are usually one-dimensional characters, often mere caricatures.[75] Although the Canadian writers questioned Hollywood's Mountie stereotypes, they never queried their own juxtaposition of a masculine Mountie to a scheming or distracting "blonde.[76] More than one older woman in *RCMP* is also described in the production notes as a "battleaxe."[77] Women might appear attractive, but then they are likely to be conniving, using their sex appeal to get their hands on something, including Gagnier – though no one ever snags this prize. Manipulative wives and hysterical women (sometimes one and the same) are common fare.[78] The wife in "The Gentle Executioner," it is implied, almost *deserves* to be poisoned. A recurrent Schamattawa character is the narrow-minded, over-sized, loud town gossip whose own daughter flees her overbearing presence – with reason, we are led to assume. Perhaps most disturbing, violence against women is not just normalized but is often depicted as their own fault. A woman's thoughtless flirtatiousness or a young teen's desire for attention might be the "understandable" cause of violence against them.[79] The stereotyping of white women is more obvious than that of Indigenous women, but this is only because there are more opportunities to caricature them. There is one small difference between the portrayal of white and Indigenous women: the latter are often portrayed as more vulnerable, more in need of RCMP protection.

Protecting women is part of Gagnier's role as guardian of the family. He is Father Confessor for families experiencing domestic strife, especially with regard to difficult children. His advice is wise, measured, designed to keep the peace but also to protect children from incompetent, uncaring adults. While firm with criminals, Gagnier's paternal compassion for women and children solidifies his fatherly role in the detachment, the town, and its environs, including the local Indian reserve. In more than one episode, he is the only reason children are placed on a better path for the future.[80] In a script prepared but not filmed, he literally saves a whole village of "Indian children" from white bank robbers/hostage takers, while their Aboriginal parents stand by, cowed into fearful acquiescence.[81] In this era of post-residential school apologies, a narrative of white authority figures "saving" reserve children from hopeless parents is especially jarring; in the 1950s, the storyline likely reflected taken-for-granted impressions of incapacitated or inept Aboriginal families.

As this storyline shows, Gagnier's paternal role extends to Indigenous peoples. Domestic violence figures prominently in one such story: the tragic tale of Johnny Wolf, a "full blooded Cree," who takes out his own failures on his wife and family. The episode is supposedly based on an RCMP case, but it was considered too violent for Australian censors, who refused to show it on television.[82] Johnny, it is established from the very first frames, seems a normal working-class Indian, but he is actually an internal mess of toxic envy and anger; he secretly "envied success and what he could not be." He could not live up to the example of his father, an accomplished artist and war hero, an "ambitious, clever Indian," with the name James Longboat. Why his father would have the name of a well-known Mohawk athlete and war hero from Ontario, while Johnny Wolf is a Cree in Saskatchewan, is never explained: race, not distinct First Nations, is the important descriptor when it came to Indigenous themes.

In many of the Indigenous stories, there is an intended message of liberal tolerance, even of criticism of white racism. As Johnny Wolf, who works as a garbage collector, is picking up the refuse of local whites, he is taunted by some nasty little neighbourhood kids who ridicule him by running around him, whooping like an Indian in a Hollywood film. In response to this juvenile racism, he becomes enraged, leaves his job, and drinks excessively, resulting in him arriving home so drunk that he smashes up his home and terrorizes his wife and two children. He lashes out at his cowering, mild-mannered wife for taking in laundry for white women: "you are doing white women's dirty work," he screams at her, "it's all your fault. You make me feel like a fool." When the police arrive at their house, Gagnier is attentive, gentle, and kind to the vulnerable wife and frightened daughter.

Fearing Johnny's drunken rage, his wife escapes to the reserve where her parents live. The RCMP officers' attempts to encourage Johnny to adopt a more truly manly role as head of the family is of little use. Johnny is haunted by his own pathetic inadequacies; he shows Gagnier his father's war medal, declaring, "He was a brave man, better than any white man." Wracked by demons of self-loathing, Johnny hunts down his wife on the reserve, killing her, her younger brother, and her parents. He then heads for the local school to get his children. After finding the carnage on the reserve, Gagnier and Scott follow in close pursuit, and high noon comes at a nearby sandpit, where Johnny is hiding with his children. He shoots Scott, though not fatally; Gagnier responds with fire and Johnny dies, clutching his father's war medals, though in one last decent act, he lets his children go. Apparently Johnny did not believe Gagnier, who repeatedly told him that, if he surrendered, "he would receive a fair trial."

Racism is an underlying theme in this episode. "This is an Indian," Scott says with derision, "this is what drink does to him." Gagnier, as the all-knowing tolerant white father, corrects Scott immediately: not true, snaps back Gagnier, who always instructs his *RCMP* sons that every person, regardless of background, has to be treated humanely. Gagnier reminds Scott that he has never stood in Johnny's Indian shoes: "Are you an Indian? What do you know about Indians' reasons?" Despite Gagnier's mild critique of Scott's knee-jerk racism, despite the fact that Johnny's drinking is not generalized to other Indians who are gentle and kind, the moral of the story is that Johnny has become the self-pitying author of his own misfortune, even in the midst of a racist town. The paternal care offered the Indian wife by Gagnier is positioned in stark contrast to the violent patriarchal deeds of Wolf: the masculinity of the white hero is selfless, while the masculinity of the Aboriginal man is self-ish. While we can't deny that Aboriginal women experienced violence within their own communities, the story does not in any way relate this violence to colonialism, and, most important, it erases any discussion of racialized violence directed at Aboriginal women by white men. In the same way as sections of the Indian Act were justified as a means of protecting Aboriginal women against unscrupulous white men, this episode suggests that Aboriginal women would find protection with the police, not with their own people on the reserve. Sadly, we know from historical research that some Aboriginal women found exactly the opposite, not only in the 1950s but long after.

Violence is not limited to Indigenous stories, but there is an assumption in the series that some groups are more prone to violence than others. They may be lower-class drug dealers, very bad criminals from the big city (Montreal) who tote guns,[83] or unassimilated, "hot headed" Ukrainians (though the word "Ukrainian" is only implied) who, in "Violence at the Wedding," cause a drunken, violent brawl with imported moonshine.[84] Indigenous peoples are just one of these groups. In "The Replacement," the bitter widow of an RCMP officer killed in the line of duty has to come to terms with the violence that claimed her husband's life. He was shot by Noel Feather, who is cast as a Métis or Indian man. Feather murders his entire family and then escapes into the bush, shooting the RCMP officer who follows in honest pursuit of justice for Feather's family. The officer's wife, who helps "man" the detachment radio, is a competent, capable woman reduced to grief and immense self-pity, but, aided by father Gagnier, she comes to see that her husband's death was not senseless and that she has a reason to live. The naming of the perpetrator of violence in this episode as Aboriginal is subtle but nonetheless establishes a connection to Johnny Wolf, who also senselessly murders his own family.

There were other stories developed for the series involving Aboriginal people, murder, and violence, though they were not used in the first season. Both researcher Alan Phillips and Crawley writers thought some "grisly" and "real blood curdling" *Quarterly* cases of murder would make good scripts,[85] but they might not have passed the RCMP litmus test for "clean," not gory, stories. Phillips had a script, "The Missing Livers" (clearly modelled on a *Quarterly* case and famous trial in 1913),[86] involving the murder and cannibalism of two priests by three Inuit men who were under extreme pressure in starvation conditions, but it is possible such scripts were vetoed because they so *overtly* suggested Indigenous people were prone to violence. Scripting stories like this one without caricaturing the Inuit as superstitious or cruel would have been difficult, although Phillips's personal take on some of the Eskimo murder cases was sympathetic to the Inuit. Gorman noted privately that the priests "both deserved it"; however, he was reluctant to produce scripts that seemed too sensational, that were not "politically acceptable" for CBC viewing.[87]

A more palatable script, "Bear Walk," which the producers favoured, was developed and written by Tilsley and only put aside because the show's consulting Indian experts had issues with its Sun Dance portions. They very much liked the message of the episode, in which a younger Indian, determined to pull his community out of superstition and backwardness, was thwarted by elders who were clinging to the traditional past. Other scripts were also commended for drawing out this theme of "modern Indians" battling "superstition" or "caught between two civilizations and unable to cope with either one."[88] The conflict between outdated tradition and modern ways, with the latter clearly the path of the future, approximated the same political thinking evident in NFB films, explaining why "Bear Walk" was far more palatable to the Crawley team than a script involving cannibalism.

Interactions between Indigenous and white were not uniformly tense: quite the contrary. A rapprochement between Native and newcomer could exist, but it was usually built either on the paternalism of the RCMP or on the mutual respect earned through the Force's masculine conquest of wilderness. This is the case in "Bad Medicine," an episode that, more than any other, establishes Gagnier as more Native than the Native. Gagnier's frontier masculinity is challenged by a corrupt, evil white man and his Indigenous accomplice, but Gagnier's skilful mastery of the northern wilderness, along with the respect he garners from his Indigenous captive, saves his life.

Gagnier is canoeing through the "North country" visiting trading posts – very dapper in full uniform, tie, and hat, one might add.[89] Eighteen days into his journey, he comes across a white man and a Métis man in an abandoned mine. Gagnier recognizes them as Burke, wanted for the murder of another white trapper, and his Métis accomplice Night

Traveller. He arrests them at gunpoint and they journey back to "civilization" together, with the arrestees only partially restrained since Gagnier needs them to help paddle the canoe. It is a test of Gagnier's will, endurance, and wilderness skill as he can't falter, sleep, or let them take his gun. It becomes apparent that Burke is manipulating Night Traveller and using him to scare Gagnier: "The Indian is an ignorant savage" who can't speak English, he tells Gagnier, "Real old-time white man hater. So you watch him."

Gagnier doubts Burke, and his respect for the older Indigenous man slowly emerges over the course of the episode: "If he could give me his word," he says, "I would untie him, as I trust him." As the viewers' doubts about Night Traveller's violent character increase, the image of Burke worsens. He admits the Métis man is his father-in-law, yet he has no respect for his own Métis wife: "she was broke and proud to marry a white man ... [W]ell, now a man that's sort of going to seed a little bit in the bush, he's got to marry *somebody*." Burke tries to bargain for his own life with that of his father-in-law, pinning the murder of the trapper on him. Burke's attempt to join racial ranks with Gagnier ("it's between us white men" he tells him) only makes Gagnier angry since this is an affront to his sense of race-neutral, unbiased justice. The court will decide, Gagnier replies "coldly" to Burke's attempt to establish a bond between the two "civilized" white men, "and the Indian will have his say." Burke is a white trash character, counterpoised to the strong, silent "noble savage" Night Traveller. In the script notes, Burke is pegged as "a bush rat or squaw man" who has "deteriorated mentally and emotionally," while Night Traveller is "well preserved of his kind," and though "silent, suspicious, untrusting," this Cree character is "intelligent" and is only withdrawn because he is quietly assessing Gagnier's character.

A denouement occurs when Burke tries to get away, and Night Traveller asserts his honour as he protects Gagnier, handing him back his gun. The stoic, silent Indian, it is suggested, might have understood English all along, or, at the very least, has come to respect Gagnier — just as Rivett-Carnac claimed "the Eskimo" respected "courageous" white men. "There was understanding in his eyes," recalls Gagnier, "was it an understanding that the white man's law would be just, or did he understand the white man's language all along?" White and Indian, a Canadian Lone Ranger and Tonto, then head off into the sunset together to face white justice. One could hardly find a more stoic Indian stereotype than Night Traveller, who *never* spoke. But Burke, too, is a stereotype: a "low-class" white who manipulates Indians, disrespects their culture, and abuses their women. Again, the show emphasizes that Indians need progressive whites like Gagnier to protect them from pernicious racist abuse. Gagnier's wilderness prowess establishes a bond between him and Aboriginal people, and his honesty and courage result in Aboriginal people respecting the fairness of Canadian law.

The notion that Aboriginal peoples deserved respect was a recurring liberal theme, one undoubtedly meant to encourage a level of tolerance for a less fortunate group in society. Humanity, as one RCMP writer later noted, was intended as one theme in the series. Teaching respect for Native peoples is part of Gagnier's fatherly role, as evidenced through his interest in Inuit culture: he collects Inuit sculpture and listens to recordings of Inuit music. His dismissive detachment sons, Scott and Mitchell, like normal teenagers, roll their eyes at this strange music, but Gagnier patiently explains why it is valuable. Gagnier's moral messages do have an impact: when Scott ventures out into the northern wildness on his own and confronts a case of white corruption involving Aboriginal people, he puts the lessons Gagnier has taught him to good use.

The episode "The Unhanged Indian," renamed "Moonshine," was one of few to make extensive use of Aboriginal actors. Scott dogsleds solo in this episode. He makes his way to a small Indian settlement with a Métis translator, Ben, in order to investigate rumours of moonshine sales. Instead, his first encounter is with Indian grandparents who have just found one of their two teenage grandsons hanging in the barn. While Scott offers condolences, he has some suspicions since "boys don't commit suicide," and grandmother Smoke at first tells the translator that they boy did not commit suicide. She adds that the local white trader, Sam Colver, had visited their house that day. Scott questions Colver, who denies this and dismisses the grandmother as a "silly old" Indian woman with no "sense of time." Colver also paints a picture of a "moody, queer" Indian child prime for suicide: "I can't say I'm surprised. Paul was the type."

Scott's investigative skills, combined with his protective impulses, raise his suspicions about Colver. He notices that the dead boy's breath smells of liquor and that the rope marks on his neck are peculiar. These clues lead to his realization that he must find the younger brother who has run away and who is perhaps in danger. When he does locate young Peter in the snowy wilderness, Scott is caring and protective; he explains that his brother had died but that he will be joining their deceased parents "so they won't be lonely." Peter spills the beans: the grandfather was helping Sam Colver make and distribute moonshine, which his brother discovered and drank, leading to his death. His hanging was a faked suicide. Grandfather Smoke was paying off a debt to the trader, who craftily persuaded him that if he did not do as he was told "he would go to prison." Grandfather Smoke is persuaded to turn Culver in, and, as the episode ends, Scott heads back to the detachment with both men under arrest. He is mildly irritated that he receives no praise over the radio from father Gagnier, only the admonition to be back in time to be on "night duty on Thursday." However, Scott has acted exactly as his RCMP father had taught him: make no distinction between Indian and white; treat racist comments about Indians with scepticism; use his objective, investigative skills; and protect those Indians who are being used and abused by avaricious whites.

The Indian who is taken advantage of by corrupt whites and in need of paternal protection is a recurring narrative in RCMP fiction. In *RCMP* this paternalism could have a stern tone: Indians are not to be let off for their crimes, but the context in which they commit them should be taken into account. This was a liberal view of criminality, not unusual in the 1950s, as progressive criminologists looked at the environment shaping criminality and talked about rehabilitation, not punishment, as the solution. Questions of context, leniency, and racism all make their way into the story of "Storm O'Brien," an episode in which Gagnier is the sole interlocutor in a dispute in a remote trapping community. While the original script did not detail that the two trappers were Aboriginal, they were cast this way. When the film company counted up the number of Indians per episode, the "Storm O'Brien" script stood at the top with thirteen.[90]

Gagnier initially goes to the northern community in order to investigate a robbery and fire at the local trading post the previous night. The owners are convinced that Jack "Storm" O'Brien (named for his quick temper) was the culprit since they heard their beloved dog bark (presumably he disliked Indians) before he perished in the fire started in the store. Storm, they admit, had a beef with them since they would not increase his credit so that he could buy the medicine he badly needed. Gagnier and the detachment's Aboriginal guide, Ben, visit Storm, who lives with his fourteen-year-old Métis nephew. Storm is now desperately ill, and they all return to the post together. After a radio call to the doctor, Storm is diagnosed with appendicitis. No plane can make it into the post in time, so Gagnier must operate by proxy, using the doctor's radioed directions. The owners of the trading post claim Storm O'Brien is not "worth taking a chance on," and they "hope he dies." It seems clear they value their deceased dog's life more than Storm's. Gagnier's instant doctoring skills, of course, save Storm's life, and, as he operates, he realizes that Storm's nephew was the robber since he knows exactly where to locate the medical supplies in the storeroom. The boy confesses (as all criminals do in this show) that he was trespassing but was just looking for some medicine for his uncle and that the fire was accidental.

Since the owners insist on pressing charges against the nephew, the story ends with him taken away for trial by Gagnier, who does advocate for leniency given the no-win position the boy faced. The ending could be read more than one way: either the boy should answer for his mistakes or the store owners brought the robbery and fire upon themselves because of their inhumane denial of medicine to the boy's uncle. There is ambiguity in some *RCMP* episodes, such as this one, distinguishing the series from law-and-order television with evil criminals and goodguy cops. My reading of the narrative is that the owners wear the black hats and Gagnier the white one; their ugly lack of compassion is unappealing, a contrast to Gagnier's empathy for the Indigenous trappers. But Gagnier's compassion must always be tempered by the rule of law, which everyone must face equally. Hence, when the owners insist they will press charges, Gagnier accedes. He and the young Métis boy again take off into the sunset, this time in a northern water plane, leaving the audience to surmise the short- and long-term outcome for Storm and his nephew.

"The Smiling People"

The original plan for *RCMP* was to provide more stories on the RCMP in the Arctic in the next season's set of episodes.[91] The producers had devised a way of doing this in the first season, even with the Schamattawa detachment as home: have Gagnier travel to his former posts in the Far North to relive cases there. "The Smiling People," written by seasoned scriptwriter George Salverson, provides an excellent prototype. Indigenous people were imported from Great Whale River, Quebec (Kuujjuarapik, Nunavik), to act in this episode, and their presence was heralded in the accompanying publicity as yet another sign of authenticity. Like the Indians recruited from Maniwaki, they were not treated as actors as much as they were employed because of their racial look. Newspaper coverage announcing "Eskimo Actors Plunged into City Civilization" make it clear that the Inuit were from the "primitive" North.[92] One publicity photo shows the woman who plays a grandmother in the episode touring the toy section of an Ottawa department store with two children. The message is that she is marvelling at the consumer benefits of civilization.

"The Smiling People" explains Gagnier's fondness for the Arctic, its Indigenous peoples, and their art and music by taking him back to imaginary Seal Bay, Northwest Territories (perhaps meant to be Inuvik), to testify in a murder case against a local Inuk woman, Koona. Koona is charged with murdering her husband with his rifle. She initially claims he was ill but later asserts that he asked her to help him commit suicide. Gagnier again plays the skilled detective and paternal father whose insightful cross-cultural observations break the case. More than in any other episode, he is the paternal protector of Indigenous women in a potentially violent world. Moreover, the Inuit are portrayed differently than *RCMP*'s northern Saskatchewan Métis and Indians: Seal Bay people

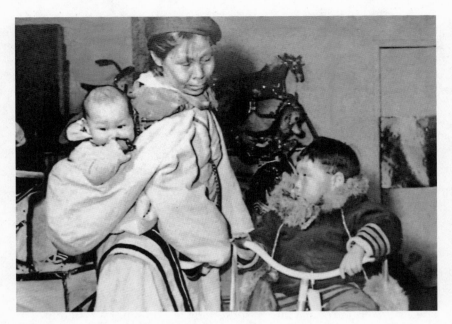

Publicity shot for "The Smiling People" shows an Innu grandmother, brought to Ottawa from Whale River for the filming, shopping in a department store. | LAC, Crawley Fonds, MG 28 III 99, box 191, publicity file

exist in a more remote, primitive, and, at the same time, more innocent context, and, as such, they need more aid assimilating into white law and order.

This episode found its origins in a case reported in the *RCMP Quarterly*, *R. v. Mafa*, though the writers had to follow the RCMP's wishes that no case file be "copied word for word." *R. v. Mafa* involves the investigation and trial of Martha Mafa who, at first, claimed she shot her sick husband on his wishes but, later, admitted another man, George Haogak, whom she subsequently married, shot him. In the production notes for the episode (modified from the *Quarterly*), Haogak kills his own wife, the implication being that George and Martha were reconstituting a family unit based on these murders. The actual case was more complicated and, indeed, was reported by the *Globe and Mail* as a trial of two Inuit women for murder. Also, there was more than one RCMP investigator, a son's testimony, and a trail of different kinds of evidence, including self-incriminating letters written in syllabic by George.[93] There was no "Eureka" breakthrough on the part of an RCMP hero, as portrayed in "The Smiling People." What the case file and the TV episode share is a common sensibility about Martha/Koona: she is portrayed as naïve, almost devoid of a sense of right and wrong. The notes on the *Quarterly* case file lead with the observation that Koona "is apparently unmoved by being held and tried for murder."[94] The RCMP record taker is astounded that the only time she cries is when she misses a trip ashore from the boat on which she is being transported.

The TV episode begins with a group of white men from "the outside" descending from a plane on a northern landing strip covered in blowing snow. The voiceover announces the arrival of "British justice" in the North: a judge, clothed imperiously in a flowing fur coat; "a Crown prosecutor, court recorder, defence counsellor," and, of course, RCMP constable Gagnier, who was to give evidence since he had been posted here a year ago.[95] Gagnier is the main prosecution witness; he also becomes Koona's source of salvation, a reminder that British (which is, simultaneously, Canadian) justice *works*. British justice also has British accents – at least, both the judge and the current RCMP officer at Seal Bay, Wymark, do, and it is represented by an all-male, predominantly white jury. Local men, such as a bush pilot/prospector passing through, are pressed into jury duty whether they like it or not as "it is hard to find a jury here." There seems to be one Inuit man on the jury, but it is hardly a jury of Koona's peers.

Gagnier's kind paternal concern for Koona is established at the very beginning of the episode, through the sweet background music, his words, and facial expressions: he asks about her children, and says he is "sorry for her troubles." Gagnier expresses concern to his fellow RCMP officer that Koona seems oblivious to the fact that his testimony might convict her, and, always observant of Indigenous others around him, he notices that the hunter Gagaluk, who lacks his own family, is shepherding Koona's three children into his tent, with the help of Koona's younger sister, Hopana. Gagnier makes inquiries with local authorities about who will look after the children if Koona is convicted: clearly, it will be Gagaluk and Hopana.

Koona is portrayed just as Inuit women were portrayed in many white women's memoires and in visual displays of the "cheerful Eskimo." She is rather stoic but always smiling, seemingly unperturbed by the seriousness of these events, and she appears to be easily led and pliable. Koona has waited at the settlement for her trial, never trying to escape. "Koona is an Eskimo," remarks a white observer, "You tell her to stay and she stays until you tell her to go." But there is an implication, as in the *Quarterly* case, that she lacks a clear moral compass. Indeed, this trial also bears a strong resemblance to that described in Elsie Gillis's *North Pole Boarding House*.[96] At the trial, Koona's sister Hopana testifies without emotion that she saw her sister shoot her husband "in the back of the head" as he slept. While Koona sits in court, ever smiling, as if unperturbed by the seriousness of the case, the all-male jury exchanges knowing glances about her guilt. Koona's vigorous defence attorney, Yahnko,[97] suggests that her confession was subtly coerced because of the difference in status and intelligence between her and her RCMP interrogators, notably Gagnier. Yahnko is sceptical that Koona understood what was transpiring when Gagnier read her her rights (admittedly through a translator): "Did you rattle this off to a simple woman in a fish camp? You in your uniform had authority here and cut quite a big figure in the eyes of an Eskimo woman ... She may not have understood you were arresting her, and the white man's power may have overwhelmed her ... [Y]ou say to a primitive woman the best thing to do is confess and [she does]." Perhaps she was "pleasing you as an outsider," he continued, thinking that you could help provide for her children. While Gagnier indignantly rejects the insinuation that he unfairly extracted a confession, Yanko's question, "What happens to a woman and children if a hunter dies?" sparks his thoughts. As he leaves the court room, he suddenly sees the truth, declaring to Wymark: "Koona is innocent!"

Gagnier has a brain wave that evening about how to uncover new evidence; he rouses others involved in the trial to help him implement his plan. In Hopana's and Koona's changing accounts of the crime, the hunter Gagaluk, who is a much superior hunter than is Koona's hapless husband, is always "three or four sleeps away" during the murder, no matter how much the rest of their story shifts. Gagnier suspects that this one unchanging element of the story suggests he was actually involved, and he devises a plan to test this theory. Gagaluk is lured to the trading post and a contrived conversation causes him to slip up on a detail about the caribou hunt he was supposedly conducting on the day of the murder. Once again, Gagnier's knowledge of the northern frontier allows him to know exactly what kind of questions to ask. It becomes clear that Gagaluk is lying and that the women are protecting him as the only option to ensure Koona's children do not starve if she goes to jail.

Gagnier rouses the local social welfare administrator, Martinson (another British-accented white male, though more professorial in appearance), who speaks Inuktitut, and they go to Koona's tent to question her again. After Martinson reassures Koona that her children will be financially cared for by the state, she breaks down and admits the truth. Gagaluk killed her husband, who was a bad hunter, and then inherited her and her family. This murder for patriarchal control, it is suggested, emerged naturally from Inuit culture. British justice, on the other hand, is not patriarchal but paternal, looking out for Koona and her family. Martinson reminds us at the end of the episode that this case is "very rare" since "these people of ours are not given to solving their problems with violence." "But I suppose they will learn from us," he concludes. At once defending the Inuit as generally peaceful, his statement cancels out tolerance with condescension. The possessive is instructive: first, "these people" are "ours," they are colonial wards, children; second, they will "learn from us" since they are less evolved when it comes to justice, law, and order.

Threads of relativism and cultural tolerance weave their way through this script. Context is shown to be critical to the crime: Koona's desperate material needs and her absolute reliance on a male hunter in an unforgiving climate led to her covering up a murderer. Her love for her children is extolled, and her lack of understanding of white cultural norms means that she *could* simply smile: she really did not understand her wrongdoing. However, innocence also suggests primitiveness, and primitiveness is equated with an outdated patriarchal culture in which women are dependent, cowed, controlled by Inuit men. RCMP law is thus progressive and modernizing. Any suggestion that violence comes from outside the Indigenous community, that Aboriginal women are vulnerable to violence by white men, or that they have some agency in their own decisions, is absent from this scenario. We thus have a tale of colonial good works: the RCMP is doing legal missionary work, aiding primitive peoples at precisely the time when the state is calling for a program of modernization in the North.

DENOUEMENT

The Crawley plan was to provide increased numbers of stories on the RCMP in the Arctic in the next set of episodes.[98] However, since the "show barely broke even,"[99] it was cancelled. The thirty-nine completed episodes were broadcast through 1959–60 in Canada, the United States, and Britain, and some global distribution followed. A second rerun was aired in the early 1960s and the 1980s on CBC. Audience research conducted in 1959 by the BBC indicates a respectable reception of the show in Britain. Two episodes scored by its Audience Research Division got marks of sixty-seven, which are comparable to other police shows, even better than a *Perry Mason* episode. The majority of viewers gave the show an "A" rating. Audience comments indicated they liked the "clever lead," Gagnier, but found that *RCMP* did not have as much "excitement or tension" as other police shows. Perhaps, one viewer commented, this was because the denouement was predetermined: "we know the Mounties always get their man." There was a positive appreciation of the show's distinction from American police shows because of its emphasis on "credibility" rather than on "artificiality."[100] The BBC was optimistic enough about the future of the show that it tried to interest the Canadians in a syndicated newspaper strip based on the series, proposed by Oldham Press. The Canadians were not enthusiastic, perhaps because they were still smarting from their earlier bad treatment by the BBC, or, as the British surmised, because McConnell, who had helped bankroll *RCMP*, had his own newspapers to think about.[101]

The Canadian reaction to the series was mixed. One audience survey ranked it seventh out of twelve shows in terms of viewing numbers.

While it could not compete with favourites like *Father Knows Best* and *Ed Sullivan*, it ranked higher than American shows *Perry Como* and *Four Just Men*.[102] Press reports claimed that a CBC audience report, based on three thousand viewers, mixed "praise with criticism." Critics of the show dismissed it as as "inauthentic and amateurish," with "muddled" plots, though other coverage asserted it had all the makings of a Hollywood production.[103] Perhaps the Crawley team intended to "tone down the heroics" with narratives that were not as violent and action-filled as those featured in American shows only to discover that even Canadian audiences wanted action and drama.[104] The creators commented on their difficulty navigating British and American input, reflecting two different kinds of cultural taste: "it is difficult to find a medium" that encompasses both the wishes of the more "gentle" English taste and the more forceful "Hollywood flair."[105] Yet subsequent Canadian shows focusing on small communities, everyday law and order, and Indigenous peoples were well received.[106] However, at the time, *RCMP* was never examined with the same critical criteria later brought to bear on shows like *North of 60* – namely, how white-Indigenous interactions were portrayed.

The exact impact of *RCMP* cannot be easily measured from the viewer's perspective, but we can identify the program's dominant themes. As a period piece, *RCMP* reflects both a liberal concern for Indigenous peoples and a colonial and masculinist view of gender and race relations. The benevolent paternalism at the heart of the program's assemblage resonates with themes found in *The Beaver* and some NFB films of the period. At precisely the point at which modernization of the northern frontier was being trumpeted by private business, journalists, and politicians,[107] *RCMP* presented a picture of the provincial and Far North, where white settlement was a fait accompli, and Indigenous peoples, marginalized by this process, needed guidance and aid. *RCMP* reproduced, in powerful fictional viewing form, prevailing views of white-Indigenous relations and of the Indian character in which colonial hierarchies were accepted, even though white racism was sometimes critiqued. This may appear contradictory, but ideology is by its very nature precisely that: messy and contradictory – and more powerful because of these apparent contradictions. Moreover, the portrayal of white-Indigenous relations through the knowledge economy of policing carried with it extra ideological weight, not simply because the police were off- and on-set advisors but also because the mis-en-scène was already established by a dominating cultural ideology in which the RCMP were heroes on the Canadian peaceable frontier.

Indigenous peoples are portrayed as a group being pushed to the margins of society, already relegated largely to a trapping or low-wage economy, on the outskirts of towns and cities. They are also socially isolated, in part due to the destructive impact of white racism. While some Aboriginal men, like Night Traveller, embody elements of a noble past – connected to the wilderness, trapping, being at one with the land – others, like Johnny Wolf, have become victims of society's scorn. *RCMP* scripts, with their negative view of white racists and their idealization of Gagnier's respect for Native peoples' culture, suggest that another future is possible. Despite this thread of hopeful liberal tolerance, the RCMP men are ultimately idealized as white frontier heroes who bring civilized British justice, law, and order to the North, just as they brought justice to the western frontier in nineteenth-century Mountie fiction. They represent British fair play and integrity; they believe in treating all Canadians equally and humanely but sternly.

Gagnier is the ultimate symbol of this process. He is a father figure in the detachment and the community, a Father Knows Best, a Father Confessor, a Father Fix-It not only to his own two detachment sons but also to the townsfolk, with their hopeless family situations. He is also a father to the most marginalized of Indigenous peoples, Indigenous women, whom he tries to protect from violence or from the miscarriage of justice. The notion that Indigenous peoples had their own equally viable systems of justice, or that Aboriginal women needed to be protected from the violence of white men, was never imagined. This made *RCMP* another ambivalent, sometimes complex, but nonetheless colonial cultural contact zone in postwar Canada.

CHAPTER FOUR

NFB Documentary, Indigenous Peoples, and Canadian Northern Policy

The histories of documentary film, Indigenous peoples, and colonialism are entwined from the very first utterance of the term "documentary," and the international story is also one in which Canada figures prominently. This chapter explores a small part of that story: the portrayal of northern Indigenous peoples in National Film Board productions dealing with northern economic development and the Inuit way of life. Both government policy goals and the NFB's actual filmmaking have to be considered since they were often compatible, though occasionally contested, increasingly so by the 1970s with the emergence of a new brand of politically engaged documentary in which Aboriginal peoples and their allies critiqued state objectives. What kind of films did government departments concerned with the Indigenous North promote, and why, and how did these goals find their way into NFB films? What kind of messages did NFB documentaries on Inuit life offer the non-Indigenous public?

While a long-standing connection between ethnographic documentaries about Indigenous peoples and colonial ways of seeing is indisputable,[1] there is another history to be considered – that of documentaries that provide openings for alternative views or that reassert Indigenous cultural values that challenge state goals. We associate the engaged cinematic politics of anti-colonial advocacy and cultural rejuvenation with more recent films, such as *Kanehsatake: 270 Years of Resistance* or *Atanarjuat*; however, there were already rumblings of anti-colonial sensibilities in the late 1960s and early 1970s. These films marked a departure from NFB films of the 1940s and 1950s, which were more attuned to salvage ethnography and to the administrative designs of state actors, particularly attempts to integrate northern Indigenous peoples into their version of a modernizing Canadian nation.

NFB films are representations of reality and forms of cultural work that are simultaneously implicated in the power relations of wider governance processes. Like other historical documents, they are constructed, mediated, incomplete evidence, valuable precisely because of their interested point of view. Despite its historic claim to reflect reality, documentary also operates as ideology – obvious, subtle, hegemonic, contested – and its social influence may be magnified precisely *because* of its claim on the real rather than on the imaginary: its "power rests on its illusory neutrality."[2] As other scholars have stressed, NFB films reflected the board's wider mandate: to create a national identity, to aid in nation building, to encourage integration and tolerance, and also to produce – in the Foucauldian sense – a certain "population" in which individual conduct intersects with national planning.[3] In analyzing this cultural work, it is critical to frame the visual, sensual, and auditory experience encapsulated in film within a social, economic, and political context. Under what economic, social, and political conditions did NFB films create their images of the North? How were the films related to wider processes of governance and socio-economic development? How did some NFB films, with their repeated calls for the equal integration of Indigenous peoples into Canadian life, culturally encode both a mission of modernization and a project of capitalist accumulation?

THE NFB DOCUMENTARY AND INDIGENOUS PEOPLES IN CANADA

John Grierson, the founding commissioner of the NFB, coined the term "documentary" in 1926 when referring to Robert Flaherty's *Moana*, a film about South Sea islanders, though Flaherty's earlier 1922 film, *Nanook of the North*, depicting the Nunavik Inuit, is often associated with the beginnings of an ethnographic documentary tradition.[4] Grierson's original description of documentary as the "creative treatment of actuality" still has some purchase, with its nod to ambiguity and invention, though some scholars also see that ambiguity as its failing because it could refer to "fiction" films as much as to "nonfiction" films.[5] Flaherty's method, which often relied on an insider's "participant observation" of the "actual" daily lives of Indigenous peoples,[6] was a model that endured well into this post-Second World War period.

Much has been written about Grierson's impact on the NFB, despite his return to Britain after the Second World War, and also about Flaherty's *Nanook* as a path-breaking, influential white rendition, if not romantic idealization, of "primitive" peoples. Grierson, initially perceived as a progressive thinker dedicated to the creation of an informed citizenship "within a liberal reformist state,"[7] has subsequently been deconstructed by critics as a conservative with little faith in the uneducated masses, as a man of influence interested in social engineering through public opinion, and as someone concerned with sustaining "international capitalism" rather than with questioning it.[8] However, the force of his vision, the impact of his chosen personnel (who remained at the NFB long after him), and the long shelf life of his recommendation that the Canadian state could use film as a mode of citizenship training were all indelibly imprinted on the NFB. In Canada, the documentary tradition and aesthetic remained strong at and beyond the NFB, and successive governments, no matter their political stripe, were convinced of the potential for film to inform and mould ideas, peoples, and the nation.

The initial postwar years were difficult for the NFB, in part because it was targeted by some government leaders, who were caught up in a paranoid security state, as a potential sanctuary for "Reds."[9] In the case of Irene Baird, discussed in Chapter 5, this was a ridiculous fantasy on the part of irrational anti-communists, and, with a few exceptions, most cases investigated were more exaggeration and fear than anything else. But these incessant ideological attacks and the purges of some workers, changes in board leadership, and wider political critiques of the NFB's work did sap its energy. So, too, did a controversial relocation from Ottawa to Montreal and various battles over managerial control. Despite these problems, the NFB survived, expanded, trained countless filmmakers, and made an astounding number of films and filmstrips.[10]

These films had an enormous influence on cultural images of the nation at home and abroad. Children growing up in the postwar period watched NFB films and filmstrips in classes, and adults saw NFB films in countless community venues as well as in some movie theatres as opening shorts. NFB photo stills were a staple in many newspapers and magazines.[11] The board created classroom study guides for its films, established local film councils, and set up film libraries. Voluntary and welfare groups were targeted by the NFB's distribution machinery. Abroad, non-Canadians watched NFB films promoted through embassies and other organizations. These films were taken to be the face of the Canadian nation exhibited for international eyes. The NFB was not only part of the "symbolic environment" shaping Canadian cultural policy,[12] it was also deeply embedded in many areas of life-long learning (e.g., the Canadian Association for Adult Education became one of the board's close collaborators in promotion). The powerful reach of the NFB over film as a form of visual education was unparalleled across the country, with only Crawley Films providing a private competitor of note; however, in Quebec, the impact of the NFB was curtailed after 1954, when Maurice Duplessis forbade its films in the classroom.

The NFB was imagined as a "citizenship building technology": its films had many goals, including laudatory ones such as creating tolerance for diversity, informing citizens of their rights, and creating "a sense of belonging."[13] NFB ethnographic documentaries of the 1940s to 1960s were often intended to promote research on Indigenous peoples, to create an open-minded understanding of Aboriginals, as well as to document disappearing races and cultures. The latter also applied to other NFB preservationist projects that filmed other "quaint," endangered groups, such as Ukrainians or Acadians, though the cultural treatment of Indigenous peoples was always distinct. As Zoe Druick argues persuasively, documentary was also a means of population governance and citizenship self-regulation. Influenced by links to both an imperial British past and to contemporary American social science discourses, the NFB exemplified a Foucauldian process of governmentalization of the population. Culture and visual display became part of a pragmatic technology of building a modern, liberal nation-state, particularly in the area of social policy.[14] Other scholars similarly employ a Foucauldian frame to examine documentary film as a site of power-knowledge shaping history, memory, and identity, including the social management of Indigenous sexuality, the body, and populations.[15]

NFB films were not bereft of all discussions of Indigenous peoples. Whether students were studying the fur trade, the early white explorers, significant Aboriginal persons like Tom Longboat, or the northern frontier, they saw and heard much about the role of Aboriginal peoples in Canadian life. Thousands of these NFB filmstrips relating to Canadian history and geography were shipped across the country and used year after year in classrooms. As instruments of acculturation, filmstrips were also integrated into the education of northern Indigenous children, lauded because they were "inexpensive to produce, light to ship, and require no complicated equipment to show."[16] Filmstrips were the "most popular" method of teaching, according to the NFB, with up to twenty-five hundred copies of well-liked strips sold and an annual distribution of twenty-seven thousand strips a year by the early 1960s.[17]

Some Aboriginal-themed films became international as well as domestic favourites. As Gary Evans's history of the NFB argues, Douglas Wilkinson's *Land of the Long Day* and *Agotee, an Eskimo Boy* came to define the NFB at home and abroad, although these "remarkable, anthropological" films, he adds, also "confirmed an international image of Canada" as a "land of Eskimos" and snow.[18] This Canadian cultural preoccupation with Indigeneity would subsequently be reinterpreted far more critically. As Margaret Atwood puts it: a "fascination with racial cross dressing ... with making the 'native' part of our culture" is also a means of "evading [our] moral responsibilities" for colonial land theft and conquest.[19] In an NFB filmstrip celebrating white explorer Alexander Mackenzie, for instance, an Aboriginal chief is featured prominently as "a man of stature among his own people ... and [with] a high degree of intelligence," but he is nonetheless a *secondary* historical character, a helpmate in the process of white exploration of First Nations lands.[20]

The Mackenzie example suggests that there were some comparable themes in NFB documentaries and Hollywood fictional versions of Indians and white settlers. In his exposé of Hollywood's Canada, Pierre Berton lays bare the many stereotypes about Aboriginal peoples in Hollywood films: the countless misrepresentations of material and cultural practices, the image of primitivism and savagery counter-posed to white (often RCMP) civilizing morals, and the portrayal of the nefarious, never-to-be-trusted Canadian "half-breed."[21] Scholars generally agree that, apart from a nostalgic romanticization of the "noble Native" and his spiritual connection to nature, the dominant themes in Hollywood films from the 1920s to the 1970s include images of Native savagism and violence, the homogenization of all Native cultures into one (usually Apache), the presentation of Native assimilation as progress, and the assumption of an enduring white paternalism.[22] Even liberal westerns, with their nascent critique of racism, assumed assimilation was the best hope for peaceful co-existence; and even the supposedly alternative rebellious treatments of Indians in the 1970s resorted to age-old stereotypes. Native women fared particularly badly, pressed into what M. Elise Marubbio calls the three faces of the "celluloid maiden": the "squaw, young [princess] maiden and the old hag."[23] In Hollywood's conflated version of sexuality and race, any union between a Native American woman and a white man becomes a "means of subsuming her vanishing culture in the dominant one," and usually such a union dictates that she perish tragically at the end of the movie.[24]

American film producers were less interested in using the Inuit North as a film backdrop than in showcasing western "cowboys-and-Indians" frontier fare. Hollywood's few films set in Alaska from the 1920s to the 1960s often reproduced popular images that were also associated with the Canadian North: the "naïve nobility" yet "childlike simplicity" of the Indigenous peoples; a focus on their "primitive practices," including the male-dominated hunt; and their life-and-death struggle for survival in a barren land.[25] Ironically, Hollywood's Alaska bore a strong resemblance to the Canadian eastern Arctic as early ethnographic films, especially *Nanook*, had set a visual template for the North in the popular imaginary. Even the RCMP was imported into Alaskan film, portrayed as stern but tolerant law enforcers in the popular 1934 Hollywood feature *Eskimo*.[26] Hollywood films *still* have some purchase as realistic portraits of Eskimo life for Indigenous Alaskans, argues Ann Fienup-Riordan, reminding us that common cultural assumptions may shape both documentary and fictional filmmaking and that dominating ideas about Indigeneity, even colonialist ones, may be adopted, managed, and internalized by colonized groups themselves.

It is likely far more Canadians imbibed Hollywood westerns than NFB films, but even if these images provide a cultural backdrop to Canadian viewing, we must still analyze NFB documentaries on their own terms. Perhaps the relative disinterest of Hollywood in the Arctic left open a small space for Canadian documentary to create its own image of Indigenous life in the North. The idea that NFB documentaries on Indigenous northerners were creative reconstructions rather than completely objective versions of northern life would be taken as axiomatic today, but this was not the dominant view in the 1940s and 1950s. Documentary was distinguished from the narrative fictional film by its claim to be a window on reality. Although some contemporary critics rejected Flaherty's *Nanook* because it was staged and/or misrepresented the Inuit (the Inuit, when they saw it later, supposedly found it laughable), in their minds there existed a true North and "real" Inuit who could be captured on film. Documentary in this period was often done in the classic expository mode, in which the world is presented in a "fresh perspective" but always with the assumption that reality is knowable:[27] facts, figures, evidence, studies, and observations (often those of experts) are mobilized to illustrate observable reality. In the expositional documentary, an all-knowing male voiceover (a "God-voice") often narrates. An authoritative Lorne Greene was perfect for this job.

Observational documentaries, showing the filmmaker as a more obvious participant, were emerging by the 1960s, but these still often carried with them an assumption of "disciplined detachment" from the issue, peoples, or events being filmed.[28] Nor were these two styles always completely antithetical: the expositional might draw on observational techniques, and, by the 1960s, more narrative "poetic" fictional filmmaking infiltrated the expository and observational documentary.[29] However, through much of the period discussed here, the classic expository documentary, offering popular but factual entertainment, was still the norm. This was particularly true of ethnographic documentary films dealing with the Inuit because these mysterious and peculiar peoples supposedly needed to be explained to southern audiences by experts. In practice, this might involve an observational technique, with white observers who lived with the Inuit translating their culture to outsiders. These white travellers, filmmakers, anthropologists, or observers, it was assumed, had "unfettered" and special access to the world of the Indigenous other.[30]

By the late 1960s and early 1970s, the classic expository tradition, the essence of the NFB's cultural "code," was increasingly challenged by filmmakers who were not comfortable with this approach.[31] An interest in cinema verité and a more consciously engaged and interactive style of documentary came to the fore both internationally and within the NFB. The assumed space between filmmaker and the subject might be collapsed, the filmmaker's voice was heard rather than that of an all-knowing commentator, and those being filmed became social actors rather than the observed. Of course, these engaged documentaries, as Paul Atkinson suggests, forwarded their own truth claims, often using an observational style that was captive to the same methods as was earlier expositional documentary.[32] After the 1970s, Indigenous filmmakers also began to use documentary to "talk back" to long-standing colonial perceptions and policies.[33] The more consciously political documentaries, made by Indigenous people and whites alike, emerged as critiques of the idea of unmediated neutrality and forwarded a different set of truth claims about Indigenous culture, survival, and state practices.

Ethnographic documentary as a whole also underwent a critical reassessment, spurred, first, by charges of its complicity in the colonial status quo and, second, by poststructuralist critiques of Enlightenment rationality and our ability to recount *any* knowable reality or disinterested position outside of representation and discourse. Anthropologists reflected critically on their past participation in the production of ethnographic photos and films that encoded or rationalized the subordination of the subaltern. Many turned to more reflexive film styles, interrogating their role in the construction of the Indigenous other.[34] While acknowledging that the collection of ethnographic visual evidence sometimes signalled a humanistic impulse to value other cultures, these scholars condemned the tradition of positivist "photographic realism" that was employed to justify white European expansionism.[35] The concept of ideological hegemony was deployed to explain this cultural complicity in orientalist ways of seeing, though Foucauldian interpretations were also used to peel back the discursive strategies of power, knowledge, and pleasure that the co-mingled "surveillance and entertainment" of ethnographic documentary provided for white middle-class audiences.[36] Ethnographic film, some argue, remains deeply "haunted" by this "colonial past." Dismissed by the most acute critics as a "festering epistemological sore," it is characterized as "nothing other than the reconstruction and redistribution of a pretended order of things" or, perhaps, a psychological compulsion to "become the Other" through the "magic" of film.[37] Less pessimistic visual scholars, however, see the possibilities in self-critical filmmaking techniques that allow us to rethink the us/them, primitive/modern dichotomies previously intrinsic to much ethnographic film.

These theoretical and political questions have reshaped the way we have seen documentary over the past thirty years. Despite more emphasis on the illusion and invention involved in documentary, Bill Nichols argues persuasively that it is preferable to characterize documentary as film that "makes an argument" rather than as film characterized by its complete fictionality or its deceptive nature. While a documentary may be "constructed as a text," just as is fiction, "at the heart of documentary is less a story and its imaginary world than an argument about the historical world."[38] Similarly, some question whether ethnographic documentary should be dismissed as "ethnofictions."[39] Questions over representation, film critics also argue, may have "liberated documentary [filmmakers]" to *be* subjective, as "objectivity no longer seems possible."[40] If we see documentary as a set of arguments, as a treatment of actuality, as film with an "inferential" rather than simply an "imaginary" relationship to society,[41] then its value as a historical source is also clear: NFB documentaries can help us see the cultural work that cinematic texts accomplished in the context of postwar northern expansionism.

INDIAN POLICY AND NATIONAL FILMMAKING

Questioning all truth claims was not on the mind of government bureaucrats and NFB personnel in the immediate postwar years. On the contrary, they saw themselves as guardians of the fact; they drew on designated experts both inside and outside of government who used scientific and social science techniques to gather evidence about the Indigenous North. Films about the North were shaped within at least three overlapping circles of influence: the Indian Affairs Branch (here shortened to IA) thinking, the goals of the northern units in the Department of Mines and Resources (renamed a number of times until it became the Department of Indian and Northern Affairs, here shortened to NA), and the NFB itself. Short- and long-term film planning was discussed by the NFB with both IA and NA – in separate committees – and these government departments used their communication budgets to facilitate the film projects they endorsed. This was one reason that the NFB listened to departmental bureaucrats: its bread and butter depended on it. During the filming of *No Longer Vanishing*, IA's Evelyn Horne was irritated when NFB director Grant McLean implied publicly that this film was an NFB project: "I find that Mr. McLean is apt to give the impression that the Film Board is making the film," she wrote, but ... "I think it should be made perfectly clear that the Film Board is making it *for* and *at the expense* of the Branch."[42]

IA, for a while situated within the Department of Mines and Resources and later (1950 to 1966) within the Ministry of Citizenship and Immigration, was not directly responsible for publications and films under the NA mandate, but its generalized influence over state thinking on Indigenous peoples was considerable because of its bureaucratic and ideological longevity on the Ottawa scene. Moreover, some of its film projects did discuss northern Indigenous peoples, and NA did consult it on film issues. For IA, films had multiple uses: they were to display the benefit of IA programs to Indigenous peoples; they informed non-Indigenous groups of the value of government policies and programs; and they would also aid in the gradual assimilation of Indians into the "normal" Canadian way of life. IA wanted to use the talents of NFB filmmakers not only to promote their own policies but also to fashion a positive view of the Canadian Indian, thinking this would not only create more understanding and tolerance but also "raise the morale" of Indians too, offering them a feeling of "worthiness and pride in their heritage."[43]

IA believed that the history and contemporary perspective it was offering was revisionist, even anti-discriminatory, a counterbalance to the "misleading treatment of Indian history to which the public has been exposed." IA workers in the field complained that they encountered too many outdated harmful stereotypes about Indians and that the media was seldom unbiased and often sensationalist, showing Indians as poverty-prone "illiterate[] misfits."[44] Such laments were common, but many IA employees displayed a contradictory point of view; on the one hand, they did not want Indians to be seen as inherently lazy or as misfits, but they were also stung by any film reporting that actually dealt with problems of poverty on reserves or IA bureaucratic mismanagement. Muckraking journalists were not welcome commentators.

There were certain NFB films that IA promoted vigorously, and there were a few they abhorred. In its discussion of what made a good film, however, IA seldom actually consulted the First Nations; rather, its first line of advice came from Indian agents and other IA employees. When the NFB was in the process of creating *No Longer Vanishing*, IA superintendent H.B. Jones urged all regional supervisors to help by sending in ideas or providing logistical aid with filming. Agents and supervisors were generally on the same page: some attention to the historic, noble Indian was worthwhile, but contemporary eyes should be focused on self-help and modernization, especially in relation to work and politics. In the latter case, IA wanted to show the value of elected band councils in contrast to customary governance processes that were unprogressive and reactionary.[45] Indian actors or participants were to be employed for dramatizations to make this point visually and emphatically, and it was taken for granted they should all be men. Women were thus visually erased from the governance roles they had and still exercise in Aboriginal communities.

Above all, economic self-help was a key virtue to be stressed. One agent from the Far North claimed his charges were at least a generation behind those in the South, but a non-Indigenous audience could imbibe a positive view by seeing both the annual caribou hunt and Indian proficiency in creating market gardens. Indian agents believed that if the educational and occupational successes of Indigenous people were exhibited, it would increase tolerance, understanding, and integration, the latter a polite word for assimilation. They had to convince both Indians and non-Indians alike that "Indians [were] already of general service to the community and ha[d] the potential to be of much more." Visual examples of Indians at work were an object lesson for Indians, showing them they *could* work, and a lesson for whites who were under the impression they *would not* work. The claim that the NFB was not particularly interested in labour-related themes in this period may be correct if labour is equated with unions.[46] Yet wage labour was a central problematic in many films on Aboriginal peoples, and the state's preoccupation with defining what "real" work was for them underscores John Lutz's claim that "different ideas about 'real' work are at the heart of colonialism."[47]

In the case of *No Longer Vanishing*, NFB writers understood from the first inception of the film that IA wanted to convey this message of Indian potential and betterment through economic progress. The latitude the NFB had was more in the realm of format: it debated whether to use a "story" or "survey documentary" approach. No matter what the format, IA understood the need for some nuance as a methodological strategy. A film designed to simply "candy-coat" Indian problems would not be effective because it would feel dishonest to the viewer; it was necessary not only to talk about Indians who had made good as "potential workers and neighbours" but also to hint – but only to hint – at continuing racism.[48] *No Longer Vanishing* was IA's all-time success story: IA recommended it for viewing, wanted it updated, showed it to parliamentarians, and, when suggestions for new films emerged, compared them to *No Longer Vanishing* – often negatively. NA shared IA's positive appraisal.

Short biographies are the medium for the film's argument. Tom Prince, who returns home to the reserve from the army, is featured first, and his story is excerpted into another NFB short, *Return of the Indian* (1955). Tom discovers new hope for economic initiative when he visits a small business just outside the reserve where his brother works, and he also notes positive political change emerging from a democratically elected band council. In keeping with sound accumulation practices, band members are now saving money for the future rather than dispersing it immediately. The film then creates a series of vignettes of other Indians in training, work, or business. Two are female, one a nurse's aide, and one a laboratory assistant, while others include one man in teacher training and far more men doing manual work, often with machinery: farmers operating threshing machines, men in logging, high steel workers, boat builders, and fishers, including one who set up his own successful small business. A few professionals are thrown in for good measure. The gendered division of labour and the male breadwinner ideology so characteristic of IA's labour placement programs are exemplified not only in the female occupations depicted (hairdressing and typing) but also in women's docile background roles.[49] Racism is not entirely ignored, but it can be overcome with willpower and the friendly aid of supportive whites. Some called me "a red Indian and savage," recounts the nurse's aide, but "I made other friends," and "I guess I was sensitive," she adds, as if turning the other cheek was the answer.

While Zoe Druick has stressed the common goals of IA and the NFB, they did have some differences. IA occasionally put its foot down, insisting that scripts be examined by it and then changed. IA was negative about a film on the Alberta Bloods as it feared it would be done as a "cultural documentary" rather than as a film with the desired IA message: Indians are "at [the] crossroads" of modernity.[50] Civil servants also "objected violently" and vociferously to the NFB's *Because They Are Different* (1964), and they punished the NFB by pulling future funding for a proposed "package" of films.[51] IA was sarcastic with the NFB employee who came to preview the film: she was told that if the NFB wanted to show the Indian as a "second class citizen," then it had done a good job.[52] The filmmakers thought they were creating a critique of white attitudes and Indian poverty that would spark debate about discrimination and racial prejudice against a "people whose land [whites] took away,"[53] but the film's unrelenting look at Native misery and its negative assessment of Indian policy damned it in IA's eyes as "atrocious."[54] The film is especially dismissive of IA's educational solutions: residential schools, for instance, had wrenched children from their culture but were resounding failures. "Residential schools are a long way from home and a long way from integration," is narrator Pierre Berton's pithy conclusion. However bleak, the film echoes the government's firmly held belief that reserves are "refuges" for the uncompetitive, that trapping and hunting as a way of life is over, and that finding an educational solution is key to progress. But it lacks that essential can-do approach of *No Longer Vanishing*, the many Horatio Alger Indian stories, and the emphasis on IA policies that *worked*.

IA claimed Indians agreed with its appraisal of the film, and it may have had a point. A few negative letters made their way directly to the NFB from white and Aboriginal viewers who objected to the portrayal of drunk Indians in the first frames and the generally negative views of Aboriginal immiseration. A welfare administrator on the Alderville reserve, Eileen Smoke, believed the film "ridiculed and belittled" Indians; its tenor was an affront to her own sense of "Indian pride." She objected to the film's focus on impoverished, remote northern reserves, which she saw as different from hers: "these Indians were pushed back into no man's land and never had the opportunity for a decent education or any facilities to help themselves. Since our land was stolen from us in the first place the least they can do is get help to Indians in the far north."[55] Even the radical Company of Young Canadians (CYC) did not see the benefit of this exposé: it asked that it be given "minimal" viewing since it "aroused unfavourable comment from Indian people."[56] It was one of the few times the CYC and IA ever agreed.

IA was also apprehensive about NFB films on community development, though the idea was welcomed in the 1960s by the head of the IA welfare division, Walter Rudnicki. Other IA officials asked instead for a new version of their favourite film, *No Longer Vanishing*. By the mid- to late 1960s, however, the NFB was pushing back on IA goals. The board was enthusiastic about community development (CD) films, to be used by community development workers "in the field" as a tool of mobilization. These were to be made not just for IA staff but also for Indian use. The NFB proposal, likely influenced by new ideas of cinema verité, advocated for more documentary realism, including depictions of the inevitable conflicts that arose between CD workers and Indian community members. The NFB proposal for CD films was not devoid of past stereotypes of Indians since the intended realism carried a moral message: self-help was the answer, leading to better wages and living conditions, dignity, and pride. The message that Indians needed to pull up their bootstraps was not new; however, the methods here – community mobilization rather than Indian agent control – did differ somewhat. IA fretted, again, about negative images preventing integration. There should be "little mention of excessive drinking" in the community development film, it urged; there should be a "quiet dignity in the people, despite their poverty."[57] That the experience of poverty might not produce dignity for anyone was not entertained. IA also urged that the problems of Native peoples not be construed as simply racial but, rather, as springing from "economic and social pressures which affect all Canadians." This was not IA's class analysis but, first, its view that progress would come from integration into the economy and, second, its desire not to segregate Indian people into a denigrated racial group.

NORTHERN DEVELOPMENT

IA influence on NFB documentaries did not stop at the tree line. Some of its NFB-developed films encompassed ideas, scenes, and images of the provincial subarctic and occasionally the Far North. IA's ideological emphasis on long-term integration was assumed to work for the northern Dene as well as for the southern Ojibway, and its understanding of positive films (*No Longer Vanishing*) versus negative ones (*Because They Are Different*) also had an influence at Northern Affairs (NA). Interaction between civil servants in NA and the NFB likewise imitated some patterns already established by IA civil servants. NA, much like IA, saw documentary film as a means of placing its policies in a positive light. As NA civil servant Irene Baird reminded her superior, film was one means to justify to the ever-critical "taxpayer the services which he is paying for."[58]

However, the relationship between the NFB and NA also differed, as did the film projects NA favoured. NA civil servants who handled the NFB film file did not seem to be weighed down so completely by the same history of antagonism and defensiveness as did IA, though discussion of certain themes unflattering to the government could elicit self-protective reactions from them, too. The northern group's film agenda reflected not only the state's immense optimism about the North as a new frontier but also a commitment to salvage ethnography, especially of the Inuit, an approach IA tended to avoid with southern Indigenous peoples. The history and heritage of Indians might be celebrated, but primarily in pageants or in costume, recalling the past. For southern Indigenous peoples, integration into contemporary life and work was stressed, while in the North, integration was yet to come or only just beginning. The NFB, for its part, had been committed since its very inception to exploring Canada *as* North; not only was the northern landscape and experience integral to the creation of Canadian identity but the Eskimo way of life was part of what defined that identity. NA and the NFB could thus agree that cinematic preservation of the Eskimo was a goal worth embracing.

Differences between IA and NA film projects must be analyzed within the context of the contemporary political economy. In the South, most Aboriginal lands had already been dealt with through treaties or appropriated for settlement and resource development, while in the Far North, control over the land was less complete and total, sometimes still contested: "original" or "primitive accumulation" was still in process.[59] Indeed, the North was seen by most elements within the state as an untapped "treasure trove" of resources, to be developed, modernized, industrialized.[60] Finding a way to develop those riches was a key goal of successive governments, and some collaboration with local Indigenous populations seemed necessary, or at least *publicly* necessary, as the use of Native land had to be justified as development. Moreover, a broader process of the "totalization" of the state's reach in the North was also under way, although it may have appeared "more benign" than past colonialism since it was accomplished through the extension of the welfare state.[61] Indigenous migrations and relocations into permanent settlements were redefining the spatial and social lives of Indigenous peoples in drastic ways that needed justification and explication, especially in terms of government policies.

Within the Department of Mines and Resources, the Editorial and Information Division usually looked after film, along with a vast range of other duties, from editing scientific reports to promoting National Parks to creating documents on northern Indigenous peoples. With Irene Baird as one key player, this group received input on film production from high-ranking department officials and the NWT Council, which was part of the department apparatus. Ideas also emanated directly from the NFB, which again coveted departmental funds as a welcome infusion of cash to its budget. The ministry was interested in films covering the environment, economic development, sovereignty, and Indigenous peoples; the scientific group also wanted films on the weather stations, scientific progress, and the natural environment of the Arctic, including birds, plant, and animal life. The discovery of minerals, the passage of ships through the Arctic seas, and the creation of new businesses were also desired topics, as they had been since films like *North West Frontier* were made in the 1930s, underscoring how critical economic development issues were to the department's public relations goals. Within this eclectic mix of films, I concentrate here primarily on some films dealing with Indigenous economic development and, in the next section, on ethnographic documentaries on the Inuit.

The exigencies and expense of northern filming meant the NFB relied heavily on NA personnel for advice. Trips were planned to collect a large amount of footage used in multiple films over the next few years. While NA wanted input and some control over filming, it could also become irritated with NFB demands for interpreters, advice, and, especially, transportation as film personnel and equipment were ferried around through government networks.[62] Planning for one such multiyear project, the NFB asked for NA comment on its extensive list of targeted themes: "the Eskimo, the Eskimo child, the Natural Economy of the Arctic, Arctic Weather Stations, Arctic Settlement." The filmmakers provided their set story board for some films. *The Eskimo Child*, for instance, was to focus on a young boy as he learned how to become a "working member of his tribe." He was thoroughly "spoilt" by his parents, a "tyrant" in the family until he matured and became deeply "reverent towards his elders." As this description indicates, filmmakers drew on popular ethnographic writing on the Inuit that was shoe-horned into somewhat predictable scenarios, particularly the primitive/modern dichotomy. They thought it important for this film, for example, to capture a picture of "Stone Age" Inuit childrearing practices since they were so different from "the ones advanced [by whites] today."[63] The Inuit clearly lived in "yesterday."

Films could be directed at both southern and northern viewers, but there were different messages for each group. Those directed at the former were supposed to showcase the state's economic development in the North positively and feature its humane treatment of Indigenous peoples, showing what Canada is doing "to provide new and better schools and educational facilities" for its "primitive peoples." This was also an international project since it would "raise our prestige" in the international community.[64] Concern for Indigenous peoples took on new public relations emphasis after the 1948 UN declaration on human rights and the emergence of human rights discussions within Canada. Cognizant of its expanded role internationally, the Canadian government was aware that it could "not criticize colonial powers elsewhere" if it was open to similar charges at home.[65]

On the other hand, when films were directed at northern Indigenous peoples, especially the Inuit, there was invariably an acculturation agenda involved: films and filmstrips were needed to help the Eskimo understand "Canadian citizenship," "how the government works," and, more generally, "how to cope with the white man's way of life." As one magazine article and a CBC script both explain, filmstrips prepared for the Eskimo could supplement the government's "Book of Wisdom for Eskimo" with "simple and basic" messages on how to keep dogs, what to purchase with family allowances, and so on. The Eskimos required paternalistic "guidance" in everyday life; for example, they "loved flour" and, without coaching, they might take all their cash to the trading post and spend wantonly on nothing but flour or perhaps misuse the baby bonus for tobacco.[66]

Reflecting internal NA debates, some NFB films stressed the need to promote the cultural makeover of the Inuit, while others were more interested in using film to record and preserve aspects of Inuit life.

The question was really one of how and when integration into Anglo-Canadian society would occur since it was assumed modernity would eventually triumph. When the acting deputy minister replied directly to the head of the NFB in 1950 about a list of suggested Arctic film topics, he explained that NA was sympathetic to a proposed documentary showing the Eskimo "in his natural state" rather than the Eskimo who is "on his way to becoming a white man." He merely cautioned that the NFB artists needed to consult northern experts about the environmental conditions, especially when the Eskimo were currently so "hard up," due largely to declining white fox fur prices. It would be "better to have recorded their lives when they were relatively prosperous,"[67] he lamented. It would have made the government look better, he might have said. Political leaders were concerned about negative images of impoverished Indigenous peoples, especially in the wake of Farley Mowat's explosive writing about Inuit starvation in the North. Irene Baird's novel about the civil service and the North, *The Climate of Power*, is on the mark in this regard. Her fictional cabinet minister responsible for the North is told by his adviser that the Canadian public is sensitive to tales of starving Eskimo and that he should shape his comments of concern to Parliament and the press accordingly.[68]

The issue of Canadian sovereignty was important to NA's public relations agenda, but it did not completely dominate NA's film program. An extended memo, "Recent Developments in the Canadian North," laid out how the editorial division saw the Arctic and how it wanted it seen by the public. This memo's distinctively poetic style strongly suggests it was penned by Baird. While she claims she wants to discourage romanticized views of the Arctic, there is a touch of the romantic in this exposition. Baird extols the North as more than space or place: she also sees it as "a habit of mind, a way of life, a frontier," and as a concept that is central to Canadian identity. However, her memo also lays bare government strategic priorities. Canada had been forced by the "bitter facts of international life" to stop ignoring the Arctic: "below the equator there is no nation of significant power. Above the equator is to be found every modern state of major influence in the world." While recognizing the importance of strategic concerns ("the arctic ocean is becoming important to world of aircraft and atomic power"), she warns that Canada should avoid an "unhealthy emphasis" on the military to the detriment of social science and scientific understandings of the North.[69] Those understandings, of course, would come from experts from the South.

This new frontier also holds out the promise of a different kind of relationship with its Indigenous peoples. "Old traditions" of imperialism are neither modern nor humane; the practice of "extermination or forcible subjection of the native inhabitants" is thankfully a thing of the past. "Amalgamation" of the Eskimo into Canadian life is inevitable, but "ruthless coercion is not." Using Cold War rhetoric to buttress her case, Baird contrasts Russian northern development to Canada's, suggesting we must eschew their practice of placing economic development over the needs of the local population and the "liberties of peoples." Bringing Indigenous peoples into the "Canadian community" is not only essential but also entirely possible: the Eskimos may be a short distance from the Stone Age but, due to their remarkable adaptability, they could transition into modernity. Since integration and adaptation are key to the future, films should explore the question of how the state could help northern Natives deal with "encroaching civilization[,] which the war" has brought closer to their doors.[70] Education is central to integration, and film is one means to education. If each northern school has a projector and filmstrips, if there are moving schools for nomadic peoples, then film, the NA suggests, could smooth the transition to modernity through the minds of children.

A new rhetoric of rights talk is also evident in Baird's document. Eskimos and whites need to plan development together, finding common ground as brothers in the community of men. However, paternalism and lingering notions of racial difference lurk below the surface. Not only would whites have to nudge the Eskimo along this path of development, but the Inuit are also often lauded for their special *inherent* virtues and "creative" talents (e.g., their innate artistic talents) based on their own racial evolution.[71] The shift in image from an "exotic people" existing where no whites could, to those "overflowing with natural artistic talent" was, by this time, a common cultural trope depicting the Inuit.[72] Not only is this optimistic message about Indigenous-white collaboration invoked more consciously in NA-sponsored films than in IA-sponsored films, but there is a simultaneous acceptance of hunting and trapping as an existing *and* continuing way of life for northern Indigenous peoples.

State and NFB collaboration are well articulated in *Canada's Awakening North*, a highly successful film considered meritorious enough to win documentary prizes at a number of festivals, including the Venice Film Festival. *Canada's Awakening North* was monitored closely throughout its creation. Initial rushes were screened not only for ministry officials and the department film committee but also for the Territorial Council, whose goal was a film showing both northerners and southerners the administrative "services provided to make the lives of northerners happier" and also showcasing economic, particularly mineral, development. At the same time, Indigenous peoples, who for "generations" had called the North "home," are featured fairly prominently. "Dogged, frugal and stalwart," these "good human people," we are told, had led a difficult, precarious existence, extracting their livelihood from the sea and the land.[73] Because winter footage was hard to secure, cameras were sent to northern residents recommended by NA to the NFB: a known photographer, a mining recorder, a local priest, a magistrate were told what to shoot. In just one example of the southern imagination shaping films about the North, amateurs were instructed on filming trapping and hunting scenes. The latter was pictured in Hollywood terms: shots were needed of a "typical young Indian stalking caribou, showing interest, alert attitude ... [G]roups of Indians bringing caribou back to camp ... [S]ame Indians being greeted by women and children." It was a version of the male breadwinner, Indian style. Some northerners politely but firmly informed the NFB that they could not film caribou being "stalked" because they were not hunted this way.[74] Yet juries awarding prizes to this film knew little about hunting; the majestic vistas, impressive wildlife photography in exotic locations, as well as the positive message about development are likely what garnered this film a prize for its scientific value.

The visual and textual composition of *Canada's Awakening North* was mapped out ahead of time with constant input from staff in the NA Editorial and Information Division. Even the deputy minister and minister eventually read the script and demanded small changes in wording. Since the film's storyline was conveyed in highly value-laden and moralistic language, it is hard to imagine that filmmakers did not understand that their documentary making was a political exercise in ideology. Pre-filming planning for this film decreed that camera shots had to convey that a "new deal" was being created for the North as "problems with the older way of life" (associated more with "the Natives") were addressed. The Native way of life on the land was "rigorous" but too "precarious," and so family life had to be "rehabilitated," reshaped into new ways. Family allowances (FA) were one method of doing this, and they were idealized as a godsend to Indigenous communities. Footage was supposed to show "close up of good-humoured recipients [of FA], general high spirits," and "individual and community purchasing" of appropriate goods.[75] Since the Inuit were only now "emerging from primitive ways," FA had to be managed by state representatives such as the RCMP, who could guide Indigenous peoples away from their practices of "easy come easy go" to carefully planned household purchasing.[76]

While Indigenous women are featured in the early scenes of whale hunting, they are relatively absent in the film, their vital labour in northern communities expunged. The only other female image originally recommended for the shoot was that of a southern white woman "rather indolently buying a fur coat." This was to remind southerners not only that they benefitted from northern resources but also "how little the average Canadian [woman?] thinks of the actual fur trade."[77] Men's resource labour is a key theme in the film, with scenes of hunting, trapping, fishing, prospecting, and mining. Resource extraction was clearly the future of the North, and this economic project would be accomplished through robust, masculine labour, ingenuity, and interracial cooperation. Private initiative and enterprise (though often on the part of individuals rather than corporations) and state regulatory aid were critical to the bustling northern "frontier." The hardy male prospector, for instance, is aided by the government geologist, and trappers of all races – "Indian, Métis, white, Eskimo" – are supported with scientific tagging of animals and trapline allocations rationally dispensed by the government.[78] In one revealing scene, Indigenous trappers sit in an elementary-style classroom and are educated about conservation by the white game warden. The image is an apt illustration of Paul Nadasdy's contention that the management of northern wildlife was key to bringing "Aboriginal peoples under the control of the state."[79] The film repeatedly features the new white order ushering in environmental planning, protecting endangered species, preventing fires, supervising game reserves, and introducing new resource possibilities, including reindeer, to Indigenous communities. It is a vivid visual representation of "colonialism through conservation."[80]

Education, missions, and health care are also featured, though even here male labour is featured: the highly skilled, multi-tasking welfare teacher is a white man, ever-tolerant of his young Indigenous students. Although it is conceded that the influx of whites resulted in devastating new diseases, a young boy suffering from TB is removed from his log shack to a clean, brightly lit hospital where his tray is piled with food and he is waited on by kindly white nurses. As scripted, the hospital scenes also show adult Indigenous patients learning English and arithmetic in order to reinforce the idea that "sickness and ignorance" could be tackled simultaneously through Indigenous self-help.[81] In this and other northern films, the portrayal of a "good" and "bad" Indigenous person, the innovative hard worker versus someone stuck in tradition, is common, just as it is in IA films. The NFB suggested that still photos could be used to close the film, showing how the modern "new order" will be "brisker, brighter." The positive "climax" of the film includes shots of the federal welfare worker making his rounds as well as shots of two promising Native boys being sent away from their hunting communities to Yellowknife to attend school. Indeed, one of the film's goals is to laud the "denominational schools" aiding Native youth.[82] This is the idealized future: resource development, government regulation, education, and, of course, hardy male breadwinners.[83]

Awakening is unusual in the amount of precise attention and advice it garnered from civil servants: the deputy commissioner of the NWT insisted that they insert language to point out that "Indian and Eskimo do not mix"; the script was checked over by IA as well as NA; even Minister Robert Winters got out his red pencil to change a few lines.[84] If this seems like propaganda to our eyes, it may not have so appeared to documentarians at the time. After all, it was hardly the only time NFB filmmakers drew on expert (white) opinion to describe northern Indigenous life. True, advice was not taken in all cases. The Anglican missionary, Reverend Donald Marsh, wanted NA to create a film for the Inuit dealing with the overhunting of the caribou since he believed they did not understand wildlife depletion. The film was to use Inuktitut narration to warn that high-powered rifles had created a crisis in caribou numbers. "Like children," he notes, "the Eskimo were willing and anxious to hear things over and over again," so the film should embrace a repetitious style.[85] NA reminded him that it had already produced a filmstrip on this topic, but it did not counter his paternalistic characterization, the classically colonial metaphor of whites as parents and Indigenous peoples as children, a view that had justified mission work for centuries. Critical historical research on wildlife conservation would also later question Marsh's confident assertions about a "caribou crisis."[86]

SALVAGE ETHNOGRAPHY

While films like *Awakening*, showcasing the emerging developing North were important to NA, there was also a consistent interest in cinematic salvage ethnography as the Inuit were seen as so removed from southern civilization that their more primitive way of life needed to be recorded for posterity.[87] Ethnographic and documentary films are often paired as similar realist projects, presenting common film choices, techniques, and goals.[88] In the mind of NFB filmmakers, the North provided an exciting opportunity to create a document of present and future value that explained the Eskimo in terms of their close relationship to the land. Such films were to "serve as a permanent record of the Eskimo way of life in all seasons of the year and portray his philosophy in relation to his environment."[89] The intent was to present things "through the eyes of the Eskimo, seeing the country as it appears to him ... how they live, work, travel," though ultimately this would also benefit whites by countering their "doubts and fears concerning the Arctic" and indicating how they could "adapt" and live there too.[90] In one case, the NFB abandoned shooting at Chesterfield since it suspected that it was not authentic and primitive enough: the film board was in search of those people "who had hardly changed their lives" at all.[91] The NFB and NA's repeated use of the term "primitive" in these descriptions requires interrogation. The word has multiple meanings. It is associated by some with Hobbesian savagism, but, conversely, it may define peoples "dwelling in nature according to nature, existing free of ... the social complexity" of Euro-Canadian society, even offering a romantic antidote to modernity.[92] The latter approximated NA's usage of "primitive."[93]

Historically, ethnographic photos and film emerged as part of a Western "middle-class need to explore the exotic":[94] amazement, wonder, unease, fascination, a sense of "wondrous difference," and even a romantic yearning for a simpler past were all invoked.[95] Yet the Eskimo was also considered part of Canadian identity. This contradictory embrace of, and differentiation from, the "primitive" North may fit well with the argument that ethnographic film performs the "magic" of becoming one with "the Other."[96] NA was particularly enamoured with *Land of the Long Day* and *Angotee: Story of an Eskimo Boy*, and it urged northern developers to show these films to Distant Early Warning (DEW) Line workers since they offered a "realistic, authentic" picture of Inuit hunting and trapping. The intent was to create "sympathetic" white attitudes towards the Inuit, while, at the same time, discouraging white contact with the Eskimo, who needed to be "insulated" (i.e., paternalistically protected) from potentially damaging modern social relations.[97]

Angotee was made with film segments shot at Chesterfield Bay by Doug Wilkinson, who had been working for the NFB since 1945, primarily on northern projects. Wilkinson's accompanying dialogue traces Angotee's life from birth to his establishment of his own independent household, with different actors playing the boy as he ages. To NA personnel like Baird, the film may have conveyed a positive message about the Inuit as an adaptable people interacting with a difficult environment in ways whites could hardly imagine. The appeal of the film is also likely due to the fact that it used the "typicality" format popular with the NFB: a compelling narrative focused on one person and her or his household, creating a storyline that humanizes and personalizes Inuit culture. It also briskly covers many aspects of Eskimo life – childbirth practices, the igloo, walrus hunting, and family relations, to name a few – in a way that emphasizes the centrality of hunting culture, precisely the image of Inuit life in much travel, ethnographic, and visual literature. To our eyes, the film may, however, convey the same "romantic preservationalism" found in Flaherty's *Nanook*.[98]

While film viewers might interpret Inuit culture as primitive, especially because of long scenes of raw meat eating, *Angotee* stresses the reassuring rationality behind Inuit social organization: keeping to one's appropriate gender, age, and family placement all mattered because of the need to survive in an inhospitable climate. There is a functional practicality to the ages and stages of Angotee's education as boy, young hunter, and father. *Angotee*, as a form of family exposition, personalizes Foucault's "deployment of alliance": the regulatory principles surrounding marriage, kinship, and family.[99] As a result of the harsh, primordial hunting economy, the family is organized around patriarchal principles. Women are important in their reproductive roles but largely lacking any agency over their own lives, and they are clearly valued less than men. Angotee's mother gives birth in an igloo quite easily, a common image of primitive women's physical closeness to nature, and his sisters are thrilled that a highly esteemed future hunter has joined the family. His grandma believes in raising him traditionally, but his mother has integrated some modern ways into the igloo, in the form of food – pablum – added to seal and caribou. In what was meant to be a humorous reversal of modernity, Angotee's father wants to eat the pablum too since he never had any as a child.

From childhood, Angotee's education is centred on survival skills: making his own small igloo, pulling the dog sleds, and aiding his father with seal hunting. Since birth, he has had a wife picked out for him by his parents. Her childhood involves learning the "tasks of women," scraping, chewing, and preparing skins and cooking. Angotee's mother dies when he is ten, and, though a "sorrowful" event, we are told the Eskimo view death through a fatalistic lens, as part of the inevitability of a harsh life: "The land is reborn only to die. No one fears death." At eighteen, Angotee marries his assigned wife in front of a priest, "and so the girl linked to him since birth is now one with destiny." However traditional the members of the Eskimo family are, they are respectably Christianized. The film ends two years later, with Angotee proudly building his own igloo and displaying his own infant son. There is a timelessness to Angotee's life, firmly situated in a premodern world: "His life will depend on his abilities as a hunter ... Little by little, he has learned his trade and together with his family he will live and multiply. They face a hard life together with good humour and boundless confidence in themselves and their land."[100]

The fatalism and optimism of the Eskimo are thus simultaneously captured in the narration. While the film adopts a highly descriptive narrative style, avoiding moralistic commentary on cultural threats and assimilation, it does perpetuate an image of the primitive family as necessarily strictly ordered, rational, and completely happy in an unsophisticated, simple way. No longer is the Inuit family portrayed as an institution of patriarchal excess, with hunter men dominating docile women, as in some earlier popular tracts; instead, a more subtle patriarchy, rationalized with a discourse of community survival, is evoked. Portraying this well-ordered functional family may have been a strategy of reassurance for, and connection to, southern viewers. By making the Inuit family similar to the white one, with a male breadwinner hunter and female homemaker child raiser, the filmmaker establishes a presumed connection across lines of culture and race.

Land of the Long Day, a film about well-known Baffin Inuit Joseph Idlout and his family, comes even more highly recommended as an educational tool about the Inuit. The film is written and directed by Doug Wilkinson and narrated by prominent Canadian actor John Drainie, though viewers are reassured of the complete authenticity of the narration: it was "told as Idlout would have told it in his native language." Some discerning Canadian film connoisseurs were not so enthusiastic, objecting to this "infantile" attempt to "talk like an Eskimo" and comparing the film unfavourably to the true "masterpiece," *Nanook of the North*.[101] Yet, internationally, the film was a large success: European countries like Denmark and Sweden wanted translated copies, it made its way into some US TV stations, American and British magazines did features on its release, and it won more than one international film award, including an honourable mention for

Joseph Idlout, the main actor in *Land of the Long Day,* looks for seals sleeping on the sea ice. | LAC, NFB Still Photography Division, R 1196–14–7-E, r002117

the Robert Flaherty documentary award. The exotic Eskimo was a truly appealing and fascinating Canadian cultural export.[102]

In 1951, Wilkinson, his wife, and cameraman Jean Roy spent fifteen months in Idlout's camp shooting film. Wilkinson then returned in 1953 to live as Idlout's son so that he could learn how to "live like an Eskimo," an experience he recounts in his memoir, *Land of the Long Day*.[103] NA gave high praise to the film as it trusted Wilkinson's insider knowledge, and, compared to many other whites, he did have language skills and sojourning experience that others did not. Wilkinson used the story of Idlout's family, part of a group of the most "northerly" Tununermiut Inuit on Baffin Island, to detail daily life in the summer months of the long day, when the sun never set. The film stresses that everyone in the family has a valuable gender- and age-specific job, but the main focus is on men hunting. In Wilkinson's book, a more extensive picture of the roles played by the entire family is outlined, though it is still clear that familial organization is patriarchal. In the film, Idlout is the undisputed head of this extended family. He makes the key decisions and takes immense pride in being the one to lead and "feed his family."[104]

Wilkinson claimed that one reason the NFB wanted the film made was that no film about Eskimo life in the Arctic had really replaced *Nanook*. There are similarities in style between *Land of the Long Day* and Flaherty's *Nanook*, perhaps one reason the former was so popular: *Nanook* had become a powerful template for future films. As with *Nanook*, so with *Land of the Long Day*: the intent was to capture the day-to-day reality of Inuit life without appearing to intrude as an outsider. The film was compelling precisely because it created the cinematic "artifice" of life-as-lived through extensive film shooting and careful editing down to a few key stories. Like *Nanook*, it emphasizes the male hunt and the theme of man versus nature, with Idlout both living with and triumphing over the latter. While scenes were undoubtedly staged, as they were for Flaherty, the film's integration of multiple side stories, from how dog harnesses work to searching for the eggs of nesting murres, makes it a visually detailed, rich description of food procurement presented in a manner that stresses the rational, utilitarian nature of Eskimo culture. Like Flaherty, Wilkinson lived with his Inuit hosts, and he wanted to present them in a humane, sympathetic manner. He did not overly romanticize them, nor was he a cultural relativist who believed all cultures were equally sophisticated. As his book makes clear, he believed that Western culture was more sophisticated than Inuit culture, both intellectually and culturally, and, as a government employee, he was later quite committed to a "modernization" agenda.[105] However, the film is an attempt to make the Inuit likeable, understandable, even heroes of their daily lives, which are so diametrically, exotically different from those of southern whites. It is meant to capture cultural difference in a way that humanizes the other, and to make it clear that whites should have a measure of humility in the face their own inability to survive in this cold climate.

One reason NA may have liked and promoted the film is the simple fact of its visual splendour: we should not forget that sensually and visually mesmerizing "spectacle," both human and landscape, especially concerning sights alien to our own surroundings, have long been part of the appeal of ethnographic documentary.[106] In contrast to some earlier NFB films, *Land of the Long Day* was shot in colour and includes panoramic scenes of icebergs, the sea, and animals – scenes that Baird would later extol in her fiction as sublime. It also has a matter-of-fact rather than a hand-wringing tenor. While *Land of the Long Day* does present a salvage perspective on a hunting-trapping culture that simply cannot last forever, it is far less preachy about the inevitable progress towards civilization, coupled with fears of Eskimo difficulty with that transition, than are some other NFB films.

While these films stand out as NA favourites, there were many other NFB films depicting Eskimo daily life circulating in the postwar period. The NFB began collecting Arctic material, often of the salvage variety, when it was founded, and this footage was sometimes reused in multiple films. As part of the Peoples of Canada series, Laura Boulton, neither a filmmaker nor an anthropologist, was sent North with cinematographer Grant McLean in 1941 to collect material from the "islands north of Hudson Bay, Baffin, Chesterfield and Fort Churchill."[107] Their film footage was used to make *Arctic Hunters* and *Eskimo Summer*, the latter produced with the ethnographic advice of Robert Flaherty. *Eskimo Summer* captures a range of Eskimo practices relating to hunting culture and features protagonists who seem relatively unaware of the filming process – the classic appeal of much ethnographic film. It appears to follow Flaherty's romanticized rendition of the "majestic" nature of primitive life as soon-to-be-history, and the commentary stresses the Inuit's oneness with nature: the Eskimo "like the animals, survive by following the seasons."[108] Eskimo survival is also shaped by primitive and strange superstition (pregnant women are not allowed in "sacred spaces") and by the bifurcation of gender- and age-related roles geared towards hunting survival. Yet Boulton's particular take on primitivism was not necessarily replicated in all NFB films. Doug Wilkinson's *How to Make an Igloo*, for instance, is quite different in that it offers a far more straightforward demonstration of how snow is chosen, located, cut, and placed, emphasizing the "ingenious" nature of Eskimo design and environmental adaptability.[109]

As late as the 1960s and early 1970s, salvage-type filming was alive and well. The Netsilik Eskimo series, produced for the Education Development Center of Massachusetts with grants from the National Science Foundation and the Ford Foundation, was shown in classrooms around North America and was advertised by the NFB.[110] Directed and produced by Quentin Brown, with academic direction by Canadian anthropologist Asen Balikci, the series charts the traditional life of the Netsilik in different seasonal hunting camps before they had modern technology such as rifles. Even though the Netsilik had been relatively isolated from white contact, in intentional salvage mode, the film turns the clock even further backward in its mis-en-scène: those who were supposedly "vanishing" from view could thus "reappear" before the camera lens as historical artefacts.[111] Postcolonial scholars would later critique this kind of ethnographic film as "nostalgic reconstructions" of the "unspoilt, authentic" premodern humanity of Indigenous peoples. To the most critical, they were forms of racial "taxidermy."[112]

The public furor that led to the banning of the series in the United States was shaped by a very different set of concerns. For conservatives, the Inuit were presented *too tolerantly*: the films represented an excess of liberal cultural relativism. Yet Balikci constructs the film storylines in tune with his own image of white southern familial norms as a deliberate attempt to make the films relevant to North American school-age child viewers, thus enhancing their cultural tolerance. Inuit subjects and practices were selected for filming if they could be connected to the lives of "American school children ... How would they [American children] compare Itimangnerk fishing and bringing his catch to his family for their food? Clearly ... the Inuit family head was the provider." Rather astoundingly – since we associate this time period with the resilience of patriarchy – Balikci muses that this ethnographic film might even "be of help in the status rehabilitation of the father figure in America."[113]

TRANSITION FILMS

In the wake of subsistence crises in the North, the movement of Indigenous peoples to settlements, and the provision of new services, the government needed to explain its policies as progressive, modern, and rational – always in the best interests of the Inuit. For NA, the inevitable incursion of whites and resource development meant that Inuit would eventually have to transition to a wage economy. In *People of the Rock*, a film made with NA aid, economic development, labour, and the clash of cultures are intertwined themes in a narrative that traces the transition from a hunting-trapping to a wage economy. Produced by NFB's Nick Bala, and written by freelance writer Monroe Scott (who also wrote for the *RCMP* series), this film uses both an Inuit and a white narrator to describe this dramatic shift from nomadic caribou hunting and "fighting polar bears" to working in a deep-shaft mine: the original title, *Modern Eskimo*, says it all.[114]

The story revolves around Kusserktok, who came to the mining camp looking for work, with his "wife, children, dogs following" him, all in a state of severe hunger. Attention is focused on the lifestyle shift for Eskimo men who can now benefit from earning "miners pay" – a white wage. Although they were not acquainted with "routine, shift work, [and] safety" concerns (not safety concerns with regard to mining any-way), they nonetheless "caught on quickly." The mine has created other (male) jobs as well, such as "air strip maintenance." Kusserktok is shown learning "the magic of [operating] the big machine." The audience is told that the Inuit are choosing their new lives – "we hunt, fish or mine, it is our choice," the Eskimo narrator says – despite the evidence already offered that lack of country food made for little choice. The Inuit men are also encouraged to be enterprising and individualistic. They are given prospecting lessons so they, too, can stake claims, presumably becoming itinerant prospectors rather than the workers – a rather far-fetched idea but one rationalized with reference to the natural "no-madic" tendencies of the Eskimo.[115]

Crafted scenes and careful dialogue suggest that working for wages does not destroy all traditional practices. A whale is sighted and the men all immediately leave work "without permission" to follow the hunt. Clearly, nomadic hunters have not yet imbibed the discipline of the time clock, but this is presented without condemnation: they will learn "to ask permission" soon enough, adds the white narrator light-heartedly. After their mining work is done, the Inuit men celebrate with a drum dance and each hunter tells his own past story with a song, but Kusserktok emphasizes that wage work is preferable to starvation: "I am happy to be here. I live in one place, and support my family. I still teach my boy to be a hunter. It is a good life."[116] The stylistic format of creating parallel narrations, one white and one Eskimo, is perhaps intended to give a voice to the Inuit, but it problematically juxtaposes two narration styles, one with short, simple sentences (Inuit) and one with more complex and expository sentences (white): the primitive and modern are thus reinforced. Ironically, it reflects the actual "racial segregation" apparent in the town and extraction process.[117] Budget files also suggest that Inuit real life actors in such films were not paid on the same scale as whites might have been.[118] The final message is one of cross-cultural collaboration, adaption, and transition. Even Farley Mowat, the NFB file indicates, applauded the Rankin effort to train and employ Inuit men on equal terms with white men.[119] In the past, the film concludes, whites had to "learn from the Eskimo how live in the North. Now we teach them how to hunt for minerals."[120] The denouement of the mine story, of course, was quite different. By 1962, the Rankin Inlet mine was closed, resulting in unemployment and "welfare dependency," precisely because many had abandoned hunting for wages.[121]

NFB filmmakers were cognizant that adaptation and transition were contentious issues. In order to create a sense of realism, it was politic to include some debate about change in the North. *Our Northern Citizen*, one segment of an NFB Perspective series produced initially for television to explore "the key factors in Canada's expanding northern development,"[122] opens with the contemporary debate about the relocation of Aklavik across the Mackenzie River. Local Aklavik men were interviewed, and while they expressed divergent views these did not fall entirely along racial lines of difference. Ultimately, white scientific experts discussing water, permafrost, building materials, and so on, had the upper discursive hand. They had facts on their side and clearly relocation was a sound scientific proposition. In both *People of the Rock* and *Our Northern Citizen*, Indigeneity and whiteness are positioned and constructed, with whiteness equated with expertise, technology, science, and governance. The very notion of "modernity," it seems, manufactured its opposite: "primitiveness."[123]

Switching to Frobisher Bay, and drawing on the research and writing of Doug Wilkinson, *Our Northern Citizen* then explores the choice Inuit men now had: either to keep to the old ways of hunting and trapping or to adapt to white man's ways of wage labour. That areas of the North had long had a mixed economy consisting of both is not stressed.[124] Moreover, the disassociation of the Inuit from modern wage labour is made abundantly clear in the film's opening scene. An Eskimo hunter is shown driving a ten-ton truck, and the narrator tells us that this is evidence of very "strange" changes in the North. In colonial imagery, as Nelson Graburn notes, reverse exoticism is often used, showing the incongruity of primitive men engaged in modern pursuits. One wonders if Homi Bhabha's claim that the colonized man could *act* but never actually *be* white was encapsulated in this and similar film shots. Nonetheless, due to Eskimo men's "adaptability, innate honesty, good humour, tolerance and acceptance of strange customs" (as they are described with almost faultless simplicity), there is hope for a transition. Eskimo men are shown performing jobs such as wood working, machine work, and service labour, though, in order to fully transition to white labour, they will need a "personality" makeover so that they can "think like we do." To rise higher in the occupational hierarchy, they would have to learn English and to overcome the limitations inherent in their culture since the Eskimo only contemplated the present, never planned for the future, and had "no system of leaders, chiefs, witch doctors or organized religion."[125]

One white journalist interviews a small group of Inuit men, asking if they would choose hunting or wage labour. His focus group, however, surprises him: they all reply, "Hunting." Not to worry: the film viewer is reassured that these men are just "nostalgic" for the past and that "subconsciously" they actually *do* want "regular" work. The final scenes show the NWT experiment with reindeer herding (footage also used in *Canada's Awakening North*), an idea imported by the federal government from Lapland in order to provide regular, "routine" employment for previously nomadic men. The NFB created a short newsreel about the reindeer project that was sold to MGM, Fox, Paramount, and Warner

Brothers and was shown in American, Canadian, and South American cinemas. The film's appeal is undoubtedly due to the incongruity of seeing the igloo-building Eskimo becoming a veritable "cowboy." Publicity called it a genuine "stampede" experience though with "Eskimo cowhands": "they may lack the regular bronco, britches and ten-gallon hat, but these Eskimo cowpokes can corral, notch and dip their antlered charges with all the speed and skill of their prairie counterparts."[126] In the wake of this small success, the NFB reminded its government funders that it had conveyed an important message to a wide public audience: smart state planning and training had created "famine insurance" for the Eskimo," helping them to adjust to stable, economically secure jobs.[127] We are left with the impression that it is an experiment, but one that the state is managing well, with the best interests of Indigenous peoples in mind.

Despite this positive message, *Our Northern Citizen* did not meet the exacting standards of influential NA official R.A.J. Phillips, who expressed his discontent to the deputy minister. After picking apart the film, his message was clear: the NFB should "never release" a film on the North without a vetting from departmental experts who, of course, would not "censor" it but simply "correct mistakes" and remove "unfortunate phrases," one of which was Doug Wilkinson's off-hand remark: "the Eskimo is an inexpensive supply of local labour." The North, bureaucrats in Ottawa felt, was such a complex place, its lands and peoples so varied, that it could not be understood by well-meaning filmmakers – only by themselves.[128]

Yet, to my eyes, there is something else that is striking about both these transition films: the erasure of women as workers. In *Our Northern Citizen*, women are almost completely invisible, except to take out the garbage or visit the trading post to sell handicrafts. Ironically, women do better in salvage films. These transition films thus offer the viewing public overlapping layers of paternalism. On the one hand, Indigenous men are unable to cope without white expertise or support, making some kind of wardship necessary. Yet Inuit men are at least *potential* "northern citizens." Masculinity is naturalized as intrinsic to citizenship, related to honest working-class labour. Women are subject to another layer of paternalism: not only is their labour erased but they are marginal to the

Moses Idlout and Rebecca Idlout soaking kamiks. Inuit women were sometimes more visible in salvage films than in transition films. | LAC, NFB Still Photography Division, R 1196–14–7-E, PA-189094

modern future. This is not akin to nineteenth-century colonial discourses in which the sexually "wild" Indigenous woman and irresponsible Indigenous family had to be tamed and remade in the image of Western bourgeois respectability. However, the equation of work and politics with men's domain nonetheless reproduced a form of masculine paternalism. Just as the Indian Act still defined an Indian patriarchal family, so the "culture-work" of film reproduced a new, double version of masculine colonial governance. Many of the same people directed, wrote, and produced these NFB films, suggesting that hegemonic ideas about the family (usually mirroring the assumed white middle-class norm) were subtly reproduced over time. These colonial ideals, however, were not without challenge, as the next section shows.

SHIFTING WINDS

Between 1964 and 1974, filmmaking about the Indigenous North shifted in approach and tenor. Consider two contrasting films dealing with Indigenous themes. *The Annanacks*, released in 1964 and co-produced with Crawley Films, is concerned with the modernization of the Nuna-tsiavut Inuit: the whites provide essential knowledge that, coupled with Indigenous resources, creates a more prosperous way of life and modern economy. Publicity for the film stressed this positive theme of adaptation, with white experts flying North to "save" the Inuit of George River from disaster.[129] The film opens with an old man, George Annanack, telling a family story in which one of his aging female ancestors is eaten so that the starving family can survive, a reminder that Inuit are not far removed from a primitive past of scarcity and want. Some are starving again, due to lack of game, so the men in the community, with women following, meet with government officials to discuss economic solutions. Two schemes are explored: the government experts explain that the Inuit can harvest their nearby trees to trade for seal meat and they might also sell Arctic char to the southern market. Self-help is important: the Inuit are told that "success rested on them."

The Inuit are initially distrustful of the whites and their alien ways – such as "living in one place" – however, white norms are presented as the way of the world. The Inuit are told that "people all over the world live like [whites do]," a rather dubious anthropological claim. Not only is expert economic advice useful but it also serves to enhance Inuit cultural preservation. Whites are clearly capable of cultural sensitivity, even when they are providing superior technical knowledge. The members of this Inuit community adapt well not only economically but also politically. Based on the tutelage of government advisors, they hold modern, democratic elections for the first time, and their new president, ironically, is George Annanack, the descendant of the people who ate their mother. Because of this terrible decision, however, the next generation is allowed to prosper, and with the economic changes in the community, they won't have to eat people again.

By the late 1960s and early 1970s, films about the Inuit moved away from the paternalism and celebration of white experts apparent in *The Annandacks*, even in some of the salvage ethnography films.[130] A dramatic contrast to *The Annandacks* was *Labrador North* (1973), made by Roger Hart within the NFB's Challenge for Change (CFC) program. This film explores the impact of the government's relocation of the

Nunatsiavut Inuit as well as community economic development and political representation. In contrast to earlier films on northern Indigenous peoples, *Labrador North* exposes the failure of institutions such as schools, and even the state, to serve Indigenous needs. While earlier films extol training and education as the economic answer in the North, this one does not. Originally imagined as a "visual record" of the Newfoundland Royal Commission on Labrador, chaired by Donald Snowden, the film shifted course when one commissioner objected to the filming. Using the footage already taken on lifestyle, social issues, and community development, Hart created a film that focuses far more on community, politics, and the state.

Families who were pressed to move south to Hopedale from more northern areas are interviewed, revealing their unhappiness, confusion, and anger. There is a strong sense of betrayal and dislocation: "We were proud of our land, we did not want to move from our land. We were separated from our relatives ... that is why we are poor here. It is like nothing; it is a void here." One displaced man admits that they are hungry for caribou meat; he claims that their old homeland still has food sources to be tapped but now people are becoming hungry for "foreign food" they cannot afford. The move has upset their diet, way of living, and the relations between parents and children as the former want to teach the latter how to hunt, but children are required by law to go to school.

Labrador North deals at length with community development issues. A white facilitator from Memorial University's Department of Extension, Ian Strachan, arrives to help the local population set up a fish plant as a cooperative, and he also encourages the formation of a local council that can interact with all levels of government. Strachan does not label Indigenous and other local inhabitants as primitive but, rather, argues that they have been isolated, without access to knowledge, and that knowledge is power. The shift to wage work was difficult, he recounts, but he advocates for a new collective "pride" in their fish plant, along with new hygienic measures that benefit the whole community. His role as white expert helping Indigenous peoples bears some similarity to that of the government experts in *The Annandacks*. Paternalism remains apparent in his comment that the locals were lacking in "responsibility" (surely the responsibilities associated with hunting have to be considered!). Yet his emphasis on community development and self-determination sets him apart. He believes people will "help themselves" by using their council to chart their own future and to lobby politicians. When the politicians do arrive on the scene, they are quite unappealing (one is decidedly bombastic and unhelpful). Finally, the film shows women who are producing their own newspaper for the Labrador coast, a more active role than women assume in many films.

Labrador North offers no cheery prognosis for the community's problems. Education, for example, is an area of conflict: parents "want [their children] to learn hunting," yet the white teacher feels they should concentrate on schoolwork in order to "make their future." Moreover, the principal understands the children's alienation from school since the books and curriculum are irrelevant to their experiences: our texts talk about "washing hands in a sink. There are no sinks in houses here."[131] These unsolved problems, as well as the depiction of the government's lack of knowledge about Inuit and local cultures, and the anguished dislocation of those who have been moved away from their traditional homes, makes this film different from earlier NFB efforts.

Newfoundland bureaucrats hated *Labrador North* about as much IA hated *Because They Are Different*. The "challenge" part of Challenge for Change hit its mark, though Hart later told an interviewer that he would have altered the film if he had anticipated such a negative reaction as he wanted it to have a full "hearing." I thought it was a relatively "tame" film he claimed, without much "editorializing."[132] Newfoundland civil servants found it offensive, not tame. The NFB had to deal with their intense anger after a showing, in part because their ire was raised at the mere sight of the community development worker Strachan. A beleaguered NFB staffer reported that thirteen senior provincial officials were "unilaterally hostile, picky, critical, cranky, incensed and bitchy in varying degrees." The fourteenth member of the group, he continued, "was a crippled old Eskimo from Nain who watched with rapt attention and was wheeled away without a world ... [A]n hour and twenty minutes later, they were still dismissing the film as narrow, one-sided, biased, predictable, unfair, distorted and a waste of taxpayers' money."[133]

The CFC program that sponsored *Labrador North* marked a shift in the political context at the NFB.[134] Set up in 1967 at the instigation of the Cabinet Secretariat and the NFB, the program was intended to stimulate social change through media work. The original focus on poverty expanded to take in Indian rights, housing, race issues, women's equality, community development, and other concerns that became more highly profiled in the wake of student, youth, and New Left activism. One of the goals was to put cameras and film planning in the hands of the citizen, not the expert; as a result, the CFC produced both activist filmmakers and active citizens. Over fourteen years, over a hundred films and videos were made, and while some, like *Labrador North*, were made by sympathetic white directors, others were created by Indigenous cultural producers. The Indian Film Crew, a collaboration of the Company of Young Canadians and the NFB, was one outcome of this program.

The CFC program was not well received by all the NA and IA civil servants who were used to dealing with the NFB. When one proposal for a film on poverty and social change came across Irene Baird's desk, her response indicated more than a little impatience: she gently lectured the NFB on its "maturity and judgment" in dealing with issues best left to the experienced policy experts and insisted that the "accent should be less on poverty and more on change."[135] IA was far more shocked and unhappy to find that it had no control over CFC films. Used to a system in which they sponsored films, bureaucrats insisted that they could "screen, edit, revise or pull from public distribution" films they did not like, such as the controversial *You Are on Indian Land*. CFC officials told them unequivocally that they could not.[136]

NA did fund some new projects initiated by the Inuit, offering an opportunity for Indigenous filmmakers to challenge and to amend the NFB message, so long entangled in paternalistic ways of seeing. In 1974, the NFB and the Department of Indian and Northern Affairs set up a filmmaking workshop for local youth in Frobisher Bay (Iqaluit), overseen by a young NFB employee, Peter Raymont, who became one of Canada's internationally renowned documentary filmmakers. The results were life changing for Raymont, whose deep concern for the

Indigenous North was carried into his later collaborative projects: award-winning, powerful documentaries that dealt with culture change, political mobilization, education, and Inuit history, to name a few areas. The Inuit who participated were able to use the camera for their own "culture-work" projects. A twenty-five-year-old Inuk man, Mosha Michael, shot, edited, and provided music for *Natsik Hunting* – a short film that lacked any commentary. Three years later, the NFB released *Asivaqtiin* (The Hunters), a lengthened version in which Moshe tells us that he was a "member," or inmate, at Ikayuktowvick in Frobisher Bay but was allowed, as part of a rehabilitation program, to accompany family members on a hunting trip "down the Bay." There is no white voice-of-god narration for his film, no John Drainie imitation of an Inuit voice: Michael Moshe is the director, writer, musician, and voice-over.

. Thematically, the film bears some similarity to earlier salvage films. There is a heavy emphasis on hunting scenes, with the same familial, gendered division of labour portrayed in Wilkinson's films. However, there is another message conveyed, in part through the intergenerational exchange of knowledge as more experienced Inuit demonstrate their hunting skills to younger people, in part through the notion of the hunt *as rehabilitation*. In order to become whole again, the Inuit need to preserve cultural ties and traditions rather than simply to transition into the (superior) wage economy. Renewed dignity depends not just on idealizing "culture" but also on the living out of collective values "rooted in both the silent and material social relations of daily life."[137]

CFC was only one element of a new Indigenous media that emerged in the 1970s as a "self-conscious engagement" with anti-colonial politics: self-determination was not just a geographical and political movement but also a cultural one.[138] Inuit filmmakers wanted to articulate an identity that was not subsumed under a Canadian version of "the Eskimo" so long promoted by the NFB and to glance back, critically, at the Canadian state. It was not just what was said but who said it that mattered as Inuit cultural producers took control of the camera. As the producer of Moshe's film, Raymont, too, represented a generational, political shift and was one of a number of white allies who were contemplating new anti-colonial perspectives. His later documentary, *Between Two Worlds*, profiles the very same Idlout first featured in Wilkinson's *Land of the Long Day*, years after Idlout had moved to a permanent settlement. Idlout's unhappy adjustment was difficult to watch, tragic in its final outcome: in keeping with a more engaged, activist style, the film raises critical questions about the human costs of colonial legacies in the Canadian North.

CONCLUSION

The emergence of new Inuit media and documentaries critical of the Canadian state's role in the North is another story, beyond the scope of this chapter. To see this shift in the 1970s as a complete break with manufactured documentary images of the 1940s and 1950s, however, oversimplifies. All documentary makes an argument, takes a stance, creates an actuality, offers either subtle or more forceful ideological claims to truth. Ending with CFC does underscore the changing economic, social, and political context shaping NFB documentaries in the postwar period. As filmmaking was severed directly from departmental budgets and agendas, the NFB had more freedom to create oppositional pieces. The political movements of resistance that arose in the long 1960s nurtured a new cadre of filmmakers, both Indigenous and white, reared on ideas of documentary activism, whose impact on film was felt for decades to come.

The earlier films of the 1940s through the 1960s reflected the political economy of Indigenous-settler relations and the prevailing dominant ideological constructions of Indigeneity. On the one hand, IA casts a long ideological shadow over NFB work. Although IA did not directly control the message about the northern Inuit, it did create, promote, and fund important filmstrips and films about Indigenous peoples that became classics and were promoted, exported, and watched again and again. IA's emphatic claim to expertise on Indigenous history, culture, and contemporary needs meant that its expertise was given serious consideration, and its budgetary support might make the difference between a film's being made or shelved. While NFB filmmakers and government bureaucrats did sometimes disagree, they often worked collaboratively, creating documentaries imbued with IA's policy goals. *No Longer Vanishing*, with its upbeat message of integration, Indians overcoming barriers to economic success, and male breadwinner families, was given IA's highest endorsement; *Because They Are Different*, with its jarring portrayal of poverty and failing state policies, was its bête noir. Some IA staff sincerely wanted to correct discriminatory stereotypes, but, in the process, they colluded in masking problems of poverty and social dislocation that did not accord with their definitions of Indian progress.

Northern films made with the collaboration of the department responsible for the North, from the Department of Mines and Resources through to the Department of Indian and Northern Development, shared some of the same goals. Again, the political and economic context was critical to filmmaking decisions. In the South, the process of dispossession and "primitive accumulation" was largely accomplished. This was not entirely true in the subarctic and Far North, so the state had to create a message about northern development that encompassed Indigenous peoples rather differently. The vast lands of the North, which Dene and Inuit knew better than many white newcomers, had yet to be vanquished. NFB films made a strong case for sovereign national control and resource development in this last Canadian frontier, with an unbridled optimism about interracial cooperation between Indigenous and white. Northern films argued that Indigenous labour and know-how would be integrated into economic development, but there was also some concession to hunting and trapping as a viable – not a bygone – way of life for Indigenous peoples. However, in both southern and northern contexts, integration was always the keyword for progress, and progress meant adapting to a wage economy, a familial model of male breadwinning, and settlement living. Indians and Eskimos would find their way in this state project through expert white guidance, training, and education – all for their own good.

From Grierson's time onwards, NFB documentary was intended as a civics lesson in tolerance and understanding, and many NA civil servants believed cultural acceptance would be aided by a better understanding of the Inuit way of life on the land. NA-NFB filmmaking collaborations thus included a salvage anthropology mentalité. While IA did not extol the "landscape where the spirits dwell," NA memos did, even if this was something of a "noble Native" romanticization. Many of NA's favoured films, like *Land of the Long Day*, celebrate the adaptable, land-based existence of the Inuit, though it assumes that their way of life also has to be recorded for posterity since it would eventually be swept away by technological modernity. There is no denying the contemporary appeal of such films. The cinematic magnificence of northern scenes and the strangeness of Inuit ways to Western eyes made them internationally popular. They also performed the cultural work of binding the image of the Eskimo with that of Canada, a coupling that functions well for the state since the latter is presented so profoundly benignly. Ironically, the iconography of the "Great White North" as northern frontier is constructed, in part, on images of Indigenous faces.[139] Indeed, to our eyes, trained to see colonial scripts and the appropriation of Indigenous identity, this merger of Indigenous with Canadian identity is artifice, and even rather cynical artifice at that.

NA wanted white Canadians to see *No Longer Vanishing* and *Angotee* in part because it believed that Inuit culture offered lessons and inspiration. Cultural relativism and a new postwar language of human rights also frames this filmmaking. *Angotee*, like Balikci's Netsilik series, might play on notions of the exotic other, but the films also try to show human connections between white and Indigenous cultures through the normality of supposedly universally shared familial relations and gender roles. Films were also meant to suggest that state modernization efforts need not totally destroy Indigenous culture: the stronger, "better" aspects of Inuit life, for instance, would be preserved. If living off the land is idealized in salvage films, however, it is also denoted as primitive as opposed to modern: it means living close to nature, free of cultural and social complexity, in groups that lack political sophistication.[140] Eskimo primitivism simply needs an infusion of education, leadership, expertise, and knowledge, an assumption that easily slides into paternalistic ways of seeing the Indigenous other. It is this notion of superior guidance that was increasingly challenged by more concerted forces of Indigenous resistance after the 1970s. This social shift coincided with alterations in NFB tactics and goals, symbolized by CFC and films like *Labrador North*. Yet the fact that new Inuit filmmaking after the 1970s might concentrate on exactly the same themes as salvage ethnography – the cultural importance of the (male) seal hunt, the dog sled, and igloo – supports the argument that ethnographic films are not merely "ethnofictions": what matters is the political process, the ends for which they are used, and "who produces which fictions about whom, and for whom."[141]

CHAPTER FIVE

Irene Baird's Northern Journeys

Asked to describe her northern travel in a CBC radio interview, author Irene Baird told the story of her encounter with a "blow," or snowstorm, while she was visiting Frobisher Bay to write a story for the federal government about local Christmas celebrations. In her educated, precise English accent, she recalled her mounting fear as she tried to make her way from the local school to her billet, blinded by thick, swirling snow. She saw a shadow and followed it until she landed at her door, relieved, but more highly attuned to the potential ferocity of the northern environment. Since she never knew who or what the shadow was, she used the incident to relay a sense of mystical awe about the North and the Inuit legend of the Blow Spirit.[1] For Baird, the story encapsulated much that inspired and fascinated her about the North: a bleak, sublime beauty, an appropriate fear of the northern elements, and a sense that this Inuit land held a certain mystery for southern visitors.

Baird's northern writing is not what she became known for in Canadian literary circles, yet her short stories, poetry, travel narratives, and novel dealing with the North probably tell us far more about her than does her famous Depression-era novel about the unemployed, *Waste Heritage*.[2] The latter is actually something of a political anomaly in her literary career.[3] Granted, there are some links between her novels, one of which was her tendency to write primarily through the voices of men. This was no accident: Baird's role as breadwinner in the family, her desire to travel in risky places, her unbridled enthusiasm for experiencing cultural difference, were all goals that, in her lifetime, were often coded masculine. In the postwar period, the North was still constructed in the South as a sphere of masculine exploration and adventure. This meant

Irene Baird, photographed by Yosef Karsh, circa 1943. |
© Estate of Yousuf Karsh

that Baird could experience the North not only as a contact zone of cultural and racial difference but also as a space of gender transcendence and personal achievement.

Baird appears in the primary sources for many chapters in this book, though often as a fleeting presence. She was an intermediary between the Department of Indian and Northern Affairs and the National Film Board; she worked directly with Donald Snowden, featured in Edith Iglauer's memoir of the North; she wrote for *The Beaver*; and she provided background material for the Royal Commission on the Status of Women (RCSW). Baird is also an in-between figure in women's history, someone who does not fit easily into existing categories, groups, and

periodizations. She identified neither with the earlier northern sojourners who accompanied husbands North nor with the later feminists who
went north with the RCSW to analyze women's status. Yet her writing
provides a rich archive of memories, ideas, and representations that il-
luminate both the individual life of a remarkable author and the more
public life of ideas about the North in the postwar period. As a raconteur
determined to capture human experience on the page, she both describes
and prescribes relationships between whites and Indigenous peoples, and,
as such, her work adds immeasurably to this exploration of the cultural
contact zones of North and South. Moreover, her total oeuvre offers
differentiated approaches, shaped by the literary medium used as well as
the time during which she wrote. While her first travel narratives laud
northern development, her poetry, short stories, and her later novel, *The
Climate of Power*, are more critical, especially with regard to the history
of Inuit-white contact.

   In contrast to other chapters, this one relies heavily on fictional and
creative writing as a historical source. Writing in a modern realist tradition, Baird would have seen a dividing line between fiction and history;
however, this does not negate the benefits of using her fictional creations
as a lens through which to view cultural understandings of the North.
Her observations are personal, shaped by her own experiences, career,
travel, and political views, but they also reveal the broader, commonly
held progressive ideas and debates of the 1950s and early 1960s. Those
who praise her writing often note her particular talent at first-hand observation: her "journalistic" eye and her ability to relay, with acuity, the
human landscape of an event or an era.[4] Although she left very few letters
behind, at least one (cited below) indicates that she enjoyed casting a
scrupulous, sardonic, and analytical eye on the Ottawa scene unfolding
around her.

   Since the nineteenth century, both literary and historical writing shared
a common interest in the art of narrative form and in expositions of the
human condition.[5] Modern twentieth-century literary theorist Raymond
Williams also interweaves his explorations of literature and history, extolling the former as the "living embodiment of past experience," while

social historian Richard Cobb writes eloquently about fiction's ability to convey the "texture," feeling, speech, movements, and attitudes of life in the past.[6] As historians, however, we do generally demarcate a difference between "what happened" and "what might have happened,"[7] between imagination as one element in historical writing and an operating principle in fiction, between the historian's assessment of historical evidence and the novelist's ability to jettison reality.[8] Indeed, at one extreme, some positivist historians are wary of any literary evidence that cannot be quantified, corroborated, compared, or verified as representative, using the historians' accepted tools of the trade.[9]

Such devotion to empiricism is rejected in poststructuralist writing that challenges the accepted notion that fictional texts are distinguishable from historical contexts since, as Hayden White puts it, the latter are themselves "fictive" in nature.[10] White's radical collapsing of the boundaries between fiction and history has not permeated historical practice, though it has encouraged a more sceptical (if debated) view of the "incommensurability" and indeterminacy of history.[11] Yet we can maintain disciplinary boundaries between history and fiction and still use fiction as a valuable historical source. Literature, argues James Smith Allen, does not provide a "storehouse of details" about the past; however, it can offer insight into the "mental world" of a particular group or era, and this may be so for "lesser" works of fiction as much, or even more, than for those designated literary "greats."[12] Literature may be a "sensitive medium" that can reflect or relay the attitudes, ideas, or reigning zeitgeist of a particular time period.[13] Baird's ability to create a sensory feeling for the North in her poetry, or a sense of "fictional believability" in her novel, was as deep a concern for her as it was for those assessing her work. In her final novel, Baird wished to weave a tale that addressed issues of human conflict and frailty as much as it did details of life in the civil service, but she also wanted to create a story that would have resonance with and seem genuine to her reading audience. To be taken seriously, Baird felt she needed to create some sense of authenticity, and she undoubtedly considered her years as a civil servant part of the long research process behind her book.

BECOMING A CIVIL SERVANT

When *The Climate of Power* was published, Irene Baird told an interviewer that "the best way to write the great Canadian novel" was to "get away from Canada."[14] In her professional and personal life, Baird had already followed this maxim, travelling and living abroad in Latin America and the United States before she settled in Ottawa. Baird came to northern travel in a happenstance manner, through her position as the information officer in the Department of Mines and Resources, which later merged into the Department of Northern Affairs and National Resources, and finally, in 1966, became the Department of Indian Affairs and Northern Development (hereafter NA).[15] How, then, did Baird move from writing a novel about the Vancouver dispossessed in the 1930s to her job as civil servant in the 1950s?

When Irene Baird published *Waste Heritage* in 1939, she was living in Victoria with her husband Robert, an engineer, and their two young children, Ronald and June. In 1919, at age nineteen, she had immigrated to British Columbia with her English-Scottish parents, who enjoyed a relatively secure, upper-middle-class lifestyle due to the family's ownership of a woollen mill in Carlyle, England. When Irene's son Ronald was young, she worked for two years at Vancouver's exclusive St. Georges School (an Anglican private school), one of the very few female teachers on staff, until she left in 1933 due to "family responsibilities."[16] However, behind the façade of this apparently privileged background lay another story: by the time of the Depression, her husband was unable to support the family, and her own parents' financial resources, which might have cushioned her, had been tapped into by her husband. Irene Baird thus needed to work to support her family.

After the publication of *Waste Heritage*, journalist Bruce Hutchinson recommended Irene for a freelance position with the *Vancouver Sun*. For just over a year, she wrote a column on the editorial page, "What Really Matters," comprised of cultural, political, social, and sometimes light-hearted comment, until, in 1942, John Grierson offered her a job with the wartime NFB. Her position led her to Washington, where she engaged in film distribution for the NFB, then on to Mexico, where she

Irene Baird and faculty at St. Georges School, circa 1933. Irene is on far left. |
Courtesy of St. Georges School, Vancouver, BC

served as the information officer for the Canadian Embassy. The ambassador, well-known diplomat Hugh Keenleyside, became a life-long friend, and Irene's teenage daughter, June, who accompanied her to Washington and Mexico, attending private schools in those locations, became friends with Hugh's sister Marion when she returned to university in Canada. Irene's ties to Hugh were particularly important. He had made discreet inquiries in Canada for her when she tried (unsuccessfully) to secure a Mexican divorce, and her letters to him indicated an admiration tinged with strong affection.

Baird's Mexico job ended precipitously when she was dismissed in 1947.[17] This was a distressing "bombshell" for Irene since her work was persistently and highly praised by the Department of External Affairs and embassy officials.[18] The minister of revenue, who was also responsible for the NFB, J.J. McCann, known as one of Canada's most ardent and irrational anti-communists, had mistakenly assumed she was a "Red" and had used his influence to have her removed.[19] When Baird wrote to Keenleyside, who had just moved back to Ottawa to become deputy minister at the Department of Mines and Resources, to tell him about her sacking, she included a hand-written postscript on the back of the letter: "I don't know how you feel about wanting to have me in your department after this but if you do still feel the same it would be wonderful."[20] Keenleyside was able to help her secure a position as an information officer in his department by having the Civil Service Commission interview only female applicants for an information officer job. Such affirmative action was extremely unusual for the time. The federal civil service had a well-entrenched "gender order" in which women were relegated to "occupational ghettos" of secretarial/clerical positions and were always pressed to resign on marriage. [21] Although some women assumed new roles during the Second World War, a "male breadwinner" model was re-imposed afterwards as the Civil Service Commission told departments to "clear their staffs" of married women.[22]

However, it was Baird's imagined politics, not her marital status, that incensed McCann, who complained to Prime Minister W.L.M. King that it was "futile" to get rid of communists in one department if they were just rehired in another, and he was not above using innuendo about Keenleyside and Baird's relationship to get his point across:

> I may say that the Deputy Minister of Mines and Resources has been particularly interested in her, an interest which has aroused considerable comment ... He did approach me when he came back to Ottawa ... requesting that she be transferred to the National Film Board here and be given a release of six months, in order that she might have an opportunity of taking over this position she now has ... I told him that I could not give any such undertaking, but said that if she wished to resign, I'd be glad to accept her resignation.[23]

Keenleyside repeatedly objected – directly to the prime minister – to accusations about Baird's politics, and he astutely had the head of the RCMP, S.W. Wood, investigate her. Wood gave her politics a clean bill of health: "We find no reason to suspect this lady has ever had Communist sympathies, or had engaged in any activities of a subversive nature."[24] If McCann had taken three seconds to read her *Vancouver Sun* columns, or considered her Ottawa friends (who included Mrs. C.D. Howe), he might have realized how silly his accusation was. Keenleyside explained to his superiors that Baird was a breadwinner for her family and that she worried that these false accusations would become public. Indeed, this incident revealed just how arbitrary and nasty the Cold War could be. When the government finally put aside its reservations and made her permanent in 1950, Baird recognized that it was Keenleyside's "tireless" behind-the-scenes lobbying that had finally won the day.[25]

Baird's work in the information section of the ministry was once interrupted with another sojourn in New York City and Latin America. By 1950, Keenleyside had left Ottawa for other diplomatic posts, first at the UN, then in Chile, so Baird sought his aid securing a job at the United Nations with a technical assistance mission destined for Columbia.[26] In 1951, she acted as a consultant for this mission, revisiting Mexico and travelling to other Spanish-speaking countries in Latin America before returning to the department. In 1962, she became the first woman to head up an information division in the federal government. Despite her role as a trailblazer, she refused a connection to feminism: "I don't believe in the feminine mystique and all that rot, and we don't need to be aggressive. We need to be well qualified,"[27] she told a newspaper interviewer in 1967. Baird clearly enjoyed some association with other professional, educated women: she was a member of the Women's Press Club, and she had toured the United States during the Second World War on behalf of a women's organization, speaking about war and reconstruction. However, her public enunciations about women's social roles could be quite contradictory, and, when interviewed in the 1960s about working women, she occasionally resorted to caricatures, claiming they "had a tendency to become too emotional" and lacked the ability to be "detached."[28] Primarily, she embraced an individualist, liberal notion of achievement: women should be judged, like men, on ability and talent. Asked for advice on women in the civil service, she quipped: "You'll never get any more cover than a man so stay out of the kitchen if you can't stand the heat."[29]

Baird's sense of gender, self, and society provided a perfect entrée to northern travel. She was eager to take risks and prove her intellectual abilities and physical stamina, yet she did not publicly extol her feats as a coup for women – something that would have not endeared her to her fellow civil servants. Her travels gave her the opportunity to experiment, explore, and experience life in new ways in an environment that was at the same time culturally strange, physically awe inspiring, and artistically invigorating.

NORTHERN TRAVEL NARRATIVES

When Keenleyside wrote to Baird in 1964, complimenting her on a poem she had published in *North*, she responded that she only had time to pen the occasional poem and that "a package" of poems had been rejected by McClelland and Stewart. "I don't have an agent now and don't have much time for writing," she lamented, though "writing still gives me more of a sense of achievement (of something concrete) than anything else I have ever done."[30] Baird's work with NA did allow her to write shorter essays for journals like *The Beaver*, the *Canadian Geographical Journal*, and the government publication *North/Nord*. These were often travel narratives and expositions on the changing North, presented with a modicum of literary flare. Given Baird's background as a journalist, she was well suited for this task, and, unlike what was possible amidst the pressures of producing a daily newspaper column, she could develop longer, more evocative and extensive commentary. These nonfiction travel pieces were a medium that encouraged – and, given her position, required – Baird's most optimistic views of development in the North. There were a number of recurring themes in these travel accounts, some of which migrated into her verse and her novel: the exhilaration of risky travel and new frontiers; the stark and frightening beauty of the land; the North as a frontier of new possibility for whites and the Inuit; and the North as a point of cultural contact, difference, and dissonance between whites and the Inuit.

Baird's first trip North, in 1955, to write a story about Christmas at Frobisher Bay, made a dramatic impression on her. She wrote about it more than once, including a retrospective piece, "You Only Take the First Trip Once." It was a time of rough travel, she recounts, yet "people who touched even the fringes of that experience of that phase of arctic experience were lucky."[31] Baird and her (all-) male compatriots travelled on a small plane, each with a sleeping bag as an essential part of her/his luggage and future accommodation. Baird found herself closely quartered with a diverse crew of men looking for money and adventure, some on their way to a job on the DEW Line. Offering a sense of the precariousness of travel, she notes lightheartedly that the pilot had to warn them that they could not all stand up at once or the plane might tip over. Three years later, she recounts, she took the trip in a "VIP aircraft," but it was hardly the same: "no style," she writes, wistfully recalling the rougher ride.[32]

Baird's accommodations were makeshift and modest. She was billeted with a local family, either white or Inuit, and, in all cases, she praised the instant hospitality provided, often by the woman of the house. Unlike some of the women's sojourning narratives discussed earlier, her accounts are not characterized by intense alienation and trepidation. Her recollections have more in common with the women who went North as part of a writing career, such as Edith Iglauer and Sheila Burnford, than with the HBC wives who followed spouses. She embraced what others commented on more uncomfortably, whether it was the smell of seal permeating the house or the cramped quarters of rough living. This was, in part, Irene's honestly felt wonder at the new, the strange, and the unknown — sensations that outweighed the physical constraints of travel. Also, the pieces in *North* were promotional, published in a government magazine; they were meant to inspire confidence, not dwell on the inhospitable and the frightening. Baird was thus less forthright than other travellers about the problems of northern travel, more insistent on the boundless possibilities of northern living.

Criticism of northern development was also muted, if mentioned at all. Contentious, failed, or destructive aspects of government policy, such as the relocations of the Inuit, were barely discussed. When Baird visits Grise Ford, for example, she mentions in passing that the two groups who moved there from Port Harrison and Pond Inlet remained socially separate. Internal departmental memos were far from open about this as a disturbing social problem.[33] Northern housing was inspected on this tour as well. There were some hitches, she admitted, with space, construction, and the crossed wires of mistaken government planning, but nothing that could not be solved with hard work and good will. This unbridled optimism did not equate with the pictures of substandard, illness-inducing housing published by the Department of Health and Welfare in 1960, to the distress of NA, which had no choice but to jointly endorse the publication.[34]

Baird also celebrates the cosmopolitan mélange of whites heading north to find their fortune, all offering their energy, know-how, and venturesome spirit. In "Working Journey" (a trip that clearly became fodder for *The Climate of Power*), she describes a group of Ottawa bureaucrats inspecting engineering projects in Pangnirtung. "What strikes you everywhere is the variety of blood stirred by whatever it is Le Grand Nord has ... [One hears] accents of Holland, Britain, Germany, Australia, Denmark, Sweden, Norway ... and the speech of Canada in three languages."[35] As in *Waste Heritage* and her other novels, Baird enjoys drawing prose pictures of memorable personalities (usually male), whether it is the young Nova Scotia man seeking his fortune in the North or the accomplished Inuit hunter. She often plays with contrasts. One piece, with photos, describes the trip of West Africans to the Arctic to participate in an experiment with new forms of protective warm clothing manufactured in France.[36] Contrast might also be evoked in the reversal of gender roles necessary on the northern frontier as men are compelled to "batch it." As Doug James, her host at one settlement, is baking bread, she wonders why she has not followed her proper gender role, offering us a subtle reminder that she is not the usual female visitor: "Why have I never learned to toss up a layer cake or make a pie?"[37]

While her contact with northerners always bred optimism, her contact with the environment did elicit some disquiet. In her piece on Frobisher Bay, Baird conveys a sense of wonder and joy, describing the Christmas party with the Inuit as a "magical" experience, with "children everywhere, skipping and darting miniatures of their parents ... the dancing, the movies and the tea kept up till the trucks came [to take people away] ... [I]t was a noisy, cheerful, wonderful party."[38] The joy of the party was a stark contrast to her experience with Arctic weather. The next day, she went to the schoolhouse to type up her story, and, when she left, she encountered the frightening blow she later described on the radio. In such a storm, visibility can disappear entirely, leaving one disoriented, frozen, unable to find home, however close it may be. Almost magically, she claimed, the shadowy Eskimo figure appeared ahead of her, leading her home. But this particular experience impressed on her how close the line was between survival and death in the precarious Arctic environs, most especially for inexperienced Kabloona (whites). She returns to this incident in her poem, "Blow Spirit," in which she emphasizes even more strongly the supernatural and mystical, suggesting that the Inuit spirit, known to guide those lost in a storm home, had been her saviour: "Man or spirit? / To this day I do not know / ... Only some few of our village Council / have met the spirit that walks in a blow / only some few of us have touched his hand / but we — these few — we know."[39]

However frightening the blow was, Baird also enjoyed abandoning the settlements for more challenging venues: "I was spoiling to explore even further into Eskimo country," she writes, and she found a means through an air inspection trip of the DEW Line.[40] This was a rugged trip, geared to the aircraft's ability to land, so that destinations were constantly shifting according to the vagaries of the weather. Acknowledging the pilot was initially deeply dismayed at the thought of a woman on board, she consented to the difficult conditions of travel without complaint and implied that she was soon accepted on the same terms as the men. When her accommodation was in a makeshift tent, she found something positive to extol: in this case, the provision of hot water.

Her own resilience in difficult or dangerous conditions was part of her self-constructed narrative. After one of her Arctic flights, she described two groups trying to make it back to the seaplane, resting on icy waters. Her group was lost, "off course ... rocking in the icy darkness," wondering where the plane was, and hoping "this [was] not the moment for an iceberg to loom before us."[41] However, Baird also conveys the feeling of community and team work that, for her, defines the northern frontier, citing not only the hospitality of those who took her in but also the camaraderie of her male companions who were "part of a team ... [W]e never heard anyone exchange a harsh work or snarl at each other." Northern work, she writes, "demanded men who could grasp the impossible, bend it their way, and make it work. It was difficult to see work in any smaller terms."[42] This was a picture of northern development – largely carried out by white men – that buttressed the government's good intentions. Northern development was celebrated as part of a brave (and masculine) endeavour, something that was part of a laudable national design.

Like other northern travel writers, Baird stresses the breathtaking beauty of a landscape that is stark and foreboding, suggesting danger, isolation, and the always imminent threat of a cold death. This captivating mix of foreboding and beauty produces a sublime visual effect. Romanticized for centuries in the Western imagination as a "grey kingdom of frozen death," the Arctic is "essentialized for poetic effect" as "eternal and unchanging" as well as awe-inspiring.[43] The lands of the eastern Arctic, Baird writes, are "tall, austere, powerfully attractive," and they could literally cast a "spell – this wide plain ... the grey, reticent sky. The absolute aloneness."[44] The landscape might also appear serene, then become more ominous. The cold air that greeted her as she left the airplane was like "iced champagne," but menacing weather might interrupt, and "the realization that you've got no more places to go and can only last a short time in that cold is a lonely moment." Air travel could be fear inducing, although the scene below inspired a calmer sense of awe: "The sky was a cold pale blue and the sun touched the ice floes and the broken blades of the sea ice with an eerie pearlish light. There are no horizons here, only distance ... It is not something you forget."[45] Even the plane wrecks visible from above became impressive scenery, akin to gigantic animals of metal, "disheveled under the snow ... [I]n winter the arctic gives all – men, beasts, machines – a decent burial."[46] Baird's description of landscape, unlike some white exploration writing, however, sometimes disassociates whites from this land, referring to it as *Inuit* land: "Nunassiag, the good land, a good land for the hunter, a good land even when life is hard. And it can be merciless."[47]

A profound sense of physical and cultural distance from life in the South is conveyed in a number of her travelogues. Baird wants her readers to imagine an Arctic absolutely "remote from day to day Canadian experience, so alien to group-think, so filled with mysteries for science to discover."[48] There is a "sense of utter separation from the [southern] world... a stolid, one-dimensional world lacking the presence of gods and spirits but high in economists, and other useful trades guaranteed to reduce the stature of poets."[49] The image of a more spiritual, less materialistic North has been a common trope in writing about the Arctic since the late nineteenth century. Baird's self-identification as a poet likely made this metaphor all the more meaningful to her. She wants the reader to know that she identifies with the poets and the spirits, not the number crunchers and rational planners.

Baird ends "A Working Journey" with a description of her prized visit to the artists' cooperative at Cape Dorset, where she admires the work of Inuit sculptors and print makers. Baird wrote about Inuit artists often, and, according to her family, spearheaded one artist's tour in the south. Her granddaughter remembers Irene bringing her and her sisters special presents from the North: Inuit sculptures. The Nunavut print makers, Baird writes, were "schooled by the land." They produced art that reflected both the "philosophical and adaptable" in their culture, pieces that were simultaneously forms of pictorial memory and expressions of rare beauty. Inuit art, Baird explains to the southern public, is a method of "story telling that blends things done, imagined and remembered ... combining solid day-to-day images of life lived with the outer space of imagination and dreams."[50] Because art is linked to our region and physical environment, "all that the [Inuit] artist makes with his hands comes out of the land," which is itself part of their long history and an "ancient past." To the Inuit, she observes, our southern environment must appear exceedingly alien, the landscape barren and strange. "The Inuit must think it bizarre that we could pass so great a part of our lives in these great buildings," seemingly substituting for cliffs and mountains. To them, we live in a "curiously flat world."[51]

North and South were not, however, inherently antagonistic, as Baird makes clear in her writing on the new northern Inuit woman. Her travelogues are stamped with the optimism of an NA bureaucrat, and they incorporate some of the same assumptions about gender roles found in NFB films and women's sojourner accounts – namely, that Inuit women now had their feet "in two worlds" and that they faced a positive transformation from life on the land,[52] subject to an arduous, premodern patriarchal culture, to a more settled, easier domestic existence. The old ways, with the looming threat of illness, starvation, and harsh living would be replaced by more modern ways of living, aided, of course, by the state, with the provision of better food, medical aid, schools, and housing. "The magic of progress" that came with a paycheque brought freedom from want and long hours of toil, though also a sense of "instability and confusion," with new leisure time, changed familial relations and modes of housekeeping. The old family ways, she adds, may have been patriarchal, but women knew they were highly valued for their survival skills. What would happen now? Baird does not avoid all social problems, noting the potential for female teens to face new "moral" dilemmas as they moved from the "tribe" to settled life.[53] Ultimately, though, optimism triumphs. Baird extols the promising emergence of the new Inuit woman: the wives, teachers, and government workers who are educated, showing "leadership" in the Inuit community, striking out on their own, often aiding their own people. One of these success stories is Paulette Anerodluk, whom I discuss in the final chapter.[54]

POETRY AND SHORT STORIES

Baird's travel writing, then, employs familiar tropes and strays little from positive messages of Inuit-white cooperation, northern economic development, state initiatives, and the integration of the Inuit into Canadian citizenship, though with elements of their culture maintained and valued. Like other southern sojourners, Baird sometimes dichotomizes the traditional (Inuit) and modern (whites) in her writing, though in contrast to other authors she does not always make this synonymous with the civilized South and the primitive North.[55] In her poetry, she begins – but only begins – to question this dichotomy. A creative and flexible medium, poetry and fiction allow her to ruminate more openly, critically, and apprehensively on the land, Inuit culture, and the relationship between white and Inuit. In her verse, there is more attention to themes of alienation and cultural dissonance as Baird reflects on the complications of cultural encounter rather than on the North as a frontier of possibility.

Some of Baird's poems are mirror descriptions of northern landscape, places, or events she describes in her travel writing. In "Eskimo Church on Christmas Morning," she depicts the church service at Frobisher Bay with the same enjoyment and wonder that she conveys in her account of her first trip to the North. For Baird, the church became a vivid mélange of colour, faces, and sound:

> the Inuit people
> families flocking
> men women children
> creating patterns of colour in the glittering snow
> reds blues greens
> coming together at the church door
> like a bright congregation of birds.

She focuses on song, Inuktitut recitations, the multitude of voices in the congregation, as well as the way in which individuals embody a small part of Inuit history:

> next to the woman an old man
> with frayed grey hair half blind eyes
> whose hard fingers have carved over the years
> – and carved exquisitely –
> the story of the life of the village
> birth death hunts celebrations
> though the light in his eyes is almost out
> this is a man with treasures to bequeath.[56]

In another poem, "The Lonely Shore," Baird describes Inuit friends who are both estranged from and close to her since they share some small vestige of common friendship.

> *I sit with joy*
> *In the tent of Koono and Kitla*
> *I cannot speak their language*
> *Yet all around*
> *Their language speaks to me*
> *I am ashamed to be tongue-tied*
> *In the presence of friendship ...*
> *As we drink black tea in peace*
> *And the life of the village goes by*
> *The reek of walrus is everywhere*
> *part of us.*[57]

Even in this poem, with its ode to human connection across cultures, the land might become ominous and threatening: "Now – suddenly – it is not peaceful / the wind is rising faster than the tide ... The bay is impatient and growing wild."[58] Baird seeks to capture both the terror and the beauty of this land:

> *a rough and lovely land*
> *open yet secret*
> *locking into the heart*
> *so that when remembrance*
> *has become a dream*
> *a scar of love remains*
> *as with all beautiful solitary and desolate places.*[59]

Other white observers often commented on the vast silence of the land, though the Inuit likely interpreted the scene, and heard actual sounds, quite differently. For Baird, the land was active, a presence with a life of its own. In the poem simply entitled "Land," it was "brooding," with a "soundlessness so utter / that the astonished ear / cause pause and listen / to the deep ring of nothing." Most important, the land is the master of men, not the other way around, and the Inuit's intimate knowledge of the land and water is all that stands between him and death:

> *a time of year a hunter may trust the ice*
> *a day too long*
> *and be betrayed by what he should have known best*
> *when the flow splits*
> *when the wind and tide*
> *drift him marooned under a frozen star.*[60]

Contrast is often used, as it was in her travel narratives, to sharpen Baird's depiction of both the land and relations between humans. In a poem that describes the scene of a Second World War airplane crash near an Inuit village ("Arctic Mobile"), she moves back and forth between the remnants of the ghostly metal machine on the hill and the Inuit village nearby, where their more distant whaling past is also a presence. The airplane wreck, "angular, apart, like a great mobile fallen from the sky," is of little concern to the Inuit villagers, yet both the village and the wreck are scenes in which humans have been subject to the "savage strike of weather." The village, now full of mechanical sounds that "rumble and clank" as trucks unload at ship time, still hold the dreamlike sounds of another distant past, that of "the great whales / who lashed and lumbered in these waters a thousand years ago."[61]

Contrast, conflict, and alienation are even stronger themes in Baird's treatment of Inuit-white relations. While her travel narratives do not look at the unpleasant underbelly of Canadian incursions into the North, her poems occasionally do. One of the most evocative is "Who Will Be I," a poem describing Pauloosie, an Inuit man who is deeply alienated by his stay in a southern sanatorium, not unlike that portrayed in Bernard Émond and Benoît Pilon's film, *Ce qu'il faut pour vivre* (the necessities of life).[62] He is cut off from the physical landscape and relationships that denote home and is literally losing his sense of self, hence his repeated question: "who is this Pauloosie?" His estrangement is physical, social, and psychological:

> *even in the night*
> *feet pass faces I cannot see*
> *the air smells of a kind of healing I do not understand*
> *I do not even understand who is this man*
> *lying in my body in this bed*
> *whose land and people are too many sleeps away.*[63]

The arrogant, superior Kabloona do not value his knowledge or recognize his role in their northern survival:

> *they come to my bedside to teach*
> *To teach me, Pauloosie*
> *Kabloona who never in a lifetime could learn all that I know — how to track food*
> *to read where the wind rises by the blowing of the fur*
> *I who guided the stumbling white man home ...*
> *my father and his father would have laughed*
> *a roaring laugh heard through the camps*
> *at such soft men.*

In order to maintain his sanity, he tries to remember his loved ones, the past, his home, otherwise he may not survive:

> *I must talk to you Pauloosie*
> *this man I used to be*
> *or one of us will die*
> *not of the sickness the Kabloona say is healing*
> *but of the other sickness of the heart.*[64]

The poem ends pessimistically, with Pauloosie clinging precipitously to his sense of self, expressing not only a deep ennui but also an acknowledgment that the Kabloona may never appreciate Inuit like him from "another world" and that the Inuit may never understand "the ways of men not living on the land."[65]

The cultural gulf laid bare in "Who Will Be I" reappears in "i don't read you charlie: a twisted tale," depicting the visit of an Inuit artist to the South, possibly based on a tour that Baird helped to orchestrate. In contrast to her article on Cape Dorset artists, in which she describes such a southern tour positively, this poem highlights cultural dissonance and makes the South uncomfortably strange, if not unwelcoming, from the view of an Inuit artist. The open space of the North has now become the claustrophobic, crowded space of the South. The art gallery was a

> *jammed babble of strange tongues*
> *heat of foreign bodies*
> *experts non experts peering stiffly*
> *as crowds do*
> *to get a look at you*
> *at your work at the work of your friends*
> *hacked out of rock*
> *in that far off arctic village*
> *(what's the name again?).*

Baird refers repeatedly to southerners' disinterest in attempting to pronounce Inuktitut words: while imbibing the fashion of Inuit art, the gallery goers are unconcerned with the artists' actual names. One journalist asks the artist if he could just change his name to an anglicized one, more easily pronounced.

The second part of the poem uses descriptions of the urban environment —"glassed in high rise boxes / sunk in concrete" — to highlight Charlie's alienation and to juxtapose Western society's cavalier disregard for the land to the Inuit's respect for it:

> *you wanta know what's the fine river*
> *over yonder*
> *Charlie that river's so polluted*
> *most of the fish died*
> *so what do we eat*
> *spaghetti meatballs hamburgers french fries.*

The narrator explains to Charlie that animals, killed in Inuit culture for sustenance, are killed in the city by mere carelessness:

a man could live here
and not see animal tracks on his way home
at night
animal tracks!
any animal dumb enough to venture onto
our superhighways
we run him down
the clown.[66]

While perceptive in its characterization of different cultural relationships to the land, this poem tends to portray the Inuit as at one with the land. This, too, is part of an established tradition of romanticizing Indigenous peoples, who are portrayed as noble anti-modernists, embracing nature and free from the materialistic, alienating tendencies of modern urban life.

Like other travellers with an artistic bent, such as photographer Richard Harrington, Baird was concerned that Inuit culture not be overwhelmed and destroyed, though her preservationist bent focused on the tangible arts rather than on seeing culture as entangled with an entire way of life. Her poetry does speak of preserving and honouring the past. The Inuit need to "keep their roots," respecting tradition, elders, and their history, including the Inuit's "long gone fathers, strong men, tough enduring ... knowing how to live in, but never tame this beautiful threatening land / Inhabiting it generation after generation / for reasons / Few kabloona will ever understand." In her poem "Keep Your Own Things" her call for the preservation of Inuit "roots" is most clearly put:

Inuit
You who call yourselves The People
Keep your own things!
Use our things if you will
Use them as you must
But only just
As they serve ends
Between friends.[67]

Baird's poetry does express some hope about bridging the cultural divide between Inuit and white — as those from the dominating group often did. Her solution, not unlike that of Sheila Burnford, is a liberal humanist one, extolling communication and respect across lines of difference:

> Inuit
> we came from rough beginnings too
> Scattered over many places
> Of many bloods
> And thicknesses of blood
> No longer of pure seed (if we ever were)
> But pollen carried on the swarming winds
> Some of us (like you) peaceful men
> Some violent
> Some wise others stupid.[68]

Like some women sojourners, she saw the mixing and shared education of children from all backgrounds as hope for the future, perhaps a way of persuading the Inuit that Kabloona were more than "rich transients" and "incomprehensible" meddlesome interlopers.[69] Divisions of race and culture are recognized but could be surmounted, power differentials even more so. Respect in her ideal world had to be earned, not because of the colour of men's skin but because of their character. Whites should be measured, she suggests, by Inuit rules and traditions, not the other way around:

> Measure us by the rods you know
> By how we guide and provide
> For our children
> What breed of companions we make
> On a rough hunt.[70]

Notably, in many of her poems, just as in her novels, it is male leadership that is probed, explored, extolled.

At her most pessimistic, however, Baird fears Inuit culture and community will crumble under the weight of the drastic changes taking place: "Your world has begun to rock and split / turned upside down by the shock of change." In "A Delicate Balance," Baird discusses the lamentable internalization of white superiority by Inuit educated in the South and the dangers of Inuit youth misled into seeing the urban white life ("ripe girls good job / those large sums of loose money") as more exciting, only to find it more corrupting, than life in the North. The poem tells the story of Johnny, whose father wants him schooled in traditional ways of the hunt but who is lured to the city, only to find doors shut in his face, poverty, "choosy girls," and a group of questionable friends who make him into a car thief: he became but a "shadow" of his former self. It was only when Johnny comes back, "drawn home by the land / knowing at last who you are," that he could find his own "balance." While Baird's poem reflects contemporary discussions about the dangers of young Inuit being caught irretrievably between two cultures, one more materialistic than the other, Johnny has more agency than the Inuit are often granted in this narrative: they are often portrayed as inherently passive and fatalistic. Not only did Johnny come to appreciate the culture of his ancestors, but the urban experience makes him stronger: he is

> *learning*
> *making choices /*
> *surviving in a rougher school than your father ever did*
> *he at least knew the ways and language of the land*
> *where the traps were set ...*
> *when you were ready — and only then*
> *you came back*
> *drawn home by the land*
> *knowing at last who you are.*[71]

Baird's short story with a similar theme, "A Learning Situation," concentrates on a scene before the fictional Johnny left home, when his parents came to ask the advice of the local government administrator, hoping he would urge their son to stay with his family. The white administrator relies completely on his Inuit translator, Simonek, who has been educated in the South and now had disdain for this "ignorant" traditional family. Baird is critical of the superior colonial perspective offered to white and Inuit alike in southern education as the lessons learned are those concerned with ruthless individualism: "If living among whites had taught Simonek anything it was to be a pragmatist. The white man's way was not the way of the shared harvest traditional among the Eskimo people ... It taught each man to reap for himself and if he could reap some of his neighbour's harvest, too, so much smarter a man was he."[72] Yet the story is not without contradiction; the administrator, despite his limitations with the language, is still portrayed as a concerned person with prestige and wisdom, someone the Inuit looked up to. At times, Baird's NA optimism and her unquestioning respect for the intelligence of northern administrators crosses over into her poetry and short stories, blunting her criticisms and closing off a critique of the actual paternalism at the heart of the state's project. Did her faith in the government's agenda not contradict her other invocations to listen to the Inuit elders?

In the poem about Johnny, there is hope for Inuit survival, yet in one of the only poems Baird wrote about a woman, the ending is more tragic. "Mary-No-More" begins with the image of a cairn, built by persons unknown, but the story shifts when the cairn is described as "small as a woman of 15," the Mary who would have been "thirty-five if she had lived." Mary's "troubles" began because her "soft heart" led her to give physical comfort to a friend: "black or white / what did it matter which you comforted in the long lonely freezing / winter night." Mary, however, confronts "shame" and blame afterwards from someone brandishing the word of God, a Western, punitive deity distinct from Inuit spirits:

> *who told you God*
> *was waiting with His rod*
> *more powerful than all your spirits ...*
> *who told you of flaming seas*
> *of fire burning forever*
> *to eat up sinners like you /*
> *so that even tornraks seemed more kind.*

The poem suggests that Mary took her own life, "acting out of terror" and fear of the Western god.[73] While circumspect and oblique, the poem suggests a condemnation of the Christian missionaries who judged Inuit sexual relations, and cross-racial relations, by their own repressive and racist standards.

THE CLIMATE OF POWER

However unconventional Baird was in her own life, she was not interested in innovating with female heroines or probing the psyche of other exceptional women. Indeed, the female characters in her novel about the civil service and the North, *The Climate of Power* (hereafter *Climate*), are unflattering, if not stereotypical, portraits. The male characters are somewhat more varied, though profoundly different from the dispossessed male underclass featured in her earlier *Waste Heritage*. *Climate* explores a more privileged and powerful group – the career civil servants running the federal government behind the scenes. Baird's focus is less on the top public servants setting the agenda, the "Ottawa men" lauded by Jack Granatstein, and more on those a step below, though both groups shared common characteristics, including WASP backgrounds and unpretentious, respectable, middle-class lifestyles.[74] Baird's familiarity with the inner workings of the civil service, her public relations management of the northern portfolio, and her travel in the North left her with a rich archive on which to draw for her novel. It is possible that some of the personalities in *Climate* came perilously close to her former colleagues as the Canadian publishers had a lawyer examine the book to check for libel: a disclaimer at the beginning, stating "all characters and the situations [in the book] are imaginary," was likely the safeguard recommended.[75]

During her time with the government, Baird had to be professionally discreet, though in a private letter to Hugh Keenleyside she expresses a certain cynicism about the situation in her ministry, also hinting at her own boredom with the "safety, comfort, security" of the civil service. She chats about the current political situation and notes that there was little money for non-military projects in the North: "the Department is being slowly drained of blood ... and without the Bureau of Mines, there is little in our shop which bears directly, or even indirectly on defense. For the time at least, the military will have most of the housekeeping money to spend in the north."[76] What is perhaps most revealing are her pithy comments on the higher-ranking bureaucrats. Her chief clearly knew how to stay in power, but out of trouble, as he was "embedded in Ottawa, as he always has been, pensionable whatever, waits daily to do as he is bid, like a sensible fellow." She imagines him as rather colourless, always "paying his bills on time," while others below him are "adrift" or even asleep: "the rest are, so to speak, old men, women and children, so short of the A bomb, what would disturb them?"[77]

After she retired in 1967 and was living in London, England, Baird cast her imagination back to these civil servant days, penning *Climate*. There is no precise equivalent in her earlier letter to George McKenna, the central character in the novel, though he may have been a composite of her previous colleagues. A senior civil servant in the imaginary Department of National Projects, George is nearing retirement but does not want to let go of the reigns of bureaucratic power or leave the job that has defined his whole identity. A tad arrogant, George believes he is indispensable; he thrives on the efficient performance of his job (and likely did pay his bills on time) and takes pride in his ability to offer the right advice to the deputy minister while keeping in touch with civil servants in the field (which, in this case, is the Canadian North). George, unlike many of the other Ottawa men, had spent considerable time in the North and was honestly concerned about the welfare of the Inuit, even if his concern is shaped by a decided paternalism. As Christina Newman observed in the late 1960s of this "Establishment" generation, their most fitting self-description and epithet would be "HE SERVED HIS MINISTER WELL."[78]

However, George was being undercut by a younger, ambitious bureaucrat hungry for power, Roy Wragge. Roy was a modernizer, intent on making George look like a dinosaur, and he was getting the approving attention of the political higher-ups, whose primary concern was always protecting Minister Peter Brock's career and reputation. With mocking wit, Baird depicts the scheming relations between the political minister and the career civil servants, and among the civil servants themselves, describing power plays over as petty a matter as who would control the department newspaper subscription. Only the civil servant who knew "no one wanted his job badly enough to sink a knife between his shoulder blades" was secure in these courteous but dangerous waters.[79] "Ottawa," she recounts, "was a capital where politics and the establishment were the main occupation, tending to make small men larger than they were and talented ones appear like statesmen and geniuses."[80] As one of the early press assessors of the manuscript put it, "our author surveys the corridors of power in a mood affectionate, but highly acid."[81]

George's undoing came on a number of fronts, both public and private. Enraged over false rumours about government incompetence causing a flu epidemic in the northern hamlet of Glasgow Bay, circulated purposely by a disreputable MP, Sheldon Watkins, and a rather unscrupulous journalist, Hawks, he physically attacks the journalist in a fit of anger at a chance meeting. It was not chance enough: cameramen on the scene captured it for TV. George is forced to take a leave, but, on his return to work, he is included in a trip north with the minister's entourage, including Roy Wagge, whose unbridled contempt for the Eskimo is well known. "They're hardly competent to judge the merits of one place or another," Wagge fumes, "As for their culture that is being destroyed anyway ... In a year or two the children will be looking down their noses at the places their parents grew up in. Museums can take care of the rest."[82] George's pride, hatred of Roy, and his fear of being cast aside become his second undoing. George, Roy, and an Inuit guide, Kunu, are on a boat trip in turbulent waters, with Roy, ever the confident braggart, standing up brandishing a gun, ignoring George's order to sit down. In a split second of murderous anger, George rocks the boat so that Roy falls into the icy water, disappearing in seconds.

George also has a personal undoing on the home front, a complicated plot only touched on here. A long-time bachelor, he was pressed into judging a civil service beauty contest and was inexplicably captivated with Flo, an attractive "girl" from the typing pool, though in reality a tawdry gold digger with a shady past looking for a secure income. In the eyes of George's middle-aged, sensibly dressed, and practical secretary, George's sudden marriage to the manipulative Flo is an abomination.

When on leave, George pampers Flo by agreeing to take dancing lessons and is tricked by the sleazy owner of the dance school (a not too subtly named Miss Brazen) into paying for private lessons for Flo, who is snuggling up to the resident male (gigilo) dance instructor, Cruise, with whom she falls into bed. George is oblivious, even when his secretary tells him that his wife is meeting her lover at the Happy Hello Motel. When he discovers the truth, there is no way out of his unhappy marriage: with guilt grating on his nerves, his sleep talk reveals his secret about Wragge's death to his scheming wife, who threatens to expose him if he leaves her.

George is relieved to be sent on another trip north; however, he physically pushes himself to the limit in an effort to reclaim his masculine pride and, against the advice of Kunu, takes his own solitary route through the snow back to the settlement. As he is about to perish in a snowstorm, he imagines the ghost of Roy Wragge pressing down on his body, taking his revenge, but he is rescued by Kunu, though not in time to save his feet, which are lost to frost bite. The book ends with him returning home, cast aside by the ministry, disabled, and facing his tortuous marriage. His minister, in contrast, is climbing the greasy pole of politics, moving on to a more prestigious cabinet post. This was not the first ending that Baird wrote. Originally, George died in a fiery car crash as he pursued his absconding wife and her lover; however, under advice from her publisher, Macmillan Britain, she created a more low-key, pathetic picture of George being put out to pasture by his superiors.

Baird's British publishers deemed her a "capable," though not "great," writer, but they appreciated her descriptions of the North and urged her to play up the theme of northern development and Inuit marginalization, something they thought would help sell the book. "All of us are interested in the Indian and Eskimo problem, that of assimilating their culture into ours," a press reader commented. His assessment drew on common tropes of colonial writing at the time, and he posed his questions more simplistically than had Baird: "is it right," he asked, "that the primitive North, with Eskimos and outdoor heroes ... should be forcibly modernized?"[83] A change in the title of the book, from Baird's original proposal, *Dinosaur*, to *Climate* underscores this enhanced focus on the changing North.

Macmillan Canada was less enthusiastic about the book. British assessors, with images of nineteenth-century Arctic polar exploration in mind, may have appreciated the romanticism of the northern theme, the Canadian editors less so. Editor Ramsay Derry found it "contrived ... old fashioned and wooden," lacking the kind of "satiric appeal of *In High Places*" and without enough "sex or associated passion."[84] One Canadian assessor, however, thought – like his British counterpart – that a book that dealt with "the Indian and Eskimo problem" would garner some interest, and he, too, felt that Baird's writing "soared" in her descriptions of the North. Reluctantly, the Canadian publisher swallowed its doubts and co-published the book, but it subsequently grumbled and squabbled with its British counterpart over various marketing issues, including the British-designed cover – an "action" picture of Roy Wragge falling from the boat, a scene Ramsay Derry dismissively told the British publisher looked "juvenile" and had countless mistakes in it.[85]

Yet Macmillan Canada's marketing of *Climate* also pushed the mysterious North theme, claiming it was a great tale of "human frailty" that "moved dramatically between the tensions of power in Ottawa and the mysterious one third of Canada within the arctic circle that only a fraction of the world has seen." Baird presented herself in the publicity as an intrepid northern traveller, the same curious Arctic explorer role she had assumed in her earlier travelogues: "I was never happier than when I could exchange a seat behind a desk for a seat in any type of aircraft heading all north ... [A]ll the action in *The Climate of Power* that takes place in the far north relates to areas I have known first hand. A frantic encounter with a storm is based on an experience I had myself ... if you're lucky enough to come through something like that and only glimpse the precipice that lies on the other side, the experience equips you with an instant course in arctic survival."[86] Like other white northern travellers (though often men), Baird, too, could exaggerate her northern survival skills for southern audiences.

Editors at Macmillan Canada were right to be apprehensive about the book's success. Baird's style was somewhat dated for the early 1970s. Her gentle, understated satire had a polite British flavour, not sharp enough for some, and George's dilemmas seemed out of sync with the times. His struggle to remain an upright bureaucrat seemed rather old-fashioned to Canadians who had witnessed the 1960s youth rebellion and the Munsinger scandal (among others).[87] Also, George's personal life approximates something from a 1940s film plot, and Flo is too much of a caricature: the flashy, conniving, and promiscuous "office gold-digger" persona that had been a staple of sexist cartoons, fiction, and film since the 1930s.[88] Reviews were few and far between. Some were unkind. John Muggeridge savaged the book, calling it the "literary whiteout of the season." George McKenna, he notes sarcastically, "is on the side of righteousness. He favours the old good North. The Eskimo like him."[89] A more generous review by Dorothy Body, who had worked for NA in the North, loved Baird's descriptions of the physical environment and conceded that she had done a good job of capturing the struggle for power between the older paternalists and the younger technocrats in the department. However, Body, representing a different generation of socially aware whites in the North, suggested that Baird misses a key issue: Ottawa's absolute power over the lives of the Inuit, now being "challenged directly by the Indians and Eskimo."[90] Baird hints at this imbalance of power, at Inuit disenchantment, but it is not a theme that is accentuated, thus reflecting a book conceived of in the 1950s rather than in the 1970s.

These reviews stand in stark contrast to Baird's aspiration to make a literary comeback, and there is a certain sad dissonance between her hopes and the reality she must have sensed – that *Waste Heritage*, her one great hit, was a book very much of the past. Nonetheless, *Climate* is a revealing historical piece that highlights images of North and South as they reverberated through the bureaucracy and into the public realm. Baird had an acute journalist's eye for the back-room machinations of Ottawa politics and the rigid gender roles defining the political sphere. The Ministry of National Projects was a predominantly masculine space in which power was negotiated, traded, and bartered for by men within the confines of a certain accepted clubby code of behaviour. This was a work environment marked by the undisputed hegemony of white men and a shared set of middle-class masculine values stressing hard work, bread-winning, and the cultural capital earned through educational professional know-how and "reasoned expertise."[91] Yet it was also one in which masculine rivalry could result in nasty power struggles. For the most part, it was a culture typified by a sense of ethnic and racial superiority to the government's Indigenous "clients" in the North. While the civil servants argued over the exact parameters of Eskimo policy, they did not question their right or ability to oversee decisions about the Inuit.

Providing support roles were the women on the margins. On the home front, wives of civil servants looked after the house and children, while the wives of politicians were preoccupied with their husbands' careers. At the ministry, a hierarchy of women worked under male authority. The French-speaking cleaning women who "chattered" and hovered near George's door after hours were at the bottom;[92] then came the young women, like Flo, in the typing pool; and then came the few older women secretaries, like George's somewhat pitiable "spinster" secretary, who had risen to the highest point most women could – namely, aiding the highest men in the ministry. Smart and perceptive, they were not without their own cynical reflections on the sometimes juvenile male power games of their bosses.[93]

In parliamentary politics, it is clear that men also rule, and, when it came to the northern portfolio, sometimes without either knowledge or integrity. Sheldon Watkins, the "cowardly" MP from Lemming Lake, is a case in point. He makes common cause with the reporter Hawks not because he actually cares about the Inuit supposedly dying of the flu but, rather, to score opposition points. Hawks knows Watkins to be "unstable," but he publishes his unsubstantiated gossip, disingenuously claiming it is a reliable source. Sheldon's fellow MPs didn't care to rein him in: they "treated him like a joke" when they were in power, but now they appreciated his "nuisance value as a busybody" stirring up trouble for their opponents.[94] Baird's picture of Sheldon is particularly unflattering. He represents politicians who, after a short time in the North, use their vaunted expertise as political capital, becoming instant "self-styled" experts on Indigenous peoples. Her description of his career also alludes to sexual corruption. Even in the 1950s, Baird must have heard stories about administrators and missionaries who abused their power and were simply moved around the North to avoid scandal. "At the time he quit his arctic teaching job" it was assumed "he had been the victim of a raw deal," "but the truth was, in an isolated location where normal diversions were few, his interest in youth activities had been a little too sincere."[95]

If Sheldon is the worst example of a white politician using the plight of Native peoples to puff up his own reputation, he is certainly not the only one to do so. Other politicians are aware that this is a hot button issue, though Baird intimates that they are more concerned with southern press coverage than with northern lives. When rumours of Inuit illness at Glasgow Bay surface, the deputy minister warns Brock, before a news conference: "at the moment adverse news affecting the Eskimo people can blow up a storm." Brock wants a quick briefing since he is "in no mood for long-winded human interest stories." He muses, in the time-honoured Canadian tradition of blaming the preceding party in power for government incompetence, that they should claim the "foul up occurred before the last election. Making it, in fact, an error of the previous government."[96] The deputy minister is sceptical since "the public has become highly emotional about the Eskimos. Where lives are involved they don't care which government it was." Brock seems mildly concerned, but he knows little about the Arctic, not even realizing that houses cannot be built in winter. All he really wants is to be able to tell the House of Commons that "action was taken." What is actually done does not concern him: "What happens to the shipment after it reaches Glasgow Bay ... whether it rots on the beaches or is built into houses is a problem for your engineers."[97]

In the midst of this controversy, Brock is challenged by the smarmy Sheldon to visit the North. Baird uses descriptions of this trip of the minister and his entourage to recount the sounds, smells, and sights of the North and, occasionally, to retell her previous positive travelogues in a more critical tone. In the travelogues, she celebrates the hardy men attracted to northern development; in *Climate*, male chatter in the plane reveals a different story. A young Maritime lad hoping to make a quick fortune just wants to be in and out: "I need the city. An' the day my contract expires I'll be on this plane heading back to Montreal with a sackful of money." What is it you're scared of?" his older companion responds, "There's nothin' in the arctic a man can't take care of just so long as he stays drunk enough."[98] Another senior civil servant, far from being overwhelmed by the beauty of the North, finds it morbid and frightening: "With the sun blown out like a candle every detail of the landscape took on a bleak grey reticence ... the arctic's a place that could grind you up and swallow you without a trace. Wipe you out in a matter of minutes."[99]

Some of Baird's small vignettes of the Inuit attempt to humanize or complicate existing images of the North. She celebrates the joyful sense of community at the party held to celebrate the minister's visit as an aging Inuit woman, a masterful accordion player, entertains, moving everyone to spontaneous dance. Her own memories of sharing tea with Inuit and white friends become scenes of McKenna doing the same. In one scene, he learns from his driver, Paulee, of the recent tragic death of his young son, who was mauled by a polar bear. That the family had four other children, Baird notes, did not make "their loss any less bitter." McKenna is saddened since he knew how "precious children were to the Eskimo."[100] While Paulee shoulders his son's death with a measure of stoicism, this is not the simple eternal fatalism implied in other sojourner accounts of the Inuit.

Writing in a time period before she would have been chastised for appropriating the Inuit voice, Baird conveys the Inuit's interpretation of events, using their thoughts to raise questions about the government's northern policies. Through the eyes of her Inuit characters, the South is made strange: the Inuit are shocked by the weird practices of whites, such as "discarding" older men like George and their arrogant disregard for Inuit knowledge;[101] however, the Inuit use silence rather than words to relay their views. The Inuit actors in the book also recognize that whites have little real interest in listening to them. When the minister asks a local Inuit interpreter, Joanassie, about the housing problem, the latter responds without a sense of deference: "[He] took the Big Shots from Ottawa without excitement. Mostly they wished to talk more than to ask Eskimo questions. For most part they were poor listeners. More interested in talking about the Eskimo than to them. It was agreed their mouths were bigger than their ears."[102]

Baird, however, does not paint a one-dimensional picture of colonial masters and oppressive relations. The ambitious Minister Brock, for instance, always has his eye on his image and future career, but, in the Arctic, when there is no press corps in sight, he asks some intelligent questions. Brock tours a new, modern school, of which the local administrator, Hemmings, is immensely proud, and, "after a critical scrutiny of the walls and the texts," asks in dismay: "What happened to the Eskimo culture? Don't these kids have one visible object to remind them when they come to school that they have a culture of their own? Artists of distinction among their own race? Anything to remind them that it's good to be born an Eskimo?" Hemmings realizes that southern school texts are a form of cultural erasure, offering Inuit children "bland narratives of blonde, apple-cheeked children, prize products of southern suburbia, with matching parents, grand-parents, and flashing traffic lights."[103]

Baird also provides jarring examples of social dislocation, never mentioned in her perky travel narratives. After the party, the minister comes across a young Indigenous man, drunk, lying in the snow in tattered clothes. When he demands an explanation, Hemmings explains that he has come to this larger settlement, Netserk, from a more isolated community, only to find there are no jobs. His mother and sisters are now alone, and his father is in an Alberta jail for murdering his brother-in-law. "Ten years ago," George mumbles, "this would not have happened."[104] While this comment may reflect Baird's romanticization of the "old" traditional North, she is reiterating the same concerns raised in her poems: that Inuit youth are caught between cultures and, without aid and education, are in danger of falling into poverty, addiction, and despair.

Perhaps most interesting are the references to the relocation of Inuit communities, the most infamous of which took place while Baird was with the ministry. In *Climate* relocation is questioned, not condemned; alluded to, not discussed at any length. The most callous statements come from the unappealing Wragge, who "found it incomprehensible that McKenna should allow his energies to be drained away by the life hazards of a pocketful of Eskimos. Few more than could be contained, dogs and all, on a good-sized surburban parking lot."[105] The young moderns in the civil service did not see the point in keeping families where they grew up: one "found it difficult to be seized by a sense of urgency over an event taking place so far off in such a totally unautomated society.

He was sympathetic towards the well-being of the Eskimos but regarded the arctic as a godforsaken spot and failed to understand why they had not harnessed up their dogs a century ago and broken out. [He] could not have found Glasgow Bay on the map."[106] McKenna, on the other hand, warns that people can't be easily moved around: "They've hunted along those coasts for years. Move them to Netserk and you destroy their whole way of life. Destroy their culture, too."[107]

On McKenna's second trip north, it is a young pilot's evocation of the new North that sparks a reconsideration of his earlier role in the relocations. A young pilot asks why he is flying to remote Gull Island when it has no valuable resources: "No one's lookin' for oil or openin' up a mine on Gull ... There's nothin' goin' on around there but people ... [H]ell, Mr McKenna, everyone these days is talkin' *re*sources. There's not much money to be made out of people."[108] McKenna's offended reaction – "aren't people important?" – suggests his more humane, less materialistic sensibilities, but he is also forced to question his own role in creating the "troubling problems" now apparent in the North. "When the relocation project was planned it seemed to him that they had most of the answers. Move the people from areas where the hunting was exhausted to where it was good. Build houses, a school, create a community ... In the first year of its life the project had attracted families [from far away]." However, the image of the homeless, drunk teenager at Netserk flashes before his eyes, reminding him that northern development and human engineering did not always go well.[109] His civil service colleagues thought such social problems were simply the inevitable "price of a better life" for the Inuit,"[110] and McKenna had convinced himself that he had cared about protecting Inuit traditions, but he now felt a nagging sense that government policy had been a failure. Although Baird may have had second thoughts about the relocation programs, her critique is still underdeveloped, and, despite her earlier observations on the military, she does not mention sovereignty considerations. As Tester and Kulchyski argue, the issue in some contested relocations was not simply good or bad intentions but, rather, ingrained colonial paternalism, bad planning, or a lack of understanding of Inuit life and culture as well as the government's concerns about security in the North.[111]

Baird's mild critique is likely another reason the book appeared dated when it was published. By the 1970s, Aboriginal activists and white critics alike were thinking in new ways about the Indigenous North: there were stronger political demands for self-determination, land claim petitions, critical writing, and an Indigenous rights movement. The cultural dissonance between white and Inuit that Baird captures in her poetry produces not only the despair and dislocation experienced by Pauloosie but also collective activism and resistance.

THE NORTH AS FICTION AND NON-FICTION

Irene Baird was a woman who thrived on ideas, adventure, and individual achievement, and her northern journeys permitted her to transcend gender conventions; however, she did not embrace or advertise her accomplishments as feminist "firsts" for women – indeed, quite the contrary.[112] Nonetheless, northern travel was still transformative for her, a personal, cultural, artistic, and intellectual experience that both inspired new appreciation of environmental beauty and raised questions about tradition and modernity, cultural dissonance between Inuit and white, the making of art, and her daily work at NA. Northern travel inspired her muse, generating the material for her last novel, along with verse, short stories, and travel commentaries that are less known to us because many were published in a government-issued publication, *North/Nord*.

This writing is not of one piece. Its one persistent thread is the awe she tries to convey vis-à-vis the sublime beauty of the North, the sense of unknown possibility, and the foreboding in an unforgiving land that was more the master of men – especially of white men – than the other way around. The travel narratives, however, embody the tone of her work with NA, offering an optimistic view of northern development that extols both those whites heading north, imbued with the spirit of adventure, as well as the traditional Inuit already there. If modernization brought problems, these are never insurmountable. Inuit artistic practice is lauded, and she remains optimistic that the Inuit could be integrated into Canadian society without the complete loss of their traditional life. Her poetry and short stories, in contrast, ask more questions and are more pessimistic. This more flexible, fictional medium permits her to question state and economic development, modernization, and cultural marginalization. All are putting the Inuit at risk. The Inuit, whose knowledge is little appreciated by whites, are culturally endangered; relations between older and younger Inuit are troubled; and, in "Mary No More," the consequence is tragic death.

These ideas are most clearly articulated in *Climate*. Through her depiction of Roy Wragge and his modernizing allies, Baird offers a critique of the ethnocentric contempt that many southerners secretly harboured for the primitive northern Inuit, and she also suggests that what southerners saw as the forces of progress could actually be a dangerous threat to the Inuit culture, disrupting a delicate balance of social and physical relations between humans and the land. Northern economic development was inevitable in her mind, but the "integration" of the Inuit into Canadian life had to be managed with care.[113] Leadership should come from enlightened white scientists, civil servants, and politicians; Baird was not at the point of imagining an Inuit-managed, Inuit-led, and Inuit-controlled territory.

Baird's writing suggests a vision of two worlds: North and South, modern and traditional, materialistic and spiritual. These binary tropes are common in other white travel writing on the North. There is also an underlying "metanarrative," often replicated in discussions of Indigenous/non-Indigenous contact *both* in the North and in the South: that of "fatal impact," with an avaricious, materialistic, and uncaring white world confronting a more holistic Native or Inuit culture, with disastrous consequences. The problem with the narrative of fatal impact, argues John Lutz, is that the complex "inbetween" accommodations and "moditional" cultural innovations of contact are obfuscated.[114] More complex, variable stories of Indigenous "coping, partially coping, not coping," adds Gerald Snider, are obscured by this linear view of historical change that implicitly verifies a modernization paradigm.[115]

Baird's fictionalized Ottawa offers a rather pessimistic view of the future of the North. White men in *Climate* are the unquestioned brokers of power, but some have little first-hand knowledge of the North, and others are only interested in northern inhabitants as a convenient political football. Civil servants take their stewardship of the "primitive" Inuit for granted, and some, like McKenna, are respectful and well intentioned; however, when the Inuit speak, the Ottawa men often don't listen. Although Baird's primary goal was not to critique race and gender relations in Ottawa politics, she inadvertently exposes these hierarchies with subtle acuity. Women in the novel have few career and life choices, and they are largely divided into wives and secretaries, each in her own way reliant on men for her social status and economic security. Some of the female characters are extremely one dimensional; Baird's portrait of Flo betrays a dislike for women who make their way in life using their bodies rather than their brains, relying on scheming rather than on achieving. Nowhere in the novel is there a woman like Baird, a woman who commands a professional, significant job in the civil service for which she requires political acumen, natural intelligence, and creative skills.

Baird's insistence on the intrinsic value of other cultures may have been linked to her primary identification as a writer and cultural producer rather than as a civil servant. She did not want to be remembered as a number cruncher but rather as an artictic creator, or, as someone who wrote about the artistic creations of others. Near the very end of *Climate* she has a French-Canadian northern administrator, LeDuc, speak in her voice. Both Baird and LeDuc might be considered outsiders in southern political circles of power, one because of her gender, one because of his language. In order to understand the Inuit, LeDuc tells a highly sceptical, pragmatic McKenna, one must listen to their legends and to "what is lying down there among the roots of their culture." LeDuc respects Inuit spiritual beliefs and tentatively suggests that, in the Arctic, "there may be influences that go beyond our poor senses of sight and hearing." Shortly thereafter, McKenna's dismissal of such "superstition" is proven false by his own encounter with the ghostly spirit of Roy Wragge on his snowy misadventure.[116]

Like Baird's poem "Blow Spirit," the book ends with a question rather than a certainty, with an invocation to heed the spirits of the ancestors. While Baird's designation of the Inuit North as more spiritual than the materialistic white South replicates common tropes about Indigenous peoples, her emphasis on their cultural self-preservation and the dangers of white colonial superiority suggests that, during her civil service years, she was developing a critical perspective on the contact zone of North and South. Her critique, however, would soon be overtaken by a subsequent generation of writers. Despite George's tragic flaws of pride and foolishness, his bureaucratic paternalism appears more attractive in *Climate* than does the callous disrespect for the Inuit articulated by the young, brash modernizers in his department. Nonetheless, paternalism is not equality. Dorothy Body's insightful review recognizes that Baird's North is part of the past: in the new North, First Nations peoples claim their own rights rather than trusting in the care of others.

CHAPTER SIX

"Mrs. Bird Flies North"

The Royal Commission on the Status of Women in the North

In the late nineteenth century, white Euro-Canadian women reformers often called for the regulation of marriage according to their definitions of proper familial social and legal norms, with the target of their concern most often working-class, Indigenous, or non-Christian people. It was not only a sense of cultural superiority but also their feminist belief in the need to protect less fortunate women from patriarchal excess that led to their calls for the state to regulate heterosexual monogamous marriage.[1] Yet, when the Royal Commission on the Status of Women (hereafter RCSW) heard testimony in the Canadian North in 1968, more than one white woman urged the state to recognize Aboriginal practices of customary marriage rather than imposing Christian norms sanctified by church and state. Was this a new sign of cultural relativism, or at least cultural sensitivity, on the part of mainstream white feminists? Have historical treatments of the women's movement, which so often imply dichotomous divisions between the colonialists and the colonized, white and racialized, neglected some nuances in feminist thought?

The answer may include nuances itself. While the call for recognition of customary marriage in 1968 may not have signalled feminists' full understanding of the history of colonialism, it did symbolize their recognition that the needs and views of Aboriginal women had not been fully integrated into the women's movement, nor had they penetrated politics and policy making. Listening to the voices of Aboriginal women may not have succeeded fully in practice, but it was part of the RCSW's claimed agenda, suggesting that the late 1960s was a transitional moment in the history of the women's movement, just as it was for the history of northern Indigenous peoples.

This chapter explores the RCSW's visit to the North, witness testimony, reflections of commissioners on Aboriginal-settler relations, expert studies, and the media treatment of the visit, all perspectives that tend to favour a non-Indigenous point of view. I examine both official and unofficial documentation of the RCSW, employing a close textual reading of the RCSW's political context, research methods and social hypotheses, as well as probing the ideological assumptions shaping the media reporting, drawing on the theoretical supposition outlined in my analysis of the *RCMP* television series. Official and unofficial record-taking also coincided with different Indigenous groups: the commission only took transcribed testimony in Yellowknife and Whitehorse, where it primarily discussed "Indian" women, while the visits to a few Nunavut Inuit settlements were not archived in written testimony.[2] Media coverage, however, corrected some of this bias, as television and radio specials on the RCSW trip to Inuit communities were aired shortly after the commissioners returned south.

The RCSW's northern hearings provide a window into changing, gendered images of the Aboriginal North in a year known globally for popular turmoil, youth rebellion, and the expression of novel and radical political ideas. 1968 did not have such a profound meaning in the case of the RCSW, but the public and behind-the-scenes commentary on the commission's northern visit suggests a small shift in how Aboriginal women and gender relations were perceived by an overwhelmingly white South. This representational shift does not dispute the dominant historiography of our times, which stresses the failure of the RCSW to think beyond the experiences of white anglophone and francophone women or to critically reflect upon its own universalist concept of gender experience.[3] Although the RCSW relayed strong concerns about Aboriginal women's marginalization, its understanding of Indigenous-white relations differed markedly from our current indictments of colonialism. Some of the same paternalist ideas characterizing the relationship between northern Aboriginal women and white women apparent in sojourners' narratives reappear in new forms in RCSW testimony. Some of the same orientalist ways of seeing Indian and Eskimo women apparent in film and television in the 1950s reappear in RCSW discussion papers, shaped by a resilient, unreflective sense of cultural superiority.

Yet RCSW documents and media coverage offer hints of alternative views and emerging challenges to white paternalism, reflecting broader shifts in the political and cultural terrain, and also suggesting that historians need a more nuanced assessment of the RCSW. The RCSW commissioners and staff knew the dominant society had been guilty of past mistakes and misinterpretations of Indigeneity that it wished to correct. Ideally, the hearings were supposed to be a space for Indigenous women to voice their own ideas and needs. Only a few did, but, supported by some white allies, these Indigenous women answered back to the long-standing images of themselves as primitive, backward, and oppressed. That answering back took on more assertive and public forms in the 1970s, though Indigenous women have never been completely silent and acquiescent to the colonial relations that characterized their lives.

"Mrs. Bird Flies North"

The *News of the North* newspaper thought itself quite witty with this announcement of the RCSW head commissioner's impending arrival in Yellowknife in the summer of 1968.[4] No doubt, at the time, the RCSW was seen as somewhat superfluous in comparison to other commissions dealing with the more important northern issues of law and governance: the Advisory Commission on the Development of Government in the NWT, headed by A.W.R. Carrothers,[5] and Judge William G. Morrow's Royal Commission on the Administration of Justice in Hay River. Nor was the North high on the RCSW's priority list. When no northern hearings were publicly listed, a telegram came from Jean Gordon, the only female member of the NWT Council, urging the commission to consider a trip north to hear from the women "who have worked and stood behind the men throughout its history,"[6] and who played an important part in the northern workforce. No mention was made of the particular needs of Indigenous women.

If it was not part of the RCSW's preliminary planning, a northern trip emerged as a "de rigueur" part of its effort to confer far and wide, especially with women whose voices were often marginalized in the mainstream. Commission staffers recognized that their claim to wide consultation was hindered by a lack of input from women in the provincial North as well as in the Far North.[7] RCSW minutes of off-the-record discussions, saved only by Commissioner Elsie MacGill, include deliberations about how to reach the "less articulate" women, not just those with the education, resources, and ability to write briefs but also "low income mothers, new Canadians, Indian women, women in prisons."[8] Indian and Eskimo women, it was suggested, had to be included as "basic variables" in all discussions about the "economic environment;" indeed, this was part of a larger philosophical discussion about whether to integrate research on marginalized women into "each section of the report" or to isolate it as a distinct category. Eventually, the latter was rejected as a segregated, supposedly negative, approach.[9]

The RCSW's integrative approach was followed more concertedly for immigrant women than for Indian and Eskimo women, and the result was the near invisibility of new Canadians in the report. Not only did the RCSW rely on 1961 census data showing Anglo and French women to be the vast majority across the country, but it was assumed that the next largest groups – namely, European immigrants – would in the long run integrate into the two founding English and French nations. Indigenous women were seen somewhat differently, and, originally, a separate section on "prejudice" was to address "special prejudices towards, Indians, Eskimo and others."[10] Up until the last moment, the commission was planning a whole chapter on women in the North; however, faced with problems putting enough research material together, it opted, literally at the last rushed minute of revisions, for sections in other chapters.[11] Nonetheless, the imperative of integrating a discussion of Indigenous women remained important for at least two of the commissioners other than Bird: Lola Lange, who had accompanied Florence Bird North, and Elsie Gregory MacGill, the most radical of the lot, who also warned, with her uncommon perspicacity, that "within a few years, the Eskimo may demand to be called Inuit. We should indicate we are not ignorant of this."[12]

How to talk to northerners without incurring massive transportation costs was the key logistical problem for the RCSW. There was not enough money allocated in the budget to take the entire commission north, but Bird, who had consulted the civil servants in the Privy Council Office who were overseeing all Royal Commissions, heard that Judge W.G. Morrow of the Territorial Court of the Northwest Territories was making a tour of the Keewatin region to hear adoption cases. Lola Lange found out he kept a residence in Edmonton as well as in Yellowknife, and she called him in Edmonton to see if the RCSW could "hitch a ride" with him. Negotiations ensued, and Morrow himself stressed the importance of commissioners actually going to the North to see the situation of women for themselves. While a trip for two commissioners to Yellowknife and Whitehorse became feasible, travelling to the hinterland of Inuit settlements seemed initially impossible since the Department of Justice might have charged the RCSW for its share of the charter aircraft. The RCSW management team at first recommended against the second leg of the trip, not only because of expense but also because it might seem perfunctory since "nobody can pretend to understand and speak on Indian and Eskimo villages after a few hours of observation."[13] Bird, too, was apprehensive about the immense costs in a time of budget restraint, and she was also concerned that the RCSW not become "another Commission on the treatment of native peoples," not only because of the "complex" problems of Indigenous women but also because of the basic barrier of language.[14]

Yet Bird understood that the RCSW would be criticized if it "relied entirely on research" and did not hear directly from "Eskimo communities." She justified the trip with precisely this rationale: "I think it is my duty to go with him [Morrow], to avoid possible criticism ... Although we will have to rely on the reports of the research people and the Department of Northern Affairs which has spent years studying Indians and Eskimos, we will at least be able to say that we took the trouble to look for ourselves. I have an idea that looking for ourselves will be a valuable

experience."[15] Whatever her sense of duty, Bird fretted about how strenu-
ous a trip it would be, consulted Morrow on her Arctic wardrobe so that
she was prepared for weather and insects, and worried about accommodation. The North in the imaginations of southerners still appeared an
intimidating, other-worldly environment. Morrow warned Bird that billeted accommodation might be make-shift, and his offer to lend her a
sleeping bag so she could sleep on someone's floor likely did not assuage
her concerns.

Commissioners were eager to tap into Morrow's northern expertise,
which he shared with them on their long plane journeys. Bird had implied in a private letter that Morrow might share his ideas on Indian and
Eskimo women with her confidentially, thus bypassing the information
doled out by the Department of Indian and Northern Affairs. Bird's
letter to that department a year later about its lack of consultation with
women over its white paper suggests that she was not entirely convinced
that it was attentive to issues of importance to Indigenous women.[16]
Judge Morrow's previous Royal Commission experience, his decisions
on the northern circuit, including the famous *Drybones* case, and his
comments on northern issues marked him as sympathetic to issues of
equal access to justice for First Nations. His later decisions on land rights
reinforced this reputation.[17] He offered advice on where to hold hearings,
lent the RCSW a court reporter, and was instrumental in facilitating
the more difficult trips to small Inuit settlements that required transla-
tors. The contact with Morrow likely reinforced for Bird the importance
of addressing the specific needs of northern Indigenous women in the
final report. However, this sense of importance did not flow two ways:
Morrow's autobiography never mentions the RCSW.

Bird travelled North with preconceived ideas about the best way to
engage northern women. As Barbara Freeman suggests, she harboured an
idealized image of universal womanhood, with women like her and Lange
specially attuned to the concerns of all the women they encountered,
despite very different backgrounds.[18] Bird thought speaking "woman to
woman" in informal northern settings was the best guarantee of good
information. When the idea of a trip North first surfaced, she told
Morrow she thought "formal hearings" in the North would be "a waste

of time "; instead, she wanted to speak personally with women after news of the RCSW was spread by word of mouth, and she suggested that perhaps Morrow himself could recommend interviews.[19] The plan shifted, however, to encompass formal hearings in two urban centres and off-the-record discussions, first in small villages just outside Yellowknife (for which she and Lange shared responsibility) and, later, in Inuit settlements and at Churchill.

Few briefs had come on their own volition from the North, so commission employees tried to scare up some more, writing to the usual suspects: government officials in the Territorial Council, established women's organizations (usually more educated, middle-class ones), and also some groups involved with First Nations peoples. The RCSW was not entirely ignorant of the bias of its selection. It knew it had to address Indigenous women's needs; however, it was not cognizant of how to do this, other than through the tried-and-true methods of hearing from those who spoke *about* Indigenous women. Since one letter had come to the RCSW from an Indian woman in Yellowknife, Bird tried to persuade her to come and speak at the hearing. According to Bird's autobiography, the woman's letter was so "moving" that she tracked her down in Yellowknife by consulting the RCMP for an address and then had a police driver take her to the woman's house in "Lowertown." She urged the Mountie to stay out of sight so as not to "give the wrong impression" to the residents, and then she persuaded the woman, living in a pathetically bare shack with only a wood stove for heat, that her appearance at the hearings "would help her people." Bird considered her visit a success since the woman's testimony got good press coverage.[20]

SEGREGATED LIVES: WOMEN'S BRIEFS AND TESTIMONY

Bird was undoubtedly referring to the letter and testimony of Mary Ann Lahache, a non-Treaty Indian who lost her Treaty rights through her husband's decision to negate his, and who was now living alone, reduced to an impoverished existence doing occasional housework since her lack of education and a disability – epilepsy – shut her out of other work. Her letter and testimony were indeed moving for she combined pathos and humility with her despondency about the predicament of Indian women in the community, many of whom were living in a "one-room house" and unable to "read or write for themselves." Lahache allowed Bird to read her letter at the hearing, citing her lack of education and retiring demeanour: "I am a shy and quiet person and can't talk for myself." However, her story still made powerful points, not only bringing home the problems with the patriarchal Indian Act but also the economic marginalization of Indian women. She did not trust welfare officials to help her as they simply wanted to "send her back" to her home. She was living on one hundred dollars a month with no security for the future, and she was consumed by worry about her medical bills. Lahache had always desired children but had not had any, and she felt she had "done the right thing" by taking her adopted son back to the authorities since she knew she could not support him properly – though this was clearly painful for her. "Really," she concluded, "I just feel like committing suicide sometimes it gets so tough, lucky I don't drink or I would have done it long ago."[21]

Mary Ann Lahache's letter and testimony had an impact on Bird because they invoked emotion, pathos, and the urgency of addressing the poverty of Indigenous women. Perhaps Lahache's statement appealed especially to the charitable instincts of liberal feminists like Bird, yet, in doing so, it also replicated a certain colonial dynamic. Still, Lahache's humble, quiet appeal may have been her way of speaking back to government power in a manner learned through years of poverty, intimidation, and fear of welfare authorities. There is no doubt that Lahache's submission contrasted sharply to that of a white witness, Alison McAteer, vice-president of the local YWCA. The RCSW staff in Ottawa originally thought hers was one of the better northern briefs, offering some of the "best" comments on training domestic workers.[22]

McAteer addressed both the need for trained household help for women in the workforce and for legislation requiring employers to provide shower facilities for men since many working-class homes did not have access to hot water. Her brief noted that water was a pressing issue for women of the North, especially "lower-class and native families." After all, it was the woman who had to deal with "dirty clothes, dishes," and so on. While Aboriginal children were being taught new lessons about "cleanliness" in the schools, they could not actually implement hygienic practices at home. She conceded that raising the wages of unskilled labour might aid in the purchase of dwellings with hot water, but providing washing facilities at work was a practical solution in the here-and-now. Her other recommendation about domestic training was intended to aid the unemployed, including Aboriginal women, though it simultaneously revealed unthinking acceptance of a race- and class-based hierarchy. Domestic work, she argued, lacked prestige, benefits, training, marketing, and a good wage: it should be reclaimed and reconfigured as valued paid labour. At the same time, she indicated that it was especially suitable for poor and Native women who had no skills or education.

Such schemes to elevate domestic workers had a century-long history, and, though sometimes initiated by working women, they were usually promoted by more affluent women who were looking for domestic help rather than engaging in it themselves for pay. McAteer's designation of housework as potential work for First Nations women contrasts sharply with Lahache's testimony that such work was their tribulation. Bird immediately picked up on this contradiction: she noted that many people wanted to train *others* to do this work, yet there was no line up to take the training. She found McAteer's claim that home help suited "certain groups who lacked the aptitude to do anything else," and the implication that these groups included "Indian women," disturbing: "Wouldn't it be more important perhaps for us to begin to find out what the aptitudes of these people are rather than to lump them all together as a group which is only suitable for domestic service?" McAteer's answers suggest that she saw Indian and Métis women as part of a group of women, including "immigrants and whites," who were just "not employable in any other field." It was a class-inflected argument that, in the North, was simultaneously racialized. The commissioners were clearly uncomfortable with this recommendation. Even staff member Monique Begin spoke up, pointing out that many working women did not make enough to pay the high wages that might have boosted the status of domestic work.[23] Yet some subsequent white witnesses did not pick up these cues and dug themselves deeper into condescending discussions of domestic work as good work for the poor and racialized. One claimed that young women especially needed more domestic training so they might take more pride in this work, "generally better for the low income, white, and native who seem to be in need of raising their status."[24]

Mary Ann Lahache's and Alison McAteer's testimonies suggest two female solitudes in the North, though briefs and testimony did not always fall so neatly into these separate silos. There was a dominant view, repeated most often, that northern Indian and Eskimo women needed to be helped as they were disadvantaged by culture, lack of education, poverty, and (sometimes) oppression within their own cultures. Yet this concern was expressed through a range of overlapping, sometimes contradictory, expressions of racism, paternalism, colonialism, critiques of racism, and moral outrage. Many people did agree that Native and white women generally led segregated lives. Bird later claimed that white women complained to her that Aboriginal women were favoured because they had access to kindergartens while white women did not (since Indigenous education was funded through the Department of Indian and Northern Affairs). The actual testimony does not suggest antagonism as much as a lament, and, in one case, a white witness argued the positive case that all children needed to learn to live together from a young age. Many briefs, however, conceded that there was little or no "social integration" of white and Indigenous, a problem Bird suggested might be attributed to the segregating effects of "reservations" and Aboriginal women's desire for cultural autonomy. Still, Bird repeatedly asked those testifying whether Native women were discriminated against, whether they were truly "accepted" in white society.

Mrs. Findlay of the Yukon Social Services Organization agreed that white women did not always welcome First Nations women and that white and native children should be better integrated in schools. She concurred that Aboriginal women were intimidated by mixed-race functions "and [that] the only time you do get them attending is if they have had quite a bit to drink and are brave enough to come."[25] Like much of the testimony, hers was contradictory, on the one hand decrying segregation and discrimination, then, on the other, offering a paternalist and/or racist explanation for it. Yet the one fact taken for granted by almost everyone testifying was that women's social existence and status was shaped by race. "The status of women in the Yukon territory seems to be quite different for the white woman than for the Indian woman," announced the same Yukon Social Services Organization at the Whitehorse hearings: "The white women have more recognition, acceptance and independence than many have experienced elsewhere. However the Indian woman is not in such a fortunate position."[26]

Not only did testimony point to a segregated and discriminatory society but it also revealed different cultural portrayals of white and Indigenous women. White women were cast, on the one hand, as intrepid and venturesome frontierswomen, courageously carving out new lives, just as white men venturing north had long done. Women who came "independently" were "more vigorous and self-asserted types," and even the ones with husbands had a little more of the "independent spirit" or they would not have agreed to go North: "Lacking this spirit, they would not stay long." One commentator understood women's paid work through this northern imaginary: like the "virile men" of the North, enterprising white woman had no trouble finding jobs – for example, as "stenographers,"[27] and so on. That this was more a function of a gender- and race-segregated labour market and demographic imbalances than a sign of women's frontier initiative was not contemplated. Bird herself absorbed this view of northern hardiness, claiming that these women "seemed to have no doubts about their own ability to do anything they wanted to do. It was quite evident that the pioneer spirit was strong in the land."[28]

At the same time, witnesses claimed that the northern environment created some specific problems for white women sojourners and settlers, particularly social isolation and difficulties adjusting to the long dark of winter. Isolation in the home, one suggested, led to white women being in the "worst position of all [compared to Native women] ... they might be better off financially but they felt trapped in [a domestic] jail," leading to depression, violence, child neglect, and alcoholism.[29] "If white women could associate more with native women," this might give them "a whole different outlook."[30] White sojourner reflections on life in the Northwest Territories in the 1950s and 1960s confirm how segregated women were:

"We were isolated, living with no connection to the women who lived in other settlements in the north ... we didn't have the opportunity to try and relate to native women. I am not saying people didn't exist and get along. I'm saying they simply had very little to do with each other."[31] Another witness claimed white women felt strong pressure to become full-time homemakers rather than employed workers; indeed, one white woman from Yellowknife wrote privately to the RCSW, chastising married white women for taking jobs away from Aboriginal youth.[32] If women did have to work, they might be shut out of government housing or retraining programs, and since few had extended family nearby, finding child care was an immense problem. Despite all these pressures, white women had a high labour force participation rate in comparison to their southern counterparts.

While written testimony did not emphasize the need for more white women émigrés to head to the North as a solution to social problems, an interview Lola Lange conducted with a northern nurse intimated that this was precisely what was needed: more white women would create more stable families and communities. Lange was told that the influx of single white male resource workers should be balanced out by more white women and family migration since the single men "upset the balance in the community when the only women in the area were Eskimo women." Lange too noted there was a "problem" with such a small proportion of white women in this Eskimo community. The implication, of course, was that whites and Eskimo should "stick to their own" rather than intermarrying.[33]

This concern about family decline took a moralistic turn with the testimony of Mrs. Parker, representing her husband, a local magistrate. She offered a lengthy discussion of criminal charges, convictions, and so on, and lamented "a deterioration" in the status of women because "marriage and the family" were "not taken seriously" enough anymore; young people were not getting married and setting up "normal families" but, rather, producing "illegitimate children." Native women's low status, in other words, was the fault of the deterioration of their traditional culture. Her evidence included "impressions" and anecdotes offered by her

magistrate husband. The brief's lament for a dissolute younger generation bore some resemblance to concerned comment across the country
on the dissipation of 1960s youth.[34]

Two female racial solitudes are also suggested by the simple fact that
the briefs were predominantly from whites, though not always from the
same ideological standpoint. Most briefs were written by individuals
or organizations connected to social services, women's organizations, or
government offices. The needs of wage-earning women were a shared
concern, though journalists noticed that those speaking out were usually
"professional" women rather than the "ordinary" (blue- and white-collar)
working woman.[35] While the sorority women from Alpha Chapter of
Beta Sigma Phi lamented the decline in status of homemaking, they did
report on a recent public panel at which women called for daycare, income tax deductions for household help, the retraining of women, and
an end to discrimination in promotions.[36] White women's briefs were
also concerned with tax issues, not only for working women but also for
northerners who needed to be compensated for the high cost of living.
Like southern presenters, many women did not fundamentally challenge
the existing sexual division of labour but, rather, advocated for better
training for women in service, white-collar, and professional occupations. Government-related briefs from the public administrator of Yukon
Territory and from Jean Gordon dealt with laws, benefits, marital status,
inheritance, and other legal issues. Doubtless, these were significant for
northern women, but who inherited wealth and who was insured to drive
an automobile were likely issues of less pressing concern to Indigenous
women.[37] These briefs assumed that property was an individual issue;
however, for the First Nations, land was often a collective political
concern.

Given that northern white women were constructed as assertive and
enterprising, it is ironic that, on more than one occasion, men spoke for
them: if white people spoke for Indigenous women, white men spoke
for white women. This was true, for instance, of the brief from the Yukon
Department of Social Welfare, delivered by Mr. O'Donaghue. After
complimenting the "phalanx of intelligent and rather good looking"

women in the room,[38] he explained that his department was not keen on providing an "official" brief but that those working in "his office" (probably many women) pressed the issue. Not surprisingly, their social welfare orientation stressed better legal means of pursuing paternal child support and economic supports for single mothers as well as legally legitimizing common law relations.

Briefs like this one assumed the shared social needs of Indigenous and low-income women: daycare should be provided, for instance, in a territory "where 17% of the population was Indian and Métis," as it was known that "under-privileged children" did badly in the early years of school. Day care would give all poor children a head start and allow their mothers to go out to work. Mr. O'Donoghue was himself conflicted about working mothers, slipping in his personal view: not only did *his* wife not work, but, "where he was brought up, the women who stay home should have the status. I am slightly appalled to think that in Canada it is those who go out who get that status." Would the women working in his office have agreed? His statement was not unusual: southern testimony similarly assumed that low-income single mothers needed to work for wages but that this was not the ideal familial arrangement. The proposition that working-class and Indigenous single mothers should be paid generous "wages for housework" so that they might be full-time home-makers like Mrs. O'Donoghue was not on the political radar of most people testifying.[39]

Northern women were thus not always discursively located in two racialized solitudes since it was assumed that the problems of "lower-class" women directly overlapped with those of Aboriginal women. It is true that both shared one problem: poverty. The repeated reference to water as a women's issue, and the desperate need for access to clean, running water, symbolized their shared predicament. More often, however, race trumped class as an explanation for social divisions in the North. There were recurring narratives that dissected, explained, and decried Aboriginal women's second-class status. Government officials focused more on legal redress; Jean Gordon, for example, suggested recognizing Native customary marriage instead of recording their children as "illegitimate," and she also recommended that unmarried Indigenous women, no matter who the partner, should have the right to register their children as Indian since this had "economic consequences" for their offspring.[40]

More often, witnesses stressed the social exclusion of Native women from mainstream society. Standard stories or accounts were reiterated, with varying conclusions drawn from them. One of the most common narratives was that of the "fallen" Native woman: it emphasized the isolation and vulnerability of all First Nations women in large urban centres like Yellowknife and Whitehorse, and it was primarily a story of sexual risk and downfall. In some presentations, white men were blamed outright; but, in most instances, it was Native women's naiveté and vulnerability that was accented. One witness constructed the common scenario around the young "Indian girl, living in a poor family situation, [who] takes the opportunity to escape" to the city but finds no work, is soon saddled with a child, and has no means of returning to school.[41] Another stressed the fatal attraction of the local bar, where men took advantage of Aboriginal women. The solution was better accommodation and welcoming Native friendship centres. In all cases, seduction, illegitimate children, addiction, and poverty are the end products of this narrative. In contrast to the "hardy" northern white women, Native women were portrayed as defenseless and easily manipulated.

The term "shacking up" was used repeatedly in northern testimony regarding Indian women's liaisons with white men. Also common were statements that Native women sought out these relationships because these partners were more likely to have money and jobs than were Native partners. But since these relationships were rarely consummated in marriage, Indian women were easily abandoned by feckless white men who were "unwilling to take their wives back to civilization with them."[42] That Aboriginal women did not marry for fear of losing their Indian status was mentioned but not taken as seriously as it should have been: to stress this would have given Indian women more agency than they were usually accorded. Some claimed that the sexual exploitation of women was simultaneously the downfall of Native men since men felt anger and resentment at being "left with the white man's leavings." As this witness put it: when these girls "lose their looks in four or five years," only then do they "settle for an Indian husband." Native masculinity was thus also in crisis since young men simply had no "incentive to improve themselves" by moving up the ladder of progress when their women "would rather have a white man for a husband."[43] This designation was particularly offensive, but others stressed that interracial marriage was not bad, it was just intrinsically unequal: it left Native women vulnerable to desertion and Native men designated as inferiors.

The common narrative about Aboriginal women's potential sexual downfall, then, was coupled with fears about the disintegration of Native families and communities. Some witnesses warned that the transition from traditional to modern living, especially in centralized settlements, was undermining Native family ties. While Indigenous women were adapting fairly well, asserted a white teacher in a Dene community, children were not learning traditional cultural and hunting skills since they had to go to school, yet older bush skills were essential not only to cultural identity but also to economic subsistence. Not surprisingly, commissioners tried to use well-known social science theories of the day regarding the dispossessed and poor. Bird wanted to know if there was a rise in female-led "matriarchal" households, as in the black United States, something clearly seen as less than desirable — just as the American Moynihan Report suggests.[44] Were Indians caught in the same place as "negroes," she asked? Were they treated as the same, en masse, "as negroes are in south Africa, in one area of town, white people in another area of town, already drawing a colour bar?" Would Native girls benefit from courses in homemaking and child psychology, as had "people in underdeveloped countries"?[45] The director of divinity of the Anglican Church, Dr. Hilda Hellaby, whose views were given considerable space in CBC reporting, stoked these fears of an emerging "matriarchy," citing the fact that women were now the "undisputed owners" of their children as one indication of this.[46] A Roman Catholic priest, whose expert knowledge on Indigenous families was taken for granted, echoed his concern that Indian men were absent and that women were left "in charge" of their communities. A white northern journalist, however, dismissed the matriarchy idea as ridiculous because, as far as she was concerned, "Indian women did all the work."[47]

While witness testimony reveals little understanding of what a matriarchy actually is, it does suggest a generalized view that Indigenous family life was in a precarious moral decline, and families on welfare were cited as evidence of this disintegration. Financial security through male breadwinners, Lola Lange mused, was still the solution, thus echoing the message of NFB films like *Our Northern Citizen*. Despite hearing that seismic shifts in the economy had upset traditional patterns of subsistence, Lange wanted to discuss cultural explanations, specifically whether the "culture of poverty" theory illuminated the Native predicament. Other witnesses echoed the image of low-income and Aboriginal families reproducing not just children but a *culture of hopelessness*: "It is very costly to continue these [poor] families generation after generation in the same situation."[48] Echoing neo-Malthusian ideas from the past, "large families" were cited as the problem rather than the inadequate two-room houses in which they lived. A higher standard of living would be facilitated by training homemakers properly, reorganizing the interior of the home, and ensuring that women learned not to budget "foolishly." Better-off "professional native homemakers" could help their less fortunate sisters.[49] At least this bootstrapping advice did not simply assume that whites would elevate Natives: Natives would also elevate natives.

Not all briefs and testimony necessarily laid the blame for violence and family fragility on the weaknesses of Native women. Marilyn Assheton-Smith, a Company of Young Canadians (CYC) worker in Yellowknife, submitted a brief and testified about the sexual abuse of Indigenous women. She used two case studies of women with whom she had come into contact to make her point: one woman suffered from alcoholism after being used by a white male "camp" worker, and the other woman had been sexually and violently abused at the hands of male oil workers. Both women, Smith stressed, were exploited, hurt, damaged. The latter woman, despite her "state of shock," refused to go to the police, indicating the distrust of Indigenous women for those supposedly protecting them. While these two narratives, especially the description of the first woman, who was still to be found "standing outside a bar with her hand out," bore some resemblance to other narratives of the fallen Native woman, Assheton-Smith's conclusion placed the blame squarely on white society.[50] Why, she asked, do we socialize our sons to treat some women as wives, others as prostitutes?

Given the company she kept, her focus on white fault and Indian exploitation was understandable. Unlike the moralistic Parker, this younger witness, shaped by the radical thinking in the CYC, made it clear she was not concerned with denouncing "immorality" or "camp followers" (as Native women were called) but, rather, with naming the male attitudes that produced Native women's misery. What "makes it possible for us to raise men, boys, who go into the camps ... [where] they will destroy women, lower class women if you like to call them that." The patriarchal sexual myths shaping society were at fault — namely, the idea that some women were pure, others not. The solution was "developing [men's] respect for women as human beings." Her practical solutions approximated those of some other social service workers: housing for single Native women, educating youth about respect, counselling services.[51] Like the more progressive Indian-Eskimo Association, she saw little use in criminalizing or jailing women: alcohol and other problems should be treated as "health and welfare" concerns, not crimes.[52]

White men are also held up to scrutiny in Bird's later autobiography. She relates an informal visit she had from some young University of British Columbia male students in the North, who came to see her at the motel as they wanted to talk "off the record." They expressed "shock" at the "treatment of Indian and Eskimo women by miners [and] construction workers" and related incidents in which these men "made [Native women] drunk ... sexually abused them" multiple times, and then "threw them out, naked, to wander about in the cold." Bird was not enamored with the students' solution — namely, licensed brothels — though she recounted their story as a compelling example of "situations which often arise" when there were unattached men "without social ties, wives and families" who lived close to others whom they felt were racially "inferior." It is interesting to note which conversations Bird chose to recount in her autobiography: this one tells the reader that not all men are tainted by patriarchal ideas as these young men objected to women's sexual exploitation. The students were of course conveniently blaming another group of men: working-class men. Yet this story of gang rape and potentially lethal abuse points to an issue underlining the recurring narrative of the fallen Native woman: racialized violence against women existed in the North. It was just a question of how it was interpreted. Was it a sign of women's vulnerability and weakness or a result of a patriarchal, racist, and colonialist mentality? The latter words would not have been used at the time, but Assheton-Smith comes closest to them.[53]

The students' story raises another repeated theme in RCSW testimony. There was an underlying assumption that others could speak for and about Aboriginal women: white experts or sojourners were constantly queried about the views and needs of Indigenous women. In this sense, the RCSW was similar to *The Beaver*'s popular anthropology or sojourner narratives of the past, though it is clear that the RCSW at least *wanted* Indigenous women to speak out. The trust commissioners placed in the opinions of well-educated observers and experts to comment on other women differentiated by language, class, and/or race was common across all the RCSW hearings, North and South. At one extreme, the RCSW's reliance on white opinion seems, at best, naïve; for example, it assumed that white priests and ministers were experts on their Aboriginal female parishioners. In other cases, such as the white Indian-Eskimo Association man who was married to a Native woman, the witness could at least cite his working relationship with the First Nations within the mixed-race alliance of the IEA.

To our thinking, the assumption that white experts could speak for Native women is egregiously arrogant. At the time, the commissioners did not see their questions as outrageous; rather, failing Indigenous witnesses, they wanted to hear from people who knew or worked with Indigenous people regarding what policies might best serve their needs. Their puzzlement was quite genuine. After Assheton-Smith warned that Indians were being put into one-dimensional cultural boxes, their needs "assumed," rather than their being asked "what they really do need," Lange peppered her with questions on how to reach out cross-culturally: How can we know what they think? "How do we learn this sort of thing? Have you any suggestions other than all joining the Company of Young Canadians?"[54]

Witnesses, however, were often asked how Indigenous women could be *helped*, a word that slipped into a highly questionable paternalism. The language of Dr. Hellaby, who also presented a brief written by Beth-Anne Exham, a missionary's wife and teacher in a Gwwich/in Dene community, is instructive. Exham, claimed Hellaby, was all too "modest" about her important role as she was one of the small group of white people who was in the North "to serve the Indians." The missionaries, teachers, nurses, and RCMP are all there "for the Indian." This relationship is thus never colonial but always beneficent. Even white witnesses' attempts to be culturally sensitive, since they knew Indigenous communities were under stress, might be entangled with an image of a ladder of modern evolutionary progress that Natives would sooner or later have to ascend. Indians "don't want the same things as we do. They don't place a high value on material possessions ... or plan for the future as we do," Hellaby explained. Despite this laudable lack of acquisitive impulse, Indigenous women had to face a transition or "social revolution," a shift to modern industrialized society, following a path white women had already "moved through years ago."[55] Hellaby did call for education for Native youth in their own culture by Native teachers, but her sense of who to consult about Indigenous lives reflected the unassailable view that whites were the experts. "If you want to know something about the Indians, ask the bachelor boys," she said, referring to white male sojourners working in the area.[56] Since Assheton-Smith had already argued that this was how Indigenous women encountered sexual exploitation, it seemed a rather inappropriate source of expertise.

Not all white experts were ideologically alike in their views. Magistrate Parker was inclined to see moral regeneration as a solution to women's problems, while Mr. McKinnon, the Whitehorse MP, managed to slip his own political agenda into his testimony, calling for more "local control" because the federal government had been an "abject failure," as evidenced by the rising crime and delinquency rates of Indigenous youth. Twelve years ago, he claimed, young Indians were "not bitter" as they are now: "it is seething and fermenting underneath and it's ready to blow." If McKinnon had conversed with Assheton-Smith and her CYC colleagues, he might have heard a political analysis of Native "bitterness" arising from long-standing colonial relations and their loss of land and livelihood. In contrast, McKinnon believed Indians should eventually move off the land, which he was clear was not *their* land, and be "integrated" into society: "There are Indian Villages where people live but these are not theirs in perpetuity as grants or reserves. I think this is a good thing and it is going to provide for an easier integration eventually."[57]

His views contrasted dramatically to those of Harry Leishman, executive secretary of the NWT Indian-Eskimo Association, a lobby group that had about one-third Indigenous, two-thirds white membership, and, when asked, saw itself as speaking not for, but on behalf of, Indigenous peoples.[58] Both the brief and the testimony stressed the imperatives of cultural validation, self-determination, education, and economic security. One of his major concerns was the hostel system experienced by young Aboriginal girls who were raised in residential schools and thus deprived of their language, culture, and families. Rather than living in hostels staffed by whites, they should encounter Native people of their own cultural background. "You can't understand their problems unless you are native ... white people cannot provide the understanding [in hostels] native kids need." The content of education was dubious too: they encountered a moralistic "sheltered" sex-segregated education about "sex and sin being synonymous" but not much in terms of job training or knowledge about the world. Lacking either new marketable skills or older cultural ones, they returned home completely alienated. Unlike others testifying, Leishman was quite critical of the churches: "Get the churches back into the church" and get them out of education was his blunt recommendation to the commissioners, who seemed somewhat surprised by his candour.

The result of a girl's inadequate and moralistic education was sexual vulnerability; she became "prey to the male community." And there is no doubt Leishman meant the white male community. To some extent, his narrative approximated that of the fallen Native woman, but his analysis also differed from that of others. "Native problems are community problems," he noted, and, although resources like counselling, friendship

centres, and accommodation might go a long way to aiding these problems, what was also needed was more "education" of white northerners.
His recipe for aiding Indian mothers was equally straightforward: they
are prematurely old not because they have too many children but because
they don't have the resources to raise them – no "fridges, running water,
electricity." The state also came in for criticism. Dividing up resources
between Treaty Indian, non-Treaty Indian, and Eskimo, he suggested,
was counter-productive in the North, in part because Indigenous people
"did not differentiate." Leishman castigated civil servants for reproducing racist ideas about welfare users: they claim Indian women "are happy
to sit around and do nothing ... that they are living a life of blissful ignorance. This is of course nonsense."

Economic stability would go some way to alleviating these social
problems. If women secured "more than a pittance" for their handicrafts,
marketed for large amounts by white intermediaries, they would have
better means to support their children. If white men were not given pref-
erence for jobs over equally qualified Native men, the latter could better
feed their families. If Native women were treated equally in courts of
law, they would not suffer the level of criminalization that was now the
case. This is not to idealize Leishman's testimony: he also made some
contradictory statements about Native children being schooled away from
their Native families and occasionally portrayed whites as those with the
moral and intellectual ability to lead. Like Lange, he was also trapped
within a male breadwinner family ideal. However, his insistence that
Indian and Eskimo problems were not individual and moral but, rather,
related to structural economic inequality and social discrimination, and
his call for whites to pay attention to Indigenous voices, suggests a less
paternalistic view than those held by other witnesses.[59] When questioned
by reporters, some white women who testified similarly echoed their
discomfort with "all the advice" given by white women to Aboriginal
women. "I don't like this ... patronizing air" of telling Native women
how to keep house, said Didi Dodds, who travelled hundreds of kilo-
metres from Hay River, a Dene community, to speak to the RCSW:
"Native women can teach us something. Until we have walked in their
shoes, we should not criticize."[60]

A small chorus of white allies like Leishman and Dodds did question stereotypes, and even the commissioners, however limited by their liberal feminist perspective, were asking questions about Aboriginal women's status that earlier women sojourners had not. Only two Indigenous women appeared, yet their testimony also marked a break from the past, including the way it was relayed to the outside world (discussed later in this chapter). When Lahache was asked how Indian women could be helped, she immediately pointed to their dire material need: they lived in poor houses, often with only two rooms, with "no running water, or anything like that, that most of the white people have."[61] Lange and Bird asked her about a suggestion offered by other witnesses: that there be "communal bath houses" with washing machines in communities without indoor plumbing as a stop-gap measure.[62] Lahache thought this would be "OK" but was not enthusiastic. Perhaps she was wondering if middle-class white women would want to have bath houses instead of their own indoor plumbing? Education was needed, Lahache agreed with some prompting, as she had only attended a one-room school house in Aklavik. Lahache was also sceptical about Indian women working at domestic labour since she only made a hundred dollars a month. Most women did not want this work unless "they got decent wages and were treated like other people."[63] Many of the commissioners' questions tried to lead Lahache in certain directions, in part because she was not talkative, in part to receive her input on the recommendations made by others.

Lahache's reticence contrasted with the more forthright tone of Rosemary Thrasher, a twenty-two-year-old Inuk who both wrote to the commission and spoke at the Yellowknife hearing. Running water opened her comments, too: Indigenous women of the North would like "better living conditions, [to] have equal housing with any other, running water and sewage." Women's domestic labour was arduous enough without having to haul "water in forty to fifty below zero weather and spilling sewage every day." Poor housing was a problem, as were job opportunities, since Indigenous girls had little education and had access only to the "jobs that no one else would take." She, too, mentioned Native women's sexual liaisons with white men, but she put them in a decidedly material context. Many young women "get picked up so that they can get a place to sleep and food to eat," or, if they have children, "they want someone to help care for them." Moreover, Thrasher circled back to the sexual harassment of single Indigenous women: "Girls should be able to live without having to have guys bug them all the time ... they sometimes threaten a girl who has no knowledge of her own rights ... [S]ome girls are scared to live alone because of this."

Rosemary Thrasher had heard Alison McAteer testify about the value of paid domestic work for Aboriginal women and she forthrightly challenged her. "Someone mentioned – Mrs. McAteer – you mentioned something about the native girls that don't really do their jobs or something?" Despite McAteer's defensive "no" emanating from the audience, Thrasher persisted: "the reason a girl would not want such a job is because she has more abilities than that role." Later, she changed her stance, saying that girls could take domestic jobs as a way to help "upgrade" themselves; however, overall, she stressed education, training, respect, and equal rights as well as material resources to improve the substandard living conditions of Indigenous women.

The commissioners immediately pegged Thrasher as a leader and role model. They saw her government job and secure living situation as a sign of success and as an indication that she might be able to counsel other girls coming to the city. While she was willing to assume that mantle, Thrasher, like Leishman and Assheton-Smith, stressed that she was not the only one to answer for "the Native": "Ask the native people want they need," she told the commission, unwilling to assume the voice of all Native peoples (and she had to remind the commissioners that she was Eskimo, *not* Indian). Interestingly, Bird mentions Lahache in her autobiography but not the feistier Thrasher. Unlike others testifying, including Lahache, Thrasher made the structural power relations of colonialism clear: "the country belonged to the native before the white man, so the best consideration should be given to them." She advised the government to turn its equality rhetoric into reality: "The government talks about equality and I think we are entitled to that too. Everyone knows this country is where red and native people lived before you came. And if you want to run the country the way you want to, then consideration should be given to native peoples."[64] No wonder the CBC reporter Ed Reid noted her unusual outspokenness.

COMMISSIONERS REINTERPRET THE NORTH

When Irene Bird and Lola Lange returned south, they relayed their thoughts on the trip to the other commissioners, with Bird later recounting hers more publicly in her memoir. Their impressionistic reports tell us something about negotiated images of the Aboriginal North, particularly how white observers drew on existing tropes and images, processing these into their own experiences. Lange's and Bird's interpretations were then incorporated into the political agenda of the RCSW's report, which was published in 1970. No doubt, the other commissioners believed that Lange's and Bird's accounts were valuable because they offered "real-life," first-person, and up-to-date reflections. It is also through these internal discussions that we hear Lange's and Bird's impressions of their trip to eastern Arctic Inuit settlements, since written testimony was not gathered at these places.

Lange taped some interviews outside of the Yellowknife and White-horse hearings, and she integrated these into her written report for her fellow commissioners. How she gathered her evidence, and who was seen as trustworthy and knowledgeable, is important to note. In order to secure more information on Indigenous life in smaller settlements, Lola Lange and Monique Begin interviewed, on the recommendation of Kay Vaydik, a CBC correspondent in the North, Father Duchaussois, a priest who had been in the NWT for over forty years. This "coffee shop conversation" in Yellowknife was supplemented with comments from Kay Vaydik and even some passers-by who happened by their table![65] Lange, Begin, and Vaydik then drove to Fort Rae, the home of a Tłįchǫ Dene community, observed the town, and interviewed two women they came across by chance in the cooperative store. It was all very impressionistic and haphazard.

Lange anticipated that her reliance on priestly views – which she also drew on heavily when in the eastern Arctic – might be queried, more because she did not interview equal numbers of Anglicans priests than because white religious men might not be the best experts on Indigenous women. Forestalling these concerns, she claimed that priests had vast experience in the North, were "knowledgeable," "very easy to interview," and were "often filling a community development function."[66] While some priests may well have been knowledgeable, it is hard to imagine that interviews with Catholic priests in the South about "what white women were really like" would have been treated so uncritically. Father Duchaussois filtered his answers to her questions through his own religious, patriarchal values. Asked about sexual relationships, he lamented the "loose" sexual liaisons that were the product of Indian women being "attracted to miners or the white men who work in the bush." He assumed Indians shared a patriarchal past, with the "strong men" leading the "tribe"; the present was thus to be lamented, given the absence of men and the emerging "matriarchal" culture. It took very little in terms of women's control over anything to raise fears about matriarchal power. Family allowances were interpreted through the moralistic lens of "traditional" family breakdown. When cash allowances replaced the practice of RCMP and local traders monitoring Indians' purchases, things fell apart: "[The Indians] gambled it or they bought liquor ... and the children never got it."[67] What the priest did share with many of Lange's other interviewees, and with some Inuit commentators of the time, was an acute concern about the decline of "traditional" bush production, which had ensured that shared family economic contributions had created bonds of social solidarity. The devastation of this way of life was creating severe distress since most Indigenous men in newly centralized settlements lacked employment, and young people, now educated "outside," could not fit in either economically or culturally when they returned North.[68]

Lange's trip to Dene territory was guided by the local white social worker. Her interview questions were shaped not only by such intermediaries but also by her own Prairie background; for example, she was interested in women's cooperatives as a path to economic improvement. Her belief in community-based initiatives resulted in her scepticism about outside experts telling northern communities how to plan – a scepticism that might have registered her sympathy for Aboriginal women's decision-making roles. However, her thinking also approximated that of Alberta Social Credit crusaders against outside scientific experts and excessive government regulation.[69] For Lange, cooperatives were a means to Aboriginal women's self-sufficiency, though still requiring white leadership. She claimed that the local cooperative in Fort Rae, established by European priests, had been run by a capable local nun who was pushed out by government experts determined to put Aboriginals in charge, and that this Native male leadership promptly lost money. The two women sewers of handicrafts whom she interviewed were portrayed as the sensible ones. They wanted the nun back in her job, replacing the hopeless men, even though they also admitted the financial rewards of handicraft making were pathetically small compared to what one could receive for wage labour. These women symbolized the North's hope for the future: they were "intelligent," capable, practical, and open to new ideas. "Are we missing the boat," Lange asked, "when we don't do something more with this type of Indian woman, offering continuous learning? It strikes me that we are ignoring a great resource."[70]

Lange's reportage on Inuit women in Nunavut was similarly skewed towards selective sources of information, often white experts and professionals such as priests, nurses, and teachers. Interviewing white northerners was not an invalid research project; it was Lange's uncritical incorporation of their reflections into her report that was problematic. She knew her ability to reach Indigenous women was "rather dubious" since the commissioners "arrived unannounced with a very young high school student to interpret."[71] Both Bird and Lange emphasized the difficulty in hearing local Indigenous voices when these were mediated by translations, cultural differences, and little time. Those who could converse in English were usually "Eskimo men in positions of power," though they, too, were assumed to be a direct entrée to the lives of Inuit women. In Coral Harbour, the local priest became Lange's informant on the changing gendered division of labour in the Arctic. You can't expect to change "the Eskimo mentality" in a few years, he warned her, pointing to the introduction of Western foods as one example of how women's domestic work had been transformed. His answer: "She [the Inuit woman] needs a white woman to show her what to do." The lack of meaningful education for Inuit girls sent out to Churchill reinforced his argument: they have imbibed "the white man's ways"; they are "useless" in terms of skills; they can't sew Eskimo clothes; and they just become a "nuisance" at home. They only thing they can do "is babysit for the whites."[72]

Lange and Bird visited the Nunavut settlements of Coral Harbour, Eskimo Point, Baker Lake, and Rankin Inlet to complete their research. Lange was disturbed by the lack of local Inuit input into the new houses provided by Ottawa. The home was the domestic workplace of women, yet they did not have any representation on local housing councils. She urged that Inuit women be added to these councils, but she also thought that local white homemakers should be trained to be community developers in the North. Lange did stress that local and regional conditions were so varied, Indian and Eskimo communities so different, that there was no one, homogenized North. Planning thus had to take gender, place, and culture into account. She took the need for Western-style modernization on faith, but her emphasis on women's self-organization repeatedly pointed to a gap in the development process: women's insights were ignored. Both Eskimo and Indian women, she warned, were "invisible, forgotten when it comes to human rights. Yet I believe that she has the abilities to change with the times if she is given the right chance."[73]

Both Lola Lange and Florence Bird expressed a certain "womanist" connection to northern Indigenous women, which, however naïve, was honestly felt. Bird believed she had an emotional connection with the Inuit women she encountered, and there is no reason to doubt the feelings she laid claim to, including her joy at seeing Inuit mothers ecstatically happy when their adoptions were completed in Morrow's courtroom: "I found that I was weeping. I was poignantly aware of the deep kinship between all women everywhere and in all ages."[74] She also believed that Eskimo women had their own innate knowledge and insights, born of everyday living in the North and related to their work as mothers. With interpreter Bob Williamson, she sat in a circle with groups of Inuit women who explained their desire for more education, literacy, and knowledge about how to feed their children with new food, how to care for houses they had moved into. They wanted wash houses, sewing machines, and radio programs in their own language. With the exception of the latter, it was mostly the material needs for survival and familial care about which they spoke.

Yet Bird's consultations were weighted heavily towards input from white experts and women sojourners. RCMP wives, teachers, nurses, and civil servants all came to talk to her privately in the room in which she was billeted. They "sat on the end of the bed and spoke off the record."[75] In her autobiography, Bird reiterates her construction of these "plucky" northern women breaking down barriers on the frontier. She came away with especially immense respect for the nurses, who were "neither dependent, passive or lacking in self confidence as many women are" but, rather, "courageous, resourceful" women who cared for whole communities, offering midwifery skills, and sometimes doing the work of doctors. They were symbols of "what happens when the abilities of women are developed."[76] The commissioners, in other words, gathered impressions that inevitably absorbed and reflected the conclusions of white northerners, while Indian and Eskimo women were essentialized as having the same universal character traits as all women. These impressions conveyed different views of NWT Indian women (who were constructed as precariously vulnerable, especially to sexual exploitation) and Eskimo women (whose idealized maternal and familial roles were stressed).

The commissioners' efforts to understand Indigenous women were not synonymous with the more "imperialist" and "assimilationist" mindset of the Women's Institutes, whose efforts to organize Indigenous northern women in the postwar period faltered on the shoals of cultural superiority, but they did share with such reform-minded white women an optimistic, if naïve, belief that universal womanly values, particularly concerning familial care, would provide an easy bridge between female solitudes.[77] Is it not possible, however, that Indigenous women were themselves using Bird's assumption of womanly commonality to press their own agenda? We should not assume they were passive in this encounter. Indeed, they may have been anxious to use this dialogue with the RCSW to make their case for the social and political priorities they saw as essential to family and community survival.

However impressionistic the commissioners' conclusions, there is some congruence between them and the writing of professional anthropologists who studied Inuit gender relations in the 1970s. They, too, commented on the cultural divide emerging between generations, the inadequacies of a transplanted educational system, and the difficulties Inuit women faced in finding their new place in an altered economy. The 1970s fieldwork of American anthropologist Anne McElroy, for instance, focuses on the gendered consequences of the transition to a wage economy from a land-based one, a shift that, she argues, seemed initially to favour men's access to jobs but, contrary to predictions, encouraged Inuit girls to delay marriage and embrace education and wage opportunities. Her later work on economic "modernization" and its social consequences posits why some Inuit women, with stronger kin and cultural ties, could weather these drastic changes better than others.[78] Women's changing generational values, the shift from traditional to modern economic activities, and the cultural difficulties with rapid change, are persisting themes for Arctic anthropologists.[79]

More recent research on Inuit women's political roles also creates an evolutionary chronology not unlike that imagined by the RCSW, from "traditional nomadic to transitional settlement life to contemporary Euro-Canadian lifestyle."[80] Unlike the RCSW, these studies, infused with a different feminist sensibility, situate women's lives in a "colonial" context, a word Bird would not have used in relation to the North. There is also a feminist reassessment of the earlier Euro-Canadian, value-laden judgments about women's traditional economic roles in the household. These are no longer seen as a sign of patriarchy but, rather, as "complementary though not identical" gender roles, even though women lacked the economic access to the public sphere enjoyed by Inuit men.[81] Gender roles were shaken up by centralized settlement, loss of subsistence, wage earning, and education, all seen at the time of the RCSW as part of an inevitable modernization process, albeit one that should be far better managed so as to aid Indigenous women.

This contemporary research is far more critical of the colonial mindset that fundamentally shaped the modernization agenda. Patriarchal, colonial ideas, scholars argue, led to the imposition of unequal gender roles: new models of governance in Nunavut were pressed upon the Inuit by white welfare officers and others who saw men as natural leaders and members of local councils. Women's current "lower elite" political participation in government is thus a consequence of the imposition of Euro-Canadian modernization models, not a reflection of patriarchal tradition.[82] Perhaps Lange's insight that Inuit women's important work roles necessitated their involvement in local councils was prescient, even if it offered a very partial solution to the problem of gender disparity.

EXPERT OPINION

The RCSW premised its views of northern Indigenous women not only on pre-existing images, public interviews, briefs, and testimony but also on research and expert opinion gathered before, during, and after its trip North. Some of this research was then recirculated into the public sphere through the report or in later publications by the commissioners.[83] A file of relevant material was collected from government departments, including one report by Irene Baird entitled "The Eskimo in Canada." RCSW staff members like Mark McClung assumed that, among the experts who should be consulted, were long-time NA administrators like Ben Sivertz, or William Taylor, head of the Human History section of the National Museum, who, in turn, recommended noted "anthropologists and sociologists."[84] Anthropological expert opinion was highly valued, and the RCSW had more than one perspective from which to choose once its studies were complete. A comparison of the submissions suggests a shift in expert understandings at the time as conventional views of primitive women jostled with more critical analyses of the colonial environment in which these women lived. In the latter case, an emerging feminist perspective was apparent, challenging the previously masculine-centred worldview of social scientists. These observers were interested in the *viability* – rather than the curiosity – of Indigenous cultures and were beginning to rethink the modernization paradigm that had governed state thinking and the public pronouncements promulgated by earlier experts.

The older view of Indigenous cultures was captured well by a study sent to the commission by Renée Dandurand on "the status of women in

Inuit women shopping in a modern store. Representation of the changing world of the "Eskimo Woman" in the new North. | Hudson's Bay Company Archives, Archives of Manitoba, 1987/363-G-100/11

the primitive societies of colonial Canada." This review of the existing research on Indigenous women in five distinct groupings, including the northern Mackenzie Indian and the Eskimo, employed highly mechanistic measures to calculate whether women had a "good status" in these societies.[85] Taking into account family and kinship (including marriage and divorce), the economy, the division of labour, ownership of surplus, and political and religious systems, Dandurand categorizes primitive peoples into groupings based on economic activity. As groups moved up the ladder of social complexity they went from (1) hunting and gathering with no surplus, to (2) hunting and gathering with surplus, to (3) hunting and gathering and engaging in agricultural cultivation with a surplus. Only the Iroquois fit into the latter group, not coincidentally being the society offering women the highest status. While Dandurand describes Eskimo women performing "complementary" economic roles with men, other practices, such as parents choosing marriage mates, male shamans, or, on rare occasions, female infanticide, indicate the "discriminatory" treatment of women.[86] This study leans heavily on earlier Arctic anthropological studies (such as Birkett-Smith's study of Eskimo infanticide) and places a strong emphasis on Western, liberal, individualist values as the measure of women's worth – for example, freedom of marriage choice, opportunities for leadership, ability to control economic surplus. This study is characterized by an implicitly evolutionary paradigm that separates "primitive" from "modern" peoples and also by an antiseptic, distanced style of presentation. Indigenous women are part of ancient and primitive cultures to be analyzed, classified, and judged – seen, in essence, through the colonial eye of white anthropologists.

Dandurand's study is never mentioned in the RCSW report, suggesting the commissioners simply put it aside as it was less sophisticated than others at their disposal. At the other end of the political spectrum, Nan Shipley's study of Manitoba Native women was not cited by the RCSW report either. This strongly argued research report discusses Indigenous women's "impoverished and underprivileged" way of life, children "forcibly removed" to schools, Native men robbed of their "pride," and the enforced poverty, "hurt[,] and injustice" felt by Native communities. The implicit critique of colonialism made this a far more difficult brief for the commissioners to absorb. While Shipley shares Eurocentric views of a universalized, transhistorical gendered division of labour in which Aboriginal men are the "providers and protectors" and women the "mother[s] and homemaker[s]," she describes social and material conditions of intense oppression. And she adds that, if the conditions for southern Manitoba Indians are reprehensible, those for the Aboriginal inhabitants of the provincial North are even more so.[87]

The RCSW drew more openly from Jean Bruce's commissioned review of Inuit women in the Keewatin Arctic. This study offers solutions more in keeping with commissioners' emphasis on educational uplift and economic training as key means of improving the lives of northern Indigenous women. Indeed, this was a solution repeatedly endorsed for *all* Canadian women. To its credit, the RCSW knew that it needed research that drew directly from interviews with Indigenous women, though Bruce's trip to eight settlements in two weeks, conducting forty-two interviews, many through a translator, indicates a rather rushed tour (something she was the first to admit). Bruce's report, which includes profiles and transcribed testimony of Inuit women, does not replicate Dandurand's stilted analysis of primitive women; however, it is less venturesome in rethinking Indigenous-settler relations than is the Lotz/ Cruikshank brief discussed below.

Jean Bruce's study indicates both the drawbacks and the unrealized potential of RCSW investigations. She drew heavily from existing government research, particularly from NA, thus reproducing its version of events (e.g., Inuit relocations) and its constructions of the important issue: namely, "adaption to settlement life" from a land- and camp-based economy.[88] This inevitably limited her ability to challenge, at a fundamental level, existing state assumptions. She did point to the recognized problems with certain government policies: northern education for Inuit girls was modelled on a white southern template, and the badly executed centralization of settlements had spawned health and housing problems. Solutions, however, remain within the bounds of Department of Indian Affairs and Northern Development thinking: create arts and crafts programs so women can use traditional skills to secure some additional income (but not, admittedly, a living wage); offer adult education so women understand child nutrition and the hygiene necessary for settlement living; and send girls out to Churchill for vocational education, even though DIAND conceded that it could not possibly provide them with employment as there were not enough "girl" jobs in the Arctic to go around.[89]

The potential of Bruce's study lay in her interviews with Inuit women, however mediated, and the understanding that their voices needed to be heard. Admittedly, some of her questions – such as "What do you know about the South?" – may have directed the focus away from the Indigenous North. The underlying Euro-Canadian assumptions of the RCSW also limited her findings: she asked Inuit women what they thought about women's "status," a concept that did not have the same resonance in cultures used to collective living and a complementary sexual division of labour as it did in Western cultures. However, women's responses did reveal their dire and immediate material needs: they wanted access to water, fuel, and food. The interviews also allowed women to express concerns about cultural loss and generational estrangement. These anxieties were most palpable in the words of older women, who understood that their children might go "outside" to school but who feared they would either not return or return with little respect for Inuit values. Regret and sorrow come through clearly in their translated voices: "Eskimo children are getting to be more like southern white people, and it is hard for their parents, who would like to teach them about the older way of life, but children will not listen to their parents anymore."[90]

It is this generational divide and consequent loss of culture that is stressed in Bruce's brief, and, as we see below, is of particular fascination to the media too. However, the RCSW narrowed Bruce's findings so that they could be adapted to a liberal individualist solution, such as adult education for Eskimo mothers. Whether adult education for Inuit women was simply a "blame-the-victim" solution, as Toni Williams suggests, is open to interpretation since many Inuit women interviewed stated their desire for education, especially with regard to English literacy. This request is also noted in the Lotz/Cruikshank study. The construction of Inuit women in Bruce's report, however, still stresses a traditional, land-based, but imperilled culture represented by older women – a culture likely to be supplanted by younger, modernized, educated women with different "choices." The question "Whose land?" is never raised, even though it was being increasingly raised by Indigenous rights groups. Bruce suggests that Inuit women should have the "freedom of choice" to "live in their Arctic homeland" under "conditions acceptable to southern standards" or be able to "participate fully in Canadian life" (the latter presenting a somewhat puzzling dichotomy).[91]

The RCSW received more than one request for copies of their most extensive research study on Indigenous women, produced by Jim Lotz, a professor in community development at the Canadian Research Centre for Anthropology at St. Paul's University (and once an NA employee) and Julie Cruikshank, his research associate. No request for access was granted. Although one internal memo suggests that this study received enough votes to get on the public publication list, it never did. Marginal comments on the draft, likely by Monique Begin, suggests some reasons:

the brief was long, extensively researched, and drew comparisons to other anthropological and sociological literature on development and cultural change. Marginal notations like "academic" and (once) "pretentious" indicate that the study was perceived to be too long, involved, and academic for popular release. Some of its critiques, like Shipley's, may have hit too close to home. Yet, by failing to publicize this study, the RCSW missed an opportunity to disseminate a politely critical view of development in the North, an emerging feminist analysis, and a view of cultural interaction that spelled the future, not the past, of anthropological research.

Lotz's funding of just over four thousand dollars allowed Julie Cruikshank to go North for three months to do participant research, after reading "under his tutelage" for a few months beforehand.[92] In retrospect, she is amazed at how easily this unfolded: "Jim Lotz, bless his heart, hired me fresh out of school with a BA in anthropology. I landed on his doorstep at the Canadian Research Centre for Anthropology run by Jim from a house in Ottawa in 1967. He applied for a grant from RCSW and then sent me off to the Yukon for three months."[93] Using a qualitative approach, Cruikshank concentrated on interviews and informal meetings, often one-on-one, with Indigenous women and supplemented these with meetings with southern Indian women (through homemakers clubs) and also used information provided by the Department of Indian Affairs and Northern Development and other government officials. Unlike government officials, however, Lotz/Cruikshank started from the premise that Indian women should define their own problems and solutions. While other writers described the Indian problem, Cruikshank queried the discourse of the "Indian problem," suggesting it erroneously assumed that the Indian, rather than the nature of white settlement and development, was the problem. Like other anthropological studies of the time, this one, too, assumes that a rapidly accelerating pace of social change – as people move "from the stone age to the jet age"[94] – is creating immense cultural and social stresses for Indigenous peoples. However, it is also critical of white assumptions about the inferiority of pre-literate cultures, and it suggests that Indigenous cultures might offer useful social alternatives to whites: by re-injecting Indigenous "history and folklore" into the classroom, "Indian, non-Indian children and teachers would benefit. Far from being outmoded, the value of Indian culture may become increasingly important to the future with the need for social cooperation."[95]

The Lotz/Cruikshank study is shaped both by a cultural relativist tradition in anthropology and by an incipient feminist critique of anthropological and historical writing that had wrongly assumed that white anthropologist/explorer/fur trader's accounts of Indigenous women could be accepted at face value.[96] Up until the 1960s, the acculturation/modernization paradigm was extremely influential in northern anthropological studies and was further entrenched in government-sponsored studies.[97] The Lotz/Cruikshank study veers in a different direction. Vast generalizations about all Indian women, and more specific statements that simply assumed their social subordination, were challenged.[98] Cruikshank recalls that her approach to research was shaped by the "grassroots" oral history literature of the time, such as "worker's history (Studs Terkel, Barry Broadfoot); African-American history (*Roots*); and especially all the new work on women's history. But I think it was also fuelled by all the ferment surrounding the 'Sixties' in general."[99] That sixties culture was challenging taken-for-granted understandings of power, culture, and colonialism.[100] While the diversity of Indian and Inuit cultures, rather than their homogenization, is stressed in their report, Lotz and Cruikshank nevertheless dispute the generalized Western notions of male superiority/female inferiority read into many Indigenous cultures based on Euro-Canadian understandings of the gendered division of labour.[101]

Cruikshank's Yukon interviews did reinforce some of the commissioners' impressions. The generation gap between older women socialized to a semi-nomadic hunting and trapping way of life, fully immersed in Native cultures, and a younger cohort, some educated in outside schools and cities, and more fluent in English, was identified as causing social tensions. But, as Lotz and Cruikshank demonstrated, despite the potential loss of culture, younger women still did not have the requisite education or skills to partake in a more affluent material existence. The sexual relationships of Indian women with white men, so often mentioned in testimony, are also discussed, though more serious attention is given to the issue of women losing official Indian status. The result of these relationships was too often a loss of pride on the part of Indian men already denigrated economically, a deep suspicion on the part of older women who saw their daughters being used and abused, and the growth of sole-support Indian women with children they could not adequately care for. Cruikshank points out that Indian Affairs' effort to create a patrilineal system within Indian cultures was, ironically, recreating a historic matrilineal system – but without the requisite material and social ingredients for a stable society.[102]

In contrast to other evidence, the Lotz/Cruikshank study positions itself more critically vis-à-vis existing ideas about development; it also tries to connect analyses of gender *and* Indian marginalization. Gender oppression is highlighted in descriptions of the northern social welfare system and the education offered to Indian women, which concentrates on domestic tasks that groom them primarily for the lowest valued and paid service jobs. "Are these girls being trained for jobs which non-Indians define as menial or for a kind of motherhood which they define as good?" it asks.[103] At the same time, the study tries to turn the tables on discriminatory stereotypes of Indigenous peoples, whether it is Indian men's laziness or Indian women's promiscuity. It challenges shibboleths, such as the perennial claim that Indian children are undisciplined, their ill health the consequence of incompetent mothering. After all, the authors point out, caring for many children in highly social communities, and in tiny houses, means germs simply cannot be contained.

Like the testimony of Assheton-Smith and Leishman, the Lotz/Cruikshank report problematizes both white attitudes and the goal of "integration" as a synonym for assimilation rather than the more positive process of two-way acculturation. As Cruikshank recounts from her conversations with Indian women, the term "white woman" was not a complimentary one: "the language had a term for white woman being a derogatory category when used in a general sense."[104] Indian women were becoming more vocal about the need for whites to listen rather than to dictate: "Their goal is to reverse the usual process of teaching the Indians and rather to educate the white man to listen."[105] This alternative construction of the Indigenous North did not let the state's ill-considered northern initiatives and paternalism off lightly. The impersonal hostel system, whereby girls boarded in cities; the lack of consultation with Indian women about housing; and the paucity of training for good employment opportunities: all these, and more, were noted.

What marks the Lotz/Cruikshank study as distinct from others is its emphasis on jettisoning the idea that Indian women need to "helped." "Helping the Native to better herself," it was clear, should no longer be the goal of white women reformers. There is a tendency, Cruikshank notes, for "whites [to] talk down to Indian women." Indian women's silence is then interpreted as agreement or acquiescence rather than as actual withdrawal from an insulting interaction.[106] The problem, in other words, is not "the Indian" but the "whiteman." White sojourners constructed their own image of northern Indians, appealing to whites in the South – the folksy image, the noble savage, perpetuated by writers like the white newspaper columnist from Old Crow.[107] Instead, Indian women should be listened to not only regarding what they want but also regarding why. Adult education, for example, had long been desired by Indian women but was "thought of solely in terms of teaching the Indians to make the best of a bad bargain while instructing them in the ways of the non-Indian."[108]

This direct challenge to white expertise was not integrated into the final RCSW report, though there were mild echoes of it, for example, in the recommendation that Indigenous women be consulted on housing issues and that more adult education should be available for them. Given the RCSW's penchant for liberal and pragmatic solutions, research that raised issues of colonial rule was sidelined in its public report. Ironically, this marginalized research was cutting edge; indeed, it was going in the direction in which new feminist anthropology was actually headed, even if it was not embraced wholeheartedly by the RCSW.

The Media Interpret the North

The levity, if not derision, with which the RCSW was treated by some reporters across the country was apparent on the northern trip, with newspaper headlines like "Sufferagettes [sic] hit town" and "Eskimo

Women Boss in the Home," which made much of Lola Lange's claim that she was the "boss" in the house, when all she was trying to do was to engage Inuit women in a conversation about the gendered division of labour in their lives.[109] There was not that much ridicule, however, for the simple reason that publicity surrounding the northern hearings was not extensive, in part due to the expense of sending reporters North. Florence Bird did not really want media representatives along for the Keewatin meetings, thinking the press would intimidate Inuit women and lead to less honest conversation. They appeared anyway. She had hoped the Canadian Press would send Rosemary Spiers, whom she saw as objective and sympathetic, but it declined. There was some coverage by local northern papers, which used the opportunity to stress northern distinctiveness, arguing that northern and southern women's issues were diametrically different one from the other.

News of the North claimed that most of the hearings in Yellowknife were taken up with discussions of Indian and Eskimo women, including sexual exploitation and, to a lesser extent, the "role of the deprived northern housewife from Southern Canada." The image of the complaining "southern" housewife may have had a certain negative public purchase, but it was not by any means the only issue explored: this ignored RCSW testimony about the poverty shared by some Indigenous and non-Indigenous women. A letter to the editor of the Whitehorse newspaper from a social services worker made it clear that daycare needs for all single mothers had also been part of the Yukon Social Services brief and that this demand should not be misinterpreted as an attack on motherhood.[110] By situating white women in the isolated housewife category and locating Native women in discussions of sexual abuse, press coverage furthered the perceived – and real – divisions between women.

In newspaper coverage, northern women's issues were not treated as peripheral or ridiculous. Rosemary Thrasher's testimony about Inuit girls needing education, jobs, and housing was relayed sympathetically, as were Harry Leishman's comments about the needs for Native-staffed friendship centres. At times, the press bought into Lange's and Bird's confident claim that women's problems were universal, but it also implicitly challenged this notion with reporting that outlined the very different interests of Indigenous and white, affluent and poor women. Bird's contention that women's problems were "all alike" was misplaced, said one reporter covering the Keewatin leg of the trip, as was indicated by the Inuit women interviewed through a translator: the "Eskimo women sitting in a circle inside a government building, their babies on their backs ... pointed out that they also have some problems quite different from those of southern women."[111] They spoke about their children's loss of cultural guideposts and the need for both Western and traditional skills and education. *News of the North* may have been at pains to show northern distinctiveness (itself a generalized category), but it was not generally sympathetic to the rights of the First Nations. The week following the RCSW, a forceful editorial denounced the idea of special status for Indians and embraced federal plans to end the Indian Act, earning a blistering letter in response from Marilyn Assheton-Smith, who criticized its embrace of a white "British" model of citizenship and the assumption that "integration" meant "becoming just like us."[112]

It is true that press coverage that reached the South was skewed towards discussions of Indian and Eskimo women. This is hardly surprising since Indigenous women had already used the hearings to air injustices, including those created by the Indian Act. Mary Axe Early and others had secured considerable notice, as had the Alberta Indian women who presented. Moreover, exposés of impoverished Aboriginal living were not uncommon in the press and on television by the 1960s: they were a staple of sensational reportage for southern pundits. Both Marilyn Assheton-Smith's testimony about the sexual exploitation of Indian women and Rosemary Thrasher's claim that Indigenous women needed jobs and housing with "running water and sewage" were given prominence. Some papers reprinted Mary Ann Lahache's entire letter, but again, arguably this tended to reproduce an image of a pathetic, oppressed woman.[113]

On the Nunavut trip, only at Eskimo Point was the press allowed into the meeting of the commissioners and local Inuit women. The images subsequently relayed to the South were remarkably consistent with earlier constructions of the Eskimo wife from other sources: they were shy women, dedicated mothers, concerned with family issues, and completely accepting of the existing sexual division of labour. Newspapers reported on Lange's belief in the usefulness of cooperatives with regard to enabling Inuit women to market their handicrafts. Inuit women's positive responses and their "love of sewing" were stressed, though papers also noted their implicit critique of the Hudson's Bay Company as it would only stock ready-made clothes, not the cloth and sewing supplies they needed.[114] Many stories stressed Eskimo mothers' concerns that they were losing touch with children educated in Churchill. Their statements went through multiple translations, first through Inuktitut and second through the press's own particular slant on this issue. Newspaper stories tended to portray Inuit women as neither political nor militant but, rather, as essentially *mothers at heart*: their emotional, caring roles and their desire to preserve something of their "heritage" were stressed. The Inuit mothers did not, apparently, denounce all southern-type education but indicated that they wanted their children not to lose all contact with their own traditions and languages. Since this goal was stated government intention (whether it was or was not is another issue), it did not seem particularly threatening or unreasonable.

Some of these themes were repeated in the radio and television coverage aired in September on CBC Radio's *Matinee* and on the popular afternoon TV show *Take Thirty*. The older medium of radio actually included more Indigenous voices as reporter Ed Reid recorded Rosemary Thrasher testifying and answering questions. His introductory conversation with *Matinee* host Pat Patterson, however, did question whether a truly representative "cross-section" of women had testified, and he included short conversation clips of Didi Dodds and Harry Leishman, who had so strongly urged whites to start listening to Indigenous voices for a change. *Matinee* also incorporated other views, including Hilda Hellaby's comment about Indian men's resentment at having to marry "the white man's leavings." A liberal concern that all sides of the story should be broadcast, as much as any sensitivity to Indigenous issues, likely shaped Patterson's presentation of the issues.

THE ROYAL COMMISSION ON THE STATUS OF WOMEN IN THE NORTH **265**

The *Take Thirty* anchors, Adrienne Clarkson and Paul Soles, made some preliminary and afterthought comments, but their show on the RCSW in the North was primarily taken up with film and reportage collected by Ed Reid. In both radio and television coverage, Reid tended to divide northern women into three discrete groups with different interests: single women, Indian and Eskimo women, and "troubled" housewives. He keyed into testimony depicting "depressed" white women sojourners unable to adjust to isolation and darkness, but Soles noted that these problems probably "[didn't] bother Eskimo women, so what of their issues?"

Reid's primary assignment for *Take Thirty* was to cover the Inuit leg of the trip; undoubtedly, the Eskimo themes were seen as exotic, foreign, and interesting in terms of visual representation. The delegation's first stop, at Coral Harbour, set the precedent for much of the *Take Thirty* show: Reid relied heavily on interviews by experts, white locals, and sometimes Lange and Bird. Male ethnologist David Mohr from Memorial University was called on in Coral Harbour to discuss the Eskimo way of life, and, like many other previous commentators, he concentrated on hunting, the use of dogs or skidoos, boats, and walrus hunts. Women's domestic labour was invisible. The government's provision of new housing was given significant prominence, suggesting that Ottawa was contributing to the rebuilding of a modern Canadian North. The government's concern and generosity were also evidenced in its efforts to save "starving" Inuit by relocating them.[115] While houses were featured in camera shots, Inuit women were only seen in the background, as part of the landscape, a common trope in the portrayal of the First Nations.[116] Was this because they preferred not to be on camera? Bird thought so, explaining in one of her on-camera interviews that she thought Eskimo women were "somewhat shy" and did not want cameras and interviewers "milling about" as they spoke.[117]

In all the RCSW whistle stops that Reid covered, the reliance on white experts continued, in part because of their command of English. In Rankin Inlet, "devastated" by the closure of the mine, Lange interviewed the Roman Catholic priest on camera about the rapid social

Florence Bird, on the right, sits in a circle listening to Inuit women, with translator
Bob Williamson. | LAC, *Take Thirty*, 17 September 1968, WO# 46904

changes taking place, especially with regard to youth and elders. The
wife of the local white administrator is also queried about her likes and
dislikes with regard to living in the North, and she speaks rather diffi-
dently of the many meetings she organized, usually two a week, but "in
May as many as five a week ... which is too many." Perhaps she was expected, as a northern wife, to participate in her husband's work with
the Inuit – but without pay. Despite the difficulties in Rankin Inlet, Lange
is convinced that this is one place where whites and Eskimo are trying to
"work together" to create a sense of "community," symbolized by camera shots of everyone at the local weekly dance.

The one meeting with Inuit women captured on film took place at
Eskimo Point. If the voices of Inuit women were desired, this would have
been the opportunity; however, allowing women to speak in their own
language, with voice-over translation, was likely perceived to be cum-
bersome (and expensive) television. In the Eskimo Point coverage, Bird

speaks at some length to expert Bob Williamson, an anthropologist living in the North and also a member of the NWT Council. Williamson translates for her, not only with regard to language but also with regard to Inuit culture. He explains the difficulties of moving from tents to wooden housing, the changes in hunting and family living patterns, even the problems of waste disposal that have occurred. Igloos may seem "romantic" to western eyes he cautions, but they also represent a time of precarious living, with a high rate of "infant mortality." Bird is rather concerned with hygiene, washrooms, and waste, and Williamson reassures her that Eskimos are not "naturally dirty" people; rather, the shift to houses has upset the whole ecosystem of daily living. He stresses the adaptability of the Inuit, their desire to partake in education and modernization, the need for equal opportunity. Bird picks up positively on the latter phrase: since "equal opportunity" is a concern of the RCSW, so, too, is the status of the Eskimo.

What is significant is not only the reliance on white experts, but Bird's repeated assurances that she understands "all women's" problems. On camera, Bird offers exactly what she later wrote in her autobiography: a story about how she told the Inuit women that she was an "old woman" because their culture respected the elders. Since people might not live past "thirty," she admits, there were few elders to respect. This rather stark admission of low life expectancy went uncommented upon. She also told the young women that she had been young once and so could understand their problems as well. Rather neatly, this made her a perfect confidant for all Inuit women. No one directly challenged her confidently universalist view, and this is perhaps all the more ironic because Bird's cultured, upper-class British accent would have put her outside the warm circle of many white working-class women as well.

Finally, the contrast between Indian and Eskimo is made very stark as the show ends with Lange and Bird in Churchill at an Indian settlement wracked by "alcoholism and social breakdown," with only one social worker to tackle these problems. Lange does not think such a position needs extensive training. The social worker agrees, though noting that you need a "feel for the people." The idea of training Native social workers and teachers is never raised in the film, though it clearly was in other

Florence Bird and Lola Lange speak with three Indigenous women at the Churchill airport. They were designated the "new women" of the North. | LAC, *Take Thirty*, 17 September 1968, WO# 46904

RCSW venues since it made its way into the report. The contrast between Indian and Eskimo is reinforced in the summation provided at the end of the television show in the form of a conversation between the anchors and Reid, who points out how very different relations are between whites and Indians and whites and Eskimo (each group homogenized, of course). Southern Indians have an unfortunate, conflictual, and contentious history with whites, but the Eskimo and whites get along better, suggesting hope for harmonious northern development.

Clarkson is struck most by the tragedy of the generation gap and the loss of Inuit culture (which she compares to the situation with "new Canadian immigrants"), and this becomes one of the RCSW report's concerns too. Loss of language and culture, however, can be "managed" within a liberal multicultural society. Neither in the RCSW report nor in the press coverage are these tragedies ever situated within a colonial context. There is no mention of forced instruction in English, as we know characterized residential schools; there is no indication that the Inuit were seen as primitives without a history, needing integration into a more developed legal system; there is never any mention of who controlled resource or land issues. The end result is a portrayal of Inuit women who are very appealing in their maternal roles yet rather passive. In the parlance of Gayatri Spivak, this Native assuredly does *not* speak.[118] Yet the last camera shot shows three young women, a typist, a steward-ess, and a nurse, all of whom represent the "modern Eskimo woman." Why were they not interviewed?

THE REPORT

The RCSW's decision to abandon a chapter on the North meant a much truncated perspective on Indigenous women, and it may also have ac-centuated the liberal, individualist tone it assumed in dealing with In-digenous issues. True, some of the RCSW recommendations came directly from presentations of Indigenous women: the demand for better cross-cultural training for whites going to the North was in a brief presented by Aboriginal women. However, the initial draft northern chapter was far more incisive than were the much-truncated sections in the final version. The former focused on Inuit women's central role in social and economic production, stressing that the family and community "could not have been sustained" without women's essential labour. While it might "super-ficially" appear that women are "subjugated," this was not so, as evi-denced by their critical role in hunting culture and in the domestic sphere, their socialization of children, and their recognized wisdom and role as bearers of culture. The shift to settlement life had eaten away at their traditional work, but modernization still held out the possibility of women's "increased influence," including with regard to questions of "community living."[119]

This earlier version also lauded the self-organization of Indian and Eskimo women who had a well-developed "practical understanding" of their own problems and had the "determination" to solve them, if society "would give them the help *they asked for*." This was reworded slightly, with severe effects: the final report states that Inuit women could solve their problems "with help," shifting the emphasis from Indigenous women's decisions to the decisions of those providing "help." Up until 25 July 1970, Elsie MacGill tried to improve the section on the North, adding language that put more power in the hands of Indigenous women: they should be "canvassed," for instance, on exactly what kind of training they needed. Some of her suggestions never made it in.[120]

When they were still working on the northern chapter, the RCSW commissioners consulted with experts in the Department of Indian Affairs and Northern Development, viewing them as critical readers. Not surprisingly, the person responsible for cooperatives recommended more emphasis be placed on training for co-op management, thus reinforcing the direction his department was taking. He also suggested that "mining and oil" exploration affected few Natives, though co-ops did – not a very prophetic comment, as it turned out.[121] In general, the RCSW drew heavily on the knowledge of experts with an advanced education and/or work experience relating to state functions. Indeed, the commission's failings vis-à-vis Indigenous women reflected some of the report's limitations with regard to class as well as with regard to gender/race.[122] The filtering process concomitant with research and writing reinforced a top-down liberal, and often middle-class, perspective, as it did in the South, but in the North it also reinforced structures of racial and colonial exclusion. Given the high percentage of First Nations women in many northern areas – yet their notable absence from hearings, testimony, commissioners' reports, and media – the erasure of their voices is especially egregious. The assumption that one could talk to a local male priest and get the inside view of Indigenous women's lives was a conceit that would not likely have been entertained for white women in the South.

The RCSW's lofty aim was the integration of all women into a Canada characterized by opportunity and equality, with the former providing a route to the latter. The commissioners recognized that Indigenous women had been historically excluded – legally, ideologically, socially – from society, in ways both purposeful and more subtle, but their solutions did not question the contradiction at the heart of an abstract, idealized liberal and capitalist order.[123] Some of the RCSW commissioners were aware of the detrimental impact of patriarchal and racist ideologies on Aboriginal women, but their solutions veered optimistically towards their integration into a more just Canadian society, aided through state initiatives. The argument of later Aboriginal feminists like Patricia Monture that the state had been irrevocably constituted as patriarchal and racist, and thus an unlikely means to women's emancipation, was far from their worldview.[124]

That the RCSW (and the media, too) tended to stress cultural reinvigoration rather than offering a radical critique of the basis for Indigenous peoples' material and social inequality is not surprising given its overall politics, but it is worth stressing nonetheless. Lamenting a generational loss of heritage and calling for a multicultural North is not the same as recognizing the social and economic basis for colonial relations. Valuing someone's culture is not the same as giving her or him full control over all the valuable resources under her/his feet. While I could not help but notice (reflecting a twenty-first-century politics) the number of times women's desperate need for clean accessible water was mentioned during testimony, this essential requirement of life was not stressed either in the media or in the report.

Still, it is too simplistic to see the RCSW process *only* as colonial paternalism; there were a range of political positions articulated in the testimony, extending from racism to paternalism to outrage about racism, and, occasionally, from both Indigenous and non-Indigenous people there were calls to abandon "helping" Indigenous women and to begin "listening" to them instead. Some non-Indigenous witnesses, better cast as allies, put more emphasis on the self-determination of the First Nations. Moreover, some liberal anti-racism of the time emphasized ignoring race divisions and concentrating on common human interests as segregation was equated with racism. When Mrs. Mandible told the commission that "we were all northerners" and that all women, "Eskimo, white, others," regardless of race, should come together to solve problems of all northern women, this was likely the sentiment intended.[125] Irene Baird expresses the same attitude in the pamphlet she

272 "MRS. BIRD FLIES NORTH"

forwarded to the RCSW as background material. While her piece on the Eskimo recognizes the past errors of whites who "talked too much about Eskimo and not enough with them," it, too, echoes the optimistic liberal vision of an Arctic where "race lines were unknown" and a brotherhood of man created a "new North."[126]

Some images of Indigenous women seemed to have immense resilience, appearing in popular accounts from the 1940s and 1950s, and being subtly reproduced in RCSW reportage: the stereotypical distinction between dispossessed and impoverished Indians, on the one hand, and primitive but helpful Eskimos, on the other, clearly persisted. Similarly, the distinction between morally compromised, sexually vulnerable Indians and shy, maternal, but cheerful Eskimo women lingered on. So, too, did the paternalistic idea that "help" adjusting to modernity could only come from white expertise. However, the RSCW offered a slight but significant modification in northern imaging. Comparing the popular 1940s anthropology of *The Beaver* and the expert reports of the RCSW, one sees a shift in academic scholarship: an incipient feminist anthropology is emerging, critical both of the colonial process of development and the male-centred approaches of past anthropologists. While this is most evident in the Lotz/Cruikshank report, even Jean Bruce's more limited study valorizes the voices of Inuit women. The importance these writers place on valuing Indigenous women's understandings of social change became a key theme in future research. Perhaps we might characterize some of the dissident views expressed by white allies in the RCSW as a form of "radical orientalism," an approach that continued to construct the traditional Indigenous North and modernized South as culturally distinct but that also tried to valorize, justify, and even idealize northern Indigenous cultural norms, making a case for their political importance and validity.[127]

The RCSW hearings revealed new political voices, whether it was Marilyn Assheton-Smith's interrogation of white male heterosexuality or Rosemary Thrasher's call for Inuit access to training and jobs (instead of the perennial occupation for poor women – domestic service). These voices were in the minority, but they were forthright in their critique. By focusing on the limitations of the RCSW, we might inadvertently obscure the agency of Aboriginal women like Thrasher, who were using the RCSW – not simply being manipulated by it – to articulate their own needs and a discourse of resistance. It is no surprise that the 1970s are often portrayed as the "awakening" point for Indigenous women's political organizing in the North.[128] Such resistance did not emerge out of nowhere, and, as the conclusion suggests, there were Indigenous women "speaking back," even before Mrs. Bird flew north.

Conclusion

Analyzing how Canadians construct the Indigenous North gives rise to two related questions. How did Indigenous northerners imagine the South? Did they ever expend near the same energy constructing a collective subjectivity that extolled "the South" as part of their cultural identity? The answer to the second question has already been provided by many Indigenous writers: No. Post-contact Inuit writing does address the colonizers' presence, often portraying "childish and bossy" whites with "critical sympathy,"[1] but the irony, as others have noted, is that Canadians are so very anxious to culturally construct a North that speaks to their distinct identity as Canadians, while Indigenous peoples living there think of it more as their homeland.[2] If Canadians saw the North as an unfinished or barren frontier, northerners experienced it as a vibrant "cultivated" space of memory, sociality, and activity in the changing relationships of humans, land, and animals.[3]

The Iconic North intentionally focuses on case studies that explore the ideological construction of the North rather than attempting to understand the ideas and responses of Indigenous northerners. That is another project, and not one that a historian of my social location is well equipped – perhaps even permitted, in some minds – to undertake. The feminist claim that we can distinguish between speaking "for" and speaking "about" others may be far more complicated and entangled than is often assumed.[4] However, we can probably distinguish between a critical assessment of the culture of colonialism and a discussion of the way it was experienced in the hearts and minds of Indigenous northerners. I have tackled the former, though having made that distinction, I do not pretend to offer a completely dispassionate, neutral, or unmediated perspective: my approach is "partial" not only in grasping only part of the picture but also in "taking sides."[5] My questions are shaped by a critique of colonialism, and my conclusions should raise troubling questions about its destructive impact on human lives.

My approach should not leave the impression that Indigenous peoples were a tabula rasa upon which ideologies were projected, a passive population accepting of their designation as a smiling people or a vanishing race. It is thus worth exploring a few brief examples of Indigenous peoples "looking back" at non-Indigenous Canada in the same time period, using cultural forms that integrated both Indigenous and Western methods of expression.

WRITING NORTH FROM AN INDIGENOUS WOMAN'S POINT OF VIEW

By the 1970s, the political organization of Indigenous peoples in the North had expanded considerably as they formed new organizations to contest colonial policies of discrimination and dispossession, and to argue for their inherent rights to land, dignity, and self-determination.[6] Some of these organizations also spoke directly to the distinct experiences and needs of Indigenous women, whose experience of colonialism was marked by particular kinds of violence and exploitation.[7] Cultural forms of expression also multiplied: northern residents took over television and radio for their own ends and in their own languages; created stories, poems, film, and photography, focusing especially on their own stories; and developed a wide range of artistic practices ranging from carving and print making to music and visual performance.[8] New forms of political and cultural expression, however, did not spring out of a vacuum: in the previous decades, Indigenous peoples, both as individual creators and as collectivities, were sustaining their own culture and also "speaking back" to non-Indigenous northerners and southerners who were intent on bringing another North into being, one more attuned to their vision of modernity, racial integration, and economic productivity. Three examples, chosen because they provide contrasting images to those discussed in this book, make this point well: the writing of Mitiarjuk Nappaaluk, the autobiography of Minnie Aodla Freeman, and what I call the lost photography of Paulette Anerodluk. Nappaaluk and Freeman are relatively well known, at least among northern scholars; Anerodluk remains an enigma, in part because she died relatively young, leaving no written archive of her thoughts or work.

Many scholars have explored the phenomenon of Inuit cultural production in the 1950s and 1960s through print making and sculpture as the state and private entrepreneurs fostered the production of handicraft goods, in part to refocus economic livelihoods from hunting and gathering to the production of saleable items for consumption in the South. Inuit art became a hot commodity. As reports on southern sales events note: "Eskimo sculpture is in fashion ... [T]here is a vitality and expressiveness in native art, coming out of what you might think to be the most primitive sites."[9] The reasons for its popularity were subsequently debated by anthropologists, some of whom stressed its inherent aesthetic appeal, others of whom noted the lingering fascination with the exotic "primitiveness" of the Inuit.[10] Fewer people were acquainted with Inuit writers, poets, and autobiographers, not only because their work did not necessarily appear in English or in mainstream publications but also because their writing might be consigned to the category of "legends" rather than literature.[11] As scholars like Robin McGrath, Penny Patrone, and others argue, Inuit cultural production includes a rich oral tradition that is sometimes expressed in writing, both in syllabics and (later) in English and French. Inuit women, however, are less likely than men to write autobiographies that draw on "epic traditions" from their culture. They have to find other cultural formats, such as fiction, within which to recount their lives.[12]

During the 1950s, for instance, Mitiarjuk Nappaaluk created a series of stories that drew on her life and that were subsequently woven into a novel, *Saanaq*. An Inuk woman living in Arctic Quebec, Nappaaluk was initially engaged by Christian missionaries to help create an Inuit-French dictionary as she was well known locally as an important repository of cultural knowledge and as someone who bridged male and female worlds: as an only child, she had learned tasks from both parents, hunting as well as sewing. She wrote her novel in pieces, compiling over a thousand pages in syllabics. Her temporary stay in a southern hospital interrupted her writing for a number of years, but the task was assumed again in the early 1960s with the aid of an anthropologist who had become fascinated with her story. A long process of translation, recording, and transliteration took place over another six years. First published in French in 1984, *Saanaq* was only recently translated for English publication.

The length of time taken to translate syllabics for English readers explains some of the gulf between Inuit literary producers and consumer-readers in southern Canada. Literary culture is not as easily commodified and marketed as is an Eskimo sculpture; moreover, what southerners want to consume may still reflect constructed images of a traditional North. We do not want realistic Inuit sculptures of hunters on snowmobiles, as Robin McGrath points out, but, rather, traditional pieces of Inuit throwing spears at walruses. In the same way, Inuit poetry that seems "sacred and unspoiled" is often embraced as a more authentic expression of Inuit culture than is Inuit poetry that addresses contemporary issues.[13]

Saanaq's author explores the lives, experiences, and relationships in an Inuit community that, at first, is relatively untouched by white interlopers; however, during the novel people are increasingly affected by changes occasioned by the newcomers. Nappaaluk's narrative draws on techniques found in many Western novels, probing the personalities, feelings, and character development of various family and community members, though her style is distinctively straightforward, disarming in its directness. She interweaves stories of family life with commentary on language use, placing both in the context of changing cultural practices and seasonal economic activities of her small community.

What is remarkable is the contrast between the visual and textual representations of gender roles in the examples I have explored, such as women's sojourning narratives, documentary and fictional film, and gender relations as portrayed in *Saanaq*. Unlike the passive Inuit woman in "The Smiling People" episode of *RCMP*, who was supposedly completely dependent on a husband or the state for survival, the heroine in *Saanaq* hunts for game when the family is in need, intervenes as a forceful presence in extended family affairs, and takes in the advice and knowledge passed on by her elders, both male and female. She is "strong willed" and a significant presence in her community; indeed, as Bernard

Saladin d'Anglure argues, her personality stands in contrast to that of many less able and competent men in the story.[14]

Sanaaq is neither a romanticized, simplified picture of idyllic life on the land before contact with whites nor a picture of unending contentiousness in Inuit-white relations afterwards. The lead character, Saanaq, has a complex relationship with her husband, involving affection as well as frustration; however, at one point he beats her severely, though he is later deeply ashamed of his uncontrolled anger. While the police intervene on her behalf to warn her husband against any future attacks, in other scenarios in the novel white newcomers are portrayed far less positively. Medical practitioners poke and probe Inuit bodies with little explanation, and the Anglican and Catholic missionaries compete unashamedly for Inuit converts, telling them that each other's missionaries are "liars."[15] Nappaaluk amusingly mocks this competition for souls when the Anglican priest tells Sanaaq judgmentally that he will not baptize her new niece, an illegitimate child who is the "fruit of sin" between an Inuk woman and a qallunaat.[16] The aunt simply says that, in that case, they will head to the Catholic priest, whom she knows will happily baptize any soul. The child being fought over by the warring priests is the product of a liaison between the HBC chief factor and Sanaaq's sister, Arnatuinnaq. Nor is their story a simple one of exploitation and abandonment. The chief factor cares for his Inuk lover and wants to marry her, but, when he is transferred against his will, he tries to make sure that Arnatuinnaq and his newborn daughter are materially looked after. His HBC replacement, however, tries to seduce Arnatuinnaq, thinking he is entitled to the same woman, only to be soundly rejected by a disgusted Arnatuinnaq. Women's agency is again stressed in a manner quite unlike anything portrayed in the non-Indigenous narratives I have examined.

Sanaaq is a work of fiction, even if elements are taken from Nappaaluk's life. Minnie Aodla Freeman's *Life among the Qallunaat* is an autobiography, a reflection on her life as a child and adolescent in Quebec's James Bay region in the 1940s and 1950s, and her later experience in the 1960s working as a translator for the Department of Indian and Northern Affairs in Ottawa.[17] It is an incredibly powerful story made all the more compelling, in my view, by its understated style and its straightforward, innocent observations about the strangeness of qallunaat life. Freeman's story was germinating at precisely the moment that Irene Baird was creating publicly appealing northern travel narratives for *North/Nord* about the government's good works in the North and at precisely the time when NFB films were detailing the North's positive economic "transition" to wage labour.

Freeman's story contradicts many of these images, not only in its largest assumptions, as it is Minnie (not her brother) who becomes the wage earner, but also in its smallest details. When an NA official insisted that NFB filmmakers show that "Indian and Eskimo do not mix," he was not describing Freeman's experience. Her family lived close to Cree people, whose language she learned and with whom she went to school. Indeed, her widowed father considered marrying a Cree woman. At residential school, it was one of her own distant cousins, whom she simply names the instigator, who became her teasing tormenter.

Freeman begins *Life among the Qallunaat* with an introduction to the unfamiliar if not bizarre landscape, sights, and sounds of Ottawa, which were completely alien to her own experience of land, family, and cultural mores. Indeed, white ways were quite incomprehensible. How did telephone and traffic lights work? What was voting? How were elevators and escalators different one from the other? As Heather Henderson points out, it was not only these strange material objects and practices of daily life but also the incomprehensible attitudes and emotions of whites that unsettled Minnie.[18] The book brilliantly makes the South and non-Indigenous life "strange," reversing the usual exoticization and othering of the Inuit.

Seen through Freeman's eyes, we are not only strange but also insensitive, unthinking, and racist. Freeman uses small incidents and interactions – such as the gift of fashionable baby doll pyjamas and her decision not to wear them – to show how foreign qallunaat social interactions were to her, even when whites were trying to be accommodating. She also details more disturbing incidents of outright racism as she is exploited by a commercial advertiser who uses her (without her consent) in a picture used to sell soft drinks. Her own employer expropriates her image in a similar fashion. Again, without her informed consent, she is photographed at her desk exhibiting government bonds that she had supposedly purchased. "I felt sick," she later remembers, "I had no idea what bonds were. My parents had never even heard about them, let alone bought them ... I was being used to show the qallunaat in the South how well the Inuit are treated in the North."[19]

Freeman introduces us to her life in the South not only with a sense of wonder and puzzlement but also with a sense of increasing alienation and unhappiness — feelings that are relayed in an understated manner, a technique that only increases the power of her words. Her reversals of the images of North and South are masterful. She points out that she and other Inuit encouraged to come to the South are given no guidance or aid with regard to strange southern ways, while whites going to the North are offered advice, seminars, manuals, and then, upon their arrival, are pampered with imported goods and luxurious living conditions (at least compared to those of their Indigenous neighbours). The fully stocked shelves of sojourners, which "looked like a full grocery store,"[20] would, for Minnie, be clear evidence of this drastically unbalanced relationship. When she describes a housing problem in the North, an issue raised both in Baird's *The Climate of Power* and in RCSW media coverage, her perspective is completely different from that of these southern observers. Freeman recalls how a high-ranking government official who visited a northern settlement insulted the local people by expressing surprise that their houses were so "clean" (exactly the concern of Florence Bird). This condescending observation is then juxtaposed to her own experience of government-built housing: first, it lacked running water, making it difficult to keep clean; and, second, failing to take into account local Inuit environmental knowledge, the government mistakenly placed houses in areas subject to flooding.[21]

Freeman's book then turns to her earlier life growing up in the North and what she calls the "truth about my people's lives," so different from the NA public relations and photographs depicting them.[22] History is literally retold as she describes her grandfather, Weetaltuk, a leader of his people, who settled a community around him on an island named for him — an island later renamed by whites. After her grandfather dies, this highly self-sufficient community is swiftly relocated, shuffled off to Great

Whale River, where this "once proud" group is reduced in stature, forced to "rely on an alien culture for survival."[23] Her description of this relocation could not be further from that provided by the ethnocentric modernizers in *Climate* who did not see any point in preserving Inuit communities (except in museums).

Minnie's own childhood is remembered fondly, though not without pain and conflict. After the death of her mother, Minnie is cared for by her grandmother, who does not want her or her brother sent away to school. Her grandfather, more inclined to give in to "authority," acquiesces to the missionaries, though the strong-minded grandmother adamantly refuses to let Minnie's brother leave.[24] Minnie spends a number of years going back and forth between her northern home and schools at Fort George and Moose Factory, and her experience at school is mixed: in some cases, the teachers are far kinder than another child — simply named the Instigator — who torments her. However difficult her adjustment, she takes a certain pride in her accomplishments and in her ability to manage new roles and situations. After she completes school, she works: first at the school, then as a nurse's aide, and then as a child minder for a local white woman, whose paranoid accusations about Minnie and her husband eventually lead to her resignation. Minnie is at one point also sent south for medical care, "shipped like cargo" to a hospital for TB.[25] However, this experience reinforces her role as an advocate and leader: she is able to intercede on behalf of other Inuit patients because of her ability to speak English.

Even after Minnie moves to Ottawa, she retains a strong attachment to, and experiences homesickness for, her family and home in the North: the tastes, smells, sense of the land, and human relations that have made her who she is. When away from her Inuit origins, she never loses a sense of being an outsider, of being someone "caught between two lives."[26] Freeman's account, barely touched on here, provides countless points of departure from the images of Inuit women relayed through non-Indigenous media. Even though she describes the ideal Inuk woman in terms not unlike those used by whites, as "gentle, kind, [and] understanding" towards her husband,[27] her autobiography offers portraits of Inuit women who counter the stereotype of female passivity. Her own relatives, and particularly her strong, determined grandmother, who was undeniably the "backbone of the family,"[28] contradict the image of the smiling, always-obedient Eskimo woman.

DESPERATELY SEEKING PAULETTE ANERODLUK

Freeman's autobiography becomes a venue for her advocacy on behalf of her people, a means of "showing the truth" about a community she loves and that she sees slipping away from her and from its own culture and history.[29] Advocacy was also intertwined in the life of Paulette Anerodluk, originally from the Coppermine area, who, when she died, probably in the 1960s, was an NA employee in Frobisher Bay.[30] Anerodluk's biography remains largely inaccessible despite my efforts to search for her in the archive, through northerners alive at the time, and through secondary sources. However, I think she is an important symbol of Inuit women who spoke back to the colonizing process at the same time as they embraced some of its tools in order to support and advocate for their people. Anerodluk was an amateur photographer, yet her photos have not been saved, archived, and displayed as they might have been if she had been a more privileged woman. Her story remains elusive but enticing, suggesting how northern history may be rewritten by Indigenous northerners if they can gather their ancestors' narratives and rescue their contributions in the same way that Project Naming is collecting names and stories, thus reversing outsiders' visual documentation of the Inuit people.

During his photographic trip to Coppermine in 1949, Richard Harrington first heard of "an Eskimo girl, Paulette," trained for five years at the Aklavik mission school, "who does photography around here, darkroom and all." Harrington surmised it would be good for a little story (none ever seem to have been published). Paulette learned her photographic skills from a local HBC trader, Lorenz A. Learmonth, who ordered her first camera for her, a Vigilante. Paulette earned money by sewing (indeed, she made caribou-skin boots and mitts for Harrington), working as an HBC bookkeeper, and possibly as a "helper" in a white

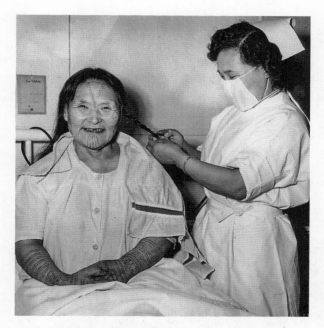

Ward aide Paulette Anerodluk looking after her mother, Eva
Kokilka, in St. Ann's Hospital. | LAC, Medical Services Branch
Photographs, R227–208–8-E, online Mikan # 3613831

household. She used her wages to order photographic supplies from
Yellowknife to pursue her passion for photography.[31] She took pictures
for Indigenous families around the settlement, never charging them, and
she did her own developing in a three-by-six darkroom with a contact
printer. Harrington was fascinated by her process, cobbled together with
limited space and materials. She "heat[ed] up dishes on an oil stove, then
transport[ed] them to her darkroom where a small 32 volt battery" gave
her some power. Paulette clearly included others in the magic as two little Inuit girls who were watching one day turned on the light, leading to
the solarization of the pictures. As a result, Paulette wrote to Kodak for a
detailed explanation of the development process.

Harrington's rendition of Paulette in his diary mixes his fascination
with Inuit women with a liking for her acculturated white ways: one senses

Paulette Anerodluk, who worked for L.A. Learmonth at the HBC Coppermine post. Paulette is carrying L.A. Learmonth's Rolloflex camera. | Nunavut Archives, Joe Osborne fonds, N-1990–006: 0052

that his attraction to her combined the exotic with white femininity. Although "her features and dress are Eskimo," he writes, her schooling and "association with whites" have changed her manners and interactions with men. She is "polite and reserved" (her Eskimo side) but can be forthright and rough in play, "making faces" at us (her white side). "How much we admire all the qualities in her – you know, *so* much like us," he comments, "God be praised." The men seemingly flirt with her, lighting her cigarette, opening doors for her. She responds in ways they think appropriate: "it seems Learmonth taught her a lot," Harrington concludes. Yet Paulette's hybrid schooling has also left her in a difficult in-between land. Native "boys" would like to marry her, says Harrington, but if this happened she could not retain her position. Whites have thought of it too but "did not have the courage." Paulette, feeling the eyes of the settlement upon her virtue, made sure she was never alone in the HBC house with a man because of what "they might say."[32]

Harrington left us with one of the most arresting pictures of Paulette as she played photographic muse for her community: she is taking a picture of Harrington taking a picture of her.[33] Indeed, it is ironic that we seem to have more pictorial than written records of Paulette, and yet we have none of her own pictures. They may have simply vanished from public view into family albums or perhaps into other venues.[34] Canon J.H. Webster, the Anglican missionary at Coppermine, was also an amateur photographer, and he and a federal Department of Transportation employee posted there, Joseph Osborne, left a number of photographs of Paulette, often posing with Webster's adopted Native daughter Ann, with the local RCMP constable, or with Osborne himself. The most compelling photo, in terms of capturing Paulette as a photographer, has the caption "Paulette was very interested in photography" and shows her happily sporting a camera around her neck, looking forthrightly into the picture-taker's lens. The other photos show a young woman engaged in talking, hanging out, and fooling around with friends about her own age. Ann and Paulette are shown playing skipping rope in the snow with Joe Osborne in front of a sleigh, with Dick Connick, the young RCMP officer posted there, and with other young men and women. There are two photos that are clearly crafted to promote HBC fur: five young Inuit women, including Ann and Paulette, are dressed up in white women's dress clothes and are swathed in beautiful furs. They are photographed both standing and sitting in front of the HBC store, with one photo playfully labelled "Coppermine Belles."[35] Three similar pictures appeared in *The Beaver*, photographed by Learmonth and Webster, but those selected by the magazine, titled "Arctic Fur Show," are slightly different, more formal and with more focus on a solo portrait of Ann Webster, an attractive woman, presumably of mixed-race ancestry, swathed in white furs. The other shots feature three of the girls, one of whom is Paulette, in a less playful, more classically posed shot.[36]

All these records omit reference to Paulette's own family and her early life on the land; yet, as other photos indicate, she could not have turned her back on these experiences. First, she later worked for NA as a nurse's aide, a common occupation educated Inuit girls were encouraged to adopt, and pictures saved by the department show her caring for her mother, a heavily tattooed Inuk, in a hospital. Second, Paulette clearly lent her services as an English-writer, and probably as a political adviser, to other Coppermine Inuit protesting the dispossession of their land. In 1953, they sent a petition to Ottawa protesting the existing social order, including the alienation of their land, which they knew was valuable in minerals. In what Peter Kulchyski and Frank Tester call a quite "remarkable petition," perhaps the first of its kind, the local Inuit lay claim to Aboriginal title: "this land is ours and we never gave it or sold it away." After a somewhat paternalistic response, which told them that the land was held in common for "Canada" and that they could stake a claim like other Canadians if they wished, a response was sent, again penned by Anerodluk, highly political in its combination of respect and determination. Paulette was likely not just a typist and interpreter but a key influence in crafting the language and approach of the petition.[37]

Paulette, when she reappears in the 1950s, is now working for the Department of Indian and Northern Affairs. She was hired in 1955 as an interpreter for the Welfare Section of the Arctic Division, staffed by Walter Rudnicki and Leo Manning.[38] She likely visited Inuit who were in southern hospitals, acting as an interpreter, and it is possible that she, too, had had TB as she had a permanent limp, which one Frobisher Bay resident attributed to this earlier illness. Four years later, she was in Frobisher Bay, still with NA, and was interviewed for Irene Baird's feature article, entitled "The Eskimo Woman and Her Changing World," published in *The Beaver* in 1959. Paulette worked as a translator for the federal government and is pictured providing soapstone to carvers at the Frobisher Bay Rehabilitation Centre, a transition centre for former and recovering TB patients. Irene offers us the only reminiscence from Paulette's youth, though refracted through her own interpretive lens. Paulette is the model "Eskimo career woman" straddling two worlds, still cognizant of the traditional but working for a living in the modern mode. In Baird's rendition, she has become an NA success story. As a translator, Paulette alternated duty at "headquarters" with trips on the Eastern Arctic Patrol and to hospitals to visit Inuit patients. Baird creates an image of her as a strong and resolute woman, pushing on the boundaries of limited gender roles from a young age, as any "career woman" might. Reassuring us that Paulette is very "feminine" to look at, Baird then relays a story from her youth: she wanted to be a boy so "she [would] not have to stay home and sew but could go hunting with her father and help drive the dogs." Since she had a brother, this was unlikely to happen, but Paulette still resolved to be "first on the scene" when her father was harnessing the dogs so that she, too, could hunt. "I don't know how the brother made out," concluded Baird lightheartedly, "bringing up the rear perhaps. Even at that early age career girl overtones were coming out."

Yet no strong Inuk woman character like Paulette appeared in Baird's *Climate*, nor were such women generally featured in NFB films.[39] Paulette, a photographer and chronicler of her own peoples' images, an advocate for her peoples' land rights, comes to us through second-hand mediations: the photos of a male sojourner, a snippet of Baird's interview, the admiring glances relayed in Harrington's diaries, promotional shots of her work for NA. Sadly, we know little of her life or of the photographs that she loved to take. She likely died while still an employee of the government. When she worked at the rehabilitation centre at Frobisher Bay, which housed people coming from sanatoriums in the South, she brought stone for men to carve, then, with the project manager, Bryan Pearson, sold the carvings at the airport at night to passengers on Pan Am and other transatlantic flights during their stopover in Frobisher Bay. We do know she had a young son who was killed and left for the dogs to maul. According to one Iqaluit resident, she died in the 1960s and is buried in the Roman Catholic cemetery in Frobisher Bay.

THE NORTH THROUGH QALLUNAAT EYES

As a translator, Paulette may have known Freeman, or possibly Baird, but I have found no records of those lives crossing. By focusing my sights on Baird and other qallunaat sojourners, filmmakers, writers, political commentators, and civil servants, I have explored the mirror opposite of Anerodluk's lost photos, asking how these groups of cultural producers constructed northern Indigenous peoples, why these representations came to the fore when they did, and what consequences they might have had. Admittedly, the varied range of cultural texts and images used in this monograph makes generalization difficult. These texts and images include forms of witnessing and personal memoires, acts of imaginative reconstruction, efforts at social and scientific documentation, and journalistic renditions of political issues. Baird's novel, *Climate*, and *The Beaver* were directed at a middlebrow reading public interested in the North, while the NFB films reached a broader audience through multiple educational outlets and in theatres. Sojourner accounts were written for the general public, not an expert audience, but they nonetheless did not have the popular, widespread impact of *RCMP*, the television show that was constructed for, and appealed to, a mass audience. The RCSW, though covered extensively in the media, was a political event that created debate as well as consensus, and it certainly eluded the interest of many northern Indigenous women who did not see its relevance to their daily lives.

However different these cultural expressions, there were linkages between them. The collective northern imaginary was shaped by expert and popular discourses, cultural production, government aspirations, and economic development objectives, all of which interacted with and upon each other. Some were directly and symbiotically related: state-funded anthropological studies undertaken by groups like the Northern Research Centre, for example, guided some northern policy thinking, while NFB filmmakers initially took many of their cues from state policy makers. Baird drew on her civil servant history to become a narrator of fictional stories about the North, and television writers incorporated long-standing mythologies promoted by the federal state's police force into their scripts. Some shared techniques of staging: both early NFB films and *The Beaver*, for instance, mixed goals of pedagogy and pleasure, used salvage paradigms, and provided a visual history of linear progress from tradition to modernity.

Perhaps most important, however diverse in their provenance and presentation, these forms of representation were all shaped within the larger context of Canadian postwar political economy, ideologies of Indigeneity, and the history of Indigenous-settler relations. The North had long played an important role in Canadian nation-building discourses, but from the 1940s onwards, it assumed new economic and political significance: the Northwest Territories was vigorously presented as the next economic frontier of resource wealth creation, and the eastern Arctic, previously unknown to many white travellers, let alone settlers, was promoted as a frontier needing both military-strategic occupation and increased benevolent intervention in the lives of Inuit who lived in precarious Stone Age conditions. Changing representations of northern Indigenous peoples cannot be hived off from this political, social, and economic scenario of northern expansion and development: they were intimately connected, mutually constituted, and cemented through the work of ideology.

All cultural formations, Raymond Williams argues, must be analyzed with attention to their "general history" and to the "whole social order, its classes and formations."[40] This emphasis on reading representations in relation to the contexts, means, and suppositions shaping their genesis and existence has shaped my conclusions more than has postcolonial theories stressing hybridity, fluidity, plurality, and indeterminacy. While indebted to some postcolonial writing on race and the orientalizing of non-Western Indigenous peoples, as well as efforts to critique the sexual and gendered underpinnings of empire, I emphasize, instead, the "work" of ideology in organizing, categorizing, and shaping ideas about the North. As Frank Tester notes with relation to cultural transformation in the Arctic, there is too much left unsaid and unexplored in postcolonial theory, including "consumption, commodities," class, and capital.[41] For Indigenous peoples, the postcolonial deconstruction of authenticity, borders, and identities poses its own political problems, particularly in relation to ongoing efforts to resist dispossession and dislocation.

Ideology is defined here not as a set of beliefs unilaterally imposed from above but, rather, as part of the fabric of everyday life, conditioned by both the material and discursive contexts within which it is bound.[42] Colonial cultures prospered not simply at the level of policy creation or high politics but also through the seemingly mundane and entertaining interpretations of history, identity, society, and humanity presented on television or in magazines.[43] Ideology, as materialist scholars suggest, exists not only as a system of signification, ideas, and belief, and as an active material force in everyday life, but also as a system of power, in this case legitimizing the interests of certain powerful social groups as opposed to others.[44] Power is expressed not only in terms of capital and class but also through ideas about gender and race ("culture" being a common stand-in for "race"). While we often take it for granted that colonialism bore the mark of racism, Canada's colonial project was also deeply gendered, whether through the RCMP's constructed heroic white masculinity or the state policy, articulated through NFB films, of creating male breadwinner Indians and Eskimo. Gender ideology shaped the differing accounts of white male and female sojourners, the testimony women gave to the RCSW, and Irene Baird's non-fiction and fictional versions of the North. Gender ideology intersected with relations of class and race and, taken together, they contradicted any idealized notion of women's shared universal identity — no matter how earnestly Florence Bird articulated its existence.

Cultural constructions did have political implications: they incited, and were shaped by, the dominant imperatives of mapping, controlling, and planning northern resources and populations between 1945 and 1970. As Robert Berkhofer notes in his path-breaking examination of the "white man's Indian," the same cultural images defining literature and social science became the "moral and intellectual justification" for state policies as well as an explanation for their successes and failures.[45] Popular and learned images of First Nations became the basis on which policy decisions about northern peoples could be rationalized, understood, and legitimated. A study of the Canadian Arctic relocations of the 1950s similarly sees culture and policy as intricately linked: past "myths and stereotypes" of the Inuit, from the film *Nanook* onwards, were "fundamental to identifying the links between imagery, popular thinking, and government policy" in the North.[46]

The European bourgeois legal ideology of terra nullius underwrote not only internal colonial relations, as it did in many other colonial contexts, but also popular imagery. Depictions of the Inuit as nomadic and primitive, with no secure geographical ties to the land, provided a rationale for resource development and, in some cases, relocations designed by the state.[47] Primitives also required an infusion of "British justice," à la RCMP, to offset a deficiency in governance and a failure to protect the weak and vulnerable – read women – in nomadic hunting cultures.[48] As we know now, migration, relocation, and centralized settlement, along with state interventions in Indian and Eskimo lives, even if well meaning in areas such as health and education, undermined existing familial, social, and community ties, resulting in social dislocation and crises that, in turn, became the focus for public debate in Canadian magazines, books, and newspapers. Some of these debates – concerning the precarious life and death of Inuit in the Arctic, whether or not welfare was needed, and who was responsible for human disasters – became political firestorms, likely providing Irene Baird with some of the events she featured in *Climate*.[49]

Nation-building discourses that emerged in the post-Second World War period did not completely ignore or omit Indigenous peoples – indeed, quite the contrary. Some integrated northern First Nations, especially the Inuit, into images of Canada that romanticized our northern landscape, celebrated the cultural and racial diversity of the nation, and extolled our adaption to a unique physical environment. Canadians, as Nellie Cournoyea comments at the beginning of this monograph, "glamourize and romanticize the Inuit ... [because they] give Canada something that other countries don't have."[50] Many of the representations discussed in the previous chapters also included articulations of tolerance, liberal pluralism, and cultural relativism. Whether it was the *RCMP* script that praised the honourable "noble-Native" and his connection to nature, *The Beaver*'s attempts to highlight the amazing adaptiveness of Inuit survival, or NFB salvage ethnographies appreciating Indigenous life on the land, this recurring theme of cultural tolerance was stressed. Nor should we see this as simply a manufactured political correctness. As some sojourner accounts indicate, those who lived in the North for some time did come to feel respect, compassion, and human connection to their neighbours, and this increased markedly in the 1960s and 1970s in the context of changing political debates about the First Nations and Indigenous organizing in Canada.

However, efforts to downplay a hierarchical relationship between Indigenous and settler populations were compromised by a persisting non-Indigenous paternalism towards northern First Nations. This paternalism, coupled with a political economy promoting inevitable development, sustained a colonial image of northern Indigenous peoples that limited their social and economic options and sustained the resilient conviction that they had to be "helped." Firmly ensconced notions of the superiority of capitalist forms of organization and Western scientific modernity were stressed again and again, and they were equated with a white settler project of good governance and enlightened governmentality. Orientalist ways of seeing Indigenous peoples thus persisted and thrived: even if they were part of the future, Indigenous peoples were simultaneously objects of an ethnographic gaze, rendered part of a nostalgic, colonial landscape. Colonialism may have modernized its form since the nineteenth century, altered its justifications, or softened its harsh racial rationales, but in the time period under study it continued to manifest a social hierarchy of progress that (albeit usually referred to as "cultural" rather than as "racial") validated a particular view of economic and social development not unlike that recommended for the Third World.[51]

Calls for cooperation, collaboration, and understanding between all races were common in public discussions of the North and were undoubtedly earnestly felt by some, but cooperation was based less on complete equality than on one group believing the other needed to take its advice, follow its lead, and listen to it. In the view of those with social and economic power, land needed to be reoriented, used in ways consonant with private accumulation and wealth generation; the skills taught needed to offer the hope of wage labour; and cultural makeovers were needed to enable modern familial living. Even those concerned with protecting Indigenous access to land-based subsistence through animal conservation viewed Indigenous hunting through "imperialist knowledge" lenses that assumed the superiority of Western science, seeing it as a necessary antidote to wasteful and "wanton" practices.[52]

Ongoing debates about the development of the North simultaneously exposed much about the cultural construction of Canadian modernity in the South (however over-generalized and inaccurate that term is). Imperialist visions often portray the metropolis as the antithesis of the colony, yet "home and away" were part of the same "field of debate."[53] At the time, most Canadians presumed that progress moved in one direction – northward – but, in fact, this very image created a dialectical relationship. By constructing the Indigenous North as primitive, the South, with its exuberant embrace of economic expansion, technology, and consumption, became the epitome of progress and development. This reciprocal construction of a primitive North in need of guidance from a modern South, of course, masked relations of ideological power that had potentially profound consequences for Indigenous peoples: what was done in the national interest of a supposedly modern, progressive state could thus be justified as being in the best interests of "less advanced" Indigenous inhabitants.

The nomenclature of primitiveness was used most especially in discussions of the Inuit, who were perceived to be a people living in harmony (if precariously and with difficulty) with nature, existing in simple societies lacking the social and intellectual complexity of Euro-Canadian society, though perhaps offering a needed cure for the negative aspects of modernity.[54] Not only did this romanticized view homogenize culturally distinct groups of northern Innu and Inuit, but it also subtly juxtaposed northern Eskimo "primitiveness" with an implied southern Indian "savagery" (again, the term "savagery" was avoided – only its connotation remained). Aside from the neglect of northern Dene and other Indian peoples that such Eskimo-focused fascination occasioned, these cultural constructions suggested a contrast between the primitive Eskimo (as a group more open and adaptable, more amenable to white newcomers) and southern Indians (a group that had been corrupted, hurt, embittered, and had been shuffled into reserves that became places of backwardness).

The pessimism and defensiveness that characterized Indian Affairs bureaucrats in comparison to the Northern Affairs ones in discussions of films is one example of this contrasting understanding of Eskimo and Indians. Their different approaches must again be contextualized in relation to the political economy of northern development. In the Far North, control over the land was neither complete nor without contest and controversy: "original," or "primitive," accumulation was still in process. The mapping, control, and development of resources by the state and capital required a public show of sensitivity towards local Indigenous populations, who were also perceived as one source of labour in the North. Moreover, a broader process of the "totalization" of the state's reach in the North was also under way, although it may have appeared "more benign" than past colonialism since it was accomplished through the extension of the "kindly" welfare state.[55]

My emphasis in this monograph on the persistence of colonial texts and images in postwar Canadian culture has three final caveats and problems. First, by focusing on textual engagement, we may become so immersed in the rhetoric of cultural difference that we seem to stress exactly what we are critiquing: namely, the labelling of economic, social, and human-made problems as *inherently* cultural problems. Culture is not the essential source of disparity, inequality, poverty, health problems, and alienation. Colonialism is a structure and set of practices as well as a defining ideology. Expressed through varied, changing cultural forms that differentiated newcomer from Native, Indian from Eskimo, and North from South, it was naturalized through culture, not simply created by it. Moreover, a focus on cultural validation may lull us into uncritically equating cultural tolerance and plurality with the end of colonial history. The seemingly progressive language of multiculturalism and tolerance, evident in global "race" thinking in the postwar period, is not to be confused with equality: cultural tolerance for the other also became an explanation for Indigenous peoples' self-imposed "underdevelopment" and a rationale for paternal colonial direction and control.[56]

Understandably, Sheila Burnford's call for respect for different cultures in the Arctic seems far more humane than does Jean Godsell's racist understanding of northern difference. The unappealing, modernizing bureaucrats in *Climate* who believed the only future for the Inuit was "in museums" seem less appealing than do those in the novel who professed respect for Inuit culture. Were these calls for tolerance and racial harmony, however, not part of a longer genealogy of liberal pluralism now heavily critiqued by some Indigenous scholars? The politics of liberal recognition and reconciliation as ends in themselves, they argue persuasively, are not just inadequate: they may "co-opt" Indigenous peoples into "neocolonial" forms of "subjectification," leaving the colonial state and primitive accumulation intact and unquestioned.[57] The validation and restoration of traditional cultures, they also point out, can be problematic without attention to the way they have become entangled with the gender inequality of the colonial state, without a conscious "re-creation" of culture to "support the well-being of all contemporary citizens."[58]

Second, contradiction and disagreement are also evident in these cultural case studies. Ideology, even a dominating ideology, is seldom monolithic and unified. It may be fractured by disagreement within the dominant group or contested by other subordinate groups. Cultural production may exist not only as an expression of power relations but also as a potential site of political contestation. Even within white settler thinking, differences clearly existed, and there were possibilities for the emergence of alternative points of view. The cultural relativism promoted by *The Beaver* may well have induced readers to develop more critical views of state policies towards Indigenous peoples; the NFB films extolling life on the land might have done the same. The trial of Koona in "The Smiling People," with a white English-speaking jury passing judgment on a woman speaking Inuktitut, may have been written by the author *and* interpreted by the viewer as a muted critique of British justice in the North as much as an endorsement of it.

Arguing that the Indigenous North was orientalized may be true but it is also an over-generalization. As a mode of culturally demarcating the superior white/West from the racialized/Indigenous other, orientalism was not universal, homogeneous, and historically static; rather, it might take on varying dogmatic, superior, romantic, critical, or questioning hues. As Judy Tzu-Chun Wu argues, anti-imperialist "second wave" feminists began to develop a different, more "radical orientalism" that revalorized the colonized or Indigenous other. They argued that colonized women did not need to be saved by white women; on the contrary, they should in fact be the ones to lead all women – politically and culturally.[59] Similar inclinations were becoming evident in discourses about the North.

Irene Baird's writing itself may be differentiated between her earlier, pleasing accounts in *North/Nord*, which gave credence and respectability to state scientific and economic projects, and her final novel, in which paternalism and racism are exposed. Her Inuit character, Joanassie, however minor in that storyline, pithily expresses Inuit cynicism about white visitors: "More interested in talking about the Eskimo than to them. It was agreed their mouths bigger than their ears."[60] Reading my sources against the grain thus throws up examples of Inuit women and men "speaking back" to the dominant images of them, even when white settlers did not comprehend Indigenous peoples' silence, refusal to work, or rejection of white ways as resistance.

The last example speaks to a final caveat: relations of gender, race, class, and colonialism are processes, not unchanging static events or "things," and there was some change over time, not only in state policy, expert discourse, and white setter perspectives but also in the forms of resistance developed by Indigenous peoples (as the opening to this chapter suggests). The emergence of some *Beaver* articles protesting the treatment of First Nations was one sign of change; so, too, were the more liberal, questioning narratives of white sojourners like Sheila Burnford and Edith Iglauer. A new genre of NFB film that emerged in the 1970s, made by politically aware white filmmakers focusing a critical eye on the state's role in the North, is another example, though what was likely even more important were the efforts by these same filmmakers to hand over the camera to the Inuit so that they could tell their own stories. By the time of the hearings on the RCSW, the gap in living conditions and perspectives between white and Indigenous women was not just more visible, it was also a public sign of shame, an issue in need of analysis and reform. No longer were the full cupboards of white women taken as an unquestioned privilege. The basic needs of Indigenous – and other impoverished – women for clean water became a clear and unacceptable dividing line in their experiences, a symbol of colonialism's past and present. Moreover, in the RCSW hearings, the resistance of Indigenous women was articulated differently, couched in the language of Aboriginal rights and entitlements, as the testimony of Rosemary Thrasher made clear. With echoes of the Paulette Anerodluk-penned petition, she asserted the Inuit right to land and livelihood: "The country belonged to the native before the white man, so the best consideration should be given to them ... [T]he government talks about equality and I think we are entitled to that too. Everyone knows this country is where red and native people lived before you came. And if you want to run the country then 'consideration' should be given to native peoples."[61] Anerodluk and Thrasher were their own spokeswomen for a new, imagined future.

Notes

INTRODUCTION

1 Quoted in Penny Petrone, *Northern Voices: Inuit Voices in English* (Toronto: University of Toronto, 1988), 286.

2 Stephen J. Harper, "Franklin Discovery Strengthens Canada's Arctic Sovereignty," *Globe and Mail*, 12 September 2014, http://www.theglobeandmail.com/news/politics/franklin-discovery-strengthens-canadas-arctic-sovereignty/article20590280/.

3 Susan Lord, "Canadian Gothic: Multiculturalism, Indigeneity and Gender in Prairie Cinema," in *Canadian Cultural Poesis: Essays in Canadian Culture*, ed. Garry Sherbert, Annie Gerin, and Sheila Petty (Waterloo: Wilfrid Laurier Press, 2006), 400. The definition draws on Mary Louise Pratt, *Imperial Eyes: Travel Writing and Acculturation* (New York: Routledge, 1992), 6–7.

4 George Mortimore, *The Indian in Industry: Roads to Independence* (Ottawa: Indian Affairs Branch, 1965), 5.

5 Patrick Wolfe, "Settler Colonialism and the Elimination of the Native," *Journal of Genocide Research* 8, 4 (2006): 388.

6 Cole Harris, *Making Native Space: Colonialism, Resistance, and Reserves in British Columbia* (Vancouver: UBC Press, 2002). On the importance of transnational circuits of colonialism, see Gurminder K. Bhambra, *Rethinking Modernity: Post-colonialism and the Sociological Imagination* (London: Palgrave Macmillan, 2013).

7 Lisa Piper, *The Industrial Transformation of Subarctic Canada* (Vancouver: UBC Press, 2009), 283, 138.

8 Peter Usher, "Northern Development, Impact Assessment, and Social Change," in *Anthropology, Public Policy, and Native Peoples in Canada*, ed. Noel Dyck and James Waldram (Montreal and Kingston: McGill-Queen's University Press, 1993), 98.

9 Harris, *Making Native Space*, 52.

10 Sarah Carter, *Lost Harvests: Prairie Indian Reserve Farmers and Government Policy* (Montreal and Kingston: McGill-Queen's University Press, 1990).

11 Kenneth Coates, *Canada's Colonies: A History of the Yukon and Northwest Territories* (Toronto: James Lorimer, 1985), 199.

12 The lineage of this ministry goes back to the nineteenth-century Department of the Interior, which had responsibility for resource development in the west and North as well as for Native affairs in some time periods. There are four federal departments in this lineage discussed in this book: Mines and Resources (1936–49), Resources and Development (1949–53), Northern Affairs and National Resources (1953–66), and Indian Affairs and Northern Development (1966). By 1936, the Indian Affairs Program was part of the Department of Mines and Resources, but, in 1949, departmental responsibilities were shifted between the Department of Citizenship and Immigration and the Department of Mines and Technical Surveys; the remaining Department of Mines and Resources functions were placed under the Department of Resources and Development. The Indian Affairs Branch remained under the Department of Citizenship and Immigration until 1966, when the Department of Indian Affairs and Northern Development was set up; the latter was also responsible for developing national parks, administering Indian and Eskimo affairs, and managing Canada's wildlife resources.

13 David Harvey, "The Body as an Accumulation Strategy," *Environment and Planning D: Society and Space* 16 (1998): 412.

14 I use the term "realist" as post-positivists do. In contrast to postmodernists, post-positivists argue that, even though all knowledge is mediated by theory, we can produce reliable knowledge and "better and worse social and political theories" and we can seek "less distorted and more objective knowledge of social phenomena by creating the conditions for the production of better knowledge." Satya P. Mohanty, "The Epistemic Status of Cultural Identity," in *Reclaiming Identity: Realist Theory and the Predicament of Postmodernism*, ed. Paula Moya and Michael P. Hames-Garcia (Berkeley: University of California Press, 2000), 41.

15 Kate Crehan, *Gramsci, Culture and Anthropology* (Berkeley: University of California Press, 2002), 71–73.

16 *Qullunaat! Why White People Are Funny*, dir. Mark Sandiford (Montreal: NFB, 2006).

17 John Sutton Lutz, *Makúk: A New History of Aboriginal-White Relations* (Vancouver: UBC Press, 2008).

18 Mary-Ellen Kelm, *A Wilder West: Rodeo in Western Canada* (Vancouver: UBC Press, 2011), 8.

19 Discussion of this issue includes Aihwa Ong, "Colonialism and Modernity: Feminist Re-presentations of Women in Non-Western Societies," *Inscriptions* 3–4 (1988): 79–93; Trinh T. Minh-Ha, *Woman, Native, Other: Writing Postcoloniality and Feminism* (Bloomington: Indiana University Press, 2009); Gayatri Spivak, "Can the Subaltern Speak?" in *Marxism and the Interpretation of Culture*, ed. Cary Nelson and Lawrence Grossberg, 271–313 (Basingstoke: Macmillan, 1988).

20 Rob Shields, *Places on the Margin: Alternative Geographies of Modernity* (London: Routledge, 1991), 29.

21 Sherrill E. Grace, *Canada and the Idea of North* (Montreal and Kingston: McGill-Queen's University Press, 1991), 15.

22 Coates, "Discovery of the North," 39.

23 On the Cold War surveillance of Arctic anthropologists, see David Price, *Threatening Anthropology: McCarthyism and the FBI's Surveillance of Activist Anthropologists* (Durham, NC: Duke University Press, 2004).

24 Hugh Brody, *Living Arctic: Hunters of the Canadian North* (Vancouver: Douglas and McIntyre, 1987), 13, 19.

25 For example, one source identifies at least nine general geographical categories of "historical Inuit occupation" in the North: Baffin Island, Caribou, Hudson Bay, Netsilik, Sadlermiut, Polar, and Mackenzie areas. Olive Dickason, *Canada's First Nations: A History of Founding Peoples from Earliest Times* (Toronto: Oxford University Press, 2002), 356.

26 Doug Wilkinson, *Land of the Long Day* (New York: Henry, Holt and Co., 1956), 21.

27 Kerry Abel, *Drum Songs: Glimpses of Dene History* (Montreal and Kingston: McGill-Queen's University Press, 1993), xv, notes six language groups. Julie Cruikshank, *Life Lived Like a Story: Life Stories of Three Native Yukon Elders* (Vancouver: UBC Press, 1990), 5, refers to eight. Also on Dene in the Yukon, see Kenneth Coates, *Best Left as Indians: Native-White Relations in the Yukon Territory, 1840–1973* (Montreal and Kingston: McGill-Queen's University Press, 1999).

28 Ella Shoat and Robert Stain, *Unthinking Eurocentrism: Multiculturalism and the Media* (London: Routledge, 1994), 18.

29 Coates, *Canada's Colonies*, 9–10.

30 Kerry Abel and Ken S. Coates, "Introduction: The North and the Nation," in *Northern Visions: New Perspectives on the North in Canadian History*, ed. Abel and Coates (Peterborough: Broadview Press, 2001), 10.

31 Joyce Green, "Towards a Détente with History: Confronting Canada's Colonial Legacy," *International Review of Canadian Studies* 12 (Fall 1995), 85.

32 Frances Abele, "Canadian Contradictions: Forty Years of Northern Political Development," *Arctic* 40, 4 (1987): 310–20.

33 Quoted in Lorenzo Veracini, *Settler Colonialism: A Theoretical Overview* (London: Palgrave Macmillan, 2010), 1.

34 Ibid., 5.

35 Patrick Wolfe, "Land, Labor and Difference: Elementary Structures of Race," *American Historical Review* 106, 3 (2001): 866–905; Marilyn Lake, "White Man's Country: The Transnational History of a National Project," *Australian Historical Studies* 122 (2003): 346–63.

36 Veracini, *Settler Colonialism*, 17.

37 Patrick Wolfe, "Race and Racialisation: Some Thoughts," *Postcolonial Studies* 5, 1 (2002): 59.

38 Veracini, *Settler Colonialism*, chap. 1.

39 Wolfe, "Settler Colonialism," 389.

40 Mel Watkins, ed., *The Dene Nation: A Colony Within* (Toronto: University of Toronto Press, 1972).

41 Robert Blauer, "Colonized and Immigrant Minorities," in *From Different Shores*, ed. Ronald Takaki 149–60 (New York: Oxford University Press, 1994); Russell Benjamin, "The American Internal Colonial Environment" in *Eternal Colonialism*, ed. Russell Benjamin and Gregory O. Hall, 3–12 (Latham, MD: University Press of America, 2010).

42 E. San Juan, *Beyond Postcolonial Theory* (New York: St. Martin's Press, 1998), 156.

43 Harold Adams, *Prison of Grass: Canada from the Native Point of View* (Saskatoon: Fifth House, 1989).

44 Shari Huhndorf, *Going Native: Indians in the American Cultural Imagination* (Ithaca, NY: Cornell University Press, 2001), 10.

45 J.S. Frideres and Renee Gadacz, *Aboriginal Peoples in Canada: Contemporary Conflicts* (Upper Saddle River, NJ: Prentice Hall, 2007).

46 Vic Satzewich and Terry Wotherspoon, *First Nations: Race, Class and Gender Relations* (Regina: Canadian Plans Research Centre, 2000), 6–8.

47 Ibid., 9–10.

48 Linda Gordon, "Internal Colonialism and Gender," in *Haunted by Empire: Geographies of Intimacy in North American History*, ed. Ann Stoler, 427–51 (Durham, NC: Duke University Press, 2007).

49 J.M. Blaut, *The Colonizer's Model of the World: Geographical Diffusionism and Eurocentric History* (New York: Guilford Press, 1993).

50 Shoat and Stain, *Unthinking Eurocentrism*, 2–3.

51 Blaut, *The Colonizer's Model of the World*, 1, 64.

52 Shoat and Stain, *Unthinking Eurocentrism*, 4.

53 Andrea Smith, *Conquest: Sexual Violence and American Indian Genocide* (Cambridge: South End, 2005); Joyce Green, *Making Space for Indigenous Feminism* (Black Point, NS: Fernwood, 2007). Indeed, to excise feminism from an analysis of colonialism may "reproduce colonizing practices." Bird Rose, quoted in Isabel Altamirano-Jimenéz, "Indigenous Women, Nationalism and Feminism," in *States of Race: Critical Race Feminism for the 21st Century*, ed. Sherene Razack, Malinda Smith, and Sunera Thobani (Toronto: Between the Lines, 2010), 115.

54 Laura Tabili, "Race Is a Relationship and Not a Thing," *Journal of Social History* 37, 1 (2003): 126.

55 Ann Stoler, *Race and the Education of Desire: Foucault's History of Sexuality and the Colonial Order of Things* (Durham, NC: Duke University Press, 1995), 27.

56 Wolfe, "Race and Racialisation," 52.

57 Renisa Mawani, *Colonial Proximities: Crossracial Encounters and Juridical Truths in British Columbia, 1871–1921* (Vancouver: UBC Press, 2009), 12.

58 Andrew Baldwin, Laura Cameron, and Audrey Kobayashi, eds., *Rethinking the Great White North: Race, Nature, and the Historical Geographies of Whiteness in Canada* (Vancouver: UBC Press, 2011).

59 Kenan Malik, *The Meaning of Race: Race, History and Culture in Western Society* (New York: New York University Press, 1996), 129.

60 Frederick Cooper and Ann Stoler, "Between Metropole and Colony: Rethinking a Research Agenda," in *Tensions of Empire: Colonial Cultures in a Bourgeois World*, ed. Cooper and Stoler (Berkeley: University of California Press, 1997), 11.

61 Shoat and Stain, *Unthinking Eurocentrism*, 21.

62 Carl Berger, *The Sense of Power: Studies in the Ideas of Canadian Imperialism, 1867–1914* (Toronto: University of Toronto Press, 1970); W.L. Morton, *The Canadian Identity* (Toronto: University of Toronto Press, 1972); D.A. West, "Re-searching the North in Canada: An Introduction to the Canadian Northern Discourse," *Journal of Canadian Studies* 36, 2 (1991): 108–19.

63 Ralph Heinimann, "Latitude Rising: Historical Continuity in Canadian Nordicity," *Journal of Canadian Studies* 28, 2 (1993): 134–39; Louis-Edmond Hamelin, *Canadian Nordicity: It's Your North* (Montreal: Harvest, 1979).

64 Grace, *Canada and the Idea of North*.

65 Shelagh Grant, "Arctic Historiography: Current Status and Blueprints for the Future," *Journal of Canadian Studies* 33, 1 (1998): 145–53; Abel and Coates, *Northern Visions*; Kenneth Coates, "Writing First Nations into Canadian History: A Review of Recent Scholarly Works," *Canadian Historical Review* 81, 1 (2000): 99–114; Kerry Abel, "Tangled, Lost and Bitter? Current Directions in the Writing of Native History in Canada," *Acadiensis* 26, 1 (1996): 92–101; Janice Cavell, "The Second Frontier: The North in Canadian Historical Writing," *Canadian Historical Review* 88, 3 (2002): 364–89; Coates, "Discovery of the North"; Kenneth Coates, "Learning from Others: Comparative History and the Study of Aboriginal-Newcomer Relations," *Native Studies Review* 16, 1 (2005): 3–13.

66 On the latter, see Frank Tester and Peter Kulychyski, *Tammarniit (Mistakes): Inuit Relocation in the Eastern Arctic, 1939–63* (Vancouver: UBC Press, 1993); Allan Marcus, *Relocating Eden: The Image and Politics of Inuit Exile in the Canadian Arctic* (Vancouver: UBC Press, 1994); David Damas, *Arctic Migrants, Arctic Villages: The Transformation of the Inuit Settlement in the Central Arctic* (Montreal and Kingston: McGill-Queen's University Press, 2002). For a first-hand account by one group, see Ila Bussidor and Ustun Bilgen-Reinart, *Night Spirits: The Story*

of the Relocation of the Sayisi Dene (Winnipeg: University of Manitoba Press, 1997). Other examples of political and economic histories include Mark Dickerson, *Whose North? Political Change, Political Development, and Self-Government in the Northwest Territories* (Vancouver: UBC Press, 1992); William Morrison, *True North: The Yukon and Northwest Territories* (Toronto: Oxford University Press, 1998); Coates, *Best Left as Indians*; and Shelagh Grant, *Sovereignty or Security: Government Policy in the Canadian North, 1936–1950* (Vancouver: UBC Press, 1988).

67 Frank Tough, *As Their Natural Resources Fail: Native Peoples and the Economic History of Northern Manitoba* (Vancouver: UBC Press, 1996), 309. For a historiographical statement on environmental history, see Sverker Sorlin, "The Historiography of the Enigmatic North," *Canadian Historical Review* 95, 4 (2014): 555–66; Graeme Wynn, "Foreword: The Enigmatic North," in John Sandlos, *Hunters at the Margin: Native People and Wildlife Conservation in the Northwest Territories* (Vancouver: UBC Press, 2007), xi-xx.

68 Bill Waiser, "A Very Long Journey: Distance and Northern History," in Abel and Coates, *Northern Visions*, 38.

69 Coates, "Discovery of the North," 37.

70 The emphasis on gender is also apparent in contemporary studies; for example, see the special issue of *Inuit Studies* 30,1 (2006).

71 Arthur Ray, *The Canadian Fur Trade in the Industrial Age* (Toronto: University of Toronto Press, 1990); Mary-Ellen Kelm, *Colonizing Bodies: Aboriginal Health and Healing in British Columbia, 1900–50* (Vancouver: UBC Press, 1998); Pat Sandiford Grygier, *A Long Way from Home: The Tuberculosis Epidemic among the Inuit* (Montreal and Kingston: McGill-Queen's University Press, 1994); Joan Ryan, *Doing Things the Right Way: Dene Traditional Justice in Lac La Martre, NWT* (Calgary: University of Calgary Press, 1995); Peter Kulchyski and Frank Tester, *Kiumajut (Talking Back): Game Management and Inuit Rights, 1900–70* (Vancouver: UBC Press, 2007).

72 On masculinity and exploration through an American lens, see Lisa Bloom, *Gender on Ice: American Ideologies of Polar Exploration* (Minneapolis: University of Minnesota Press, 1993); Michael F. Robinson, *The Coldest Crucible: Arctic Exploration and American Culture* (Chicago: University of Chicago Press, 2006).

73 Kerry Abel, *Drum Songs: Glimpses of Dene History* (Montreal and Kingston: McGill-Queen's University Press, 1993); Louis-Jacques Dorais, *Quaqtaq: Modernity and Identity in an Inuit Community* (Toronto: University of Toronto Press, 1997).

74 Nancy Wachowich, in collaboration with Apphia Agalakti Awa, Rhoda Kaukjak Katsak, and Sandra Pikujak Katsak, *Saqiyuq: Stories from the Lives of Three Inuit Women* (Montreal and Kingston: McGill-Queen's University Press, 1999).

75 Charlotte Gray, *Gold Diggers* (Toronto: HarperCollins, 2011).

76 Two examples are J.D.H. King and Henrietta Lidchi, eds., *Imaging the Arctic* (Vancouver: UBC Press, 1998); and Anne Feinup-Riordan, *Freeze Frame: Alaska Eskimos in the Movies* (Seattle: University of Washington Press, 1995). There is extensive writing around certain themes, such as Robert Flaherty's *Nanook of the North*. See, for example, Julia Emberly, "Colonial Governance and the Making and Unmaking of the Bourgeois 'Eskimo' Family: Robert Flaherty's *Nanook of the North*," in *Indigeneity: Construction and Re/presentation*, ed. James Brown and Patricia Sant, 95–118 (Commack, NY: Nova Science Publishers, 1999); Huhndorf, *Going Native*.

77 Adams, *Prison of Grass*, 147.

78 Allan J. Ryan, *The Trickster Shift: Humour and Irony in Contemporary Native Art* (Vancouver: UBC Press and University of Washington Press, 1999); Molly Blyth, "Tricky Stories Are the Cure: Contemporary Indigenous Writing in Canada" (PhD diss., Trent University, 2009).

79 Daniel Francis, *The Imaginary Indian: The Image of the Indian in Canadian Culture* (Vancouver: Arsenal Pulp Press, 1992), 5–6.

80 Elizabeth Bird, "Savage Desires: The Gendered Construction of the American Indian in Popular Media," in *Selling the Indian: Commercializing and Appropriating American Indian Culture*, ed. Carter Jones Meyer and Diana Royer (Tucson: University of Arizona Press, 2001), 63.

81 Philip Deloria, *Playing Indian* (New Haven, CT: Yale University Press, 1998), 115. See also Robert Berkhofer, *The White Man's Indian: Image of the American Indian from Columbus to the Present* (New York: Alfred Knopf, 1978).

82 Deloria, *Playing Indian*; Huhndorf, *Going Native*.

83 Francis, *Imaginary Indian*, 8. For a much earlier discussion of images, see Ronald Haycock, *The Image of the Indian* (Waterloo: Wilfrid Laurier University Press, 1971).

84 Anna Johnston and Alan Lawson, quoted in Veracini, *Settler Colonialism*, 9 (emphasis added).

85 Sharon Tiffany and Kathleen Adams, *The Wild Woman: An Inquiry into the Anthropology of an Idea* (Cambridge, MA: Schenkman, 1985).

86 Gail Guthrie Valaskakis, *Indian Country: Essays on Contemporary Native Culture* (Waterloo: Wilfrid Laurier University Press, 2005), chap. 5; Rayna Green, "The Pocahontas Perplex: The Images of the Indian Woman in American Vernacular Culture," *Massachusetts Review* 16, 4 (1976): 698–714; Patricia Albers and William James, "Illusion and Illumination: Visual Images of American Indian Women in the West," in *The Women's West*, ed. Susan Armitage and Elizabeth Jameson, 35–50 (Norman: University of Oklahoma Press, 1987); Karen Anderson, *A Recognition of Being: Reconstructing Native Womanhood* (Toronto: Second Story Press, 2000).

87 Sarah Carter, *Capturing Women: The Manipulation of Cultural Imagery in Canada's Prairie West* (Montreal and Kingston: McGill-Queen's University Press, 1997), 10.

88 Victoria Freeman, "Attitudes toward 'Miscegenation' in Canada, the United States, New Zealand and Australia, 1860–1914," *Native Studies Reviews* 16,1 (2005): 41–70; Pamela White, "Restructuring the Domestic Sphere: Prairie Indian Women on Reserves – Image, Ideology and State Policy, 1880–1930" (PhD diss., McGill University, 1987); Mary Jane McCallum and Aroha Harris, "Assaulting the Ears of Government: The Indian Homemakers Clubs and the Maori Women's Welfare Leagues in their Formative Years," in *Indigenous Women and Work: From Labor to Activism*, ed. Carol Williams, 225–39 (Urbana: University of Illinois Press, 2013).

89 Zoe Druick, *Projecting Canada: Government Policy and Documentary Film at the National Film Board of Canada* (Montreal and Kingston: McGill-Queen's University Press, 2007); Carol Payne, *The Official Picture: The National Film Board of Canada's Still Photography Division and the Image of Canada, 1941–1971* (Montreal and Kingston: McGill-Queen's University Press, 2013).

90 Carol Payne, "Lessons with Leah: Re-Reading the Photographic Archive of Nation in the National Film Board of Canada's Still Photography Division," *Visual Studies* 21, 1 (2006), 8. See also Payne, *Official Picture*.

91 Payne, "Lessons with Leah," 4–21.

92 Eva Mackey, *The House of Difference: Cultural Politics and National Identity in Canada* (New York: Routledge, 1999), 38.

93 Makin, *Meaning of Race*, 169.

94 Carter, *Capturing Women*, 10.

95 Peter Geller, *Northern Exposures: Photographing and Filming the Canadian North, 1920–45* (Vancouver: UBC Press, 2004).

96 Hugh Brody, "In Conclusion: The Power of the Image," in King and Lidchi, *Imaging the Arctic*, 227.

97 J.C. King and Henrietta Lidchi, "Introduction," in King and Lidchi, *Imaging the Arctic*, 13.

98 Bart Moore-Gilbert, *Postcolonial Theory: Contexts, Practices, Politics* (London: Verso, 1997), 11.

99 Bhambra, *Rethinking Modernity*, 18.

100 As scholars of postcolonial theory have noted, Said's concept of orientalism maintains some debt to Gramsci's concept of ideological hegemony, though integrating Foucault's attention to discourse and power. See Moore-Gilbert, *Postcolonial Theory*. However, many critics also point to Said's oversimplification of and distance from historical materialism.

101 Ania Loomba, *Colonialism/Postcolonialism* (London: Routledge, 1998), 37.

102 Reina Lewis, *Gendering Orientalism: Race, Femininity and Representation* (London: Routledge, 1996), 3.

103 One problem with discussions of postcolonialism and history concerns the vastly overgeneralized terms used to explain the benefits of postcolonialism; often these could just as easily apply to other theories, like Marxism or feminism. For example, one author equates postcolonialism with a "concern with the contingencies and specificities of historical change within particular imperial frames." Angela Woollacott, "Postcolonial Histories and Catherine Hall's *Civilising Subjects*," in *Connected Worlds: History in Transnational Perspective*, ed. Ann Curthoys and Marilyn Lake, 63–74 (Sydney: ANU Press, 2005).

104 "Postcolonialism's genealogies, boundaries, fields, locations, and ideologies have all [been] found to be problematic." Paul Tiyambe Zeleza, "The Troubled Encounter between Postcolonialism and African History," *Journal of the Canadian Historical Association* 17, 2 (2006): 92.

105 Sara Ahmed, *Strange Encounters: Embodied Others in Post-Coloniality* (London: Routledge, 2000), 10.

106 Arif Dirlik, *The Postcolonial Aura: Third World Criticism in the Age of Global Capitalism* (Boulder, CO: Westview Press, 1997); Benita Parry, "Problems in Current Theories of Colonial Discourse," *Oxford Literary Review* 9 (1987): 27–58; Ella Shoat, "Notes on the Postcolonial," *Social Text* 31–32 (1992): 99–113; Patrick Wolfe, "History and Imperialism," *American Historical Review* 102, 2 (1997): 388–420; Benita Parry, *Postcolonialism: A Materialist Critique* (London: Routledge, 2004); Vivek Chibber, *Postcolonial Theory and the Specter of Capital* (London: Verso, 2013); Ellen Meiksins Wood and John Bellamy Foster, eds., *In Defense of History* (New York: Monthly Review Press, 1997).

107 Parry, "Problems in Current Theories"; Albert Memmi, *The Colonizer and the Colonized* (Boston: Beacon, 1965), 84.

108 Glen Coulthard, "Subjects of Empire: Indigenous Peoples and the 'Politics of Recognition' in Canada," *Contemporary Political Theory* 6 (2007): 437–60.

109 San Juan, *Beyond Postcolonial Theory*, 6–7.

110 Aziz Ahmed, *In Theory: Classes, Nations, Literatures* (London: Verso, 1992).

111 San Juan, *Beyond Postcolonial Theory*, 8.

112 Arif Dirlik, "The Past as Legacy and Project: Postcolonial Criticism in the Perspective of Aboriginal Historicism," in *Contemporary North American Political Issues*, ed. Troy Johnson, 73–98 (Walnut Creek, CA: Altamira Press, 1999).

113 Shoat, "Notes," 105.

114 Glen Coulthard, *Red Skin, White Masks: Rejecting the Colonial Politics of Recognition* (Minneapolis: University of Minnesota Press, 2014), chap 2.

115 Philip Deloria, "Places Like Homes, Banks, and Continents: An Appreciative Reply to the Presidential Address," *American Quarterly* 58, 1 (2006): 23–29.

116 Grace, *Canada and the Idea of North*.

117 Renée Hulan, *Northern Experience and the Myths of Canadian Culture* (Montreal and Kingston: McGill-Queen's University Press, 2002), 17.

118 Janet Mancini Billson and Kyra Mancini, *Inuit Women: Their Powerful Spirit in a Century of Change* (Lanham, MD: Rowman and Littlefield, 2007), 54–55.

119 Sara Mills, *Gender and Colonial Space* (Manchester: Manchester University Press, 2005), 10.

120 Frederick Cooper and Anne Stoler, "Between Metropole and Colony," in Cooper and Stoler, *Tensions of Empire*, 11.

121 Jenny Sharpe, *Allegories of Empire: The Figure of Woman in the Colonial Text* (Minneapolis: University of Minnesota Press, 1993), 9.

122 Antonio Gramsci, *Selections from Cultural Writings*, ed. David Forgacs and Geoffrey Nowell-Smith (Cambridge: Harvard University Press, 1985), 112.

123 Frank Tester, "Iglu to Iglurjuag," in *Critical Inuit Studies: An Anthology of Contemporary Arctic Ethnography*, ed. Pamela Stern and Lisa Stevenson, 230–52 (Lincoln: University of Nebraska Press, 2006). "Events in themselves" is from Lisa Stevenson, "Introduction," in Stern and Stevenson, *Critical Inuit Studies*, 8.

CHAPTER ONE | NARRATING THE NORTH

1 Wanda N. Tolboom, *Arctic Bride* (New York: William Morrow and Co, 1956), 37.

2 Although I use both the term "travel" and the term "sojourning" to describe these books, I concentrate more on women sojourners – that is, those who lived for a time in the North, though they did not necessarily intend to go as permanent settlers. Granted, the distinction was sometimes blurred. I concentrate on texts published between 1940 and 1970, though a broader sample of northern travel writing has been consulted. Those most intensely cited were chosen because of their date of publication, their public reception, and to show a range of occupations. They are: Marjorie Hinds, *School-House in the Arctic* (London: Geoffrey Bles, 1958); Katharine Scherman, *Spring on an Arctic Island* (Boston: Little Brown and Co, 1956); Mrs. Tom Manning, *Summer on Hudson Bay* (London: Hodder and Stoughton Ltd., 1949); Mrs. Tom Manning, *Igloo for a Night* (Toronto: University of Toronto Press, 1946); Elsie Gillis with Eugenie Myles, *North Pole Boarding House* (Toronto: The Ryerson Press, 1951); Donalda McKillop Copeland (as told to Eugenie Myles), *Remember, Nurse* (Toronto: The Ryerson Press, 1960); Mena Orford, *Journey North* (Toronto: McClelland and Stewart, 1957); Miriam MacMillan, *Greens Seas and White Ice* (New York: Dodd, Mead and Co, 1948); Jean Godsell, *I Was No Lady: I Followed the Call of the Wild* (Toronto: The Ryerson Press, 1959); Edith Iglauer, *The New People: The Eskimo's Journey into Our Time* (New York: Doubleday, 1966); Sheila Burnford, *Without Reserve* (Boston: Atlantic Monthly

Press, 1969); Sheila Burnford, *One Woman's Arctic* (Toronto: McClelland and Stewart, 1973). Others consulted include Betty Lee, *Lutiapik* (Toronto: McClelland and Stewart, 1975); Eva Alvey Richards, *Arctic Mood* (Caldwell, Idaho: Caxton, 1949); William Ashley Anderson, *Angel of Hudson Bay: The True Story of Maud Watt* (Toronto: Clarke, Irwin and Co., 1961); Constance and Harmon Helmricks, *We Live in the Arctic* (New York: Little Brown and Co., 1947); Doug Wilkinson, *Land of the Long Day* (Toronto: Clarke, Irwin and Co.,1955); Ritchie Calder, *Men against the Frozen North* (London: George Allen and Unwin, 1957); Frank Illingworth, *Highway to the North* (New York: Philosophical Library, 1955); Joseph P. Moody, *Arctic Doctor* (New York: Dodd Mead and Co., 1953); Duncan Pryde, *Nunaga: Ten Years of Eskimo Life* (New York: Walker and Company, 1971); and one travel narrative of northern Ontario – Gordon Langley Hall, *Me Papoose Sitter* (New York: Thomas Crowell Co., 1955).

3   Deidre David, *Rule Britannia: Women, Empire and Victorian Writing* (Ithaca: Cornell University Press, 1995), 5. Women's travel narratives were a popular form of writing extending back to Upper Canada and the early west: for example, Anna B. Jameson *Winter Studies and Summer Rambles* (Toronto: McClelland and Stewart, 1965); Georgina Binnie-Clark, *Wheat and Woman* (Toronto: University of Toronto Press, 1979); Agnes Deans Cameron, *The New North: An Account of a Woman's 1908 Journey through Canada to the Arctic* (Saskatoon: Western Producer Prairie Books, 1986). For analysis, see Marian Fowler, *The Embroidered Tent: Five Gentlewomen in Early Canada* (Toronto: Anansi Press, 1982); Jennifer Henderson, *Settler Feminism and Race Making in Canada* (Toronto: University of Toronto Press, 2003); Barbara Kelcey, *Alone in Silence: European Women in the Canadian North before 1940* (Montreal and Kingston: McGill-Queen's University Press, 2001).

4   Copeland, *Remember*.

5   James Frideres, *Native People in Canada: Contemporary Conflicts*, 2nd ed. (Scarborough: Prentice-Hall Canada, 1993), 295.

6   David Spurr, *The Rhetoric of Empire: Colonial Discourse in Journalism, Travel Writing and Imperial Administration* (Durham, NC: Duke University Press, 1993).

7   Hugh Brody, *The People's Land* (London: Penguin Books, 1975), 79. On orientalism, see Edward Said, *Orientalism* (New York: Vintage Books, 1979); Reina Lewis, *Gendering Orientalism: Race, Femininity and Representation* (London: Routledge, 1996).

8   Alfred Memmi, *Colonizer and the Colonized* (New York: Beacon Press, 1965), 85.

9   Library and Archives Canada (LAC), Richard Harrington Diaries, MG 31, C5, vol. 1, Port Harrison trip, 1948. Of course, Harrington, too, generalized – for example, about the inherent shyness of the Eskimo.

10 Mary Louise Pratt, *Imperial Eyes: Travel Writing and Transculturation* (London: Routledge, 1992), 7. Other works include Inderpal Grewal, *Home and Harem*

(Durham, NC: Duke University Press, 1996); Sara Mills, *Discourses of Difference* (London: Routledge, 1991); Dea Birkett, *Spinsters Abroad* (Oxford: Blackwell, 1989); Alison Blunt, *Travel, Gender and Imperialism: Mary Kingsley and West Africa* (New York: Guildford Press, 1994); Helen Callaway, *Gender, Culture and Empire* (London: Macmillan, 1987); Antoinette Burton, *Burdens of History* (Chapel Hill: University of North Carolina Press, 1994); Ellen Jacobs, "Eileen Power's Asian Journey, 1920–1: History, Narrative and Subjectivity," *Women's History Review* 7, 3 (1998): 295–319; Laura Donaldson, *Decolonizing Feminisms: Race, Gender and Empire Building* (Chapel Hill: University of Northern Carolina Press, 1992); Antoinette Burton, ed., *Gender, Sexuality and Colonial Modernities* (London: Routledge, 1999); Clare Midgley, ed., *Gender and Imperialism* (Manchester: Manchester University Press, 1998); Anne McClintock, *Imperial Leather: Race, Gender and Sexuality in the Colonial Context* (London: Routledge, 1995); Ann L. Stoler, *Race and the Education of Desire: Foucault's History of Sexuality and the Colonial Order of Things* (Durham, NC: Duke University Press, 1995).

11   Ann Stoler, "Making Empire Respectable: The Politics of Race and Sexual Morality in 20th-Century Colonial Cultures," *American Ethnologist* 16, 4 (1989): 634–59; Ruth R. Pierson and N. Chaudhur, "Introduction," in *Nation, Empire and Colony: Historicizing Gender and Race*, ed. Ruth R. Rierson and N. Chaudhur (Bloomington: Indiana University Press, 1998), 4; Jane Haggis, "Gendering Colonialism or Colonizing Gender: Recent Women's Studies Approaches to White Women and the History of British Colonialism," *Women's Studies International Forum* 13, 1 (1990): 105–15; Angela Woolcott, "All This Is Your Empire, I Told Myself: Australian Women's Voyages 'Home' and the Articulation of Colonial Whiteness," *American Historical Review* 102, 4 (1997): 1003–29.

12   Peter Usher, "Northern Development, Impact Assessment, and Social Change," in *Anthropology, Public Policy, and Native Peoples in Canada*, ed. Noel Dyck and James Waldram (Montreal and Kingston: McGill-Queen's University Press, 1993), 115.

13   Mills, *Discourses of Difference*, 22. See also Lisa Bloom, *Gender on Ice: American Ideologies of Polar Expeditions* (Minneapolis: University of Minnesota Press, 1993).

14   Steve Clark, "Introduction," in *Travel Writing and Empire: Postcolonial Theory in Transit*, ed. Steve Clark (London: Zed Books, 1999), 3.

15   Some had precise descriptions of northern flora and birds (Manning), others offer more direct opinions (Hinds), while some attempt a more light-hearted description of northern life (Gillis).

16   Copeland, *Remember*, 5.

17   Eva Becket, "Review of *School-House in the Arctic*," *The Beaver* (hereafter *TB*) (Winter 1959): 59.

18 Gillis, *North Pole*, 6.

19 Burnford was from Scotland. Iglauer was an American who subsequently moved to Canada and wrote other books about the North.

20 E.W. Manning, "Review of *Green Seas and White Ice*, by Miriam MacMillan," *TB* (September 1950): 47.

21 S.A. Hewitson, "Review of *Arctic Bride*, *TB* (Autumn 1957): 55.

22 Becket, "Review of *School-House*."

23 P.M. Bennett, "Review of *Igloo for the Night* and *A Summer on Hudson Bay*," *Arctic* (August 1950): 117.

24 B.G. Sivertz, "Review of *The New People*," *North* 13, 3 (1966): 43. Sivertz was at the time commissioner of the Northwest Territories.

25 C.H.J. Winter, "Review of *Igloo for the Night*," *TB* (December 1944): 42.

26 Sylvia Seeley, "Review of *Journey North*," *Canadian Geographic Journal* (March 1959): xiii.

27 Tolboom, *Arctic Bride*, 3.

28 Burnford, *Without Reserve*, 29.

29 Copeland, *Remember*, 6–7.

30 Pratt, *Imperial Eyes*, 84.

31 Gillis, *North Pole*, 10, 124.

32 Godsell, *I Was No Lady*, 48.

33 Godsell, *I Was No Lady*. Manning refers briefly to such conflicts in *Summer*, 53.

34 Godsell, *I Was No Lady*, 35.

35 Ibid., 95.

36 Ibid., 55.

37 Provincial Archives of Manitoba (PAM), Hudson's Bay Company Papers (HBC), Wolstoneholme Post Journal, B 397/a/9. January 1940.

38 Orford, *Journey North*, 17.

39 Gillis, *North Pole*, 88.

40 Godsell, *I Was No Lady*, 45.

41 Hinds, *School-House*, 15.

42 Burnford, *Without Reserve*, 20–21.

43 Miriam MacMillan, *Greens Seas*, 75.

44 Scherman, *Spring on an Arctic Island*, 105.

45 Ibid., 188.

46 Gillis, *North Pole*, 165.

47 Pryde, *Nunaga*.

48 LAC, Richard Harrington Diary, Igloolik trip, December 1952-March 1953.

49 Spurr, *Rhetoric of Empire*, 61–75.

50 E. Wallace Manning, "Explorer's Wife," *TB* (September 1942): 12.

51 MacMillan, *Green Seas*, 32,

52 Gillis, *North Pole*, 15. The incident is also mentioned in men's narratives. See Moody, *Arctic Doctor*, 9.

53 Peter Freuchen, *I Sailed with Rasmussen* (New York: Julian Messner, 1959). On the themes of death, mystery, and violence in popular narratives, see Sherrill Grace, *Canada and the Idea of the North* (Montreal and Kingston: McGill-Queen's University Press, 2001), 179.

54 Godsell, *I Was No Lady*, 37.

55 Copeland, *Remember*, 1.

56 Ibid., 63.

57 Ibid., 164–65.

58 Gillis, *North Pole*, 48.

59 Shelagh Grant, *Arctic Justice: On Trial for Murder, Pond Inlet, 1923* (Montreal and Kingston: McGill-Queen's University Press, 2002).

60 "The Cheerful Eskimo," *TB* (March 1952): 7–15. Photo credits: Richard Harrington.

61 Sherman, *Spring on an Arctic Island*.

62 Ibid.,180.

63 Ibid., 138.

64 MacMillan, *Green Seas*.

65 Spurr, *Rhetoric of Empire*, 167.

66 Manning, *Summer*, 26.

67 Hinds, *School-House*, 190.

68 Ibid.,127.

69 Gillis, *North Pole*, 184.

70 Hinds, *School-House*, 161.

71 David M. Quiring, *CCF Colonialism in Northern Saskatchewan: Battling Parish Priests, Bootleggers, and Fur Sharks* (Vancouver: UBC Press, 2004).

72 Copeland, *Remember*, 9.

73 Arthur Ray, *The Canadian Fur Trade in the Industrial Age* (Toronto: University of Toronto Press, 1990).

74 Tolboom, *Arctic Bride*, 173.

75 Gillis, *North Pole*, 9; Scherman, *Spring on an Arctic Island*, 192.

76 Frank Tester and Peter Kulchyski, *Tammarniit (Mistakes): Inuit Relocation in the Eastern Arctic, 1939–63* (Vancouver: UBC Press, 1994), chap. 2.

77 Tolboom, *Arctic Bride*, 106–7.

78 Timothy Kadloo and Sam Arnakallak (Pond Inlet), quoted in Grant, *Arctic Justice*, 232.

79 *Qalluaat! Why White People Are Funny* (NFB, dir. Mark Sandiford, 2006).

80 Tester and Kulchyski, *Tammarniit*, 93, 139.

81 Iglauer, *The New People*, opening page.
82 Tester and Kulchyski, *Tammarniit*, 173.
83 Iglauer, *New People*, 93.
84 Iglauer continued to keep in touch with Snowden (see LAC, MG 31, D 163, box 1, file 19, for her letters) and later wrote on other northern themes. See Edith Iglauer, *Denison's Ice Road* (Vancouver: Harbour Publishing, 1975).
85 MacMillan, *Green Seas*, 52.
86 Hinds, *School-House*, 45.
87 Burnford, *Without Reserve*, 67.
88 Pratt, *Imperial Eyes*, 84.
89 Scherman, *Spring on an Arctic Island*, 117.
90 Ibid., 138.
91 Also, to be uninterested in European labour was simply to "be indolent." John Lutz, *Makuk: A New History of Aboriginal White Relations* (Vancouver: UBC Press, 2008), 35.
92 Orford, *Journey North*, 95. The critical view of Inuit fatalism was also found in Betty Lee, *Lutiapik* (Toronto: McClelland and Stewart, 1975).
93 Manning, *Summer*, 140.
94 Craig Campbell, "A Genealogy of the Concept of 'Wanton Slaughter' in Canadian Wildlife Biology," in *Cultivating Arctic Landscapes: Knowing and Managing Animals in the Circumpolar North*, ed. David G. Anderson and Mark Nuttall, 154–71 (New York: Berghahn Books, 2004).
95 Hinds, *School-House*, 154 (emphasis mine).
96 This would echo some of Homi Bhabha's characterizations. The Native might be anglicized but could never be "English.'" Bart Moore-Gilbert, *Post Colonial Theory* (London: Verso, 1997), 120.
97 David Damas details why "preservationalism" (keeping Inuit in their camps) fell out of favour in *Arctic Migrants/Arctic Villagers: The Transformation of Inuit Settlement in the Central Arctic* (Montreal and Kingston: McGill-Queen's University Press, 2002), 190–91.
98 Scherman, *Spring*, 188.
99 Iglauer, *New People*, 195.
100 Ibid., 63, 40, 45
101 Notably, Duncan Pryde's description of his own participation in spouse swamping in *Nunaga*.
102 Notions of proper domesticity were central to many other colonial projects: Jean Comaroff and John Comaroff, *Ethnography and the Historical Imagination* (Boulder, CO: Westview Press, 1992); K. Hansen, ed., *African Encounters with Domesticity* (New Brunswick, NJ: Rutgers University Press, 1992); Amy Kaplan, "Manifest Domesticity," *American Literature* 70, 3 (1998): 581–606.

103 Patricia Jasen, "Race, Culture and the Colonization of Childbirth in Northern Canada," in *Rethinking Canada: The Promise of Women's History*, ed. V. Strong-Boag, M. Gleason, and A. Perry, 353–66 (Toronto: Oxford University Press, 2002).

104 Judith Bender Zelmanovitz, "Midwife Preferred: Maternity Care in Outport Nursing Stations in Northern Canada," in *Women, Health and Nation: Canada and the United States since 1945*, ed. Georgina Feldberg, Molly Ladd-Taylor, Alison Li, and Kathryn McPherson, 161–95 (Montreal and Kingston: McGill-Queen's University Press, 2003).

105 Manning, *Igloo*, 55.

106 Orford, *Northern Journey*, 113.

107 This story is a bit incredible since the doctor supposedly served in the Boer War. Whether that was true or not, Watt clearly valued the midwife over the doctor. Anderson, *Angel of Hudson Bay*, 141.

108 Tolboom, *Arctic Bride*, 102. Since these women did not discuss their own sexuality, one can only infer from other vague references to their premarital "shyness" their belief in sex only after marriage. The fact that their sexuality was not mentioned but that of Inuit women was again placed the latter in the category of a more sexualized "other."

109 Tolboom, *Arctic Bride*, 62.

110 Gillis, *North Pole*, 57, 75.

111 Ibid., 151.

112 This may not have been in response to their proximity to less affluent Inuit but because, after a radio message home, he worried that everyone knew their business. "If you ever mention food again ... I'll kill you." Was the author aware how negative a view she presented of her husband? Gillis, *North Pole*, 62, 75.

113 Hinds, *School-House*; Kulchyski and Tester, *Tammarniit*, 85.

114 Iglauer, *New People*, 198.

115 Manning, *Igloo*, 21.

116 Gillis, *North Pole*, 95.

117 Helen Callaway, "Dressing for Dinner in the Bush: Rituals of Self-Definition and British Imperial Authority," in *Dress and Gender: Making and Meaning*, ed. Ruth Barnes and Joanne B. Eicher (New York: Berg Books, 1992), 236.

118 Godsell, *I Was No Lady*, 201.

119 Ibid., 137.

120 A review by anthropologist Douglas Leechman of Gillis's book in *Canadian Geographic Journal*, February 1952, ix, notes that her description of the oddities of the Eskimos made it "an entertaining book."

121 As Grace points out, mimicry is unstable and uncontrollable; it can also "backfire on the mimics." Grace, *Canada*, 100. See also Diana Fuss for a discussion of differences between feminist characterizations of mimicry as "dissent" and the

different characterization of Bhabha: "Interior Colonies: Frantz Fanon and the Politics of Identification," *Diacritics* 24 (1994): 20–42.

122 Tolboom, *Arctic Bride*, 93.

123 For earlier images, see Sarah Carter, *Capturing Women: The Manipulation of Cultural Imagery in Canada's Prairie West* (Montreal and Kingston: McGill-Queen's University Press, 1997). And, on twentieth-century images of Indians, see Douglas Francis, *The Imaginary Indian: The Image of the Indian in Canadian Culture* (Vancouver: Arsenal Pulp Press, 1992).

124 Hugh Brody, *The Other Side of Eden* (Toronto: Douglas and McIntyre, 2000), 263.

125 Tolboom, *Arctic Bride*, 225.

126 Pryde, *Nunaga*.

127 Gillis, *North Pole*, 90.

128 Burnford, *Without Reserve*, 145; Burnford, *One Woman's Arctic Journey*, 47.

129 Orford, *Journey North*, 20.

130 Ibid., 70–72.

131 "Review of *I Was No Lady*" by H.S.M. Kemp," *TB* (Winter 1959): 57.

132 Alberta, Calgary Glenbow Archives, Philip Godsell Fonds, MS 33, file 337, Godsell, P/B, biographical clippings, Jean Godsell. These reviews were in a range of newspapers: *Winnipeg Tribune*, *Herald Magazine*, *Calgary Herald*, *Lethbridge Herald*. Philip Godsell was considered an expert on Indian artefacts and culture, and a promoter of Indian heritage.

133 Diana Rowley, "Review of *I Was No Lady*," *Canadian Geographic Journal* 60 (March 1960): xvi.

134 Godsell, *I Was No Lady*, 45.

135 Book jacket, *Without Reserve*.

136 Ronald Haycock, *The Image of the Indian* (Waterloo: Wilfrid Laurier Press, 1971), 28.

137 For example, John Howard Griffin, *Black Like Me* (New York: Houghton Mifflin, 1961).

138 Burnford, *Without Reserve*, 49.

139 Ibid., 119.

140 Ibid., 81.

141 Ibid., 140. While relayed somewhat obliquely, it seems that she suspects that the guardian was abusing the ward sexually.

142 Burnford, *One Woman's Arctic*, 39.

143 Ibid., 186.

144 Ibid., 91, 188.

145 Ibid., 192

146 Brody, quoted in Grant, *Arctic Justice*, 17.

147 Hinds, *Arctic School-House*, 57. Hinds discusses her first assignment as a welfare teacher at Fort McPherson, but most of the book deals with Port Harrison.
148 Catherine Scott, *Gender and Development: Rethinking Modernization and Dependency Theory* (London: Routledge, 1996).

CHAPTER TWO | THE BEAVER

1 Photo credit: Norman Ross, *The Beaver* (hereafter *TB*), March 1943: 40.
2 Jane Collins and Catherine Lutz, *Reading National Geographic* (Chicago: University of Chicago Press, 1993), 2; Peter Hervik, "The Mysterious Maya of National Geographic," *Journal of Latin American Anthropology* 4, 1 (1999): 166–97.
3 Brian Dippie, *The Vanishing American: White Attitudes and US Indian Policy* (Middletown: Wesleyan University Press, 1982), 281–82.
4 W. Jackson Rushing, *Native American Art and the New York Avant-Garde* (Austin: University of Texas, 1995), 192–24.
5 Daniel Francis, *The Imaginary Indian: The Image of the Indian in Canadian Culture* (Vancouver: Arsenal Pulp Press, 1992); Sarah Carter, *Capturing Women: The Manipulation of Cultural Imagery in Canada's Prairie West* (Montreal and Kingston: McGill-Queen's University Press, 1997); Eva Mackey, *The House of Difference: Cultural, Political and National Identity* (Toronto: University of Toronto Press, 2002); Edward Said, *Orientalism* (New York: Vintage Books, 1979).
6 Fatima Tobing Roy, *The Third Eye: Race, Cinema and Ethnographic Spectacle* (Durham, NC: Duke University Press, 1996), 5.
7 Kate Crehan, *Gramsci, Culture and Anthropology* (Berkeley: University of California Press, 2002), 108.
8 Collins and Lutz, *Reading National Geographic*, 167, 170.
9 Public Archives of Manitoba (PAM), RG 2/3/13, Hudson's Bay Company Archives (HBCA), Canadian Committee Records, series 3, *Beaver* file, "Mr Klein Speaks," *The Bayonet*, 1934.
10 PAM, Clifford Wilson Fonds, E 95/8, letter to Clifford Wilson from Ted Vogel, 10 December 1954 (emphasis in original).
11 This appeared many times. For example, *TB* (Winter 1964): 1.
12 Alan Sekula, "Photography between Labour and Capital," in *Mining Photographs and Other Pictures: A Selection from the Negative Archives of Shedden Studio, Glace Bay, Cape Breton*, ed. Don Macgillivray and Allan Sekula (Sydney: UCCB Press, 1983),198, 193.
13 PAM, Wilson Fonds, E95/3, and Malvina Bolus Fonds, biographical sketch, *Canadian Who's Who, 1936–37*, vol. 2 (Toronto: International Press, 1937). Douglas MacKay attended Woodstock College, University of Toronto, and Columbia

University and worked as a journalist for Canada Steamship Lines and the Seigniory Club in Montreal. Wilson came from an English Westmount family, attended Upper Canada College and McGill. Both had written popular versions of HBC history. Bolus was educated in England. After immigrating to Canada in 1926, she worked for Agnes Macphail and, later, for the *Canadian Geographical Journal*. She wrote on landscapes and landmarks as well as Eskimo art, and she edited fur trade history.

14 Letter sent by Winston Churchill to Sir Ashley Cooper, displayed in *TB* (June 1945): 4.

15 PAM, Bolus Fonds, E 380, box 1, a dissertation on *The Beaver* by the editor, ca.1971, file "editing, writing *The Beaver*."

16 PAM, Wilson Fonds, E 95/52, "Why Teach Children History?"; Clifford Wilson, *Adventurers All: Tales of Forgotten Heroes in New France* (Toronto: Macmillan, 1933); Clifford Wilson, ed., *Northern Treasury: Selections from* The Beaver (Toronto: Baxter Publishing 1954); Clifford Wilson, ed. *Pageant of the North: A Photographic Adventure into Canada's Northland* (Toronto: The Ryerson Press, 1957); Clifford Wilson, "History in Motion Picture," *Canadian Historical Review*, 23 (March 1942): 65–68.

17 Alan Cairns, *Citizens Plus: Aboriginal Peoples and the State* (Vancouver: UBC Press, 2000), 23.

18 Marjorie Wilkins Campbell, "Her Ladyship, My Squaw," *TB* (September 1954): 14–17. Women's history was clearly an interest of other authors too. See Grace Lee Nute, "Journey for Frances," *TB* (June 1954): 12–15, and her "Down North in 1892," *TB* (June 1948): 42–45.

19 Diamond Jenness, "Among the Eskimos," *TB* (Winter 1954): 27, 30.

20 Peter Kulchyski, "Anthropology in the Service of the State: Diamond Jenness and Canadian Indian Policy," *Journal of Canadian Studies* 28, 2 (1993): 21–50.

21 Robert Hancock, "The Potential for Canadian Anthropology: Diamond Jenness' Arctic Ethnography" (MA thesis, University of Victoria), 1999.

22 D.B. Marsh, "The Anglican Missionaries," *TB* (Winter 1954): 32.

23 Arthur Thibert, "The Roman Catholic Missionaries," *TB* (Winter 1954): 36.

24 P.A.C. Nichols, "The Fur Traders," *TB* (Winter 1954): 37–38.

25 Ann Fienup-Riordan, *Eskimo Essays: Yup'ik Lives and How We See Them* (New Brunswick, NJ: Rutgers University Press, 1990), 16–17.

26 Peter Fruechen, "Out of the Stone Age," *TB* (September 1951): 5.

27 Hugh Brody, *The Other Side of Eden* (Toronto: Douglas and McIntyre, 2000), 263.

28 Joanna de Groot, "Conceptions and Misconceptions: The Historical and Cultural Context of Discussion on Women and Development," in *Women, Development and Survival in the Third World*, ed. Haleh Afshar (London: Longman, 1991), 118

(emphasis in original); Ann Stoler, "Making Empire Respectable: The Politics of Race and Sexual Morality in 20th-Century Colonial Cultures," *American Ethnologist* 16, 4 (1989): 634–59.

29   Regna Darnell, *And Along Came Boas: Continuity and Revolution in Americanist Anthropology* (Philadelphia: John Benjamins Publishing Co., 1998), 40.

30   David Spurr, *The Rhetoric of Empire: Colonial Discourse in Journalism, Travel Writing and Imperial Administration* (Durham, NC: Duke University Press, 1996), 62, 69.

31   Marius Barbeau, "Old Port Simpson," *TB* (September 1940): 23

32   Andrew Nurse, "But Now Things Have Changed: Marius Barbeau and the Politics of Amerindian Identity," *Ethnohistory* 48, 3 (2001): 433–72; Derek Smith, "The Barbeau Archives at the Canadian Museum of Civilization: Some Current Research Problems," *Anthropologica* 43 (2001): 191–200.

33   H.B. Hawthorn et al., *The Indians of British Columbia: A Study of Contemporary Social Adjustment* (Toronto: University of Toronto Press, 1960); H.B. Hawthorn, *A Survey of Canada: A Report on Economic, Political, Educational Needs and Policies* (Ottawa: Indian Affairs Branch, 1966).

34   H.B. Hawthorn, "Enter the European IV: Among the Indians of Canada," *TB* (Summer 1954): 3–7.

35   On Hawthorn's place in the history of Canadian anthropology and policy making, see Noel Dyck, "Canadian Anthropology and the Ethnography of Indian Administration," in *Historicizing Canadian Anthropology*, ed. Julia Harrison and Regna Darnell, 78–92 (Vancouver: UBC Press, 2006); and Julia Harrison and Regna Darnell, "Historicizing Traditions in Canadian Anthropology," in Harrison and Darnell, *Historicizing Canadian Anthropology*, 3–18.

36   Margaret Mead, "The Eskimos," *TB* (Autumn 1959): 32–41.

37   Margaret Mead, "Into the South Pacific," *TB* (June 1953): 7–9.

38   Katherine Pettipas, *Severing the Ties That Bind: Government Repression of Indian Religious Ceremonies on the Prairies* (Winnipeg: University of Manitoba Press, 1994), 194.

39   Douglas Leechman, "The Trappers," *TB* (Winter 1957): 24–31; Douglas Leechman, "The Painted Skins," *TB* (March 1948): 14–18.

40   Alison Griffiths, *Wondrous Difference: Cinema, Anthropology and Turn-of-the-Century Visual Culture* (New York: Columbia University Press, 2002); Anna Grimshaw, *The Ethnographer's Eye: Ways of Seeing in Modern Anthropology* (Cambridge: Cambridge University Press, 2001).

41   Regna Darnell, *Invisible Genealogies: A History of Americanist Anthropology* (Lincoln: University of Nebraska Press, 2001), 7–8.

42   For example, see June Helm and Vital Thomas, "Tales from the Dogrib," *TB* (Winter 1966): 16–20.

43 Morris Schumiatcher "The Buckskin Curtin," *TB* (Autumn 1959): 12–15. See also L.H. Nicholson, "The Problem of the People," *TB* (Spring 1959): 20–24.

44 The anthropologist was an American, working with James Van Stone in the Arctic, under the auspices of the federal government. Wendall Oswalt, "Caribou Eskimo without the Caribou" *TB* (Autumn 1960): 13.

45 George Woodcock, "Louis Riel: Defender of the Past," *TB* (Spring 1960): 24.

46 W.L. Morton, "The Canadian Métis," *TB* (September 1950): 3.

47 W.L. Morton, "The 1870 Outfit at Red River," *TB* (Spring 1970): 7.

48 Frederick Tisdall and Elizabeth Robertson, "Voyage of the Medicine Men," *TB* (December 1952): 42–46.

49 Wilma Raynor, "Windigo Woman," *TB* (Summer 1957): 32–33. On ethnic tourists, see V. Smith, *Hosts and Guests: The Anthropology of Tourism* (Philadelphia: University of Pennsylvania Press, 1977).

50 Resident Nurse, "Medicine Man," *TB* (June 1943): 24–25.

51 Ibid.

52 I have not discussed nature photography here: another topic in itself. Note that the magazine also used the work of professional American nature photographer Lorene Squire, who contributed many powerful pictures of Inuit life. Although she died in 1942, *The Beaver* managed to acquire many of her photos, which it continued to use in the postwar period.

53 James R. Ryan, *Picturing Empire: Photography and the Visualization of the British Empire* (Chicago: University of Chicago Press, 1997), 17, 19.

54 A. Apter, "On Imperial Spectacle: The Dialectics of Seeing in Colonial Nigeria," *Comparative Studies in Society and History* 44, 2 (2002): 564–96; Grace Lee Nute "Down North in 1892," *TB* (June 1948): 43.

55 Philip Godsell, "Warriors of the Plains," *TB* (June 1952): 7. See also Philip Godsell, *Arctic Trader: The Account of Twenty Years with the Hudson's Bay Company* (New York: C.P. Putman, 1934).

56 "The Cheerful Eskimo," *TB* (March 1952): 7–15. Photo credits: Richard Harrington.

57 The chapter was entitled "Portrait of Famine: Padlei, 1950." See Richard Harrington, *The Face of the Arctic* (New York: Abelard-Schuman, 1952).

58 Ann Fienup-Riordan, *Freeze Frame: Alaska Eskimos in the Movies* (Seattle: University of Washington Press, 1995).

59 Ryan, *Picturing Empire*, 140.

60 Doug Wilkinson, "A Vanishing Canadian," *TB* (Spring 1959): 25–29.

61 Douglas Leechman, "The Savages of James Bay," *TB* (June 1945): 14.

62 Brian Tobin, "Hudson's Bay House," *TB* (March 1944): 30.

63 Ibid., 34.

64 "Here and There," *TB* (June 1944): 48. No photo credit.

65 Chantel Nadeau, *Fur Nation: From the Beaver to Brigitte Bardot* (New York: Routledge, 2001).

66 *TB* (March 1948) : 2, photo credit: International News Photos.

67 Sawchuk claims that Canadians "merely adopted those [explorers] of foreign extraction." While it is true that men like Peary and Franklin have claimed far more historical attention, Canadian popular writing absorbed some British men *as* Canadian (e.g., fur traders) and they did celebrate some Canadian narratives, such as those by Vilhajalmur Stefansson. Christina Sawchuk, "An Arctic Republic of Letters in Early Twentieth-Century Canada," *Nordlit* 23 (2008): 274.

68 Mary Louise Pratt, *Imperial Eyes, Travel Writing and Transculturation* (London: Routledge, 1992), 7.

69 Nute, "Down North," *TB* (June 1948): 44.

70 Campbell, "Her Ladyship," 14–15; Sylvia Van Kirk, *Many Tender Ties: Women in Fur Trade Society, 1670–1870* (Winnipeg: Watson and Dwyer, 1980). More contemporary accounts of women sojourners in the North were also published. Marjory Hinds, for example, recounted her experience of running Canada's "northernmost school in Arctic Bay," the article a precursor to her later memoir: Marjorie Hinds, "School in the High Arctic," *TB* (Winter 1959): 13–17; and Marjorie Hinds, "April in the Arctic Zone," *TB* (Spring 1964): 26–31.

71 Roy, *Third Eye*, 79–80.

72 Ibid., 80.

73 Mrs. J.S.C. Watt, "The Long Trail," *TB* (March 1943): 50.

74 Renate Rosaldo, *Culture and Truth: The Remaking of Social Analysis* (Boston: Beacon Press, 1993).

75 Diane Eaton and Sheila Urbanek, *Paul Kane's Great Nor-West* (Vancouver: UBC Press, 1995).

76 Gillian Poulter, "Representation as Colonial Rhetoric," *Canadian Journal of Art History* 16, 1 (1994): 11–25; Elwood C. Parry III, "Cooper, Cole and the Last of the Mohicans," in *Art and the Native American: Perceptions, Realities and Influences*, ed. Mary Louise Krumrine and Susan Scott (University Park: Penn State University Press, 2001), 165–67; Robert Berkhofer, *The White Man's Indian: Image of the American Indian from Columbus to the present* (New York: Alfred Knopf, 1978).

77 For a discussion of the use of the naked Indigenous female body in *National Geographic*, see Lisa Bloom, *Gender on Ice: American Ideologies of Polar Exploration* (Minneapolis: University of Minnesota Press, 1993), 273–76.

78 John Hongimann, "Dance of the Ancients," *TB* (Autumn 1968): 46. On Honigmann's extensive use of photography in his ethnographies, see Brian Cummins, *Faces of the North: The Ethnographic Photographs of John Hongimann* (Toronto: Natural Heritage Books, 2004).

79 As other authors have noted, Aboriginal cultural performance that appeared to be staged or stereotypical might also be a way to "preserve culture, bolster self-esteem and affect observers." Mary-Ellen Kelm, *A Wilder West: Rodeo in Western Canada* (Vancouver: UBC Press, 2011), 228. On posing for whites, see Nelson Graburn, "The Present as History: Photography and the Inuit, 1959–94," in *Imaging the Arctic*, ed. J.C.H. King and Henrietta Lidchi (Seattle/Vancouver: University of Washington Press/UBC Press, 1998), 163.

80 Francis, *Imaginary Indian*, 36.

81 Irene Baird, "Land of the Lively Arts," *TB* (Autumn 1961): 17. Of course, this promotion reflected government priorities (including getting the Inuit off welfare) as well. For an overview of the groups and motives involved in Inuit art, and also the way in which the Inuit themselves used art as a statement about identity, see Nelson Graburn, "Authentic Inuit Art: Creation and Exclusion in the Canadian North," *Journal of Material Culture* 9, 2 (2004): 141–59.

82 George Swinton, "Eskimo Carving Today," *TB* (Spring 1958): 41.

83 *TB* (Autumn 1967). Covers, too, began to use more Indigenous art instead of tourist-like poses of Indians and Eskimo.

84 Marion Nichols, "Hudson's Bay Bride," *TB* (June 1942): 40–41.

85 Pratt, *Imperial Eyes*, 78.

86 Raymond Bell, "Indian Wedding," *TB* (June 1942): 28–29.

87 Catherine Scott, *Gender and Development: Rethinking Modernization and Dependency Theory* (London: Routledge, 1996), 24, 27; Marianne Marchand and Jane Parpart, eds., *Feminism/Postmodernism/Development* (London: Routledge, 1995).

88 John Isbister, *Promises Not Kept: The Betrayal of Social Change in the Third World* (Bloomfield, CT: Kumarian Press, 2001), 33–34.

89 R. G. Robertson, "Promise of the Canadian North," *TB* (Autumn 1958): 8–9.

90 "Transition," *TB* (Summer 1958): 29.

91 William Morrow, "Arctic Circuit," *TB* (Winter 1966): 37.

92 Sergeant W.H. Nevin, "Policing the Far North," *TB* (September 1945): 7.

93 Ibid., 9.

94 Noel Dyck's term is an incredibly apt characterization of many such accounts. Noel Dyck, *What Is the "Indian Problem": Tutelage and Resistance in Canadian Indian Administration* (St. John's: Institute for Economic and Social Research, 1992).

95 Jean Lesage, "Enter the European: V-Among the Eskimos (Part II)," *TB* (Spring 1955): 7.

96 Toshio Yatsushiro, "The Changing Eskimo," *TB* (Summer 1962): 19, 22.

97 Irene Baird, "Inuvik, Place of Man," *TB* (Autumn 1960): 16.

98 George Michie and Eric Neil, "Cultural Conflict in the Eastern Arctic," *Canadian Geographer* 5 (1955): 33–34; Diamond Jenness, "Among the Eskimos," *TB* (Winter 1954): 30.

99 Hugh Brody, *The People's Land* (London: Penguin Books, 1975), 77–78.
100 Yatsushiro, "Changing Eskimo," 22, 24.
101 Douglas Leechman, "Beauty's Only Skin Deep," *TB* (September 1951): 38–40.
102 "Here and There," photo caption, *TB* (March 1947): 35, photo credit: R. Harrington.
103 Paige Raibmon, "Theatres of Contact: The Kwakwaka'wakw meet Colonialism in BC and at the Chicago World Fair," *Canadian Historical Review* 81, 2 (2000): 157–90; David MacDougall, "Whose Story Is It?" in *Visualizing Theory: Selected Essays from VAR, 1990–94*, ed. Lucien Taylor, 27–36 (New York: Routledge, 1994).
104 Indigenous stereotypes were also highly marketable. The magazine's own use of advertising images like that of the feathered Indian smoking his traditional pipe suggested that, for many readers, "the best Indian was the historical Indian": Francis, *Imaginary Indian*, 176.
105 de Groot, "Conceptions and Misconceptions," 115.
106 Winona Stevenson, "Colonialism and First Nations Women in Canada," in *Scratching the Surface: Canadian Anti-Racist Feminist Thought*, ed. Enakshi Dua and Angela Robertson (Toronto: Women's Press, 1999), 49–82. It is likely that the Inuit (as opposed to Indian) hunting family may long have been viewed, perhaps with some longing, by white observers as ordered and patriarchal. Shari M. Hundorf, *Going Native: Indians in the American Cultural Imagination* (Ithaca: Cornell University Press, 2001), 87, argues that, to white men, this was precisely the appeal of "going Native" in the North in the interwar years.
107 R.G. Robertson, The promise of the Canadian North," *TB* (Autumn 1958): 4–11.
108 "Red and White," *TB* (March 1946): 27.
109 Peter Geller, "Northern Exposures: Photographic and Filmic Representations of the Canadian North, 1920–45" (PhD diss., Carleton University, 1975).
110 Sekula, "Photography between Labour and Capital," 201.
111 Carol Williams, "Beyond Illustration: Illuminations of the Photographic Frontier," *Journal of the West* 46, 2 (2007): 38.
112 Richard Harrington "Madonna of the Peace," *TB* (June 1950): 25.
113 Don Blair, "Summer Voyage in Hudson Bay," *TB* (September 1954): 35. Note one difference: a later sketch on the cover shows the Inuit woman with a child in her hood, though again it is a highly idealized picture of health and happiness. See Bettina Steinke, *TB* (Winter 1966): 1.
114 Collins and Lutz, *Reading National Geographic*.
115 "Children of the North," *TB* (Winter 1962): 40–47.
116 Collins and Lutz, *Reading National Geographic*, 167.
117 "Here and There," photo caption, *TB* (December 1947): 45.
118 One exception is "Arctic Fur Show," a picture of "Paulette, Doris" and "Ann Webster" modelling fur. Paulette Anerodluk is discussed in the conclusion. *TB* (December 1945): 38. Photo captions: L.E. Learmonth and J.H. Webster.

119   Frederica Knight, "The New Kayak," *TB* (Spring 1960): 30–37.

120   While photographs taken by Indigenous people were very rare, the occasional well-known photographer was published. For example, Pitsulak's photos were featured in one issue: *TB* (September 1946): 20–21.

121   *TB* (Spring 1959):13, photo credit: Charles Gimpel.

122   *TB* (December 1944): 18, photo credit: D.B. Marsh.

123   Graburn, "Present as History," 165.

124   "Our Way of Living," *TB* (Spring 1959): 29–36, photo credits: Mary-Rousselière, OMI.

125   "Journey from the Igloo," *TB* (Spring 1959): 12.

126   Irene Baird, "The Eskimo Woman," *TB* (Spring 1959): 49–52

127   Ibid., 52.

128   Edward Said, "Representing the Colonized," 216.

129   Carol Williams, *Framing the West: Race, Gender and the Photographic Frontier on the Pacific Northwest* (New York: Oxford University Press, 2003), 9.

130   Etienne Anaveluk, "Eskimo Week," *TB* (Autumn 1954): 42.

131   Markoose, "In the Pilot's Seat," *TB* (Spring 1970): 4–11.

132   Said, *Orientalism*; Edward Said, "Representing the Colonized: Anthropology's Interlocuters," *Critical Inquiry* 15, 2 (1989): 205–25; Roy, *Third Eye*.

133   James Clifford, "Of Other Peoples: Beyond the 'Salvage Paradigm,'" in *Discussions in Contemporary Culture*, ed. Hal Foster (Seattle: Bay Press, 1987), 121–22.

134   For example, the work of Milton Freeman or Harvey Feit. On their relation to changing scientific paradigms, see Stephen Bocking, "Indigenous Knowledge and the History of Science, Race and Colonial Authority in Northern Canada," in *Rethinking the Great White North: Race, Nature, and the Historical Geographies of Whiteness in Canada*, ed. Andrew Baldwin, Laura Cameron, and Audrey Kobayashi (Vancouver: UBC Press, 2001), 50.

135   George Woodcock, "A Northern Journal," *TB* (Summer 1969): 6.

136   Noel Dyck and James Waldram, "Anthropology, Public Policy and Native Peoples: An Introduction to the Issues," in *Anthropology, Public Policy and Native Peoples in Canada*, ed. Noel Dyck and James Waldram (Montreal and Kingston: McGill-Queen's University Press, 1993), 16.

137   M.J. Hewitt, "A Kabloona Hunts with the Inlanders," *TB* (Spring 1968): 33.

138   Crehan, *Gramsci*, 103.

CHAPTER THREE | NORTH OF SCHAMATTAWA

1   Library and Archives Canada (LAC), Crawley Film Fonds, MG 28 III 99 (hereafter Crawley), vol. 48, file 2, Dorothy Hatton to Budge Crawley, 4 July 1958;

LAC, Crawley, vol. 48, file 2, Cock to Hatton 16 July, 1958. The handwritten memo is probably written by Crawley but could be by Cock.

2 Michael Dawson, *The Mountie: From Dime Novel to Disney* (Toronto: Between the Lines, 1998); Keith Walden, *Visions of Order: The Canadian Mounties in Symbol and Myth* (Toronto: Butterworths, 1982); Daniel Francis, *The Imaginary Indian: The Image of the Indian in Canadian Culture* (Vancouver: Arsenal Pulp Press, 1992), chap 4.

3 David Buxton, *From the Avengers to Miami Vice: Form and Ideology in Television Series* (Manchester: Manchester University Press, 1990), 16.

4 Political economy is defined here as "the study of social relations, particularly the power relations that mutually constitute the production, distribution and consumption of resources, including communication resources." Vincent Moso, *The Political Economy of Communication* (London: Sage, 2009), 2. See also Robert Babe, "Political Economy and Cultural Studies Column: Political Economy, Cultural Studies and Postmodernism," *Topia* 15 (2006): 91–100.

5 For a listing of Canadian shows, see David Skene-Melvin, *Canadian Crime Fiction* (Shelburne: Battered Silicon Dispatches, 1996).

6 CBS, *Father Knows Best* (1954–60); Nina Leibman, *Living Room Lectures: The Fifties Family on Film and Television* (Austin: University of Texas Press, 1995).

7 One could go further back to the Frankfurt School and its influence as well. A few recent overviews of this literature include: Jonathan Gray and Amanda D. Lotz, *Television Studies: A Short Introduction* (Malden, MA: Polity Press, 2012); Jennifer Holt and Alisa Perren, *Media Industries: History, Theory, Method* (Malden, MA: Blackwell, 2009).

8 Ron Lembo, *Thinking through Television* (Cambridge: Cambridge University Press, 2000), 59.

9 Douglas Kellnor, "Media Industries, Political Economy, and Media/Cultural Studies: An Articulation," in Holt and Perren, *Media Industries*. As he argues, "There is no communication without culture and no culture without communication, so drawing a rigid distinction" is myopic (102–3).

10 Ibid., 103.

11 Lembo, *Thinking through Television*, 55. See also John Fiske, *Television Culture* (New York: Methuen, 1987).

12 Elizabeth Furniss, *The Burden of History: Colonialism and Frontier Myths in a Rural Community* (Vancouver: UBC Press, 1990), 187.

13 Pierre Berton, *Hollywood's Canada: The Americanization of Our National Image* (Toronto: McClelland and Stewart, 1975).

14 Christopher P. Wilson, *Cop Knowledge* (Chicago: University of Chicago Press, 2000), 5.

15 Ian Loader, "Policing and the Social: Questions of Symbolic Power," *British Journal of Sociology* 48, 1 (1997): 3-4.

16 For an exception, see Arthur Lower, "Is the RCMP a Threat to Our liberty?" *Maclean's Magazine*, 6 July 1957, 8. However, the more popular view was represented in Alan Phillips's article on the RCMP, in which their anti-radical work was lauded: "The Thirty Years War with the Commies," *Maclean's Magazine*, 1 September 1954: 17–20, 56–62.

17 Steve Hewitt, *Riding to the Rescue: The Transformation of the RCMP in Alberta and Saskatchewan, 1914–1939* (Toronto: University of Toronto Press, 2006); Reginald Whitaker, Gregory Kealey, and Andrew Parnaby, *Secret Service: Political Policing in Canada from the Fenians to Fortress America* (Toronto: University of Toronto Press, 2012).

18 William R. Morrison, *Showing the Flag: The Mounted Police and Canadian Sovereignty in the North* (Vancouver: UBC Press, 1985), 179.

19 For one example, see Shelagh Grant, *Arctic Justice: On Trial for Murder, Pond Inlet, 1923* (Montreal and Kingston: McGill-Queen's University Press, 2002).

20 Morrison, *Showing the Flag*, 179.

21 Ibid., 143.

22 Lorna Roth, *Something New in the Air: The Story of First Peoples Television Broadcasting in Canada* (Montreal and Kingston: McGill-Queen's University Press, 2005), 18.

23 William Bleasdell Cameron, "Peaceful Invasion," *The Beaver* (March 1948): 36–39; "The Redcoats Are Ready," *Forest and Outdoors* (March 1950): 14–15; Alan Phillips, "The Toughest Beat in the World," *Maclean's Magazine*, 15 September 1954, 51–2.

24 Francis, *Imaginary Indian*, 1.

25 Margery Fee, "Romantic Nationalism and the Image of Native People in Contemporary English-Canadian Literature," in *The Native in Literature*, ed. Thomas King, Cheryl Calver, and Helen Hoy (Toronto: ECW Press, 1987), 24.

26 On Crawley, see Barbara Wade Rose, *Budge: What Happened to Canada's King of Film* (Toronto ECW Press, 1998).

27 LAC, Crawley, vol. 48, file 1, memo by Harry Horner, 13 November 1959.

28 David Hogarth, *Documentary Television in Canada: From National Public Service to Global Marketplace* (Montreal and Kingston: McGill-Queen's University Press, 2002), 5.

29 For example, the *Ottawa Citizen* featured a regular series on RCMP cases in 1957. See Trent University Archives (hereafter TU), Monroe Scott Fonds, 99–001 (hereafter Scott), vol. 14, file "*RCMP* General," clippings. The Phillips *Maclean's* articles, advertised as a "gripping series" on the RCMP, began 1 July 1954 and

included quotes that later appeared in Crawley background documents, so the research exchange between Phillips and Crawley was quite direct.

30 LAC, Crawley, vol. 48, file 1, Charles Jennings to Budge Crawley, 20 March 1956.

31 LAC, Crawley, vol. 49, file 1, draft letter to Richard Dorso, Ziv Television, n.d. and Crawley to Nicholson, 19 January 1956.

32 Ibid., Crawley to Donald Carter, 3 October 1957 and George Gorman to Robert Yamin, Ziv Television, 4 February 1957.

33 LAC, Crawley, vol. 48, file 2, notes on a meeting with Ralph Levy; LAC, Crawley, vol. 49, file 8 (also listed as file P1500B).

34 LAC, Crawley, vol. 48, file 1, Donald Carter to F.R. Crawley, 3 October 1957.

35 Paul Litt, *The Muses, the Masses, and the Massey Commission* (Toronto: University of Toronto Press, 1992).

36 LAC, Crawley, vol. 49, file 6, Crawley press release, n.d.

37 Rose, *Budge*, 97. This likely comes from an interview since there is no discussion of this issue (and Crawley's anger with the BBC) in the Crawley Fonds. The BBC's actions are described in more detail in James A. Forrester, *Budge: F.R. Crawley and Crawley Films, 1939–1982* (Lakefield: IRS, 1988), again based on an interview with Budge Crawley.

38 LAC, Crawley, vol. 49, file 6, CBC information services *RCMP* series, n.d.

39 LAC, Crawley, vol. 48, file 1, Crawley to Nicholson, 19 January 1956 and Crawley to Weller Kreever, 19 September 1956.

40 Charles Edward Rivett-Carnac replaced Nicholson when he resigned in 1959 after a federal-provincial spat over use of RCMP in a Newfoundland labour dispute. See Blair Fraser, "Will the Provinces Reject the RCMP?" *Maclean's Magazine*, 25 April 1959, 2; "Police Contracts at Stake: Could This Doom *RCMP*?" *Financial Post*, 4 April 1959, 30.

41 LAC, Crawley, vol. 48, file 1, Crawley to Richard Dorso, draft, n.d.

42 LAC, Crawley, vol. 49, file 9, Gray Campbell, "First Detachment," 17 August 1958.

43 LAC, Crawley, vol. 48, file 5, Horner to Marjorie Cresswell, 2 July and 19 August 1959. Cresswell was Tilsley's research assistant.

44 LAC, Crawley, vol. 49, file 8 (R 1500B), Vincent Tilsley to George Gorman, attached to letter from Reta Wheatley to Gorman, n.d.

45 BBC Archives, T23/208 TV Publicity *RCMP*, 1958–60. Tilsley was a respected scriptwriter who worked on classics such as *Jane Eyre*, and also wrote for *The Yorkey*, *The Third Man*, *Sherlock Holmes*, and *The Forsythe Saga* series.

46 LAC, Crawley, vol. 48, file 2, Harry Horner to Inspector Bayfield, 21 April 1958.

47 LAC, Crawley, vol. 48, file 1, Crawley to Rivett-Carnac, 10 November 1959.

48 Ibid., Quentin Brown to Crawley, 4 November 1955.

49   LAC, Crawley, vol. 49, file 8, Kemp to Tilsley, 5 September 1956.

50   LAC, Crawley, vol. 48, vol. 5, Horner to Tilsley, 14 September 1959.

51   Ibid., file 2, "Statement of Purpose and Format."

52   TU, Scott, 99–001, box 14, file "*RCMP* General."

53   LAC, Crawley, vol. 49, file 8 (R1500B), Tilsley to Crawley, 11 September 1958.

54   Mary Jane Miller notes that *RCMP* emphasized "human decency and detection rather than violent plot resolutions." However, this seems to be based on secondary sources rather than a viewing of the episodes, as none is cited. Mary Jane Miller, *Turn Up the Contrast: CBC Television Drama since 1952* (Vancouver: UBC Press, 1987), 30. See also Mary Jane Miller, *Outside Looking In: Viewing First Nations Peoples in Canadian Dramatic Television Series* (Montreal and Kingston: McGill-Queen's University Press, 2008), 114–15.

55   LAC, "Breakout," VI 2912–07–0007. When *RCMP* hero Gagnier reminds another officer that a criminal is still a "human being," the effect is to make Gagnier look humane.

56   Ibid., vol. 48, file 2, Tilsley to Crawley, 10 September 1959.

57   LAC, Crawley, vol. 48, file 1, *RCMP* television series.

58   TU, Scott, box 14, file "*RCMP* General."

59   Monroe Scott, *Corpus Delectable*, produced by Theatre Aquarius, 11 March 1995. My thanks to Monroe Scott for giving me a copy of his play.

60   TU, Scott, box 14, file "*RCMP* General."

61   Ibid.

62   Ibid.

63   LAC, Crawley, vol. 191, Fan letters file, Marguerite Broomhead to Mr. Everett, 07/1964.

64   Many other notable Canadian actors appeared once or more in the series: John Vernon, Frances Hyland, Bruno Gerrusi, Toby Ryans, John Drainie, and more.

65   LAC, Crawley, vol. 184, file 15, "Sun Dance," E.S.W. Cole to Crawley, 1 January 1954.

66   LAC, Crawley, vol. 49, file 8 (P1500B), internal memo, GMG to Budge, 23 November 1955.

67   LAC, Crawley, vol. 49, file 12, "Difficult Northern Journey Story Idea" by Deputy Commissioner Rivett-Carnac.

68   Ibid.

69   LAC, Crawley, vol. 48, file 5, Crawley to Girard, 9 December 1958. Nicholson talked to Budge Crawley and asked him to look into a new title.

70   Mark Cronlund Anderson and Carmen Roberston, *Seeing Red, a History of Natives in Canadian Newspapers* (Winnipeg: University of Manitoba Press, 2011). It is important to note that there is some historical debate about the public image of Aboriginal peoples in this postwar period, some arguing that, after a period of

relatively more positive coverage during the war, there was new attention to Aboriginal issues, others suggesting strong continuities with racist themes and motifs evident since the nineteenth century. See Scott Sheffield, *The Red Man's on the Warpath: The Image of the "Indian" and the Second World War* (Vancouver: UBC Press, 2004); Jim Miller, *Skyscrapers Hide the Heavens* (Toronto: University of Toronto Press, 2000).

71 LAC, Crawley, vol. 49, file 7, script meeting, 19 March, 1959.

72 LAC, Crawley, vol. 48, file 5, Girard to Gorman, 24 November 1958.

73 LAC, Crawley, vol. 48, file 1, Gorman to Girard, 24 November 1958. For the few Aboriginal actors who were principals, see vol. 191, Actors Pay Sheets file. Not all those cast as Aboriginal principals were Aboriginal (e.g., the actor [Larry Zahab] who played Johnny Wolf was not).

74 LAC, Crawley, vol. 191, file Angus Baptiste, letters dated from 25 May 1959 to 20 December 1959.

75 Paul Rutherford, *When Television Was Young: Primetime Canada, 1952–1967* (Toronto: University of Toronto Press, 1990).

76 Ward Alexander Foster, "Blondes and the Men of the RCMP," *Saturday Night*, 6 March 1948, 22–23.

77 TU, Scott, vol. 14, file "The Marked Man"; file "Legacy."

78 LAC, "Poison Pen," 7907–0389.

79 See LAC, "The Piggybank Robbery" (7907–0384) and "Day of Reckoning" (7907–0399). "Mop Up" was a compendium of everyday cases, one of which involved Gagnier reconciling a dueling couple. "I did not mean to hit her," was the husband's reaction. Hers was more chilling: "I don't mind a beating or two but I don't want him going around killing anyone." LAC, "Mop Up," (7907–0379).

80 In "The Gunslinger" (7907–0400) and "The Cattle Rustler" (79-7-0392) fathers have failed to father properly. In "Back to School" (7907–0379) Gagnier becomes a surrogate father/adviser to a new recruit. In "The Third Question" (7907–0382) he also becomes a surrogate father to a child having trouble in school because of language difficulties. In "Little Girl Lost," he notes that the parents are to blame for the child's disappearance because of their constant fighting. If the parents do not stop, he predicts, the daughter will certainly end up a "juvenile delinquent: "Little Girl Lost" (2005–07–0023).

81 LAC, Crawley, vol. 49, file 12, future *RCMP* stories.

82 LAC, vol. 191, files 2–3, David Stone, Australian Broadcasting Commission, to C.M. Everett, 10 July 1961; Everett to Stone 20 July, 1961. The Australian censors objected because "Father threatened to kill own family and general aspect of poor family life." Everett claimed that the ending "compensated" for the violence in the episode, but they had to rescind some of the money the Australians had paid for the episode.

83 LAC, "Tourist Bait" (7907–0408).

84 LAC, "Violence at the Wedding" (7907–0403). See also LAC, Crawley, vol. 50, "Violence at the Wedding" script file. The script notes say: "No mention is made in the script of the word 'Ukrainian' although this is what the people are." There are other themes in this episode, including distinctions between the older and younger Ukrainians, the unassimilated and the more "white" ones, but the character profiles make it clear that ethnic stereotypes were alive and well. A discussion of the interconnected themes of women, ethnicity, and race in *RCMP* is not possible here – but needed.

85 TU, Scott, Box 14, file "*RCMP* General," memo re: "The Husband Killer," and Scott to Lister Sinclair, 6 September 1957.

86 LAC, Crawley, vol. 49, file 9, A digest of twenty-eight stories by Alan Phillips, "The Missing Livers"; "The Five-Thousand Mile Innocence Patrol"; "Case no. 21," "Believe or Be Killed."

87 LAC, Crawley, vol. 49, file 8 GMG Memo to Crawley, 23 November 1955.

88 LAC, Crawley, vol. 48, file 1, comments on "Bear Walk," and vol. 48, file 5, Girard to Crawley, Re: *RCMP* scripts, BBC comments, 18 November 1958.

89 This was supposed to be part of his character: he was "fastidious in his personal habits," always clean-shaven (even in the bush), with clean nails and "no trace of stubble on his face." TU, Scott, box 14, file "*RCMP* General."

90 LAC, Crawley, vol. 48, file 1 "The Following Indians have been used in RCMP Stories." There is no indication why they were listing them. It was likely for payment purposes.

91 LAC, Crawley, vol. 49, file 11, media release n.d.

92 LAC, Crawley, vol. 191, publicity file, clipping, n.d.

93 The notes supposedly taken from the quarterly report also differed from newspaper coverage. The *Globe and Mail* claimed that George and Martha married but that George's wife subsequently killed him and was tried for murder. *Globe and Mail*, 27 August 1946, 7.

94 LAC, Crawley, vol. 49, file 9, *R. v. Mafa.*

95 All quotes from the episode, LAC, VI 9101–0018, "The Smiling People."

96 Elsie Gillis and Eugenie Myles, *North Pole Boarding House* (Toronto: The Ryerson Press, 1951), 38.

97 The fact that she is not defended by someone with an Anglo name may be significant since such names were still associated to some degree with those who were "outsiders" vis-à-vis the ruling class. This is evident in another *RCMP* episode: "Violence at the Wedding."

98 LAC, Crawley vol. 49, file 11, media release, n.d.

99 Wade, *Budge.*

100 BBC Archives, Audience Research Reports, week 8 and week 28.

101 BBC Archives, TV publicity *RCMP* T23/208, John Walters, Odhams Press Limited to Ronnie Waldman, BBC, 30 October 1958, and a series of other letters on this issue.

102 LAC, Crawley, vol. 191, publicity file, audience report for 3–9 April 1960.

103 "TV Critics Shoot Down RCMP Series," *Vancouver Sun*, 28 January 1960; "RCMP Operations TV Serial," *Regina Leader Post*, 24 October 1959.

104 "RCMP Series on TV Tones Down Heroics," *Montreal Gazette*, 22 October 1959.

105 LAC, Crawley, vol. 48, file 13, Harry Horner to Vincent Tilsley, 14 September 1959.

106 Mary Jane Miller, in *Outside Looking In*, looks at *Caribou Country*, *The Beachcombers*, and *North of 60* (the latter, of course, belongs to an entirely different cultural and political moment).

107 Pierre Berton, "The Mysterious North," *Maclean's Magazine*, 15 November 1954, 13–14.

CHAPTER 4 | NFB DOCUMENTARY

1 I use Alison Griffiths's definition of ethnographic documentary, which is more open and flexible than others. It does not presume a professional anthropological intent in the film. Ethnographic documentary refers to "actuality films produced by anthropological, amateur or commercial means." The definition rests on the relationship between the filmed and those filming. Alison Griffiths, *Wondrous Difference: Anthropology and Turn-of-the-Century Visual Culture* (New York: Columbia University Press, 2002), xxix. Others see ethnographic film more as a genre of anthropology. See Rosalind Morris, *New Worlds from Fragments: Film, Ethnography and the Representation of Northwest Coast Cultures* (Boulder, CO: Westview Press, 1994), 12.

2 Carol Payne, *The Official Picture: The National Film Board's Still Photography Division and the Image of Canada, 1941–1971* (Montreal and Kingston: McGill-Queen's University Press, 2013), 180.

3 Foucault's notion of "biopower over humans" stressed their membership in certain groups of "populations"; the process of governmentality was one in which "individual conduct" was shaped to accord with "national conduct." Graham Burchell, Colin Gordon and Peter Miller, *The Foucault Effect: Studies in Governmentality* (Chicago: University of Chicago Press, 1991), 5.

4 *Nanook of the North*, dir. Robert Flaherty, 1922. *Nanook* almost has an industry of academic discussion behind it. Two examples include William Rothman, "Robert Flaherty's Nanook of the North," in *Documenting the Documentary: Close Readings of Documentary Film and Video* (Detroit: Wayne State University, 2014), 1–18; Sherrill Grace, "Exploration as Construction: Robert Flaherty and *Nanook of the North*," *Essays on Canadian Writing*, 59 (Fall, 1996): 123–46.

5 Jane M. Gaines, "Political Mimesis," in *Collecting Visible Evidence*, ed. Jane M. Gaines and Michale Renov (Minneapolis: University of Minnesota Press, 1995), 84.

6 Fatima Tobing Rony, *The Third Eye: Cinema and Ethnographic Spectacle* (Durham, NC: Duke University Press, 1996), 123.

7 Brian Winston, *Claiming the Real: The Documentary Film Revisited* (London: British Film Institute, 1995), 40.

8 Joyce Nelson, *The Colonized Eye: Rethinking the Grierson Legend* (Toronto: Between the Lines, 1988). Grierson has been intensely studied. See one bibliography: http://www.lib.berkeley.edu/MRC/documentarybib.html#grierson (viewed 16 February 2015). For a few Canadian pieces, see Gary Evans, *John Grierson and the National Film Board: The Politics of Wartime Propaganda* (Toronto: University of Toronto Press, 1984); Peter Morris, "Rethinking Grierson: The Ideology of John Grierson," in *Dialogue Canadian and Quebec Cinema*, ed., Pierre Veronneau, Michael Dorland, and Seth Feldman, 21–56 (Montreal: Mediatext, 1987); Peter Morris, "After Grierson: The National Film Board, 1945–1953," in *Take Two: A Tribute to Canadian Film*, ed. Seth Feldman, 182–94 (Toronto: Irwin, 1984). On Canadian documentary, see Jim Leach and Jeannette Sloniowski, eds., *Candid Eyes: Essays on Canadian Documentaries* (Toronto: University of Toronto Press, 2003).

9 Reginald Whitaker and Gary Marcuse, *Cold War Canada: The Making of a National Insecurity State, 1945–57* (Toronto: University of Toronto Press, 1994).

10 Gary Evans, *In the National Interest: A Chronicle of the National Film Board of Canada from 1949 to 1989* (Toronto: University of Toronto Press, 1991).

11 Payne, *Official Picture*.

12 Michael Dorland, "Introduction," in *Cultural Industries in Canada: Problems, Policies and Prospects*, Michael Dorland, ed. (Toronto: Lorimer, 1996), xii.

13 Zoe Druick, *Projecting Canada: Government Policy and Documentary Film at the National Film Board* (Montreal and Kingston: McGill-Queen's University Press, 2007), 4.

14 Druick, *Projecting Canada*.

15 Julia Emberly, "Colonial Governance and the Making and Unmaking of the Bourgeois 'Eskimo' Family: Robert Flaherty's *Nanook of the North*," in *Indigeneity: Construction and Representation*, ed. James Brown and Patricia Sant, 95–118 (Commack, NY: Nova Science Publishers, 1999).

16 LAC, RG 22, Department of Mines and Resources (this section of the department was later integrated into the Department of Resources and Development, then into the Department of Northern Affairs and National Resources and finally, in 1966, into the Department of Indian Affairs and Northern Development),vol. 144, MF 4-1-44, press release, 21 November 1950.

17 LAC, RG 22, vol. 164, Dorothy Macpherson, NFB to H.M. Jones, Indian Affairs Branch, 17 August 1961.

18 Evans, *In the National Interest*, 32.

19 Margaret Atwood, *Strange Things: The Malevolent North in Canadian Literature* (Oxford: Clarendon Press, 1995), 39.

20 Note that, in the script, the Indian women are described as "docile, hard working, silent." Another chapter could be written on NFB history education. LAC, RG 10 Indian Affairs Branch, within Dept. of Citizenship and Immigration, vol. 8813, file 1/12–11–3, History series script "Lord of the North."

21 Pierre Berton, *Hollywood's Canada: The Americanization of Our National Image* (Toronto: McClelland and Stewart, 1975), 99.

22 There is a large body of literature on this theme. A few examples are: Edward Buscombe, *'Injuns!': Native Americans in the Movies* (Cornwall: Reaktin Books, 2006); Angela Aleiss, *Making the White Man's Indian: Native Americans and Hollywood Movies* (Westport, CT: Praeger, 2005); Jacqueline Kilpatrick, *The Celluloid Indian: Native Americans and Film* (Lincoln: University of Nebraska Press, 1990); Peter Rollins and John E. O'Connor, eds., *Hollywood's Indian: The Betrayal of the Native American in Film* (Lexington: University Press of Kentucky, 2003); Ward Churchill, *Fantasies of the Master Race: Literature, Cinema, and the Colonization of American Indians* (San Francisco: City Lights Books, 1998).

23 E. Elise Marubbio, *Killing the Indian Maiden: Images of Native American Women in Film* (Lexington: University Press of Kentucky, 2006), 4.

24 Ibid., 7,19, 220. Despite the "complex, versatile, remolded" view of the celluloid Indian maiden over time, Marubbio concludes certain myths remain, even in the more recent Native-centred filmmaking

25 Ann Fienup-Riordan, *Freeze Frame: Alaska Eskimos in the Movies* (Seattle: University of Washington Press, 1995), 8, 83.

26 Fienup-Riordan, *Freeze Frame*, 83.

27 Bill Nichols, *Representing Reality: Issues and Concepts in Documentary* (Bloomington: University of Indiana Press, 1991), 32.

28 On these definitions, see Nichols, *Representing Reality*, 32–33.

29 Peter Stevens, *Brink of Reality: New Canadian Documentary Film and Video* (Toronto: Between the Lines, 1993), 30.

30 Nichols, *Representing Reality*, 43.

31 Leach and Sloniowksi, "Introduction," *Candid Eyes*, 4.

32 Paul Atkinson, *The Ethnographic Imagination* (New York: Routledge, 1990), 148.

33 Faye Ginsberg, "Native Intelligence: A Short History of Debates on Indigenous Media and Ethnographic Film," in *Made to Be Seen: Perspectives on the History of*

Visual Anthropology, ed. Marcus Banks and Jay Ruby, 234–55 (Chicago: University of Chicago Press, 2011).

34 Griffiths, *Wondrous Difference*, 315.

35 Elizabeth Edwards, *Anthropology and Photography, 1860–1920* (New Haven/ London: Yale University Press/The Royal Anthropological Institute, 1992), 5.

36 Rony, *Third Eye*.

37 Johannes Fabion, Trinh T. Minh-ha, and Michael Taussig, quoted in Michael Renov, "Domestic Ethnography and the Construction of the 'Other' Self," in Gaines and Renov, *Collecting Visible Evidence*, 140–41.

38 Nichols, *Representing Reality*, 11.

39 Harald E.L. Prins, "The Paradox of Primitivism: Native Rights and the Problem of Imagery in Cultural Survival Films," *Visual Anthropology* 9 (1997): 250.

40 Leach and Sloniowksi, "Introduction," 5.

41 Keith Beattie, *Documentary Screens: Non-Fiction Film and Television* (London: Palgrave Macmillan, 2004), 15.

42 LAC, RG 10, vol. 8813, file 1/12–11–3, Evelyn Horne to Col. Acland, 27 August 1954 (emphasis in original).

43 LAC, RG 10, vol. 8813, file 1/12–11–1, R.F. Davey to NFB, 28 November 1962.

44 LAC, RG 10, vol. 8813, file 1/12–11–1, F.B. McKinnon to J.H. Gordon, 30 October 1963.

45 LAC, RG 10, vol. 8813, file 1/12–11–1, G.L. Charbonneau to Leo Vonnah, n.d.

46 Malek Khouri, *Filming Politics: Communism and the Portrayal of the Working Class at the National Film Board of Canada, 1939–46* (Calgary: University of Calgary Press, 2007).

47 John Lutz, *Makúk: A New History of Aboriginal-White Relations* (Vancouver: UBC Press, 2008), 6. Note also that northern themes have been less visible in labour, with some exceptions: William Morrison and Ken Coates, *Working the North: Labor and the Northwest Defence Projects 1942–46* (Fairbanks: University of Alaska Press, 1994), 1–2.

48 LAC, RG 10, vol. 8813, file 1/12–11–1, G.I. Fairholm to Mr. L.A. Leblanc, 2 December 1965.

49 On placement programs see Joan Sangster, *Transforming Labour: Women and Work in Postwar Canada* (Toronto: University of Toronto Press, 2011), chap. 6; Mary Jane McCallum, *Indigenous Women, Work and History, 1940–1980* (Winnipeg: University of Manitoba Press, 2014), chap.2.

50 LAC, RG 22, Vol. 141, file MF 4-1-6, H. Jones to Guy Roberge, NFB, 18 March 1957.

51 NFB, *Because They Are Different* file, George Pearson to Grant MacNeill, 23 April, 1968.

52 LAC, RG 10, vol. 8813, file 1/12–11–1, W.O. Brennan to Mr. Battle, Assistant Deputy Minister, 16 December 1964.

53 NFB, *Because They Are Different* file, Post production script, 2 and Grant McLean to Grant Rayson, 7 December 1964; Guy Laberge to C.M. Isbister, 23 Dec 1964.

54 LAC, RG 10, vol. 8813, file 1/12–11–1, Memo for file from R.F. Battle, 11 January 1965.

55 NFB, *Because They Are Different* file, letter of Eileen Smoke to NFB, 10 December 1964.

56 Kelly Pineault, "Shifting the Balance: Indigenous and non-Indigenous Activism in the Company of Young Canadians, 1966–1969" (MA thesis, Trent University, 2011), 165–66. Jerry Gambill, associated with the All Indian Film Crew, claimed one of the songs in the film, "One Little Indian," was used as an "extermination song" in the nineteenth century.

57 LAC, RG 10, vol. 8813, file 1/12–11–1, minutes, Liaison meeting re: NFB Community Development Film, 29 March 1964.

58 LAC, RG 22, vol. 140, MF 4.1.11, Irene Baird, memo to deputy minister, n.d.

59 Marx's term "original accumulation" was translated as "primitive accumulation," but the meaning is what is important: this refers to the first, or original, appropriation of land and the means of subsistence of subaltern groups, and the privatization of communal lands, with the result that inhabitants must find other ways – such as wage labour – to subsist. Michael Perelman, *The Invention of Capitalism* (Durham, NC: Duke University Press, 2000). For a discussion in the Canadian context, see Glen Sean Coulthard, *Red Skin White Masks: Rejecting the Colonial Politics of Recognition* (Minneapolis: University of Minnesota Press, 2014), 7–11.

60 Peter Usher, "Northern Development, Impact Assessment, and Social Change," in *Anthropology, Public Policy, and Native Peoples in Canada*, ed. Noel Dyck and James Waldram (Montreal and Kingston: McGill-Queen's University Press, 1993), 109.

61 Frank Tester and Peter Kulchyski, *Tammarniit (Mistakes): Inuit Relocation in the Eastern Arctic, 1939–63* (Vancouver: UBC Press, 1994), 6.

62 This was true of a film on Cape Dorset: LAC, RG 85, vol. 1956, file A-1003–19, pt. 1, G.L. Donovan, NFB to R.A.J. Phillips, Assistant Director, Northern Administration Branch, 19 March 1962, and following memos, including "Memo for the Director" by C.M. Bolger, Administrator of the Arctic, 31 May 1962.

63 LAC, RG 22, vol.142, MF 4.1.24, Film Project: The Eskimo Child.

64 LAC, RG 22, vol. 142, MF 4.1.24, Donald Fraser to Irene Baird, 8 November 1947.

65 Allice Legat, *Walking the Land, Feeding the Fire: Knowledge and Stewardship among the Tlicho Dene* (Tucson: University of Arizona Press, 2012), 113.

66 LAC, RG 22, vol. 144, MF 4.1.44, "Films for Eskimo" by Phil Shackleton, clipping from the *Vancouver Sun Magazine* and CBC News Roundup script, with attached letters of Irene Baird to Mr. Baxter, 23 March 1950, and Memo for R.A. Gibson, 25 May, 1950.

67 LAC, RG 22, vol. 161, file "Films," C.W. Jackson to Irwin, 11 May 1950.

68 Irene Baird, *The Climate of Power* (Toronto: Macmillan, 1971), 42.

69 LAC, RG 22, vol. 142, MF 4.1.24, 12 May 1949. All quotes from "Recent Developments in the Canadian North."

70 LAC, RG 22, vol. 142, MF 4.1.24, film proposal, Government Services in NWT.

71 Irene Baird, *Canada's North: A Land on the Move* (Ottawa: DIAND, 1972), 6.

72 Nelson Graburn, "The Present as History: Photography and the Inuit, 1959–94," in *Imaging the Arctic*, ed. J.C.H. King and Henrietta Lidchi (Seattle/Vancouver: University of Washington Press/UBC Press, 1998), 164.

73 NFB, *Canada's Awakening North* (dir. Ronald Dick, 1951).

74 LAC, RG 22, RG 144, MF 4-1-24, Geddes Webster, Mining Recorder to R.S. Dick, NFB, 3 April 1950.

75 LAC, RG 22, Vol. 143, MF 4.1.25, "Northern Film Project."

76 NFB, *Canada's Awakening North*.

77 LAC, RG 22, vol. 143, MF 4.1.25, "Northern Film Project."

78 NFB, *Canada's Awakening North*.

79 Paul Nadasdy, *Hunters and Bureaucrats: Power, Knowledge, and Aboriginal-State Relations in the Southwest Yukon* (Vancouver: UBC Press, 2004), 199.

80 Stephen Bocking, "Indigenous Knowledge and the History of Science, Race, and Colonial Authority in Northern Canada," in *Rethinking the Great White North: Race, Nature and the Historical Geographies of Whiteness in Canada*, ed. Andrew Baldwin, Laura Cameron, and Audrey Kobayashi (Vancouver: UBC Press, 2001), 44.

81 LAC RG 22, vol.161, R.S. Dick, NFB, to Arctic Division, 27 October 1950.

82 LAC, RG 22, vol. 143, MF 4.1.25, "Northern Film Project."

83 LAC, RG 22, vol. 142, MF 4.1.24, outline treatment for film on the Mackenzie District.

84 LAC, RG 22, vol. 143, Irene Baird to R.A. Gibson, 21 February 1950; C.W. Jackson to R.A. Gibson, 16 May 1950; Baxter to Mr. McClelland, NFB, 29 December 1950.

85 LAC, RG 22, vol. 141, MC 4-1-6, D.B Marsh to R.G. Robertson, Commissioner, NWT, 15 November 1955.

86 Peter Usher, "Caribou Crisis or Administrative Crisis? Wildlife and Aboriginal Policies on the Barren Grounds of Canada, 1947–60," in *Cultivating Arctic Landscapes: Knowing and Managing Animals in the Circumpolar North*, ed. David G. Anderson and Mark Nuttall, 172–99 (New York: Berghahn Books, 2004).

87 Salvage ethnography is often related to the term "salvage anthropology," utilized after the 1960s as a means of critiquing modern anthropologists of the late nineteenth and early twentieth centuries who collected artefacts, images, and stories of (largely Indigenous) peoples who were likely to suffer cultural extinction in the face of modernity.

88 Prins, "Paradox of Primtivism"; Jean-Pierre Olivier de Sardan, "The Ethnographic Pact and Documentary Film," *Visual Anthropology*, 12 (1999):13–25.

89 LAC, RG 22, vol. 142, MF 4.1.24, Ross McLean to R.A. Gibson, 18 May 1949.

90 LAC, RG 22, vol.142, MF 4.1.24, "Film Project: The Eskimo."

91 LAC, RG 22, Vol. 142, MF 4.1.24, Ross McLean to R.A. Gibson, 18 May 1949.

92 Berkhofer, quoted in Prins, "Paradox of Primitivism," 244.

93 Ironically, the "noble savage" concept has been redeployed more recently in some Indigenous-made films "for their own political ends," as a form of "cultural resistance." See Berkhofer, quoted in Prins, "Paradox of Primitivism," 244.

94 Jay Ruby, *Picturing Culture: Explorations of Film and Anthropology* (Chicago: University of Chicago Press, 2000), 168.

95 Griffiths, *Wondrous Difference*.

96 Michael Taussig, quoted in Renov, "Domesticating Ethnography," 141.

97 LAC, RG 22, vol. 141, MC 4-1-6, A.J. Baxter, NA, to Mr. L.W. Chatwin, NFB, 9 November 1955.

98 Rony, quoted in Keith Beattie, *Documentary Screens: Non-Fiction and Fiction Film and Television* (London: Palgrave Macmillan, 2004), 49.

99 Michel Foucault, *The History of Sexuality*, vol. 1 (New York: Pantheon Books, 1984), pt 4, chap. 3.

100 NFB, *Angotee: Story of an Eskimo Boy* (dir. Doug Wilkinson,), 1953.

101 NFB, *Land of the Long Day* file, Toronto Film Society Members Evaluation Form.

102 NFB, *Land of the Long Day* (dir. Wilkinson), 1952.

103 Doug Wilkinson, *Land of the Long Day* (New York: Henry Holt and Company, 1955).

104 NFB, *Land of the Long Day*.

105 Frank Tester, "Iglu to Iglurjuag," in *Critical Inuit Studies: An Anthology of Contemporary Arctic Ethnography*, ed. Pamela Stern and Lisa Stevenson (Lincoln: University of Nebraska Press, 2006), 236.

106 Elizabeth Cowie, *Recording Reality, Desiring the Real* (Minneapolis: University of Minnesota Press, 2011).

107 Whether she was a favourite of Grierson, or simply a self-promoter, her appointment as a filmmaker remains a historical "mystery" since she was neither a film expert nor an anthropological expert. See Robert McMillan, "Ethnography and the NFB: The Laura Boulton Mysteries," *Canadian Journal of Film Studies* 1, 2 (1991): 67–78.

108 NFB, *Eskimo Summer* (dir. Laura Boulton), 1944.

109 NFB, *How to Make an Igloo* (dir. Douglas Wilkinson, 1949).

110 Because this series has been discussed by other scholars, I limit my remarks here.

111 Griffiths, *Wondrous Difference*, 314.

112 Rony, *Third Eye*, 195.

113 Asen Balikci, "The Netsilik Film Series," *Visual Anthropology* 22 (2009): 388.

114 NFB, *People of the Rock* file, working title *Modern Eskimo*.

115 NFB, *People of the Rock* file, *NFB Film Study Guide:* People of the Rock.

116 NFB, *People of the Rock* (dir. Clarke Da Prato), 1961.

117 Tara Cater and Arn Keeling. "'That's Where Our Future Came From': Mining, Landscape, and Memory in Rankin Inlet, Nunavut," *Études/Inuit/Studies* 37, 2, (2013): 65.

118 The total cast budget for *People of the Rock* seems to be three hundred dollars. One note mentions paying the lead Inuit man twenty dollars per day.

119 NFB, *People of the Rock* file, excerpt from Farley Mowat, "Eskimo at Rankin Inlet," typescript, n.d.

120 NFB, *People of the Rock*.

121 Cater and Keeling, "That's Where," 65; Tester and Kulchyski, *Tammarniit*, 349.

122 NFB, Perspectives North of 60 file.

123 Gerald Sider, *Skin for Skin: Death and Life for Inuit and Innu* (Durham, NC: Duke University Press, 2014), 165.

124 Morrison and Coates, *Working the North*, 116.

125 NFB, *Our Northern Citizen* (dir. John Howe), 1956.

126 LAC, RG 22, vol. 161, file 5-0-1-42, NFB release, "Reindeer Round up on an Arctic Island." Ironically, the history of Aboriginal peoples in rodeo was assumed not to exist. For a discussion of this history, see Mary-Ellen Kelm, *The Wilder West: Rodeo in Western Canada* (Vancouver: UBC Press, 2011).

127 LAC, RG 22, vol. 161, file 5-0-1-42, Allan Stark to R.A. Gibson, 3 October 1950.

128 LAC, RG 85, Department of Indian Affairs and Northern Development, vol. 2054, file NR 5/2-3, RAJP to Deputy Minister, 11 April 1956.

129 NFB, the Annanacks file, "The Annanacks," press release.

130 In *The Netsilik Today* (1971), for instance, filmmakers follow Zachary Itiminak, his wife, and his child through a typical day after they had moved from a hunting camp into the Pelly Bay settlement. A cinema verité ambiance presents life in the pace it is lived, dialogue is in Inuktitut, and one version has no expert voiceover.

131 NFB, *Labrador North* (dir. Roger Hart), 1973.

132 NFB, *Labrador North* file, "Comments from Roger Hart on *Labrador North*." The interviewer is unknown, but his/her writing on the margins of the printed interview indicate his/her scepticism about whether any film is devoid of politics or point of view.

133 NFB, *Labrador North* file, letter of Wally Wason, Saint John, NB, to Roger Hart, Challenge for Change, Montreal, 29 January 1974.

134 Thomas Waugh, Michael Brendan Baker, and Ezra Winton, eds., *Challenge for Change: Activist Documentary at the National Film Board of Canada* (Montreal and Kingston: McGill-Queen's University Press, 2010).

135 LAC, RG 22, vol. 684, file F-1270–6, Baird to NFB, 28 March 1967. Others working in the NA area were more sympathetic. See LAC, RG 85, vol. 2054, file FR 5/2–3, "Notes on Challenge for Change" by H. Shuurman, Research Northern Science Research Group.

136 Pineault, "Shifting the Balance," 165.

137 Sider, *Skin for Skin*, 145.

138 Shari Huhndorf, "*Atanarjuat*, the Fast Runner: Culture, History and Politics in Inuit Media," *American Anthropologist* 105, 4 (2003): 823.

139 Kay Anderson, "Extremity: Theorizing from the Margins," in *Rethinking The Great White North*, 261.

140 Berkhofer, quoted in Prins, "Paradox of Primitivism," 244.

141 Ibid., 249.

CHAPTER 5 | IRENE BAIRD'S NORTHERN JOURNEYS

1 Irene Baird, "Blow Spirit," *North/Nord* 13, 1 (1966): 18–19. My thanks to Baird's granddaughter, Nora Spence, who gave me a copy of the radio interview.

2 Most critical scholarship has been on *Waste Heritage*. Irene Baird's writing has been studied as an exemplar of modern-realist Canadian fiction or assimilated into the collective oeuvre of the Popular Front literary left in Canada. Colin Hill, "The Modern Realist Movement in English-Canadian Fiction, 1919-1950" (PhD diss., McGill University, 2003), 229; Roger Hyman, "Wasted Heritage for *Waste Heritage*: The Critical Disregard for an Important Novel," *Journal of Canadian Studies*, 17, 4 (1982–83): 74–87; Robin Mathews, "Canada's Hidden Working Class Literature," *Canadian Dimension* 31, 6 (1997): 37-39; James Doyle, *Progressive Heritage: The Evolution of a Politically Radical Literary Tradition in Canada* (Waterloo: Wilfrid Laurier Press, 2002); Carmen Irr, *The Suburbs of Dissent: Cultural Politics in the US and Canada During the 1930s* (Durham, NC: Duke University Press, 1998).

3 For an overview of Baird's life, see Joan Sangster, "Creating a Writers Archive: Irene Baird's Work and Writing, 1940-1970," *Journal of Historical Biography* 10 (Fall 2012): 34–69; and Colin Hill, "Introduction," *Waste Heritage* (Ottawa: Ottawa University Press, 2007), ix-li. For discussions of Baird's progressive politics and writing, see Douglas Parker, "Women in Communist Culture in Canada, 1932-1937" (MA thesis, McGill University, 1994); Malek Khouri, *Filming Politics: Communism and the Portrayal of the Working Class at the National Film Board of Canada, 1939-1946* (Calgary: University of Calgary Press, 2007), 80, 94; Candida

Rifkind, *Comrades and Critics: Women, Literature and the Left in 1930s Canada* (Toronto: University of Toronto Press, 2009). Baird's political ambivalence is best discussed in Rifkind and in Jody Mason, "'Siddown Brother, Siddown': The Problems of Commitment and the Publishing History of Irene Baird's *Waste Heritage*," *Papers of the Bibliographic Society of Canada* 45, 2 (2007): 143–62.

4 Rifkind, *Comrades and Critics*, 164. It is also important to note Baird's own work as a journalist for Vancouver newspapers. See Sangster, "Creating a Writers Archive."

5 Lionel Gossman, *Between History and Literature* (Cambridge: Harvard University Press, 1990), 228; Morroe Berger, *Real and Imagined Worlds: The Novel and Social Science* (Cambridge: Harvard University Press, 1977), 215.

6 Raymond Williams, "Thomas Hardy and the English Novel," in *The Raymond Williams Reader*, ed. John Higgins, 119-40 (Oxford: Blackwell, 2001); Raymond Williams, quoted in John Higgins, *Raymond Williams, Literature, Marxism and Cultural Materialism* (London: Routledge, 1999), 11; Richard Cobb, *Promenades: A Historian's Appreciation of Modern French Literature* (Oxford: Oxford University Press, 1986), 2. See also Jerome Blum, "Fiction and the European Peasantry: The Realist Novel as a Historical Source," *Proceedings of the American Philosophical Society* 126, 2 (1982): 122–39.

7 Berger, *Real and Imagined Worlds*, 177.

8 As Gossman points out, even R.G. Collingwood accepted the role of imagination in historical writing, but he also believed that the historical imagination was "bound to work from evidence." Gossman, *Between History and Literature*, 248.

9 Peter Laslett, "The Wrong Way through the Telescope: A Note on Literary Evidence in Sociology and in Historical Sociology," *British Journal of Sociology* 27, 3 (1976): 319–42.

10 Hayden White, "The Historical Text as Literary Artifact," in *The Writing of History: Literary Form and Historical Understanding*, ed. Robert Canary and Henry Kozicki (Madison: University of Wisconsin Press, 1978), 42.

11 On the problems with such incommensurability, see Gossman, *Between History and Literature*, 293–307. For a critique of such postmodernist conflations of fiction and history, see Richard Price, "Postmodernism and History," in *Language and Labour*, ed. Neville Kirk and John Belchem, 11-43 (Aldershot, UK: Ashgate Press, 1997).

12 James Smith Allen, "History and the Novel: Mentalité in Modern Popular Fiction," *History and Theory* 22, 3 (1983): 249, 238.

13 Berger, *Real and Imagined*, 189.

14 McMaster University (MU), Macmillan Fonds (MF), box 65, "Climate of Power" file, clipping, "Recipe for Writing a Successful Novel," *Toronto Star Weekly*, 24 April 1971. All subsequent citations from this box and file unless noted otherwise.

15 Baird was in the Department of Indian Affairs and Northern Development when
she retired, but she was originally hired into the Department of Mines and Resources (1936–49), which became the Department of Resources and Development
(1949–53), the Department of Northern Affairs and National Resources (1953–66),
and the Department of Indian Affairs and Northern Development (1966).

16 St. Georges Anglican School, Yearbook, 1933: "It is with great regret that we say
good-bye to Mrs. Baird this term as a full time teacher, who finds looking after her
form as well as her family too great a strain. She is, however, reluctant to sever her
connection with St. George's altogether and is coming to look after her form on
three afternoons a week." E-mail from Elizabeth Knox to Joan Sangster, 19 November 2010. My thanks to St. George's School for locating this material for me.

17 Library and Archives Canada (LAC), Hugh Keenleyside Fonds, MG 31, E 102
(Keenleyside), vol. 7, Baird file, Pearson to Ross McLean, 6 March 1947, McLean
to Pearson, 20 March 1947, McLean to Baird, 20 March 1947.

18 LAC, Keenleyside, vol. 7, Baird file, Baird to Keenleyside, 25 March 1947.

19 LAC, William Lyon Mackenzie King correspondence, MG 26- J1, reel C11048,
J.J. McCann to King, 30 July 1947.

20 LAC, Keenleyside, Baird file, Baird to Keenleyside, 25 March 1947.

21 Judy Fudge, "From Segregation to Privatization: Equality, the Law and Women
Public Servants, 1908-2001," in *Privatization, Law and the Challenge to Feminism*, ed.
Brenda Cossman and Judy Fudge (Toronto: University of Toronto Press, 2002), 87.

22 Ibid., 91. See also Kathleen Archibald, *Sex and the Public Service* (Ottawa:
Queen's Printer, 1970).

23 LAC, King correspondence, McCann to King, 30 July 1947.

24 LAC, Keenleyside, Baird file, Keenleyside to King, 5 May 1948, with letter from
S.T. Wood to Keenleyside, 4 May 1948.

25 LAC, Keenleyside, Baird file, Baird to Keenleyside, n.d.

26 LAC, Keenleyside, Baird file, Keenleyside to Baird. These letters were marked
"personal" but had no dates, making it hard to confirm who wrote them and
when. But the second said, "In response to your letter of Sunday," presumably
referring to Baird's original letter written a few days before.

27 "Civil Servant Retires after 25 Years Service," *Globe and Mail*, 10 July 1967.

28 "Senior Federal Post Tops Varied Career," *Globe and Mail*, 18 December 1962.

29 "Women in Canada's Public Service," *Globe and Mail*, 26 May 1966.

30 LAC, Keenleyside, file B, personal correspondence, Baird to Keenleyside, 19
November 1964.

31 Irene Baird, "You Only Take the First Trip Once," *North/Nord* 13, 6 (1966): 26.

32 Baird, "You Only Take," 27. In 1962, Baird accompanied Lady Eaton on a trip to
the Arctic. It is likely this is the "VIP" trip to which she is referring: "Lady Eaton
Describes Her Trip to the Arctic," *Toronto Star*, 19 March 1963.

33 Baird, "Diary of a Working Journey," *North/Nord* 12, 1 (1965): 22.

34 Frank Tester, "Iglu to Iglurjuag," in *Critical Inuit Studies: An Anthology of Contemporary Arctic Ethnography*, ed. Pamela Stern and Lisa Stevenson, 424-44 (Lincoln: University of Nebraska Press, 2006).

35 Baird, "Diary," 16.

36 Baird, "Les Africains Visit the Eskimos," *North/Nord* 8, 4 (1961): 20–24. Pictures credits are uncertain, but it seems Baird may have taken them.

37 Baird, "Dairy," 20.

38 Ibid, 28.

39 Irene Baird, "Blow Spirit," *North/Nord* 13, 1 (1966): 18–19.

40 Baird, "You Only Take," 29.

41 Baird, "Diary," 22

42 Baird, "You Only Take," 29.

43 John McCannon, *A History of the Arctic: Nature, Exploration and Exploitation* (London: Reaktion Books, 2012), 7.

44 Baird, "Diary," 17, 19.

45 Baird, "You Only Take," 29.

46 Ibid.

47 Baird, "Diary," 18.

48 Ibid.

49 Baird, "Dairy," 18–19.

50 Baird, "Cape Dorset Man," *Canadian Geographical Journal* 71, 5 (1965): 173. This article likely refers to the tour Baird's family noted. The artist Kanangenak is brought south by Northern Affairs for a show in Stratford and an opening at the Canadian Handicraft Guild. It also likely inspired the poem "i don't read you charlie."

51 Ibid., 175.

52 Irene Baird, "The Eskimo Woman: Her Changing World," *The Beaver* (Spring 1959): 50.

53 Ibid., 52.

54 Ibid., 54.

55 There are some exceptions to this but they are not generally the rule. For an exception, see her comment in "Diary" that the Inuit cannot go back to the Stone Age. This piece uses the language of "primitivism."

56 Baird, "Eskimo Church on Christmas Morning," *North/Nord* 17, 6 (1970): 14–15.

57 Baird, "The Lonely Shore," *North/Nord* 10, 3 (1963): 34.

58 Ibid., 35.

59 Baird, "Land," *North/Nord* 11, 6 (1964): 16–17.

60 Ibid.

61 Baird, "Arctic Mobile," *North/Nord* 9, 6 (1962): 45.
62 *Ce qu'il faut pour vivre/The Necessities of Life*, dir. Benoît Pilon (2008).
63 Baird, "Who Will Be I," *North/Nord* 13, 5 (1966): 16.
64 Ibid.
65 Ibid., 17
66 Baird, "I don't read you charlie: a twisted tale," *North/Nord* 19, 2 (1972): 10–11.
67 Baird, "Keep Your Own Things," *North/Nord* 11, 2 (1964): 11.
68 Ibid.
69 Baird, "Diary," 16.
70 Baird, "Keep Your Own Things," *North/Nord* 11, 2 (1964): 10–11.
71 Baird, "A Delicate Balance," *North/Nord* 20, 3 (1973): 13–15.
72 Baird, "A Learning Situation," *North/Nord* 14, 6 (1967): 11.
73 Baird, "Mary No More," *North/Nord* 18, 6 (1971): 17.
74 Jack Granatstein, *The Ottawa Men: The Civil Service Mandarins* (Toronto: Oxford University Press, 1982), chap. 1
75 MU, MF, Donald Sutherland, manager, Trade Department, Macmillan Canada, to James Wright, Macmillan Britain, 7 April 1970. The disclaimer is on the copyright page.
76 LAC, Keenleyside, Baird file, Baird to Keenleyside, 10 December (likely 1955). Baird likely knew of Keenleyside's disillusion with the new minister, Robert Winters, whose conservative outlook had made it difficult for Keenleyside to implement a reform agenda. See Keenleyside, *Memoires*, 2:357. Keenleyside's references to his differences with Winters are understated, but they are covered in Shelagh Grant, *Sovereignty or Security? Government Policy in the Canadian North, 1936-1950* (Vancouver: UBC Press, 1988), 234–35. Janice Cavell and Jeff Noakes, *Acts of Occupation: Canada and Arctic Sovereignty, 1918–25* (Vancouver: UBC Press, 2010), also argue that Keenleyside suggested that public attention be shifted "from military and strategic aspects of northern development to work being done by scientists, explorers, administrators, missionaries, doctors, social workers" (255).
77 LAC, Keenleyside, Baird to Keenleyside, December 10 (likely 1955).
78 Christina Newman, "The Establishment that Govern Us," *Saturday Night*, May 1968, 24.
79 Irene Baird, *The Climate of Power* (Toronto: Macmillan, 1971), 25.
80 Ibid, 71.
81 MU, MF, Derrick report on Dinosaur, 6, ix, 1969.
82 Baird, *Climate*, 60.
83 MU, MF, Jarrett assessment, 6, ix, 69
84 MU, MF, Ramsay Derry to Sutherland or other editors, 16 April 1970.
85 MU, MF, Sutherland to Derry, 5, x, 1970; Sutherland to James Wright, 22 June 1970.

86 MU, MF, box 71, *Climate* file, promotion brochure.

87 Bryan Palmer, *Canada's 1960s: The Ironies of Identity in a Rebellious Era* (Toronto: University of Toronto Press, 2009).

88 Julie Berebitsky, *Sex in the Office: A History of Gender, Power and Desire* (New Haven: Yale University Press, 2012), chap. 4.

89 John Muggeridge, "Corridors of Power, "*Saturday Night*, May 1971: 29–30.

90 Dorothy Body, "North from Ottawa," *Books in Canada* 1, 1 (1971): 23.

91 Christopher Dummitt, *The Manly Modern in Postwar Canada* (Vancouver: UBC Press, 2007), 152.

92 Baird, *Climate*, 23.

93 Ibid., 96.

94 Ibid., 53.

95 Ibid.

96 Ibid., 39.

97 Ibid., 42.

98 Ibid., 223.

99 Ibid., 168.

100 Ibid., 238.

101 Ibid., 169.

102 Ibid., 138.

103 Ibid., 187.

104 Ibid., 155.

105 Ibid., 60.

106 Ibid., 62.

107 Ibid., 60.

108 Ibid., 231 (emphasis in original).

109 Ibid.

110 Ibid., 232.

111 Frank Tester and Peter Kulchyski, *Tammarniit (Mistakes): Inuit Relocation in the Eastern Arctic, 1939–63* (Vancouver: UBC Press, 1994).

112 "Senior Federal Post Tops Career," *Globe and Mail*, 18 December 1962; "Civil Servant Retires after 25 Years Service," *Globe and Mail*, 10 July 1966; "Women in Canada's Public Service," *Globe and Mail*, 26 May 1966.

113 These views on integration were similar to those of her mentor, Keenleyside. Both Keenleyside and Baird saw integration (which was not entirely different from assimilation) as inevitable, but they were also concerned with preserving some forms of Indigenous culture. As Shelagh Grant points out, there was paternalism involved, though their views were "progressive" in comparison to some others of the time who stressed only the value of modernizing primitive peoples. See Grant, *Sovereignty or Security*, 198.

114 John Lutz, *Makúk: A New History of Aboriginal-White Relations* (Vancouver: UBC Press, 2008), 43, 23.

115 Gerald Sider, *Skin for Skin: Death and Life for Inuit and Innu* (Durham, NC: Duke University Press, 2013), 6.

116 Baird, *Climate*, 239.

CHAPTER 6 | "MRS. BIRD FLIES NORTH"

1 Sarah Carter, *The Importance of Being Monogamous: Marriage and Nation Building in Western Canada to 1915* (Edmonton: Athabasca University Press, 2008), 91–92, 272–73.

2 The RCSW's homogenized use of the word "Indian" makes it difficult to identify the First Nations to which it is referring as well as to which witnesses it is referring. In some instances, such as its visit to Ford Rae, I can be more specific; in other cases, I must rely on its homogenized categorization. Given the areas the RCSW is usually talking about, the word "Indian" likely often meant "Dene."

3 Some examples include Toni Williams, "Re-Forming 'Women's' Truth: A Critique of the Report of the Royal Commission on the Status of Women," *Ottawa Law Review* 22/3 (1990): 725–59; Patricia Monture-Okanee, "The Violence We Women Do: A First Nations View," in *Challenging Times: The Women's Movement in Canada and the United States*, ed. Constance Backhouse and David Flaherty, 193–204 (Montreal and Kingston: McGill-Queen's University Press, 1992).

4 "Mrs. Bird Flies North Next Week," *News of the North*, 1 August 1968.

5 Mark Dickerson, *Whose North? Political Change, Political Development, and Self-Government in the Northwest Territories* (Vancouver: UBC Press, 1992), 84.

6 Library and Archives Canada (LAC), Royal Commission on the Status of Women Fonds, RG 33–89 (hereafter RCSW), vol. 35, NWT Hearings file, telegram of Gordon and response, n.d.

7 LAC, Elsie Gregory MacGill Fonds, MG 31, K 7 (MacGill), vol. 4, minutes, 13-15 March 1968.

8 LAC, MacGill, vol. 3, minutes, 15–16 February 1968.

9 LAC, MacGill, vol. 4, minutes, 26–27 September 1968; 13–14 December 1968; 30–31 October 1968.

10 LAC, MacGill, vol. 4, proposed amendments to first proposals for report from MacGill, 27 August 1968.

11 With a 1 August deadline, the separate chapter was only abandoned in July. LAC, MacGill, vol. 5, minutes, 15–17 July 1970.

12 Ibid., vol. 5, minutes, 7 August 1970.

13 LAC, RCSW, vol. 35, NWT Hearings, Begin memo to commissioners, 29 May 1968.

14 Ibid., Bird memo for Begin re: visit to the Yukon and NWT, 17 May 1968.

15 LAC, RCSW, vol. 35, Bird to Commissioners, 24 June 1968.

16 LAC, MacGill, vol. 3, minutes, 24–26 September 1969.

17 Morrow made a number of sympathetic decisions about Indigenous rights, first the *Drybones* case, which used the Bill of Rights to overturn discriminatory regulations about Aboriginal drinking, and later a decision on Dene land rights (*Re Paulette et al.* and *Registrar of Titles 1974*), though the latter was overturned at a higher court level. Morrow also insisted on the need for a legal aid program in the North. On Morrow, see Dorothy Harley Eber, *Images of Justice* (Montreal and Kingston: McGill-Queen's University Press, 1997), 156–57; William G. Morrow, *Northern Justice: The Memoirs of Justice William G. Morrow* (Toronto: University of Toronto Press, 1995); John David Hamilton, *Arctic Revolution: Social Change in the Northwest Territories, 1935-1994* (Hamilton: Dundurn, 1994), 124; and Dickerson, *Whose North*, 101.

18 Barbara Freeman, *The Satellite Sex: The Media and Women's Issues in English Canada, 1966-71* (Waterloo: Wilfrid Laurier Press, 2001), 205–6.

19 LAC, RCSW, vol. 35, NWT Hearings, Bird to Morrow, 17 October 1967.

20 Florence Bird, *Anne Francis: An Autobiography* (Toronto: Clarke, Irwin and Co, 1974), 279.

21 LAC, RCSW, vol. 17, brief 394.

22 LAC, RCSW, vol.35, NWT Hearings, memo from Angela Burke to Mrs. Bird, 2 July 1968.

23 LAC, RCSW, vol. 10, Yellowknife testimony, Bird, McAteer, Begin (hereafter Yellowknife and name of person testifying).

24 LAC, RCSW, Yellowknife, Mrs. Mandible.

25 LAC, RCSW, vol. 10, Whitehorse testimony (hereafter Whitehorse and name of person testifying), Mrs. Findlay.

26 Ibid.

27 LAC, Whitehorse, Mr. O'Donoghue.

28 Bird, *Anne Francis*, 278.

29 LAC, Yellowknife, Mrs. Mandible.

30 Ibid.

31 Lynn Brooks, "Guided by Our Bellies," in *Gossip: A Spoken History of Women in the North*, ed. Mary Crnkovich, 37–42 (Ottawa: Canadian Arctic Resources Committee, 1990). "I think this changed very slowly, but increasingly so in the 1970s as native women self-organized into their own associations" (Brooks, "Guided," 39).

32 LAC, RCSW, vol. 8, NWT letters file.

33 LAC, RCSW, vol. 35, Report of Commissioner Lola Lange on Northwest Territories trip.

34 LAC, RCSW, Yellowknife, Mrs. Parker.

35 CBC Matinee, 9 September 1968.

36 LAC, RCSW, vol. 12, brief 122.

37 LAC, RCSW, vol. 12, brief 111.

38 CBC *Matinee*. Bird got a laugh from the room by interjecting, "only 'rather' good looking?"

39 LAC, Whitehorse, O'Donaghue.

40 LAC, vol. 18, brief 411.

41 LAC, Whitehorse, Findlay.

42 LAC, RCSW, vol. 35, Lange Report.

43 LAC, RCSW, Whitehorse, Hellaby.

44 Daniel Patrick Moynihan, *The Negro Family: The Case for National Action* (Washington, DC: Department of Labor, 1965).

45 LAC, RCSW, Yellowknife, Bird.

46 CBC *Matinee*.

47 LAC, vol. 35, Lang Report on NWT trip, Lang quoting Kay Vaykik.

48 LAC, RCSW, Whitehorse, Findlay.

49 LAC, RCSW, Yellowknife, Wilbe.

50 LAC, RCSW, vol. 17, brief 352.

51 LAC, RCSW, Yellowknife, Marilyn Assheton-Smith.

52 Ibid.

53 Bird, *Anne Francis*, 279.

54 LAC, Yellowknife, Assheton-Smith; Lange.

55 LAC, Whitehorse, Hellaby.

56 Ibid.

57 LAC, Whitehorse, McKinnon.

58 Leishman did not have time to clear his brief with the executive of the IEA, so he presented it as a private brief, but he noted that he was "confident" the IEA would go along with the majority of his comments. LAC, RCSW, vol. 35, NWT file, n.d.

59 LAC, Yellowknife, Leishman. His comments on taking away children from Native families for reasons of education seem contradictory. He is generally very critical of this, but later says briefly they should be sent to schools, though these schools needed Native counsellors.

60 CBC *Matinee*.

61 LAC, Yellowknife, LaHache.

62 LAC, Yellowknife, Lange.

63 LAC, Yellowknife, LaHache.

64 LAC, RCSW, brief 419 and Yellowknife, Thrasher testimony.

65 LAC, vol. 35, Lange report on trip to NWT.

66 Ibid.

67 Father Duchaussois quoted in Lange Report.
68 Abe Okpik, "Bewildered Hunters in the Twentieth Century," in *Canada's Changing North*, ed. William Wonders, 191–99 (Montreal and Kingston: McGill University Press, 2003 [1966]).
69 Brian Thorn, "Visions of the New World Order: Women and Gender in Radical and Reactionary Movements in Post-World War II Western Canada" (PhD diss., Trent University, 2006), chap. 2.
70 LAC, RCSW, vol. 35, Lange Report.
71 Ibid.
72 Father Massart, quoted in Ibid.
73 Ibid.
74 Bird, *Anne Francis*, 281.
75 Ibid., 283.
76 Ibid., 284.
77 Linda Ambrose, "Our Last Frontier: Imperialism and Northern Canadian Rural Women's Organization," *Canadian Historical Review* 86, 2 (2005): 263, 269.
78 Anne McElory, "Canadian Arctic Modernization and Change in Female Inuit Role Identification," *American Ethnologist* 2, 4 (1975): 662–86; and Anne McElory, "Ooleepeeka and Mina: Contrasting Responses to Modernization of Two Baffin Island Women," in *Being and Becoming Indian: Biographical Studies of North American Frontiers*, ed. James Clifton, 290–318 (Prospect Heights, IL: Waveland Press, 1993).
79 For example, a three-generational study conducted for the Royal Commission on Aboriginal Peoples traces different life experiences, styles of storytelling, and understandings of identity, relayed by a grandmother, mother, and daughter. See Nancy Wachowich in collaboration with Apphia Agalakti Awa, Rhoda Kaukjak Katsak, and Sandra Pikujak Katsak, *Saqiyuq: Stories from the Lives of Three Inuit Women* (Montreal and Kingston: McGill-Queen's University Press, 1999).
80 Tina Moore, "Political Participation of Inuit Women in the Government of Nunavut," *Wicazo Sa Review* (Spring 2002): 65.
81 Ibid., 87.
82 Ibid., 85. On the debate about political gender parity, see Laakuluk Jessen Williamson, "Inuit Gender Party and Why It Was Not Accepted in the Nunavut Legislature," *Études Inuit Studies* 30, 1 (2006): 51–68.
83 For example, one study contributed to Julie Cruikshank's master's thesis, "The Role of Northern Canadian Indian Women in Social Change" (MA thesis, University of British Columbia, 1969). Some parts of her joint study with Jim Lotz also inform his later book, *Northern Realities: The Future of Northern Development in Canada* (Toronto: New Press, 1972).

84 LAC, RCSW, vol. 35, NWT Hearings, Mark McClung to Executive Secretary, memo on Research Program on Indigenous Populations, 6 October 1967.
85 LAC, vol. 8, Renée Dandurand, "The Status of Women in the Primitive Societies of Pre-Colonial Canada," 3.
86 Ibid., vol. 8,18.
87 LAC, RCSW, vol. 28, Nan Shipley, "Report on the Status of the Indian and Métis Women of Manitoba," 1, 2, 21.
88 LAC, RCSW, vol. 25, Jean Bruce, "A Study of Eskimo Women in the Keewatin Region of the Northwest Territories," 1.
89 Jean Bruce, "Study of Eskimo Women," 16. The official from NA noted that there were only sixty-five jobs available for "Eskimo women," and he foresaw a shortage of jobs for "trained Eskimo girls" in the future.
90 Ibid., 27.
91 LAC, RCSW, Bruce, "Study of Eskimo Women," 16.
92 LAC, MacGill, vol. 3, minutes, 15–16 February 1968. The contract for Lotz was to explore "the changing role of Indian women and the problems they are facing." Lotz had come highly recommended by NA.
93 E-mail correspondence from Julie Cruikshank to Joan Sangster, 09/12/2013.
94 LAC, RCSW, vol. 28, Julie Cruikshank and Jim Lotz, "Changing Role of Canadian Indian Women," 42.
95 Ibid., 76.
96 Ibid., 13.
97 As Cruikshank later reflected in "The Politics of Ethnography in the Canadian North," in *Anthropology, Public Policy and Native Peoples in Canada*, ed. Noel Dyck and James Waldram (Montreal and Kingston: McGill-Queen's University Press, 1993). 136. See also Peter Usher, "Northern Development, Impact Assessment and Change," in the same volume, 109.
98 This clearly acted as a corrective to traditional observers who saw men as hunter-providers and women's contributions as "minor." See, for example, Asen Balikci, *Vunta Kutchin Social Change: A Study of the People of Old Crow, Yukon Territory* (Ottawa: Northern Co-ordination and Research Centre, Department of Northern Affairs and National Resources, 1963), 33.
99 E-mail correspondence, Cruikshank to Sangster, 09/12/2013
101 Bryan Palmer, *Canada's 1960s: The Ironies of Identity in a Rebellious Age* (Toronto: University of Toronto Press, 2009), chap. 10.
101 LAC, RCSW, Cruikshank and Lotz, "Changing Role," 16.
102 Ibid., 51
103 Ibid., 101.
104 Ibid., 79.

105 Ibid., 40.

106 Ibid., 85.

107 Note that this same charge was repeated in Lotz's *Northern Realities*, 221–23.

108 LAC, Cruikshank and Lotz, "Changing Role," 110.

109 "Homes under Petticoat Rule," *Winnipeg Free Press*, 4 September 1968; "Eskimo Women Boss in the Home," *Telegraph Journal*, 21 August 1968.

110 Letter to the editor, *Whitehorse Star*, 26 September 1968

111 "Status of Keewatin Women," *News of the North*, 29 August 1968.

112 Letter to the editor, *News of the North*, 15 August 1968.

113 "Northern Native Women Want Housing Equality," *Corner Brook Western Star*, 24 August 1968; "Indian Girl Uneducated, Has Problems," *Pembroke Observer*, 25 August 1968.

114 "Northern Women Speak Up," *Western Producer*, 29 August 1968.

115 Frank Tester and Peter Kulchyski, *Tammarniit (Mistakes): Inuit Relocation in the Eastern Arctic, 1939–63* (Vancouver: UBC Press, 1994); Janet Mancini Billson, "Opportunity or Tragedy: The Impact of Canadian Resettlement Policy on Inuit Families," *American Review of Canadian Studies* 20, 1 (1990): 187–218.

116 Jonathan Bordo, "Jack Pine: Wilderness Sublime or the Erasure of the Aboriginal Presence from the Landscape," *Journal of Canadian Studies* 27, 4 (1992): 98–128.

117 CBC, *Take Thirty*, 17 September 1968. Nor did she think civil servants should be pressed to speak on camera.

118 Gayatri Chakravorty Spivak, "Can the Subaltern Speak?" in *Marxism and Interpretations of Culture*, ed. C. Nelson and L. Grossberg, 271–313 (Bassingstoke: Macmillan Educational, 1988).

119 LAC, MacGill, vol. 5 minutes, 29 April–1 May 1970.

120 Ibid., 26 June 1970.

121 Ibid., 27–29 May 1970.

122 The filtering role that such knowledge claims had on the commission was found in other areas, such as labour. Joan Sangster, *Transforming Labour: Women and Work in Postwar Canada* (Toronto: University of Toronto Press, 2010), chap.7.

123 Adele Perry, "Women, Racialized People and the Making of the Liberal Order in Northern North America," in *Liberalism and Hegemony: Debating the Canadian Liberal Revolution*, ed. Jean-Francois Constant and Michel Ducharme, 274–97 (Toronto: University of Toronto Press, 2009). See also Robin Jarvis Brownlie, "A Persistent Antagonism: First Nations and the Liberal Order," same volume, 298–321. Both these articles suggest to me that race and gender exclusions are a significant problem, with an overarching "liberal order framework," for all of Canadian history.

124 Patricia Monture-Angus, *Thunder in My Soul: A Mohawk Woman Speaks* (Halifax: Fernwood, 1995).

125 LAC, Yellowknife, Mrs. Mandible.

126 LAC, RCSW, vol. 20, Documentation and Research: Women in the NWT and Yukon File, Irene Baird, "The Eskimo in Canada," 4. This was, of course, a pamphlet originally written for public, not private, circulation, and she quoted one of her superiors approvingly on the ideal of a "raceless" North.

127 Judy Tzu-Chun Wu, *Radicals on the Road: Internationalism, Orientalism, and Feminism during the Vietnam Era* (Ithaca: Cornell University Press, 2013), 4. Wu argues that radical orientalism was used not only by Western activists to question colonialism but also by the colonized as a means of gathering support for their struggles.

128 Brooks, "Guided by Our Bellies," 39.

CONCLUSION

1 Robin McGrath, "The European in Inuit Literature," in *The Canadian North: Essays in Culture and Literature*, ed., Jorn Carlsen and Bengt Streijffert (Lund: Nordic Association for Canadian Studies, 1989), 117.

2 Renée Hulan, citing Thomas Berger, *Northern Experience and the Myth of Canadian Culture* (Montreal and Kingston: McGill-Queen's University Press, 2002), 96.

3 David Anderson, "Reindeer, Caribou and 'Fairy Stories' of State Power," in *Cultivating Arctic Landscapes: Knowing and Managing Animals in the Circumpolar North*, ed. David G. Anderson and Mark Nuttall (New York: Berghahn Books, 2004), 2.

4 Linda Alcoff, "The Problem of Speaking for Others," *Cultural Critique* 20 (Winter 1991-92): 3-22.

5 Following from Gerald Sider's description of his approach in *Skin for Skin: Death and Life for Inuit and Innu* (Durham, NC: Duke University Press, 2013).

6 In 1969, the Indian Brotherhood of the NWT was founded, followed by COPE (Committee for Original Peoples Entitlement) in 1970, Inuit Tapirisat of Canada in 1971, and the Métis Association of the NWT in 1971.

7 Mary Crnkovich, ed., *Gossip: A Spoken History of Women in the North* (Ottawa: Canadian Arctic Resources Committee, 1990).

8 Some Inuit photographers, like Peter Pitseoluk, also became relatively well known by the 1970s as their work was collected, shown, and reproduced with the aid of non-Indigenous scholars. See Peter Pitseolak with Dorothy Eber, *People from Our Side* (Edmonton: Hurtig, 1976).

9 "Choice Work by Eskimo on View Here," *Montreal Star*, 14 November 1953, quoted in "Historical Notes," *Inuit Art Quarterly* 2, 1 (1987): 15.

10 Nelson Graburn, "Inuit Art and Canadian Nationalism," *Inuit Art Quarterly* 1, 3 (1986): 5-6; and Joan Vastokas, "A Reply to Nelson Graburn," *Inuit Art Quarterly* 2, 1 (1987): 15-16.

11 Robin McGrath, "Inuit Literature in English," *Canadian Review of Comparative Literature*, 1–2 (1989): 702.

12 Robin McGrath, "Circumventing the Taboos: Inuit Women's Autobiographies," in *Regard sur l'avenir/Looking to the Future*, ed. Marie-Josée Dujour and François Thérien (Québec: Université Laval, 1992), 216.

13 McGrath, "Inuit Literature in English," 702.

14 Bernard Saladin d'Anglure, "Introduction" to Mitiarjuk Nappaaluk, *Sanaaq* (Winnipeg: University of Manitoba Press, 2014), xii-xviii.

15 Nappaaluk, *Sanaaq*, 114.

16 Ibid., 192.

17 Two autobiographical accounts of men's lives are Maurice Metalyer, trans., *I Nuligak* (Toronto: Peter Martin Associates, 1966); Abtgibt Aoajarj Thrasher, *Thrasher: Skid Row Eskimo* (Toronto: Griffin House, 1976).

18 Heather Henderson, "North and South: Autobiography and the Problems of Translation," in *Reflections: Autobiography and Canadian Literature*, ed. K.P. Stich, 61–69 (Ottawa: University of Ottawa Press, 1988). Freeman's book is also discussed in Renée Hulan, *Northern Experience and the Myths of Canadian Culture* (Montreal and Kingston: McGill-Queen's University Press, 2002), 84–87; and Sherrill Grace, *Canada and the Idea of North* (Montreal and Kingston: McGill-Queen's University Press, 2001).

19 Minnie Aodla Freeman, *Life among the Qallunaat* (Edmonton: Hurtig, 1978), 65. As others have pointed out, her play, *Survival in the South*, was even more openly critical of the Qallunaat. See McGrath, "European," 114.

20 Elsie Gillis and Eugenie Myles, *North Pole Boarding House* (Toronto: The Ryerson Press, 1951), 57, 75.

21 Freeman, *Life*, 63–64.

22 Ibid., 65.

23 Ibid., 184.

24 Ibid., 112,

25 Ibid., 176.

26 Ibid., 38.

27 Ibid., 187.

28 Ibid., 124.

29 Ibid., 65.

30 Telephone conversation with Bryan Pearson, Iqaluit, July, 2014. This is not confirmed since I have yet to find a record of death.

31 Canon Webster does not discuss Paulette's friendship with his daughter in his correspondence. Anglican Church of Canada General Synod Archives, J.H. Webster Fonds, correspondence files.

32 LAC, Richard Harrington Diaries, MG 31, C 5, Coppermine visit, 1949. Paulette is also mentioned briefly in Richard Harrington, *The Face of the Arctic* (Toronto: Thomas Nelson and Sons, 1952), 26–27.

33 LAC, Indian and Northern Affairs, Department Library Photo Albums, Album 44 (1949, Western Arctic), photo credit: R. Harrington.

34 It is revealing that some archives indicate that women's picture taking was absorbed into other people's (i.e., men's) collections. For example, L.A. Learmonth's substantial collection of photos in the Northwest Territories Archives notes that his partner took some of the photographs. A collection of government-sponsored photos in Library and Archives Canada, ostensibly taken by Richard Harrington, includes the note: "Mrs. Baird took fifteen of the photos." Which Mrs. Baird? When? Archivists were completely unable to offer answers to the latter questions.

35 Prince of Wales NWT Heritage Centre, Osborne Collection, photos N-1900–006, nos. 0052, 0122, 0187, 0219,0269, 0277, 0280, 0290,0298, 0441, 0443.

36 A third picture dealt with the actual work of fur, showing it being baled for shipment. "Arctic Fur Show," *The Beaver* (December 1945): 38. Photo credits: L.A. Learmonth and J.H. Webster.

37 Peter Kulchyski and Frank Tester, *Kiumajut (Talking Back): Game Management and Inuit Rights, 1900-70* (Montreal and Kingston: McGill-Queen's University Press, 1998), 244–50.

38 Pat Sandiford Grygier, *A Long Way from Home: The Tuberculosis Epidemic among the Inuit* (Montreal and Kingston: McGill-Queen's University Press, 1994), 81.

39 With one or two exceptions, such as the film *Eskimo Artist: Kenojuak,* dir. J. Feeney, NFB,1963.

40 Raymond Williams, *Culture* (Glasgow: Fontana Paperbacks, 1981), 85.

41 Frank Tester, "Can the Sled Dog Sleep? Postcolonialism, Cultural Transformation and the Consumption of Inuit Culture," *New Proposals: Journal of Marxism and Interdisciplinary Inquiry* 3, 3 (2010): 9.

42 My definition is taken from Terry Eagleton, *Ideology: An Introduction* (London: Verso, 1991), 194–95.

43 Elizabeth Furniss, *The Burden of History: Colonialism and Frontier Myths in a Rural Community* (Vancouver: UBC Press, 1990), 187.

44 Eagleton, *Ideology,* 112–23.

45 Robert Berkhofer, *The White Man's Indian: Images of the American Indian from Columbus to the Present* (New York: Alfred Knopf, 1978), 114.

46 Alan Marcus, *Relocating Eden: The Image and Politics of Inuit Exile in the Canadian Arctic* (Hanover: University Press of New England, 1995), 3.

47 Mary-Ellen Kelm, "Change, Continuity, Renewal: Lessons from a Decade of Historiography on the First Nations of the Territorial North," in *Northern*

Visions: New Perspectives on the North in Canadian History, ed. Kerry Abel and Ken S. Coates (Peterborough: Broadview Press, 2001), 80.

48 LAC, VI 9101–0018, "The Smiling People."

49 For example, the controversy over Farley Mowat's writing. See Marcus, *Relocating Eden*.

50 Nellie Cournoyea, "The Independent Inuit," *Maclean's*, 14 July 1986, quoted in Penny Petrone, *Northern Voices: Inuit Voices in English* (Toronto: University of Toronto, 1988), 286.

51 Catherine Scott, *Gender and Development: Rethinking Modernization and Dependency Theory* (London: Routledge, 1996); Marianne Marchand and Jane Parpart, eds., *Feminism/Postmodernism/Development* (London: Routledge, 1995).

52 Craig Campbell, "A Genealogy of the Concept of 'Wanton Slaughter,' in Canadian Wildlife Biology," in *Cultivating Arctic Landscapes: Knowing and Managing Animals in the Circumpolar North*, ed. David G. Anderson and Mark Nuttall (New York: Berghahn Books, 2004), 154–71.

53 Antoinette Burton, "Rule of Thumb: British History and Imperial Culture in Nineteenth- and Twentieth-Century Britain," *Women's History Review* 3/4 (1994): 483.

54 Berkhofer quoted in Harald E.L. Prins, "The Paradox of Primitivism: Native Rights and the Problem of Imagery in Cultural Survival Films," *Visual Anthropology* 9 (1997): 244

55 Frank Tester and Peter Kulchyski, *Tammarniit (Mistakes): Inuit Relocation in the Eastern Arctic, 1939-63* (Vancouver: UBC Press, 1994), 6.

56 Kenan Malik, *The Meaning of Race: Race, History and Culture in Western Society* (New York: New York University Press, 1996), 169–70.

57 Glen Coulthard, *Red Skin, White Masks: Rejecting the Colonial Projects of Recognition* (Minneapolis: University of Minnesota Press, 2014), 156.

58 Ibid., chap.3; Leanne Simpson, *Dancing on Our Turtle's Back* (Winnipeg: Arbeiter Ring Publishing, 2011), 51.

59 Judy Tzu-Chun Wu, *Radicals on the Road: Internationalism, Orientalism, and Feminism during the Vietnam Era* (Ithaca: Cornell University Press, 2013).

60 Irene Baird, *The Climate of Power* (Toronto: Macmillan, 1971).

61 LAC, Royal Commission on the Status of Women, RG 33–89, vol. brief 419 and Thrasher testimony, Yellowknife.

Bibliography

ARCHIVAL SOURCES

Anglican Church of Canada General Synod Archives
  J.H. Webster Fonds, Correspondence Files

British Broadcasting Company (BBC) Archives
  Audience Research Reports and TV Publicity Files T23/208

Glenbow Archives of Calgary
  Philip Godsell Fonds

Library and Archives Canada (LAC)
  "Back to School" (7907–0379)
  "Breakout" (VI 2912–07–0007)
  "The Cattle Rustler" (79-7-0392)
  Crawley Film Fonds, MG28-III99
  "Day of Reckoning" (7907-0399)
  Department of Indian Affairs and Northern Development Fonds, RG10
  Department of Mines and Resources Fonds, RG 22
  Donald Snowden Fonds, MG 31, D 163
  Elsie Gregory MacGill Fonds, MG 31, K7
  "The Gunslinger" (7907-0400)
  Hugh Keenleyside Fonds, MG 31, E 102
  Indian and Northern Affairs, Department Library Photo Albums, Album 44
  "Little Girl Lost" (VI 2005-07-0023)
  "Mop Up" (7907-0379)
  Northern Affairs Program Fonds, RG 85
  "The Piggybank Robbery" (7907-0384)
  "Poison Pen" (7907-0389)
  Richard Harrington Diaries, MG 31, C 5
  Royal Commission on the Status of Women Fonds, RG 33-89

"The Smiling People" (VI 9101-0018)
"The Third Question" (7907-0382)
"Tourist Bait" (7907-0408)
"Violence at the Wedding" (7907-0403)
William Lyon Mackenzie King Fonds, MG 26-J13

National Film Board Archives (NFB)

Prince of Wales NWT Heritage Centre
Osborne Photos Collection

McMaster University Archives (MU)
Macmillan Company of Canada Fonds

Public Archives of Manitoba (PAM)
Bolus Fonds, E 380
Clifford Wilson Fonds, E 95/8
Hudson's Bay Company Fonds

Trent University Archives (TU)
Monroe Scott Fonds

NEWSPAPERS AND PERIODICALS

The Beaver
Canadian Dimension
Corner Brook Western Star
Globe and Mail
Financial Post
Forest and Outdoors
Maclean's Magazine
Montreal Star
News of the North
Ottawa Citizen
Pembroke Observer
Saturday Night
Telegraph Journal
Toronto Daily Star
Toronto Star
Toronto Star Weekly
Western Producer
Winnipeg Free Press Weekly

MOTION PICTURES AND TELEVISION

Blais, Gilles, dir. *Yesterday – Today: The Netsilik Eskimo*. NFB, 1971.
Boulton, Laura, dir. *Arctic Hunters*. Ottawa, NFB, 1944.
Boulton, Laura, dir. *Eskimo Summer*. Ottawa: NFB, 1944.
CBC Matinee. Toronto: CBC Radio Archives, 1968.
Da Prato, Clarke, dir. *People of the Rock*. Ottawa: NFB, 1961.
Flaherty, Robert, dir. *Nanook of the North*, 1922.
Greenwald, Barry, dir. *Between Two Worlds*. NFB, 1990.
Hart, Roger. *Labrador North*. Ottawa: NFB, 1973.
Howe, John, dir. *Our Northern Citizen*. Ottawa: National Film Board, 1956.
James, Ed, creator. *Father Knows Best*. Los Angeles: CBS Productions, 1954–60.
McLean, Grant, dir. *No Longer Vanishing*. Ottawa: National Film Board, 1955.
Michael, Moshe. *The Hunters (Asivaqtiin)*. NFB, 1977.
Ransen, Mort, dir. *The Transition*. Ottawa: National Film Board, 1964.
Sandiford, Mark, dir. *Qullunaat! Why White People are Funny*. Ottawa: NFB, 2006.
Take Thirty. Toronto: Canadian Broadcasting Corporation, 1962–84.
Wilkinson, Doug, dir. *Angotee: Story of an Eskimo Boy*. Ottawa: National Film Board, 1953.
—. *How to Make an Igloo*. Ottawa: National Film Board, 1949.
—. *Land of the Long Day*. Ottawa: National Film Board, 1952.

SECONDARY SOURCES

Abel, Kerry. *Drum Songs: Glimpses of Dene History*. Montreal and Kingston: McGill-Queen's University Press, 1993.
—. "Tangled, Lost and Bitter? Current Directions in the Writing of Native History in Canada." *Acadiensis* 26, 1 (1996): 92–101.
Abel, Kerry, and Ken S. Coates, eds. *Northern Visions: New Perspectives on the North in Canadian History*. Peterborough: Broadview Press, 2001.
Abele, Frances. "Canadian Contradictions: Forty Years of Northern Political Development." *Arctic* 40, 4 (1987): 310–20.
Adams, Harold. *Prison of Grass: Canada from the Native Point of View*. Saskatoon: Fifth House, 1989.
Ahmad, Aijaz. *In Theory: Classes, Nations, Literatures*. London: Verso, 1992.
Ahmed, Sara. *Strange Encounters: Embodied Others in Post-Coloniality*. London: Routledge, 2000.
Albers, Patricia, and William James. "Illusion and Illumination: Visual Images of American Indian Women in the West." In *The Women's West*, ed. Susan

Armitage and Elizabeth Jameson, 35–50. Norman: University of Oklahoma Press, 1987.

Alcoff, Linda. "The Problem of Speaking for Others." *Cultural Critique* 20 (Winter 1991–92): 3–22.

Aleiss, Angela. *Making the White Man's Indian*. Santa Barbara: Praeger, 2005.

Altamirano-Jiménéz, Isabel. "Indigenous Women, Nationalism and Feminism." In *States of Race: Critical Race Feminism for the 21st Century*, ed. Sherene Razack, Malinda Smith, and Sunera Thobani, 111–25. Toronto: Between the Lines, 2010.

Alvey Richards, Eva. *Arctic Mood*. Caldwell, ID: Caxton, 1949.

Ambrose, Linda. "Our Last Frontier: Imperialism and Northern Canadian Rural Women's Organization." *Canadian Historical Review* 86, 2 (2005): 257–84.

Anderson, David. "Reindeer, Caribou and 'Fairy Stories' of State Power." In *Cultivating Arctic Landscapes: Knowing and Managing Animals in the Circumpolar North*, ed. David G. Anderson and Mark Nuttall, 1–16. New York: Berghahn Books, 2004.

Anderson, Karen. *A Recognition of Being: Reconstructing Native Womanhood*. Toronto: Second Story Press, 2000.

Anderson, William Ashley. *Angel of Hudson Bay: The True Story of Maud Watt*. Toronto: Clarke, Irwin and Co., 1961.

Apakark Thrasher, Anthony. *Thrasher: Skid Row Eskimo*. Toronto: Griffin House, 1976.

Apter, A. "On Imperial Spectacle: The Dialectics of Seeing in Colonial Nigeria." *Comparative Studies in Society and History* 44, 2 (2002): 564–96.

Archibald, Kathleen. *Sex and the Public Service*. Ottawa: Queen's Printer, 1970.

Atkinson, Paul. *The Ethnographic Imagination*. New York: Routledge, 1990.

Atwood, Margaret. *Strange Things: The Malevolent North in Canadian Literature*. Oxford: Clarendon Press, 1995.

Babe, Robert. "Political Economy and Cultural Studies Column: Political Economy, Cultural Studies and Postmodernism." *Topia* 15 (2006): 91–100.

Baird, Irene. "Les Africaines Visit the Eskimos." *North/Nord* 8, 4 (1961): 20–24.

–. "Arctic Mobile." *North/Nord* 9, 6 (1962): 45.

–. "Blow Spirit." *North/Nord* 13, 1 (1966): 18–19.

–. "Cape Dorset Man." *Canadian Geographical Journal* (November 1965): 5.

–. *The Climate of Power*. Toronto: Macmillan, 1971.

–. "A Delicate Balance." *North/Nord* 20, 3 (1973): 13–15.

–. "Diary of a Working Journey." *North/Nord* 12, 1 (1965): 22.

–. "Eskimo Church on Christmas Morning." *North/Nord* 17, 6 (1970): 14–15.

–. "I Don't Read You Charlie: A Twisted Tale." *North/Nord* 19, 2 (1972): 10.

—. "Keep Your Own Things." *North/Nord* 11, 2 (1964):10–11.

—. "Land." *North/Nord* 11, 6 (1964): 16–17.

—. "A Learning Situation." *North/Nord* 14, 6 (1967): 11.

—. "The Lonely Shore." *North/Nord* 10, 3 (1963): 34.

—. "Mary No More." *North/Nord* 18, 6 (1971): 17.

—. *Waste Heritage*. Ottawa: Ottawa University Press, 2007.

—. "Who Will Be I." *North/Nord* 13, 5 (1966): 16.

—. "You Only Take the First Trip Once." *North /Nord* 13, 6 (1966): 26.

Baldwin, Andrew, Laura Cameron, and Audrey Kobayashi, eds. *Rethinking the Great White North: Race, Nature, and the Historical Geographies of Whiteness in Canada*. Vancouver: UBC Press, 2011.

Balikci, Asen. "The Netsilik Film Series." *Visual Anthropology* 22 (2009): 384–92.

—. *Vunta Kutchin Social Change: A Study of the People of Old Crow, Yukon Territory*. Ottawa: Northern Co-ordination and Research Centre, Department of Northern Affairs and National Resources, 1963.

Beattie, Keith. *Documentary Screens: Non-Fiction Film and Television*. London: Palgrave Macmillan, 2004.

Bender Zelmanovitz, Judith. "Midwife Preferred: Maternity Care in Outpost Nursing Stations in Northern Canada." In *Women, Health and Nation: Canada and the United States since 1945*, ed. Georgina Feldberg, Molly Ladd-Taylor, Alison Li, and Kathryn McPherson , 161–95. Montreal and Kingston: McGill-Queen's University Press, 2003.

Benjamin, Russell. "The American Internal Colonial Environment." In *Eternal Colonialism*, ed. Russell Benjamin and Gregory O. Hall, 3–12. Latham, MD: University Press of America, 2010.

Bennett, P.M. Reviews of *Igloo for the Night* and *A Summer on Hudson Bay*. *Arctic* (August 1950): 117.

Berebitsky, Julie. *Sex in the Office: A History of Gender, Power and Desire*. New Haven: Yale University Press, 2012.

Berger, Carl. *The Sense of Power: Studies in the Ideas of Canadian Imperialism, 1867–1914*. Toronto: University of Toronto Press, 1970.

Berger, Morroe. *Real and Imagined Worlds: The Novel and Social Science*. Cambridge: Harvard University Press, 1977.

Berkhofer, Robert. *The White Man's Indian: Images of the American Indian from Columbus to the Present*. New York: Alfred Knopf, 1978.

Berton, Pierre. *Hollywood's Canada: The Americanization of Our National Image*. Toronto: McClelland and Stewart, 1975.

Bhambra, Gurminder K. *Rethinking Modernity: Postcolonialism and the Sociological Imagination*. London: Palgrave Macmillan, 2013.

Binnie-Clark, Georgina. *Wheat and Woman*. Toronto: University of Toronto Press, 1979.

Bird, Elizabeth. "Savage Desires: The Gendered Construction of the American Indian in Popular Media." In *Selling the Indian: Commercializing and Appropriating American Indian Culture*, ed. Carter Jones Meyer and Diana Royer, 62–98. Tucson: University of Arizona, 2001.

Bird, Florence. *Anne Francis, an Autobiography*. Toronto: Clarke, Irwin and Co., 1974.

Birkett, Dea. *Spinsters Abroad*. Oxford: Blackwell, 1989.

Blauer, Robert. "Colonized and Immigrant Minorities." In *From Different Shores*, ed. Ronald Takaki, 149–60. New York: Oxford University Press, 1994.

Blaut, J.M. *The Colonizer's Model of the World: Geographical Diffusionism and Eurocentric History*. New York: The Guilford Press, 1993.

Bloom, Lisa. *Gender on Ice: American Ideologies of Polar Exploration*. Minneapolis: University of Minnesota Press, 1993.

Blum, Jerome. "Fiction and the European Peasantry: The Realist Novel as a Historical Source." *Proceedings of the American Philosophical Society* 126, 2 (1982): 122–39.

Blunt, Alison. *Travel, Gender and Imperialism: Mary Kingsley and West Africa*. New York: Guildford Press, 1994.

Blyth, Molly. "Tricky Stories Are the Cure: Contemporary Indigenous Writing in Canada." PhD diss., Trent University, 2009.

Bocking, Stephen. "Indigenous Knowledge and the History of Science, Race and Colonial Authority in Northern Canada." In *Rethinking The Great White North: Race, Nature, and the Historical Geographies of Whiteness in Canada*, ed. Andrew Baldwin, Laura Cameron, and Audrey Kobayashi, 39–61. Vancouver: UBC Press, 2001.

Body, Dorothy. "North from Ottawa," *Books in Canada* 1, 1 (May 1971): 23.

Bordo, Jonathan. "Jack Pine: Wilderness Sublime or The Erasure of the Aboriginal Presence from the Landscape." *Journal of Canadian Studies* 27, 4 (1992): 98–128.

Brody, Hugh. *Living Arctic: Hunters of the Canadian North*. Vancouver: Douglas and McIntyre, 1987.

—. *The Other Side of Eden*. Toronto: Douglas and McIntyre, 2000.

—. *The People's Land*. London: Penguin Books, 1975.

Brooks, Lynn. "Guided by Our Bellies" In *Gossip: A Spoken History of Women in the North*, ed. Mary Crnkovich, 37–42. Ottawa: Canadian Arctic Resources Committee, 1990.

Burnford, Sheila. *One Woman's Arctic*. Toronto: McClelland and Stewart, 1973.

—. *Without Reserve*. Boston: Atlantic Monthly Press, 1969.

Burton, Antoinette. *Burdens of History*. Chapel Hill: University of North Carolina Press, 1994.

–. "Rule of Thumb: British History and Imperial Culture in Nineteenth and Twentieth Century Britain." *Women's History Review* 3, 4 (1994): 483–501.

Burton, Antoinette, ed. *Gender, Sexuality and Colonial Modernities*. London: Routledge, 1999.

Buscombe, Edward. *"Injuns!": Native Americans in the Movies*. Cornwall: Reaktin Books, 2006.

Bussidor, Ila, and Ustun Bilgen-Reinart. *Night Spirits: The Story of the Relocation of the Sayisi Dene*. Winnipeg: University of Manitoba Press, 1997.

Buxton, David. *From the Avengers to Miami Vice: Form and Ideology in Television Series*. Manchester: Manchester University Press, 1990.

Cairns, Alan. *Citizens Plus: Aboriginal Peoples and the State*. Vancouver: UBC Press, 2000.

Calder, Ritchie. *Men against the Frozen North*. London: George Allen and Unwin, 1957.

Callaway, Helen. "Dressing for Dinner in the Bush: Rituals of Self Definition and British Imperial Authority." In *Dress and Gender: Making and Meaning*, ed. Ruth Barnes and Joanne B. Eicher, 232–47. New York: Berg Books, 1992.

–. *Gender, Culture and Empire*. London: Macmillan 1987.

Campbell, Craig. "A Genealogy of the Concept of 'Wanton Slaughter' in Canadian Wildlife Biology." In *Cultivating Arctic Landscape: Knowing and Managing Animals in the CircumpolarNorth*, ed. David G. Anderson and Mark Nuttall, 154–71. New York: Berghahn Books, 2004.

Carter, Sarah. *Capturing Women: The Manipulation of Cultural Imagery in Canada's Prairie West*. Montreal and Kingston: McGill-Queen's University Press, 1997.

–. *Lost Harvests: Prairie Indian Reserve Farmers and Government Policy*. Montreal and Kingston: McGill-Queen's University Press, 1990.

Cater, Tara, and Arn Keeling. "'That's Where Our Future Came From': Mining, Landscape, and Memory in Rankin Inlet, Nunavut." *Études/Inuit/Studies* 37, 2 (2013): 59–82.

Cavell, Janice. "The Second Frontier: The North in Canadian Historical Writing." *Canadian Historical Review* 88, 3 (2002): 364–89.

Chibber, Vivek. *Postcolonial Theory and the Specter of Capital*. London: Verso, 2013.

Churchill, Ward. *Fantasies of the Master Race: Literature, Cinema, and the Colonization of American Indians*. San Francisco: City Lights Books, 1998.

Clark, Steve. "Introduction." In *Travel Writing and Empire: Postcolonial Theory in Transit*, ed. Steve Clark, 3. London: Zed Books, 1999.

Clifford, James. "Of Other Peoples: Beyond the 'Salvage Paradigm.'" In *Discussions in Contemporary Culture*, ed. Hal Foster, 121–22. Seattle: Bay Press, 1987.

Coates, Kenneth. *Best Left as Indians: Native-White Relations in the Yukon Territory, 1840–1973*. Montreal and Kingston: McGill-Queen's University Press, 1991.

—. *Canada's Colonies: A History of the Yukon and Northwest Territories*. Toronto: James Lorimer, 1985.

—. "The Discovery of the North: Towards a Conceptual Framework for the Study of Northern/Remote Regions." *Northern Review* 12/13 (Winter 1994): 15–43.

—. "Learning from Others: Comparative History and the Study of Aboriginal-Newcomer Relations." *Native Studies Review* 16, 1 (2005): 3–13.

—. "Writing First Nations into Canadian History: A Review of Recent Scholarly Works." *Canadian Historical Review* 81, 1 (2000): 99–114.

Cobb, Richard. *Promenades: A Historian's Appreciation of Modern French Literature*. Oxford: Oxford University Press, 1986.

Collins, Jane, and Catherine Lutz. *Reading National Geographic*. Chicago: University of Chicago Press, 1993.

Comaroff, Jean, and John Comaroff. *Ethnography and the Historical Imagination*. Boulder, CO: Westview Press, 1992.

Cooper, Frederick, and Ann Stoler. "Between Metropole and Colony: Rethinking a Research Agenda." In *Tensions of Empire: Colonial Cultures in a Bourgeois World*, ed. Frederick Cooper and Ann Stoler, 1–56. Berkeley: University of California Press, 1997.

Coulthard, Glen Sean. *Red Skin White Masks: Rejecting the Colonial Politics of Recognition*. Minneapolis: University of Minnesota Press, 2014.

—. "Subjects of Empire: Indigenous Peoples and the 'Politics of Recognition' in Canada." *Contemporary Political Theory* 6 (2007): 437–60.

Cowie, Elizabeth. *Recording Reality, Desiring the Real*. Minneapolis: University of Minnesota Press, 2011.

Crehan, Kate. *Gramsci, Culture and Anthropology*. Berkeley: University of California Press, 2002.

Crnkovich, Mary, ed. *Gossip: A Spoken History of Women in the North*. Ottawa: Canadian Arctic Resources Committee, 1990.

Cronlund Anderson, Mark, and Carmen Roberston. *Seeing Red: A History of Natives in Canadian Newspapers*. Winnipeg: University of Manitoba Press, 2011.

Cruikshank, Julie. *Life Lived Like a Story: Life Stories of Three Native Elders*. Vancouver: UBC Press, 1990.

—. "The Role of Northern Canadian Indian Women in Social Change." MA thesis, University of British Columbia, 1969.

Cummins, Brian. *Faces of the North: The Ethnographic Photographs of John Hongimann*. Toronto: Natural Heritage Books, 2004.

Damas, David. *Arctic Migrants/Arctic Villagers: The Transformation of Inuit Settlement in the Central Arctic.* Montreal and Kingston: McGill-Queen's University Press, 2002.

Darnell, Regna. *And Along Came Boas: Continuity and Revolution in Americanist Anthropology.* Philadelphia: John Benjamins Publishing Company, 1998.

—. *Invisible Genealogies: A History of Americanist Anthropology.* Lincoln: University of Nebraska Press, 2001.

David, Deirdre. *Rule Britannia: Women, Empire and Victorian Writing.* Ithaca, NY: Cornell University Press, 1995.

Dawson, Michael. *The Mountie: From Dime Novel to Disney.* Toronto: Between the Lines, 1998.

Deans Cameron, Agnes. *The New North: An Account of a Woman's 1908 Journey through Canada to the Arctic.* Saskatoon: Western Producer Prairie Books, 1986.

de Groot, Joanna. "Conceptions and Misconceptions: The Historical and Cultural Context of Discussion on Women and Development." In *Women, Development and Survival in the Third World,* ed. Haleh Afshar, 107–35. London: Longman, 1991.

Deloria, Philip. "Places like Homes, Banks and Continents: An Appreciative Reply to the Presidential Address." *American Quarterly* 58, 1 (2006): 23–29.

—. *Playing Indian.* New Haven: Yale University Press, 1998.

Dickerson, Mark. *Whose North? Political Change, Political Development and Self Government in the Northwest Territories.* Vancouver: UBC Press, 1992.

Dippie, Brian. *The Vanishing American: White Attitudes and US Indian Policy.* Middletown: Wesleyan University Press, 1982.

Dirlik, Arif. "The Past as Legacy and Project: Postcolonial Criticism in the Perspective of Aboriginal Historicism." In *Contemporary North American Political Issues,* ed. Troy Johnson, 73–98. Walnut Creek, CA: Altamira Press, 1999.

—. *The Postcolonial Aura: Third World Criticism in the Age of Global Capitalism.* Boulder, CO: Westview Press, 1997.

Donaldson, Laura. *Decolonizing Feminisms: Race, Gender and Empire Building.* Chapel Hill: University of Northern Carolina Press, 1992.

Dorais, Louis-Jacques. *Quaqtaq: Modernity and Identity in an Inuit Community.* Toronto: University of Toronto Press, 1997.

Dorland, Michael, ed. *Cultural Industries in Canada: Problems, Policies and Prospects.* Toronto: Lorimer, 1996.

Doyle, James. *Progressive Heritage: The Evolution of a Politically Radical Literary Tradition in Canada.* Waterloo: Wilfrid Laurier Press, 2002.

Druick, Zoe. *Projecting Canada: Government Policy and Documentary Film at the National Film Board of Canada.* Montreal and Kingston: McGill-Queen's University Press, 2007.

Dummitt, Christopher. *The Manly Modern in Postwar Canada*. Vancouver: UBC Press, 2007.

Dyck, Noel. "Canadian Anthropology and the Ethnography of Indian Administration." In *Historicizing Canadian Anthropology*, ed. Julia Harrison and Regna Darnell, 78–92. Vancouver: UBC Press, 2006.

–. *What Is the "Indian Problem"? Tutelage and Resistance in Canadian Indian Administration*. St. John's: Institute of Social and Economic Research, Memorial University, 1991.

Dyck, Noel, and James Waldram, eds. *Anthropology, Public Policy and Native Peoples in Canada*. Montreal and Kingston: McGill-Queen's University Press, 1993.

Eagleton, Terry. *Ideology: An Introduction*. London: Verso, 1991.

Eaton, Diane, and Sheila Urbanek. *Paul Kane's Great Nor-West*. Vancouver: UBC Press, 1995.

Edwards, Elizabeth. *Anthropology and Photography, 1860–1920*. New Haven/Yale University Press and London/Royal Anthropological Institute, 1992.

Emberly, Julia. "Colonial Governance and the Making and Unmaking of the Bourgeois 'Eskimo' Family: Robert Flaherty's *Nanook of the North*." In *Indigeneity: Construction and Re/presentation*, ed. James Brown and Patricia Sant, 95–118. Commack: Nova Science Publishers, 1999.

Eriksen, Thomas H., and Finn Sivert Nielsen. *A History of Anthropology*. London: Pluto Press, 2001.

Evans, Gary. *In the National Interest: A Chronicle of the National Film Board of Canada from 1949 to 1989*. Toronto: University of Toronto Press, 1991.

Fee, Margery. "Romantic Nationalism and the Image of Native People in Contemporary English-Canadian Literature." In *The Native in Literature*, ed. Thomas King, Cheryl Calver, and Helen Hoy, 15–33. Toronto: ECW Press, 1987.

Fienup-Riordan, Ann. *Eskimo Essays: Yup'ik Lives and How We See Them*. New Brunswick: Rutgers University Press, 1990.

–. *Freeze Frame: Alaska Eskimos in the Movies*. Seattle: University of Washington Press, 1995.

Fiske, John. *Television Culture*. New York: Methuen, 1987.

Forrester, James A. *Budge: F.R. Crawley and Crawley Films, 1939–1982*. Lakefield: IRS, 1988.

Foucault, Michel. *The History of Sexuality*, vol. 1. New York: Pantheon Books, 1984.

Fowler, Marian. *The Embroidered Tent Five Gentlewomen in Early Canada*. Toronto: Anansi Press, 1982.

Francis, Daniel. *The Imaginary Indian: The Image of the Indian in Canadian Culture*. Vancouver: Arsenal Pulp Press, 1992.

Freeman, Barbara. *The Satellite Sex: The Media and Women's Issues in English Canada, 1966–71.* Waterloo: Wilfrid Laurier Press, 2001.

Freeman, Minnie Aodla. *Life among the Qallunaat.* Edmonton: Hurtig, 1978.

Freeman, Victoria. "Attitudes toward 'Miscegenation' in Canada, the United States, New Zealand and Australia, 1860–1914," *Native Studies Reviews* 16, 1 (2005): 41–70.

Freuchen, Peter. *I Sailed with Rasmussen.* New York: Julian Messner, 1959.

Frideres, J.S., and Renee Gadacz. *Aboriginal Peoples in Canada: Contemporary Conflicts.* Scarborough: Prentice Hall, 2007.

Frideres, James. *Native People in Canada: Contemporary Conflicts.* 2nd ed. Scarborough: Prentice-Hall Canada, 1993.

Fudge, Judy. "From Segregation to Privatization: Equality, the Law and Women Public Servants, 1908–2001." In *Privatization, Law and the Challenge to Feminism,* ed. Brenda Cossman and Judy Fudge, 86–127. Toronto: University of Toronto Press, 2002.

Furniss, Elizabeth. *The Burden of History: Colonialism and Frontier Myths in a Rural Community.* Vancouver: UBC Press, 1990.

Fuss, Diana. "Interior Colonies: Franz Fanon and the Politics of Identification." *Diacritics* 24 (1994): 20–42.

Gaines, Jane M. "Political Mimesis." In *Collecting Visible Evidence,* ed. Jane M. Gaines and Michale Renov, 84–102. Minneapolis: University of Minnesota Press, 1995.

Geller, Peter. "Northern Exposures: Photographic and Filmic Representations of the Canadian North, 1920–45." PhD diss., Carleton University, 1975.

—. *Northern Exposures: Photographing and Filming the Canadian North, 1920–45.* Vancouver: UBC Press, 2004.

Gillis, Elsie, and Eugenie Myles. *North Pole Boarding House.* Toronto: The Ryerson Press, 1951.

Ginsberg, Faye. "Native Intelligence: A Short History of Debates on Indigenous Media and Ethnographic Film." In *Made to Be Seen: Perspectives on the History of Visual Anthropology,* ed. Marcus Banks and Jay Ruby, 234–55. Chicago: University of Chicago Press, 2011.

Godsell, Jean. *I Was No Lady: I Followed the Call of the Wild.* Toronto: The Ryerson Press, 1959.

Godsell, Philip. *Arctic Trader: The Account of Twenty Years with the Hudson's Bay Company.* New York: C.P. Putman, 1934.

Gordon, Linda. "Internal Colonialism and Gender." In *Haunted by Empire: Geographies of Intimacy in North American History,* ed. Ann Stoler, 427–51. Durham, NC: Duke University Press, 2007.

Gossman, Lionel. *Between History and Literature*. Cambridge: Harvard University Press, 1990.

Graburn, Nelson. "Authentic Inuit Art: Creation and Exclusion in the Canadian North." *Journal of Material Culture* 9, 2 (2004): 141–59.

–. "Inuit Art and Canadian Nationalism." *Inuit Art Quarterly* 1, 3 (1986): 5–6.

–. "The Present as History: Photography and the Inuit, 1959–94." In *Imaging the Arctic*, ed. J.C.H. King and Henrietta Lidchi, 160–67. Seattle/Vancouver: University of Washington Press/UBC Press, 1998.

Grace, Sherrill E. *Canada and the Idea of North*. Montreal and Kingston: McGill-Queen's University Press, 1991.

–. "Exploration as Construction: Robert Flaherty and Nanook of the North." *Essays on Canadian Writing* 59 (1996): 123–46.

Gramsci, Antonio. *Selections from Cultural Writings*, ed. David Forgacs and Geoffrey Nowell-Smith. Cambridge: Harvard University Press, 1985.

Granatstein, Jack. *The Ottawa Men: The Civil Service Mandarins*. Toronto: Oxford University Press, 1982.

Grant, Shelagh. "Arctic Historiography: Current Status and Blueprints for the Future." *Journal of Canadian Studies* 33, 1 (1998): 145–53.

–. *Arctic Justice: On Trial for Murder, Pond Inlet, 1923*. Montreal and Kingston: McGill-Queen's University Press, 2002.

–. *Sovereignty or Security: Government Policy in the Canadian North, 1936–1950*. Vancouver: UBC Press, 1988.

Gray, Charlotte. *Gold Diggers*. Toronto: HarperCollins, 2010.

Gray, Jonathan, and Amanda D. Lotz. *Television Studies: A Short Introduction*. Malden, MA: Polity Press, 2012.

Green, Joyce. *Making Space for Indigenous Feminism*. Black Point, NS: Fernwood, 2007.

–. "Towards a Détente with History: Confronting Canada's Colonial Legacy." *International Review of Canadian Studies* 12 (Fall 1995): 85–105.

Green, Rayna. "The Pocahontas Perplex: The Image of the Indian Woman in American Vernacular Culture." *Massachusetts Review* 16, 4 (1976): 698–714.

Grewal, Inderpal. *Home and Harem*. Durham, NC: Duke University Press, 1996.

Griffin, John Howard. *Black Like Me*. New York: Houghton Mifflin, 1961.

Griffiths, Alison. *Wondrous Difference: Cinema, Anthropology and Turn-of-the-Century Visual Culture*. New York: Columbia University Press, 2002.

Grimshaw, Anna. *The Ethnographer's Eye: Ways of Seeing in Modern Anthropology*. Cambridge: Cambridge University Press, 2001.

Grygier, Pat Sandiford. *A Long Way from Home: The Tuberculosis Epidemic among the Inuit*. Montreal and Kingston: McGill-Queen's University Press, 1994.

Haggis, Jane. "Gendering Colonialism or Colonizing Gender: Recent Women's Studies Approaches to White Women and the History of British Colonialism." *Women's Studies International Forum* 13, 1 (1990): 105–15.

Hall, Stuart. "Gramsci's Relevance for the Study of Race and Ethnicity." In *Stuart Hall: Critical Dialogues in Cultural Studies*, ed. David Morley and Kuan-Hsing Chen, 411–40. London: Routledge, 1996.

Hamelin, Louis-Edmond. *Canadian Nordicity: It's Your North*. Montreal: Harvest, 1979.

Hamilton, John David. *Arctic Revolution: Social Change in the Northwest Territories, 1935–1994*. Hamilton: Dundurn, 1994.

Hancock, Robert. "The Potential for Canadian Anthropology: Diamond Jenness' Arctic Ethnography." MA thesis, University of Victoria, 1999.

Hansen, K. ed. *African Encounters with Domesticity*. New Brunswick, NJ: Rutgers University Press, 1992.

Harley Eber, Dorothy. *Images of Justice*. Montreal and Kingston: McGill-Queen's University Press, 1997.

Harrington, Richard. *The Face of the Arctic*. Toronto: Thomas Nelson and Sons, 1952.

Harris, Cole. *Making Native Space Colonialism: Resistance and Reserves in British Columbia*. Vancouver: UBC Press, 2002.

Harrison, Julia, and Regna Darnell. "Historicizing Traditions in Canadian Anthropology." In *Historicizing Canadian Anthropology*, ed. Julia Harrison and Regna Darnell, 3–18.Vancouver: UBC Press, 2006.

Harvey, David. "The Body as an Accumulation Strategy." *Environment and Planning D: Society and Space* 16 (1998), 401–21.

Hawthorn, H.B. *A Survey of Canada: A Report on Economic, Political, Educational Needs and Policies*. Ottawa: Indian Affairs Branch, 1966.

Hawthorn, H.B., C.S. Belshaw, and S.M. Jamieson. *The Indians of British Columbia: A Study of Contemporary Social Adjustment*. Toronto: University of Toronto Press, 1960.

Haycock, Ronald. *The Image of the Indian*. Waterloo: Wilfrid Laurier Press, 1971.

Heinimann, Ralph. "Latitude Rising: Historical Continuity in Canadian Nordicity." *Journal of Canadian Studies* 28, 2 (1993): 134–39.

Helmricks, Constance, and Harmon Helmricks. *We Live in the Arctic*. New York: Little Brown and Co., 1947.

Henderson, Heather. "North and South: Autobiography and the Problems of Translation." In *Reflections: Autobiography and Canadian Literature*, ed. K.P. Stich, 61–69. Ottawa: University of Ottawa Press, 1988.

Henderson, Jennifer. *Settler Feminism and Race Making in Canada*. Toronto: University of Toronto Press, 2003.

Hervik, Peter. "The Mysterious Maya of National Geographic." *Journal of Latin American Anthropology* 4, 1 (1999): 166–97.

Hewitt, Steve. *Riding to the Rescue: The Transformation of the RCMP in Alberta and Saskatchewan, 1914–1939*. Toronto: University of Toronto Press, 2006.

Higgins, John. *Raymond Williams: Literature, Marxism and Cultural Materialism*. London: Routledge, 1999.

Hill, Colin. "The Modern Realist Movement in English-Canadian Fiction, 1919–1950." PhD diss., McGill University, 2003.

Hinds, Marjorie. *School House in the Arctic*. London: Geoffrey Bles, 1958.

Hogarth, David. *Documentary Television in Canada: From National Public Service to Global Marketplace*. Montreal and Kingston: McGill-Queen's University Press, 2002.

Holt, Jennifer, and Alisa Perren. *Media Industries: History, Theory, Method*. Malden, MA: Blackwell, 2009.

Huhndorf, Shari. "Atanarjuat, The Fast Runner: Culture, History and Politics in Inuit Media." *American Anthropologist* 105, 4 (2003): 822–26.

–. *Going Native: Indians in the American Cultural Imagination*. Ithaca: Cornell University Press, 2001.

Hulan, Renée. *Northern Experience and the Myths of Canadian Culture*. Montreal and Kingston: McGill-Queen's University Press, 2002.

Hyman, Roger. "Wasted Heritage for Waste Heritage: The Critical Disregard for an Important Novel." *Journal of Canadian Studies* 17, 4 (1982–83): 74–87.

Iglauer, Edith. *Denison's Ice Road*. Vancouver: Harbour Publishing, 1975.

–. *The New People: The Eskimo's Journey into Our Time*. New York: Doubleday, 1966.

Illingworth, Frank. *Highway to the North*. New York: Philosophical Library, 1955.

Irr, Carmen. *The Suburbs of Dissent: Cultural Politics in the US and Canada During the 1930s*. Durham: Duke University Press, 1998.

Isbister, John. *Promises Not Kept: The Betrayal of Social Change in the Third World*. Bloomfield, CT: Kumarian Press, 2001.

Jackson Rushing, W. *Native American Art and the New York Avant-Garde*. Austin: University of Texas, 1995.

Jacobs, Ellen. "Eileen Power's Asian Journey, 1920–1: History, Narrative and Subjectivity." *Women's History Review* 7, 3 (1998): 295–319.

Jameson, Anna B. *Winter Studies and Summer Rambles*. Toronto: McClelland and Stewart, 1965.

Jasen, Patricia. "Race, Culture and the Colonization of Childbirth in Northern Canada." In *Rethinking Canada: The Promise of Women's History*, ed. Veronica

Strong-Boag, Mona Gleason, and Adele Perry, 353–66. Toronto: Oxford University Press, 2002.

Kaplan, Amy. "Manifest Domesticity." *American Literature* 70, 3 (1998): 581–606.

Kelcey, Barbara. *Alone in Silence: European Women in the Canadian North before 1940*. Montreal and Kingston: McGill-Queen's University Press, 2001.

Kellnor, Douglas. "Media Industries, Political Economy, and Media/Cultural Studies: An Articulation." In *Media Industries: History, Theory, and Method*, ed. Jennifer Holt and Alisa Perren, 95–107. Malden, MA: Wiley-Blackwell, 2009.

Kelm, Mary-Ellen. "Change, Continuity, Renewal: Lessons from a Decade of Historiography on the First Nations of the Territorial North." In *Northern Visions*, ed. Kerry Abel and Kenneth Coates, 77–90. Toronto: University of Toronto Press, 2002.

—. *Colonizing Bodies: Aboriginal Health and Healing in British Columbia, 1900–50*. Vancouver: UBC Press, 1998.

Khouri, Malek. *Filming Politics: Communism and the Portrayal of the Working Class at the National Film Board of Canada, 1939–1946*. Calgary: University of Calgary Press, 2007.

Kilpatrick, Jacqueline. *The Celluloid Indian: Native Americans and Film*. Lincoln: University of Nebraska Press, 1990.

King, J.D.H., and Henrietta Lidchi, eds. *Imaging the Arctic*. Vancouver: UBC Press, 1998.

Kulchyski, Peter. "Anthropology in the Service of the State: Diamond Jenness and Canadian Indian Policy." *Journal of Canadian Studies* 28, 2 (1993): 21–50.

Kulchyski, Peter, and Frank Tester. *Kiumajut (Talking Back): Game Management and Inuit Rights, 1900–70*. Vancouver: UBC Press, 2007.

Laakuluk, Jessen Williamson. "Inuit Gender Party and Why It Was Not Accepted in the Nunavut Legislature." *Études Inuit Studies* 30, 1 (2006): 51–68.

Lake, Marilyn. "White Man's Country: The Transnational History of a National Project." *Australian Historical Studies* 122 (2003): 346–63.

Langley Hall, Gordon. *Me Papoose Sitter*. New York: Thomas Crowell Co., 1955.

Laslett, Peter. "The Wrong Way through the Telescope: A Note on Literary Evidence in Sociology and in Historical Sociology." *British Journal of Sociology* 27, 3 (1976): 319–42.

Leach, Jim, and Jeannette Sloniowski, eds. *Candid Eyes: Essays on Canadian Documentaries*. Toronto: University of Toronto Press, 2003.

Lee, Betty. *Lutiapik*. Toronto: McClelland and Stewart, 1975.

Legat, Allice. *Walking the Land, Feeding the Fire: Knowledge and Stewardship among the Thico Dene*. Tucson: University of Arizona Press, 2012.

Leibman, Nina. *Living Room Lectures: The Fifties Family on Film and Television*. Austin: University of Texas Press, 1995.

Lembo, Ron. *Thinking through Television*. Cambridge: Cambridge University Press, 2000.

Lewis, Reina. *Gendering Orientalism: Race, Femininity and Representation*. London: Routledge, 1996.

Litt, Paul. *The Muses, the Masses, and the Massey Commission*. Toronto: University of Toronto Press, 1992.

Loader, Ian. "Policing and the Social: Questions of Symbolic Power." *British Journal of Sociology* 48, 1 (1997): 1–18.

Loomba, Ania. *Colonialism/Postcolonialism*. London: Routledge, 1998.

Lord, Susan. "Canadian Gothic: Multiculturalism, Indigeneity and Gender in Prairie Cinema." In *Canadian Cultural Poesis: Essays in Canadian Culture*, ed. Garry Sherbert, Annie Gerin, and Sheila Petty, 400. Waterloo: Wilfrid Laurier Press, 2006.

Lotz, Jim. *Northern Realities: Canada-US Exploitation of the Canadian North*. Toronto: Follett, 1971.

Lutz, John Sutton. *Makúk: A New History of Aboriginal-White Relations*. Vancouver: UBC Press, 2008.

MacDougall, David. "Whose Story Is It?" In *Visualizing Theory: Selected Essays from VAR, 1990–94*, ed. Lucien Taylor, 26–36. New York: Routledge, 1994.

Mackey, Eva. *The House of Difference: Cultural Politics and National Identity in Canada*. New York: Routledge, 1999.

MacMillan, Miriam. *Greens Seas and White Ice*. New York: Dodd, Mead and Co., 1948.

Malik, Kenan. *The Meaning of Race: Race, History and Culture in Western Society*. New York: New York University Press, 1996.

Mancini Billson, Janet. "Opportunity or Tragedy: The Impact of Canadian Resettlement Policy on Inuit Families." *American Review of Canadian Studies* 20, 1 (1990): 187–218.

Mancini Billson, Janet, and Kyra Mancini. *Inuit Women: Their Powerful Spirit in a Century of Change*. Lanham: Roman and Littlefield, 2007.

Manning, Mrs. Tom. *Igloo for a Night*. Toronto: University of Toronto Press, 1946.

–. *Summer on Hudson Bay*. London: Hodder and Stoughton, 1949.

Marchand, Marianne, and Jane Parpart, eds. *Feminism/Postmodernism/Development*. London: Routledge, 1995.

Marcus, Allan. *Relocating Eden: The Image and Politics of the Inuit Exile in the Canadian Arctic*. Vancouver: UBC Press, 1994.

Marubbio, M. Elise. *Killing the Indian Maiden: Images of Native American Women in Film*. Lexington: University Press of Kentucky, 2006.

Mason, Jody. "'Siddown Brother, Siddown': The Problems of Commitment and the Publishing History of Irene Baird's *Waste Heritage*." *Papers of the Bibliographic Society of Canada*, 45, 2 (2007): 143–62.

Mawani, Renisa. *Colonial Proximities: Crossracial Encounters and Juridical Truths in British Columbia, 1871–1921*. Vancouver: UBC Press, 2009.

McCallum, Mary Jane, and Aroha Harris. "Assaulting the Ears of Government: The Indian Homemakers Clubs and the Maori Women's Welfare Leagues in their Formative Years." In *Indigenous Women and Work: From Labor to Activism*, ed. Carol Williams, 225–39. Urbana: University of Illinois Press, 2013.

McClintock, Anne. *Imperial Leather: Race, Gender and Sexuality in the Colonial Context*. London: Routledge, 1995.

McElroy, Anne. "Canadian Arctic Modernization and Change in Female Inuit Role Identification." *American Ethnologist* 2, 4 (1975): 662–86.

—. "Ooleepeeka and Mina: Contrasting Responses to Modernization of Two Baffin Island Women." In *Being and Becoming Indian: Biographical Studies of North American Frontiers*, ed. James Clifton, 290–318. Prospect Heights, IL: Waveland Press, 1993.

McGrath, Robin. "Circumventing the Taboos: Inuit Women's Autobiographies." In *Regard sur l'avenir/Looking to the Future*, ed. Marie-JoséeDujour and François Thérien, 215–25. Quebec: Université Laval, 1992.

—. "The European in Inuit Literature." In *The Canadian North: Essays in Culture and Literature*, ed., Jorn Carlsen and Bengt Streijffert, 109–18. Lund: Nordic Association for Canadian Studies, 1989.

—. "Inuit Literature in English." *Canadian Review of Comparative Literature* 1–2 (1989): 700–6.

McKillop Copeland, Donalda. *Remember, Nurse*. Toronto: The Ryerson Press, 1960.

McMillan, Robert. "Ethnography and the N.F.B.: The Laura Boulton Mysteries." *Canadian Journal of Film Studies* 1, 2 (1991): 67–78.

Meiskins Wood, Ellen, and John Bellamy Foster, eds. *In Defense of History*. New York: Monthly Review Press, 1997.

Memmi, Albert. *Colonizer and the Colonized*. New York: Beacon Press, 1965.

Metalyer, Maurice, trans. *I Nuligak*. Toronto: Peter Martin Associates, 1966.

Michie, George, and Eric Neil. "Cultural Conflict in the Eastern Arctic." *Canadian Geographer* 5 (1955): 33–34.

Midgley, Clare, ed. *Gender and Imperialism*. Manchester: Manchester University Press, 1998.

Miller, Jim. *Skyscrapers Hide the Heavens*. Toronto: University of Toronto Press, 2000.

Miller, Mary Jane. *Outside Looking In: Viewing First Nations Peoples in Canadian Dramatic Television Series*. Montreal and Kingston: McGill-Queen's University Press, 2008.

—. *Turn Up The Contrast: CBC Television Drama Since 1952*. Vancouver: UBC Press, 1987.

Mills, Sara. *Discourses of Difference*. London: Routlege, 1991.

—. *Gender and Colonial Space*. Manchester: Manchester University Press, 2005.

Minh-ha, Trinh T. *Woman, Native, Other: Writing Postcoloniality and Feminism*. Bloomington: Indiana University Press, 2009.

Mitchell, W.J.T. *Picture Theory: Essays on Verbal and Visual Representation*. Chicago: University of Chicago Press, 1994.

Mohanty, Satya P. "The Epistemic Status of Cultural Identity." In *Reclaiming Identity: Realist Theory and the Predicament of Postmodernism*, ed. Paula Moya and Michael P. Hames-Garcia, 29–66. Berkeley: University of California Press, 2000.

Monture-Angus, Patricia. *Thunder in My Soul: A Mohawk Woman Speaks*. Halifax: Fernwood, 1995.

—. "The Violence We Women Do: A First Nations View." In *Challenging Times: The Women's Movement in Canada and the United States*, ed. Constance Backhouse and David Flaherty, 193–204. Montreal and Kingston: McGill-Queen's University Press, 1992.

Moody, Joseph P. *Arctic Doctor*. New York: Dodd Mead and Co., 1953.

Moore, Tina. "Political Participation of Inuit Women in the Government of Nunavut." *Wicaẓo Sa Review* 17, 1 (Spring 2002): 65–89.

Moore-Gilbert, Bart. *Postcolonial Theory: Contexts, Practices, Politics*. London: Verso, 1997.

Morris, Peter. "After Grierson: The National Film Board, 1945–1953." In *Take Two: A Tribute to Canadian Film*, ed. Seth Feldman, 182–94. Toronto: Irwin, 1984.

—. "Rethinking Grierson: The Ideology of John Grierson." In *Dialogue Canadian and Quebec Cinema*, ed. Pierrre Veronneau, Michael Dorland, and Seth Feldman, 24–56. Montreal: Mediatext, 1987.

Morris, Rosalind. *New Worlds from Fragments: Film, Ethnography and the Representation of Northwest Coast Cultures*. Boulder: Westview Press, 1994.

Morrison, William R. *Showing the Flag: the Mounted Police and Canadian Sovereignty in the North*. Vancouver: UBC Press, 1985.

—. *True North: The Yukon and Northwest Territories*. Toronto: Oxford University Press, 1998.

Morrow, William G. *Northern Justice: The Memoirs of Justice William G. Morrow*. Toronto: University of Toronto Press, 1995.

Mortimore, George. *The Indian in Industry: Roads to Independence.* Canada: Indian Affairs Branch, 1965.

Morton, W.L. *The Canadian Identity.* Toronto: University of Toronto Press, 1972.

Moso, Vincent. *The Political Economy of Communication.* London: Sage, 2009.

Moynihan, Daniel Patrick. *The Negro Family: The Case for National Action.* Washington, DC: Department of Labor, 1965.

Nadasdy, Paul. *Hunters and Bureaucrats: Power, Knowledge, and Aboriginal-State Relations in the Southwest Yukon.* Vancouver: UBC Press, 2004.

Nadeau, Chantal. *Fur Nation: From the Beaver to Brigitte Bardot.* New York: Routledge, 2001.

Nelson, Joyce. *The Colonized Eye: Rethinking the Grierson Legend.* Toronto: Between the Lines, 1988.

Nichols, Bill. *Representing Reality: Issues and Concepts in Documentary.* Bloomington: University of Indiana Press, 1991.

Nichols-Pethick, Jonathan. *TV Cops: The Contemporary American Television Police Drama.* New York: Routledge, 2012.

Nurse, Andrew. "But Now Things Have Changed: Marius Barbeau and the Politics of Amerindian Identity." *Ethnohistory* 48, 3 (2001): 433–72.

Okpik, Abe. "Bewildered Hunters in the Twentieth Century." In *Canada's Changing North,* ed. William Wonders, 191–99. Montreal and Kingston: McGill-Queen's University Press, 2003.

Olivier de Sardan, Jean-Pierre. "The Ethnographic Pact and Documentary Film." *Visual Anthropology* 12 (1999):13–25.

Ong, Aihwa. "Colonialism and Modernity: Feminist Re-presentations of Women in Non Western Societies." *Inscriptions* 3–4 (1988): 79–93.

Orford, Mena. *Journey North.* Toronto: McClelland and Stewart, 1957.

Palmer, Bryan. *Canada's 1960s: The Ironies of Identity in a Rebellious Age.* Toronto: University of Toronto Press, 2009.

Parker, Douglas. "Women in Communist Culture in Canada, 1932–1937." MA thesis, McGill University, 1994.

Parry, Benita. *Postcolonialism: A Materialist Critique.* London: Routledge, 2004.

—. "Problems in Current Theories of Colonial Discourse." *Oxford Literary Review* 9 (1987): 27–58.

Parry III, Elwood C. "Cooper, Cole and the Last of the Mohicans." In *Art and the Native American: Perceptions, Realities and Influences,* ed. Mary Louise Krumrine and Susan Scott, 165–67. University Park: Penn State University Press, 2001.

Payne, Carol. "Lessons with Leah: Re-reading the Photographic Archive of Nation in the National Film Board of Canada's Still Photography Division." *Visual Studies* 21, 1 (2006): 4–21.

—. *The Official Picture: The National Film Board of Canada's Still Photography Division and the Image of Canada, 1941–1971*. Montreal and Kingston: McGill-Queen's University Press, 2013.

Perry, Adele. "Women, Racialized People and the Making of the Liberal Order in Northern North America." In *Liberalism and Hegemony: Debating the Canadian Liberal Revolution*, ed. Jean-Francois Constant and Michel Ducharme, 274–97. Toronto: University of Toronto Press, 2009.

Petrone, Penny. *Northern Voices: Inuit Voices in English*. Toronto: University of Toronto, 1988.

Pettipas, Katherine. *Severing the Ties That Bind: Government Repression of Indian Religious Ceremonies on the Prairies*. Winnipeg: University of Manitoba Press, 1994.

Pierson, Ruth R. "Introduction." In *Nation, Empire and Colony: Historicizing Gender and Race*, ed. Ruth R. Pierson and N. Chaudhur, 1–20. Bloomington: Indiana University Press, 1998.

Pineault, Kelly. "Shifting the Balance: Indigenous and non-Indigenous Activism in the Company of Young Canadians, 1966–1969." MA thesis, Trent University, 2011.

Piper, Liza. *The Industrial Transformation of Subarctic Canada*. Vancouver: UBC Press, 2009.

Pitseolak, Peter, and Dorothy Eber. *People from Our Side*. Edmonton: Hurtig, 1976.

Poulter, Gillian. "Representation as Colonial Rhetoric." *Canadian Journal of Art History* 16, 1 (1994): 11–25.

Pratt, Mary Louise. *Imperial Eyes: Travel Writing and Acculturation*. New York: Routledge, 1992.

Price, David. *Threatening Anthropology: McCarthyism and the FBI's Surveillance of Activist Anthropologists*. Durham: Duke University Press, 2004.

Price, Richard. "Postmodernism and History." In *Language and Labour*, ed. Neville Kirk and John Belchem, 11–43. Aldershot, UK: Ashgate Press, 1997.

Prins, Harald E.L. "The Paradox of Primitivism: Native Rights and the Problem of Imagery in Cultural Survival Films." *Visual Anthropology* 9 (1997): 243–66.

Pryde, Duncan. *Nunaga: Ten Years of Eskimo Life*. New York: Walker and Company, 1971.

Quiring, David M. *CCF Colonialism in Northern Saskatchewan: Battling Parish Priests, Bootleggers, and Fur Sharks*. Vancouver: UBC Press, 2004.

Raibmon, Paige. "Theatres of Contact: The Kwakwaka'wakw Meet Colonialism in BC and at the Chicago World Fair." *Canadian Historical Review* 81, 2 (2000): 157–90.

Ray, Arthur. *The Canadian Fur Trade in the Industrial Age*. Toronto: University of Toronto Press, 1990.

Renov, Michael. "Domestic Ethnography and the Construction of the 'Other' Self." In *Collecting Visible Evidence*, ed. Jane Gaines and Michael Renov, 140–55. Minneapolis: University of Minnesota, 1999.

Rifkind, Candida. *Comrades and Critics: Women, Literature and the Left in 1930s Canada*. Toronto: University of Toronto Press, 2009.

Robinson, Michael P. *The Coldest Crucible: Arctic Exploration and American Culture*. Chicago: University of Chicago Press, 2006.

Rollins, Peter and John E. O'Connor, eds. *Hollywood's Indian: The Betrayal of the Native American in Film*. Lexington: University Press of Kentucky, 2003.

Rosaldo, Renate. *Culture and Truth: The Remaking of Social Analysis*. Boston: Beacon Press, 1993.

Roth, Lorna. *Something New in the Air: The Story of First Peoples Television Broadcasting in Canada*. Montreal and Kingston: McGill University Press, 2005.

Rothman, William. "Robert Flaherty's *Nanook of the North*." In *Documenting the Documentary: Close Readings of Documentary Film and Video*, ed. Barry Keith Grant and Jeannette Sloniowski, 1–18. Detroit: Wayne State University, 2014.

Rowley, Diana. Review of *I Was No Lady*. *Canadian Geographic Journal* 60 (March 1960): xvi.

Ruby, Jay. *Picturing Culture: Explorations of Film and Anthropology*. Chicago: University of Chicago Press, 2000.

Rutherford, Paul. *When Television Was Young: Primetime Canada, 1952–1967*. Toronto: University of Toronto Press, 1990.

Ryan, Allan J. *The Trickster Shift: Humour and Irony in Contemporary Native Art*. Vancouver: UBC Press, 1999.

Ryan, James R. *Picturing Empire: Photography and the Visualization of the British Empire*. Chicago: University of Chicago Press, 1997.

Ryan, Joan. *Doing Things the Right Way: Dene Traditional Justice in Lac La Martre, NWT*. Calgary: University of Calgary Press, 1995.

Said, Edward. *Orientalism*. New York: Vintage Books, 1979.

—. "Representing the Colonized: Anthropology's Interlocuters." *Critical Inquiry* 15, 2 (1989): 205–25.

Saladin d'Anglure, Bernard. "Introduction." In Mitiarjuk Nappaaluk, *Sanaaq*, xii–xviii. Winnipeg: University of Manitoba Press, 2014.

Sandiford Grygier, Pat. *A Long Way from Home: The Tuberculosis Epidemic among the Inuit*. Montreal and Kingston: McGill-Queen's University Press, 1994.

Sangster, Joan. "Creating a Writers Archive: Irene Baird's Work and Writing, 1940–1970." *Journal of Historical Biography* 10 (Fall 2012): 34–69.

—. *Transforming Labour: Women and Work in Postwar Canada*. Toronto: University of Toronto Press, 2010.

San Juan, E. *Beyond Postcolonial Theory*. New York: St. Martin's Press, 1998.

Satzewich, Vic, and Terry Wotherspoon. *First Nations: Race, Class and Gender Relations*. Regina: Canadian Plains Research Centre, 2000.

Sawchuk, Christina. "An Arctic Republic of Letters in Early Twentieth-Century Canada." *Nordlit* 23 (2008): 273–92.

Scherman, Katharine. *Spring on an Arctic Island*. Boston: Little Brown and Co., 1956.

Scott, Catherine. *Gender and Development: Rethinking Modernization and Dependency Theory*. London: Routledge, 1996.

Scott, Monroe. *Corpus Delectable*. Prod: Hamilton: Theatre Aquarius, 1995.

Seeley, Sylvia. Review of *Journey North*. *Canadian Geographic Journal* 58 (March 1959): xiii.

Sekula, Alan. "Photography between Labour and Capital." In *Mining Photographs and Other Pictures: A Selection from the Negative Archives of Shedden Studio, Glace Bay, Cape Breton*, ed. Don Macgillivray and Allan Sekula, 193–202. Sydney: UCCB Press, 1983.

Sharpe, Jenny. *Allegories of Empire: The Figure of Woman in the Colonial Text*. Minneapolis: University of Minnesota Press, 1993.

Sheffield, Scott. *The Red Man's on the Warpath: The Image of the 'Indian' and the Second World War*. Vancouver: UBC Press, 2004.

Shields, Rob. *Places on the Margin: Alternative Geographies of Modernity*. London: Routledge, 1991.

Shoat, Ella. "Notes on the Postcolonial." *Social Text* 31, 32 (1992): 99–113.

Shoat, Ella, and Robert Stain. *Unthinking Eurocentrism: Multiculturalism and the Media*. London: Routledge, 1994.

Sider, Gerald. *Skin for Skin: Death and Life for Inuit and Innu*. Durham, NC: Duke University Press, 2013.

Simpson, Leanne. *Dancing on Our Turtle's Back*. Winnipeg: Arbeiter Ring Publishing, 2011.

Sivertz, B.G. Review of *The New People*. *North* 13, 3 (1966): 43.

Skene-Melvin, David. *Canadian Crime Fiction*. Shelburne: The Battered Silicon Dispatches, 1996.

Smith, Andrea. *Conquest: Sexual Violence and American Indian Genocide*. Cambridge: South End, 2005.

Smith, Derek. "The Barbeau Archives at the Canadian Museum of Civilization: Some Current Research Problems." *Anthropologica* 43 (2001): 191–200.

Spivak, Gayatri Chakravorty. "Can the Subaltern Speak?" In *Marxism and Interpretations of Culture*, ed. C. Nelson and L. Grossberg, 271–313. Bassingstoke: Macmillan Educational, 1988.

Spurr, David. *The Rhetoric of Empire: Colonial Discourse in Journalism, Travel Writing and Imperial Administration*. Durham, NC: Duke University Press, 1996.

Stevens, Peter. *Brink of Reality: New Canadian Documentary Film and Video*. Toronto: Between the Lines, 1993.

Stevenson, Lisa. "Introduction." In *Critical Inuit Studies: An Anthology of Contemporary Arctic Ethnography*, ed. Pamela Stern and Lisa Stevenson, 1–22. Lincoln: University of Nebraska Press, 2006.

Stevenson, Winona. "Colonialism and First Nations Women in Canada." In *Scratching the Surface: Canadian Anti-Racist Feminist Thought*, ed. Enakshi Dua and Angela Robertson, 49–82. Toronto: Women's Press, 1999.

Stoler, Ann. "Making Empire Respectable: The Politics of Race and Sexual Morality in 20th Century Colonial Cultures." *American Ethnologist* 16, 4 (1989): 634–59.

—. *Race and the Education of Desire: Foucault's History of Sexuality and the Colonial Order of Things*. Durham: Duke University Press, 1995.

Tabili, Laura. "Race Is a Relationship and Not a Thing." *Journal of Social History* 37, 1 (2003): 125–30.

Tester, Frank. "Can the Sled Dog Sleep? Postcolonialism, Cultural Transformation and the Consumption of Inuit Culture." *New Proposals: Journal of Marxism and Interdisciplinary Inquiry* 3, 3 (2010): 7–19.

—. "Iglu to Iglurjuag." In *Critical Inuit Studies: An Anthology of Contemporary Arctic Ethnography*, ed. Pamela Stern and Lisa Stevenson, 230–52. Lincoln: University of Nebraska Press, 2006.

Tester, Frank, and Peter Kulchyski. *Tammarniit (Mistakes): Inuit Relocation in the Eastern Arctic, 1939–63*. Vancouver: UBC Press, 1993.

Thorn, Brian. "Visions of the New World Order: Women and Gender in Radical and Reactionary Movements in Post-World War II Western Canada." PhD diss., Trent University, 2006.

Tiffany, Sharon, and Kathleen Adams. *The Wild Woman: An Inquiry into the Anthropology of an Idea*. Cambridge: Schenkman, 1985.

Tiyambe Zeleza, Paul. "The Troubled Encounter between Postcolonialism and African History." *Journal of the Canadian Historical Association* 17, 2 (2006): 89–129.

Tobing Rony, Fatimah. *The Third Eye: Race, Cinema and Ethnographic Spectacle*. Durham, NC: Duke University Press, 1996.

Tough, Frank. *As Their Natural Resources Fail: Native Peoples and the Economic History of Northern Manitoba*. Vancouver: UBC Press, 1996.

Tzu-Chun Wu, Judy. *Radicals on the Road: Internationalism, Orientalism, and Feminism during the Vietnam Era*. Ithaca: Cornell University Press, 2013.

Usher, Peter. "Caribou Crisis or Administrative Crisis? Wildlife and Aboriginal Policies on the Barren Grounds of Canada, 1947–60." In *Cultivating Arctic Landscapes: Knowing and Managing Animals in the Circumpolar North*, ed.

David G. Anderson and Mark Nuttall, 172–99. New York: Berghahn Books, 2004.

—. "Northern Development, Impact Assessment, and Social Change." In *Anthropology, Public Policy, and Native Peoples in Canada*, ed. Noel Dyck and James Waldram, 98–130. Montreal and Kingston: McGill-Queen's University Press, 1993.

Valaskakis, Gail Guthrie. *Indian Country: Essays on Contemporary Native Culture*. Waterloo: Wilfrid Laurier University Press, 2005.

Van Kirk, Sylvia. *Many Tender Ties: Women in Fur Trade Society, 1670–1870*. Winnipeg: Watson & Dwyer Publishing, 1980.

Vastokas, Joan. "A Reply to Nelson Graburn." *Inuit Art Quarterly* 2, 1 (1987): 15–16.

Veracini, Lorenzo. *Settler Colonialism, a Theoretical Overview*. London: Palgrave Macmillan, 2010.

Wachowich, Nancy, Apphia Agalakti Awa, Rhoda Kaukjak Katsak, and Sandra Pikujak Katsak. *Saqiyuq: Stories from the Lives of Three Inuit Women*. Montreal and Kingston: McGill-Queen's University Press, 1999.

Wade Rose, Barbara. *Budge: What Happened to Canada's King of Film*. Toronto: ECW Press, 1998.

Walden, Keith. *Visions of Order: The Canadian Mounties in Symbol and Myth*. Toronto: Butterworths, 1982.

Watkins, Mel, ed. *The Dene Nation: A Colony Within*. Toronto: University of Toronto Press, 1972.

Waugh, Thomas, Michael Brendan Baker, and Ezra Winton, eds. *Challenge for Change: Activist Documentary at the National Film Board of Canada*. Montreal and Kingston: McGill-Queen's University Press, 2010.

West, D.A. "Re-Searching the North in Canada: An Introduction to the Canadian Northern Discourse." *Journal of Canadian Studies* 36, 2 (1991): 108–19.

Whitaker, Reginald, and Gary Marcuse. *Cold War Canada: The Making of a National Insecurity State, 1945–57*. Toronto: University of Toronto Press, 1994.

Whitaker, Reginald, Gregory Kealey, and Andrew Parnaby. *Secret Service: Political Policing in Canada from the Fenians to Fortress America*. Toronto: University of Toronto Press, 2012.

White, Hayden. "The Historical Text as Literary Artifact." In *The Writing of History: Literary Form and Historical Understanding*, ed. Robert Canary and Henry Kozicki, 41–62. Madison: University of Wisconsin Press, 1978.

White, Pamela. "Restructuring the Domestic Sphere: Prairie Indian Women on Reserves: Image, Ideology and State Policy, 1880–1930." PhD diss., McGill University, 1987.

Wilkinson, Doug. *Land of the Long Day*. Toronto: Clarke Irwin and Co., 1955.

Williams, Carol. "Beyond Illustration: Illuminations of the Photographic Frontier." *Journal of the West* 46, 2 (2007): 29–40.

—. *Framing the West: Race, Gender and the Photographic Frontier on the Pacific Northwest*. New York: Oxford University Press, 2003.

Williams, Raymond. *Culture*. Glasgow: Fontana Paperbacks, 1981.

—. "Thomas Hardy and the English Novel." In *The Raymond William Reader*, ed. John Higgins, 119–40. Oxford: Blackwell, 2001.

Williams, Toni. "Re-Forming 'Women's' Truth: A Critique of the Report of the Royal Commission on the Status of Women." *Ottawa Law Review* 22, 3 (1990): 725–59.

Wilson, Christopher P. *Cop Knowledge*. Chicago: University of Chicago Press, 2000.

Wilson, Clifford. *Adventurers All: Tales of Forgotten Heroes in New France*. Toronto: Macmillan, 1933.

—. "History in Motion Picture." *Canadian Historical Review* 23 (March 1942): 65–68.

—. *Northern Treasury: Selections from* The Beaver. Toronto: Baxter Publishing, 1954.

—. *Pageant of the North: A Photographic Adventure into Canada's Northland*. Toronto: The Ryerson Press, 1957.

Winston, Brian. *Claiming the Real: The Documentary Film Revisited*. London: British Film Institute.

Wolfe, Patrick. "Land, Labor and Difference: Elementary Structures of Race." *American Historical Review* 106 (2001): 866–905.

—. "Race and Racialisation: Some Thoughts." *Postcolonial Studies* 5, 1 (2002): 51–62.

—. "Settler Colonialism and the Elimination of the Native." *Journal of Genocide Research* 8, 4 (2006): 387–409.

Woollacott, Angela. "All This Is Your Empire, I Told Myself: Australian Women's Voyages Home and the Articulation of Colonial Whiteness." *American Historical Review* 102, 4 (1997): 1003–29.

—. "Postcolonial Histories and Catherine Hall's *Civilising Subjects*." In *Connected Worlds: History in Transnational Perspective*, ed. Ann Curthoys and Marilyn Lake, 63–74. Sydney: ANU Press, 2005.

Index

Note: The page number for an illustration is indicated in bold type.

186–87; indeterminacy of, 187; Inuit, 186, 199, 204, 300n25; northern, 19–21, 186; oral, 259, 276; and progress, 34–35; rewritten, 280–81, 282; women's, 73, 185–86. *See also* historical nostalgia

Hogarth, David, 109

Hollywood: Alaska of, 144; disinterest in the Arctic, 145; and the RCMP, 111, 113, 122; and *RCMP* television series, 115; treatment of Indigenous peoples, 78, 82, 143–44

homogenization, of Indigenous peoples, 10–11, 120–21, 123, 268

Hongiman, John, 86

Horne, Evelyn, 148

Horner, Harry, 111

housing, 250, 280

How to Make an Igloo (film), 168

Hudson's Bay Company (HBC): critiques of, 264; museum holdings of, 83, 92, 93–99; and nation building, 70, 71–72; and Paulette Anerodluk, 285; public relations, 72–73, 78; public relations vehicle (*see The Beaver*); representations of, 49, 76–77, 80; traders, 50, 75; and white women sojourners, 33, 49

Huhndorf, Shari, 14

Hulan, Renée, 29

Hutchinson, Bruce, 188

"i don't read you charlie: a twisted tale" (by Irene Baird), 202–3

ideology: of Canadian northernness, 69–71, 94, **95**, 106–7; of classification, 76; of colonial domination, 10, 13, 23–24, 242–43; cultural, 120, 137–38; defined, 289–90; of gender, 23; hegemonic, 70–71; of integration, 153; male breadwinner, 151, 239, 244; of multiculturalism, 24–25; political, and filmmaking, 140; of terra nullius, 6, 33,

40, 291; text and image as, 70–71, 101; work of, 289

Idlout, Joseph, 47, 165, **166,** 167, 180

Idlout, Moses, **174**

Idlout, Rebecca, **174**

Iglauer, Edith, 37, 39, 43, 51–52, 56, 58, 61, 185, 193, 296, 310n19, 312n84

Indian Act, 230, 263

Indian Affairs Branch (IA): and community development films, 152; in federal departments, 7, 148; influence on NFB documentaries, 148–49, 151, 153; objections to *Because They Are Different,* 151–52; objections to *Labrador North,* 177; view of reserves, 152; views of Indigenous people, 149

Indian-Eskimo Association, 240, 241, 243, 345n58

Indian Brotherhood of the NWT, 349n6

Indian Film Crew, 178

Indigeneity: cultural construction of, 21–23, 171–72, 180–81; cultural preoccupation with, 143

Indigenous art. *See* Inuit art

Indigenous cultures: family life, 56–57, 238–39, 313n107; loss of, 268; state intervention in, 49–55, 58, 65, 89–91, 291, 345n58; understandings of, 71–82, 92, 144, 258–59

Indigenous labour: and wage economy, 121–22, 169–70, 327n73, 336n118; white reliance on, 47, 51, 55, 65, 66, 85

Indigenous peoples: as actors, 327n73, 336n118; as artefacts of history, 82; cultural construction of, 4–5, 10, 105–6, 118–22, 335n93; erasure of, 85; as filmmakers, 178–79; generational divide, 257, 259, 268; homogenization of, 10–11, 120–21, 123, 268; marginalization of, 78–79; political organization of, 275; postwar public image of, 326n70; relocations of (*see* relocation); speaking back, 275; state categorization

discrimination in, 232–33 (*see also* racialization; racism); and sense of mystical awe, 184, 195, 196; *vs.* South, 202–4, 220; understandings of, 37, 94, 154, 173, 215, 287–97; visual and textual representations of, 100–1

North Pole Boarding House (by Elsie Gillis and Eugenie Myles), 43, 134

northern development, 193–94, 196, 208–9, 218; political economy of, 294

North/Nord, 192, 296

NWT Council, 155, 225

Ojibway people, 153

One Woman's Arctic (by Sheila Burnford), 65–66

Orford, Mena, 37, 39, 40, 57, 62

orientalism, 26–27, 35–36, 39–40, 47–48, 70, 100, 224–25, 292, 305n100, 349n127; radical, 295–96

othering, 22–23, 279

Ottawa Citizen, 324n29

Our Northern Citizen (film), 171–72, 173, 239

Parry, Benita, 27

paternalism: in anthropology, 74; and celebration of white experts, 175; challenged, 225; *vs.* equality, 222–23; of government agenda, 49–55, 58, 90–91, 160, 207; and Indigenous-settler relations, 179–80, 182–83, 242, 265–66, 292; and marginalization of women, 173–74; of missionaries, 68; *vs.* patriarchy, 135; presumed need for, 129–32, 156, 160, 162, 176–77; racialization and, 158–59; in *RCMP* television series, 123–24; of RCSW process, 265–66, 270–71; and respect, 128

patriarchy, 92–93, 135

Patrone, Penny, 276

Patterson, Pat, 264

Payne, Carol, 24

Pelletier, Gilles, **116**

People of the Rock (film), 170, 171, 336n118; Inuit actors, 171

Perkins, John, 117

Phillips, Alan, 109–10, 125, 126, 324n16, 324n29

Phillips, R.A.J., 173

photographers: amateur, 81–82, 97; HBC, 93; Indigenous, 322n120; Inuit, 282–87, 350n8; women, 282–87, 351n34

photographic realism, 147

Piper, Lisa, 6

Pitseoluk, Peter, 350n8

Pitsulak, 322n120

political economy, 105–6, 294, 323n4

postcolonialism, 26–29, 289, 306nn103–4

postmodernism, 25, 299n14

poverty: and access to water, 230–36; and dignity, 153; of Indigenous women, 230, 237; masking, 181; RCSW testimony on, 262; sensational reporting on, 263; state interference and, 157, 176, 244; and subsistence crises, 169, 170, 175

power: archival holdings and, 72; biopower, 329n3; ideology and, 71, 290, 293; and material life, 5; of naming, 108; relations of, 24, 85; of the state, 220–21; of television, 106–7. *See also The Climate of Power*

Pratt, Mary Louise, 40, 84

primitive accumulation, 154, 181

primitiveness/primitivism, 79, 135, 163, 172, 293; language of, 47–48, 65, 67, 74, 156, 163, 293, 333n59, 340n55

Prince, Tom, 150

progress: assimilation as, 144, 181; economic, 150–51, 153; evolutionary, 254; hierarchy of, 52, 292; and paid labour, 198; problems of, 99

Printed and bound in Canada by Friesens

Set in Akzidenz-Grotesk, Fournier, and Zurich Ultra Black
by Artegraphica Design Co. Ltd.

Copy editor: Joanne Richardson

Proofreader and indexer: Dianne Tiefensee